ADVANCE PRAISE FOR *OMAR KHADR, OH CANADA*

"Some cases enshrine the defining moments of their time. Omar Khadr's is one. Future generations will rightly judge our shocking derelictions of responsibility in this matter. Here is an anthology that strips bare our collective Canadian failure to extend justice and humanity to a child soldier. Read this brilliant, powerful, compelling collection and weep." CONSTANCE BACKHOUSE, distinguished university professor and university research chair in the Faculty of Law, University of Ottawa.

"*Omar Khadr, Oh Canada* is a very important contribution to this very serious matter of a Canadian whose fundamental human rights have been abused with official complicity." REG WHITAKER, distinguished research professor emeritus at York University and adjunct professor of political science at the University of Victoria

"This book is an emphatic response to Omar Khadr's cry 'Nobody cares about me.' Omar's ongoing story is one that brings shame to Canada, but one that we cannot forget. He has suffered unspeakable harms and the least we can do is learn from them. Many Canadians believe that Omar Khadr is a terrorist who deserves the treatment that he has received. This book chronicles the many inhumanities that he has borne. It offers gripping, stimulating, and shocking facts and arguments about Omar's family history, his plight as a child soldier, his torture, his legal battles and the many violations of law that occurred in the process. It should go a long way to changing people's minds." NATASHA BAKHT, associate professor in the Faculty of Law, University of Ottawa, and editor of *Belonging and Banishment: Being Muslim in Canada*

"Williamson has drawn together a remarkable multidisciplinary collection of essays, poetry, and drama, which traces the complexities and contradictions of the still unfolding Omar Khadr story. Provocative and compelling, this book exposes both the plight of children trapped by conflict and the uneven and fragile terrain of contemporary Canadian citizenship." JANINE BRODIE, distinguished university professor, University of Alberta

"*Omar Khadr, Oh Canada* acts as a Canadian social prism through which we may finally begin to see important glimmers of the life of Omar Khadr beyond the moral panic of media accounts and the sterile analysis of judicial decisions. This introspective, nuanced, and multi-dimensional consideration of Omar's story inescapably confronts us with Canada's willful involvement in a racist system that has denied and continues to deny Omar's humanity." YAVAR HAMEED, human rights lawyer

Omar Khadr, Oh Canada

EDITED BY JANICE WILLIAMSON

McGill-Queen's University Press
Montreal & Kingston • London • Ithaca

© McGill-Queen's University Press 2012

ISBN 978-0-7735-4022-4

Legal deposit third quarter 2012
Bibliothèque nationale du Québec

Printed in Canada on acid-free paper that is 100% ancient forest free (100% post-consumer recycled), processed chlorine free

This book has been published with the help of a grant from the University of Alberta's Faculty of Arts, Vice-President (Research).

McGill-Queen's University Press acknowledges the support of the Canada Council for the Arts for our publishing program. We also acknowledge the financial support of the Government of Canada through the Canada Book Fund for our publishing activities.

Copyright page continued on page 449.

Library and Archives Canada Cataloguing in Publication

Omar Khadr, Oh Canada / edited by Janice Williamson.

Includes bibliographical references.
ISBN 978-0-7735-4022-4

1. Khadr, Omar, 1986– . 2. Khadr, Omar, 1986– – Literary collections. 3. Political prisoners – Cuba – Guantánamo Bay Naval Base – Biography. 4. Child soldiers – Canada – Biography. 5. Canadians – Legal status, laws, etc. – United States. 6. Child soldiers – Legal status, laws, etc. – United States. 7. Canada – Politics and government – 2006– . 8. Afghan War, 2001– – Prisoners and risons, American. I. Williamson, Janice

HV9468.K53043 2012 341.6'50973 C2012-902277-2

This book was typeset by Interscript in 10.5/13 Sabon.

Become the sky. Take an axe to the prison wall.
Escape.
Walk out like someone suddenly born into colour.
Do it now.

Rumi

When I heard pigeons cooing in the trees,
Hot tears covered my face.

When the lark chirped, my thoughts composed
A message for my son.

Mohammad, I am afflicted.
In my despair, I have no one but Allah for comfort

The oppressors are playing with me,
As they move freely about the world ...

They have monuments to liberty
And freedom of opinion, which is well and good.

But I explained to them that
Architecture is not justice.

... After the shackles and the nights and the suffering and the tears
How can I write poetry?

Sami al Haj

Contents

PART TWO OMAR KHADR IN GUANTÁNAMO: ARCHITECTURE IS NOT JUSTICE

Acknowledgments

After Omar Khadr's 2002 capture in Afghanistan, my engagement with the issue was minimal and restricted to signing petitions from time to time. In mid-November 2009, I was one of about 250 who stood in the chill of an outdoor rally and marched in support of Omar Khadr at Edmonton's Churchill Square. This interfaith activist event was a collaboration organized by Charlene Schraf of Amnesty International, the Generation of Change Group at Al Rashid Mosque (Canada's first mosque established in 1938), and students from the Micah Action and Awareness Student Society (MAASS) at the King's University College, a Christian-based institution.

Inspired by this gathering, I sent out an invitation to contribute to a book about Omar Khadr. A few weeks later, the distinguished Canadian writer George Elliott Clarke was the first to promise a poem.

In April 2010, I attended his Banff Centre workshop on creative non-fiction where I wrote about Omar Khadr in the company of a wonderful group of women writers and with the support of workshop leader Mark Abley. Soon after, this project met a deadline when Mark extended an invitation to submit a proposal to McGill-Queen's University Press.

In May, Edmonton's Westwood Unitarian Congregation gave me an opportunity to talk about what Omar Khadr's story teaches Canadians. Generous members of Middle Eastern and North African Music volunteered to play their beautiful music during the service; I am grateful to the group's director, ethnomusicologist Michael Frishkopf, and fellow musicians, Dr Ashraf El Assaly, Nadir Bellahmer, and Abdel Hadi Wajdoni. Afterwards they told me that hearing someone talk about the Omar Khard case was deeply meaningful. And I regretted my comfortable detachment from the Khadr issue earlier. We talked about human rights abuses and Islamophobia in the post-9/11 environment of fear. It was then I realized the importance of bringing this issue to public debate.

An anthology is by definition collaborative, and I give special thanks to the generous contributors for their work and dedication. We are fortunate to benefit from McGill-Queen's University Press's interest in producing a collection that is eclectic and wide-ranging in genre and approach. This book has been sharpened and improved by Mark Abley's excellent writerly advice, editorial and translation skills, and enthusiastic commitment to the project. The press's high standards benefit this volume in many ways from the striking cover and design to the editorial expertise of Maureen Garvie and Ryan Van Huijstee. The external readers offered insight and productive critique that nudged the manuscript in important ways. I take responsibility for errors or omissions.

I collaborated earlier on a book about Canadian women and peace with Deborah Gorham, who taught me my first interdisciplinary undergraduate course; her enduring friendship, engaged work, and collaborative spirit nourish me. Decades ago, my teachers and fellow graduate students at York University showed me what cross-disciplinary intellectual and creative work could yield. While preparing this manuscript, I have been grateful for helpful dialogues with Karyn Ball, Karin Buss, Constance Brissenden, Janine Brodie, Shelagh Campbell, Leilei Chen, Victoria Clarke, Pat Clements, Linda Duncan, Kim Echlin, Caterina Edwards, Deborah Gorham, Isobel Grundy, Ellen Homola, Marco Katz, Michael Keefer, Margaret Macpherson, Amin Malak, Sheila Pratt, Helen Sadowski, Douglas Spaner, Ollie Williamson Shakotko, Susan Shirriff, Meenal Shrivastava, Malinda Smith, Jane Springer, Fred Wah, and Arlette Zinck. Jane Springer went beyond the call of friendship to lend her excellent editorial eye. Sandy Kachmar, Cec Ochmann, and Susan Sauve offered loving support to my family. And grateful thanks go to Angela Van Essen, a fine scholar and research assistant.

My work on this book is dedicated to my daughter, Bao, and to my students, like contributor Hasnain Khan, the generation coming of age in the era of Omar Khadr. May they seek and find justice, not war.

Omar Khadr's future remains uncertain as this book is published. In one of his handwritten notes in 2006, he wrote, "Excuse me, Mr Judge ... I say with my respect to you and everybody else here that I'm boycotting these procedures until I be treated humanely and fairly." After a decade of mistreatment, Omar Khadr deserves what has escaped him for too long – humane care, freedom, and an education.

Omar Khadr: A Timeline

1975–77: Ahmed Said Khadr emigrates from Egypt to Canada. He studies computer science at the University of Ottawa and marries Maha Elsamnah.

1980s: After the Soviet invasion of Afghanistan, Muslims from around the world go there to fight with the rebels.

1985: Ahmad Khadr sets up a humanitarian organization in Peshawar, Pakistan, not far from the Afghan border.

19 September 1986: Omar Khadr is born in Toronto, the fifth of seven children. The family moves often between Canada and Pakistan.

1995–96: Ahmed Khadr is arrested and accused of complicity in a terrorist bombing of the Egyptian Embassy in Pakistan. He begins a hunger strike. After Canadian Prime Minister Jean Chrétien raises the case with his Pakistani counterpart, Benazir Bhutto, Khadr is released.

17 November 2001: Two months after the terrorist attacks on New York and Washington, the Taliban regime in Kabul falls to the US-backed Northern Alliance. Taliban fighters continue to operate in much of southern Afghanistan. Ahmed Khadr's name now appears on a US list of suspected terrorists.

27 July 2002: Omar Khadr, aged fifteen, is arrested in the ruins of a compound in Afghanistan after a firefight with US troops. He is

severely injured in the fight and loses sight in one eye. No others from his side survive the battle. He will be charged with throwing a hand grenade that fatally wounded Sgt Christopher Speer, a Delta Force strategic forces soldier and medic.

27 July–October 2002: Omar is held captive under extreme conditions in the US Bagram Air Base in Afghanistan.

October 2002: He is transferred to the Guantánamo Bay military complex in Cuba. As the detention camp is officially considered outside US legal jurisdiction, prisoners are not entitled to Geneva Convention protection.

February 2003: CSIS and Foreign Affairs agents spend parts of four days interrogating Omar in the company of a US agent. At this point he has received no visits from any Canadian consular official.

2 October 2003: Ahmed Khadr is one of eight fighters killed in a battle with Pakistani forces in the Waziristan region of northwestern Pakistan. Omar's fourteen-year-old brother Abdulkareem is wounded in the battle and left paralyzed.

8 August 2005: The Federal Court of Canada issues an interim injunction prohibiting the Canadian government from further interrogation of Omar Khadr.

7 November 2005: Omar is charged with murder by an unprivileged belligerent, attempted murder by an unprivileged belligerent, conspiracy, and aiding the enemy. Deemed an "enemy combatant," he is the only Canadian among roughly 660 prisoners at Guantánamo. He is the only child housed with adults.

9 January 2006: US authorities announce that Omar will appear that month before a military commission.

6 February 2006: Stephen Harper is sworn in as prime minister of a minority Conservative government.

6 April 2006: The Canadian Bar Association urges Prime Minister Harper to ask the United States to obey the rule of law and stop holding foreigners in Guantánamo without charge.

29 June 2006: The US Supreme Court releases its decision in the *Hamdan v. Rumsfeld* case. It rules that President Bush did not have authority to set up war crimes tribunals, thus invalidating the system of military commissions. The judgment says that military commissions do not conform to acts of Congress and finds them illegal under the Geneva Conventions.

17 October 2006: President Bush signs into law a new Military Commissions Act, its purpose being "to authorize trial by military commission for violations of the law of war, and for other purposes."

February 2007: Under the Military Commissions Act, Omar Khadr is again charged with murder, attempted murder, conspiracy, providing material support for terrorism, and spying.

14 June 2007: Sixteen NDP MPs, nine non-govermental organizations in Canada, and 110 academics and lawyers sign an open letter to Prime Minister Harper requesting that he repatriate Omar without delay.

29 June 2007: A US military judge dismisses all charges against Omar: he is an "enemy combatant," but military commissions can deal only with "unlawful enemy combatants."

3 July 2007: The US government appeals the dismissal.

12 August 2007: The Canadian Bar Association asks Prime Minister Harper to negotiate with the United States to repatriate Omar "to face due process under Canadian law."

25 September 2007: A three-member appeal panel reverses the ruling of 29 June 2007 and reinstates the charges against Omar.

27 September 2007: Opposition leader Stéphane Dion meets Omar's US defence counsel, Lt-Cmdr William Kuebler, and calls for Khadr's release: "Canada is alone among Western nations in not having secured the release from Guantánamo of one of its nationals."[1]

4 February 2008: Documents that are mistakenly released during a military tribunal hearing show that another fighter was still alive inside the Afghan compound where Omar was captured. Earlier it

had been alleged that Omar alone survived the US bombardment, making him the only suspect in the death of Sgt Speer.

March 2008: In an affidavit, Omar Khadr says that US military interrogators at Bagram Air Base in Afghanistan threatened him with rape and tortured him into making false statements.

17 April 2008: A letter submitted in court filings by Omar's defence lawyers reveals that Canada's previous Liberal government had asked the United States not to send him to Guantánamo after his capture in Afghanistan.

28 April 2008: Former Minister of Foreign Affairs Bill Graham expresses regret that Canada has not been "more vigilant" on Omar's behalf.

23 May 2008: The Supreme Court of Canada rules that Canadian officials took part in an "illegal" process by sharing information about Omar with the United States. The court orders the government to give Omar's legal team the secret files that CSIS and Foreign Affairs compiled from their interrogation at Guantánamo.

29 May 2008: The Pentagon abruptly replaces the military judge presiding over the case.

3 June 2008: Foreign Affairs documents reveal that US soldiers guarding Omar at Guantánamo have called him a "good kid" and "salvageable," but warn that prolonged detention could radicalize him.

17 June 2008: The Canadian government says it has resisted repatriating Omar over fears he would reconnect with his family, described as "terrorist."

10 July 2008: Prime Minister Harper again vows to leave the case in the hands of the US military, despite reports a day earlier that Canadian officials knew Omar was being harshly treated by US forces at Guantánamo.

15 July 2008: Video is made public of Canadian agents interrogating the sixteen-year-old Omar at Guantánamo in February 2003.

20 July 2008: Former prime minister Paul Martin says Canada should lobby to bring Omar home. Former Liberal ministers Anne McLellan, Irwin Cotler, and Stéphane Dion all now say they were unaware of the extent of the abuse allegations involving Omar and/or that he should be tried in a Canadian court.

9 August 2008: Omar's Canadian lawyers, Dennis Edney and Nate Whitling, file a lawsuit against Prime Minister Harper to try to force him to intervene in the case and repatriate Omar. The lawsuit says the federal government has ignored its obligation to help rehabilitate and reintegrate children illegally used in armed conflict, and that Omar has suffered torture in American hands.

23 November 2008: Harper says he will not lobby to have Omar repatriated to Canada.

28 November 2008: Irwin Cotler, former minister of Justice, writes: "Other western nations ... have evidently realized what our government has not. There is no justice in waiting for an unjust criminal process to unravel. There is no justice in acquiescing in the inhumane treatment of our citizen. And until the government starts realizing that its duty to protect Canadians cannot wait for illegal judicial processes to run their course, our citizens will remain at risk."[2]

12 December 2008: Omar Khadr's military-appointed lawyer tells a pre-trial hearing at Guantánamo that a photograph and an American soldier's testimony prove Khadr could not possibly have thrown the grenade that killed Sgt Speer.

19 January 2009: FBI special agent Robert Fuller testifies that the fifteen-year-old Omar, while being held at Bagram Air Base, identified Canadian Maher Arar as a man he saw in an al-Qaeda "safe house" in Afghanistan. Cross-examined, Fuller admits that Omar took a lot of time to identify Arar and only said he "might have seen him." It was information given by Canadian officials to the United States that led Arar to be deported to his native Syria. Arar was cleared of terrorist links by a judicial inquiry in 2006 and later awarded compensation. According to Omar's defence team, this false FBI information supports the claim that US authorities coerced him into making untrue statements.

22 January 2009: Having promised during his presidential campaign that he would close the Guantánamo detention camp and reject the Military Commissions Act, the newly inaugurated Barack Obama instructs the Secretary of Defense that no new charges should be sworn and that all military commission proceedings should be halted.

February 2009: France's Foreign Minister Bernard Kouchner asks US Secretary of State Hilary Clinton to intervene in Omar's case while discussing Guantánamo, which Clinton called "a cancer." WikiLeaks will eventually release a US cable about the meeting: "The FM [Kouchner] handed the Secretary a paper concerning Omar Khadr, a 15-year old Muslim of Canadian origin. The Secretary agreed to review the case ... Leading figures in allied governments were pressing Washington over the case of a Canadian citizen – even though Canada's government was not."[3]

24 March 2009: The Canadian House of Commons passes New Democrat MP Wayne Marston's motion calling for Omar's immediate repatriation. "It is now the will of the House that the child soldier Omar Khadr be repatriated," Marston says. "It is time for the Prime Minister to bring Omar Khadr home."[4]

April 2009: US authorities remove Omar's military defence lawyer, Lt-Cmdr Bill Kuebler, from the case. Kuebler had lodged a complaint about his superior, saying that the Pentagon's chief defence lawyer, Col. Peter Masciola, supported the prosecution of Omar while overseeing his defence. A few days later, Kuebler is reinstated to the case.

23 April 2009: Federal Court Justice James O'Reilly rules that the federal government has violated the Charter rights of Omar Khadr by refusing to seek his release. He writes: "Clearly Canada was obliged to recognize that Mr. Khadr, being a child, was vulnerable to being caught up in armed conflict as a result of his personal and social circumstances in 2002 and before."

24 April 2009: Amnesty International launches a campaign to pressure the Canadian government into repatriating and rehabilitating Omar.

28 April 2009: A US military judge says that hearings against Omar will begin in June.

7 May 2009: Eighteen members of the University of Saskatchewan's law faculty and sixty-one of the province's trial lawyers sign an open letter saying that Canada's failure to seek Omar Khadr's repatriation goes against principles of fundamental justice.

24 June 2009: Federal lawyers file an appeal of the court ruling ordering Canada to seek Omar's return to this country. The repatriation order is put on hold pending the outcome of the appeal.

15 July 2009: The Security Intelligence Review Committee, the watchdog for Canada's spy agency, says CSIS ignored human rights concerns by interrogating Omar when he was a teenager in Guantánamo. The government says it is "reviewing the report with interest."

14 August 2009: A Federal Court of Appeal judge upholds a ruling ordering the government to repatriate Omar.

25 August 2009: Ottawa promises to fight the decision in the Supreme Court of Canada. Ten days later the Supreme Court grants the government's request for an appeal.

13 November 2009: The United States says it will soon move Omar from Guantánamo to a military prison within the United States to stand trial before a military tribunal.

4 December 2009: Colonel Patrick Parrish, the US military judge, says he wants to fix a trial date and gives the lawyers two weeks to propose schedules.

15 December 2009: Omar is among the Guantánamo prisoners set to be immediately transferred to the maximum-security Thomson Correctional Center in Illinois. This does not happen, and the Thomson Center will eventually be closed.

29 January 2010: In a unanimous ruling the Supreme Court of Canada refuses to order the Harper government to seek Omar Khadr's

repatriation. But it also declares that federal government actions have violated and continue to violate Omar's constitutional rights, and that Canada should rectify the wrongs committed against him.

3 February 2010: The Harper government again declares it will not seek Omar's repatriation from Guantánamo.

16 February 2010: The federal government sends a diplomatic note to the United States asking that information from Omar's interviews with Canadian interrogators not be used against him, as the Supreme Court of Canada found his Charter rights had been violated.

7 March 2010: A high-ranking source says officials in the Obama administration are looking for ways to repatriate Omar out of fear that the military commissions at Guantánamo will be further discredited. "They don't have the stomach to try a child for war crimes," the source says.

28 April 2010: Pretrial proceedings for Omar finally begin in Guantánamo. Prosecutors say he could face a prison term of twenty-five to forty years.

5 July 2010: The Federal Court of Canada gives the Harper government seven days to remedy the violations of Omar's constitutional rights.

7 July 2010: Omar fires his three American lawyers, throwing his upcoming trial into doubt.

12 July 2010: He tells the US military judge that he will boycott the trial, calling it a "sham." The judge refuses to let him fire his military lawyer, Lt-Col Jon Jackson. The same day the government of Canada says it will appeal the Federal Court order of July 5.

9 August 2010: The presiding judge at the trial decides to allow the use of evidence the defence has said was the product of torture. Omar pleads not guilty to five charges of war crimes.

12 August 2010: The trial begins. The military commission deciding Omar's fate consists of a judge and jury of eight officers.

13 October 2010: Omar agrees to a plea bargain. He pleads guilty to five charges, including murder, as part of a deal that avoids a war-crimes trial. He also admits to planting improvised explosive devices and to receiving weapons training from a terrorist network. Under an agreement worked out between the US and Canada, he must now begin to serve an eight-year sentence in Guantánamo. In a diplomatic note, the Harper government agrees to "favourably consider" an application for his repatriation after a year. Despite this, the US military jury chooses to sentence him to forty years' imprisonment.

7 March 2011: President Obama announces the resumption of Guantánamo military commissions to prosecute alleged terrorists.

3 August 2011: Omar fires his Canadian lawyers, Dennis Edney and Nate Whitling. He writes to them: "Although I feel deeply indebted to you for your dedication, changing counsel at this time is in my best interests. I have the highest praise and respect for you both." In their place Omar appoints John Norris and Brydie Bethel.

6 September 2011: Prime Minister Harper announces that his government will reinstate the anti-terrorism clauses brought in after 11 September 2001 and that expired in 2007. His rationale? "The major threat is still Islamicism."[5] Anne McLellan and John Manley, former Chrétien-era Liberal ministers responsible for the original clauses, reaffirmed their support. Bob Rae, the current Leader of the Liberals, objected – along with the NDP.

1 November 2011: Lawyer John Norris says that Omar Khadr has asked to return to Canada to serve the rest of his sentence here. Norris hopes the transfer will occur "very soon," but government officials have given no assurance of this. The process may take up to eighteen months, according to news reports.

31 December 2011: President Obama signs the 2012 National Defense Authorization Act (NDAA), which may make it possible to accelerate Omar Khadr's transfer.

11 February 2012: Access to Information requests make public two documents Public Safety Minister Vic Toews wrote to CSIS director Richard Fadden. On 7 December 2010 Toews said that "under exceptional circumstances" CSIS could share information based on third-party torture. The directive lets CSIS decide whether to reveal how or why the evidence was obtained. A July 2011 four-page directive advised CSIS to release information to foreign governments even when torture is a "substantial risk."[6]

NOTES

This timeline is derived from elements in the Omar Khadr story developed in Dr Audrey Macklin's University of Toronto Law timeline, the *National Post* timeline, the CBC timeline, the PBS timeline, Global News timeline, and other news and political websites.

1 CTV New Staff, "Dion Meets with Khadr's Lawyers, Seeks Action," 20 September 2007, http://www.ctv.ca/CTVNews/Politics/20070919/Omar_Khadr_070919/ (accessed 30 August 2011).

2 Irwin Cotler, "Omar Khadr, a Canadian Responsibility," *National Post*, http://network.nationalpost.com/np/blogs/fullcomment/archive/2008/11/28/irwin-cotler-omar-khadr-a-canadian-responsibility.aspx (accessed 30 August 2011).

3 Campbell Clark, "France Pressed U.S. on Khadr as Ottawa Stood Silent: WikiLeaks," *Globe and Mail*, 1 December 2010 (updated 25 April 2011), http://www.theglobeandmail.com/news/politics/france-pressed-us-on-khadr-as-ottawa-stood-silent-wikileaks/article1820952/ .

4 "Marston's Khadr Motion Passes: Repatriation Urged," press release, http://www.ndp.ca/press/marston-s-khadr-motion-passes-repatriation-urged.

5 "Harper Says 'Islamicism' Biggest Threat to Canada," CBC News, 7 September 2011, http://www.cbc.ca/news/politics/story/2011/09/06/harper-911-terrorism-islamic-interview.html (accessed 8 September 2011).

6 Canadian Press, "CSIS OK'd to share data despite torture risk," *CBC News*, 2 March 2012, http://www.cbc.ca/news/canada/story/2012/03/02/csis-torture-information-directive.html.

EDITOR'S NOTE

In late October 2011, Omar Khadr was eligible to be transferred to Canada to serve the rest of his sentence. There seemed to be progress five months later after a long silence.

On 24 March 2012 (when this book was about to be printed), a *New York Times* article quoted several US officials including Guantánamo's chief military prosecutor and a Bush-era Pentagon official who registered concern that delays in transferring Omar Khadr might threaten the Guantánamo plea bargain progress – it would not be credible unless governments "follow through" on their promise to transfer prisoners. Journalist Charlie Savage concluded Omar Khadr's "limbo status is the result of bureaucratic delays in processing his application to transfer, especially within the Canadian government." However a spokesman for Canadian Public Safety Minister Vic Toews noted Omar Khadr's "file has not come to the minister's office for review," implying the delay was on the US side.

On 28 March, US Defense Secretary Leon Panetta said: "Obviously we will approve the transfer to Canada," and indicated he would soon sign the agreement. The same day in the Canadian House of Commons, Toews said that if a US application for Khadr's transfer from Guantánamo "were received, it will be determined in accordance with the law." That evening, Canadian Press reported that Ottawa would indeed approve the transfer.

Should this occur, President Obama is required to give the US Congress thirty-days notice of the transfer – and due to the pre-trial agreement, Congress cannot stop it.

It thus appears that Omar Khadr may return to Canada in late May 2012.

Two portraits of Omar Khadr by Heather Spears

OMAR KHADR, OH CANADA

Introduction: The Story So Far

JANICE WILLIAMSON

THE INSIDE STORY

The cover of this anthology pictures a sharp dialogue – a twinned trajectory investigating Omar Khadr's experience and the Canadian world to which he expects to be released. We have gazed at images of Omar in photographic portraits and court drawings, but the screen-capture shots of his Guantánamo interrogation in 2003 provide an especially disturbing trace of the story – a diptych that displays the prisoner's gestures of despair in a freeze-framed record of traumatic breakdown.

Omar Khadr's critics look at his picture and see a man justifiably treated. Neither an innocent nor a victim, he is for them "the enemy" whose punishment cleanses us all. But others see Omar Khadr as a man – at first a boy – whose last decade has been barely a life. Canadian citizen and child soldier, Omar Khadr speaks back to many of us in the troubling echo of our national anthem's opening words. In the title of this collection, the phrase "Oh Canada" is a direct address that asks us to reflect on what has been done in our name during the era of Omar Khadr, not only to the person but to our country. "To what world am I being released?" Omar asked in 2010 – and, we might add, to what country?

In 2005 the headline on a *Globe and Mail* editorial, "Omar Khadr's Limbo," condemned the Canadian government's paralysis: "Fighting terrorism does not justify discarding the rule of law ... Canada, unlike Britain and Australia, has made little attempt to secure the release or speak for the due-process rights of its lone citizen at Guantánamo ... There is not and may never be a groundswell of opinion that Omar Khadr's rights need protection. But they do. The Canadian government's eagerness to exploit Guantánamo in the case of a Canadian teenager incarcerated since he was 15 is shameful."[1]

But Omar Khadr and others held in Guantánamo are not so much in an in-between "limbo" as in "organized oblivion."[2] Guantanámo is "a space of exception,"[3] where people can be imprisoned indefinitely without trial, a penal institution that disappears citizens beyond the law of any nation.

Omar Khadr's case represents "the first modern-day prosecution of a child soldier and the only captive to be held responsible for a battlefield killing of a US service member in Iraq or Afghanistan."[4] A prisoner from 2002 until the time of this writing, almost a decade later he is the only citizen of a Western country remaining in Guantánamo. In an October 2010 US Military Commission that played by its own rules, he plea-bargained for one more year in Guantánamo and an additional seven years in a Canadian prison. Back in 2002, then Opposition leader Stephen Harper mused about trucking and transport and national security in relation to Omar Khadr's capture.[5] Almost ten years later as leader of the governing party, Harper has not advocated for Omar's transfer back to Canada, even though this is now part of a high-level diplomatic and legal commitment that is expected to take place sometime in 2012.[6]

For years, as though exiled, Omar Khadr disappeared below the radar of what matters. Why? Philosopher Simone Weil believed that we create distance between ourselves and those who suffer. Weil asked, "What is the reason that as soon as one human being shows he needs another (no matter whether his need be slight or great), the latter draws back from him?" She answered, "Gravity."[7]

If the gravity of violence and suffering makes us avert our eyes, this anthology reminds us of our responsibility to not look away. Collective stories of human rights abuses demand our attention.

As I write these words, we still await Omar Khadr's return to Canada. And many questions remain – about his child soldier status, the meaning of Canadian citizenship, his near-decade of imprisonment without trial, and the legitimacy of the justice meted out by a Guantánamo Military Commission.

A STORY IN FIVE PARTS

What do we know about Omar Khadr? And how do we know it? The young man himself is a stranger to us, kept in solitary confinement and prison throughout his youth and young adult life. What is his story? What is his legal status as a child soldier? What Canadian policies made his life in prison possible? What roles do racism and Islamophobia play in his treatment? How did our government become accessories to torture? What is the value of Canadian citizenship? What does it mean to be Canadian?

This book attempts to answer these questions. A multi-disciplinary and multi-genre approach draws on many areas of expertise to document, analyze, critique, speculate upon, and interpret Omar Khadr's story. Why include poetry, drama, a screenplay, and imaginative essays in a book that could easily be confined to analysis and "the facts"? Because poetry puts language itself in relief, and literary prose narrates events and affective patterns that can articulate connections between individual stories and cultures. Whether interpreted by the poet, visual artist, screenwriter, dramatist, novelist, documentarian, or prose stylist, the creative texts here navigate tales told on the front page of newspapers through forms that help us imagine the world of the prison cell, courtroom, battleground, interrogation, or trial.

My own understanding of Omar Khadr's life is embedded in Canadian literature, where readers discover networks of connection that make up a country's social and cultural life. Along with tales of celebration and community, our literary history chronicles hierarchies of difference and power linked to ongoing injustices against First Nations peoples, African Canadians, Asian Canadians, and others.[8] Post-9/11, Muslims and Arab-looking people have been particularly targeted in a decade shaped by Islamophobia's fear and ignorance.

One of the epigraphs to this book is "Humiliated in the Shackles," a poem written by Sami al Haj, a Sudanese cameraman for the Al Jazeera network who was wrongfully imprisoned in Bagram and Guantánamo between 2001 and 2008. He was released without charge, and WikiLeaks documents reveal his arrest was not in error but strategically planned in order to obtain information about Al Jazeera.[9]

Dozens of Guantánamo inmates wrote poetry during their imprisonment. Because of the proliferating allusions and metaphorical nature of the art form, the US military decided that poetry presented a "special risk" lest it communicate coded messages.[10] Writing can be dangerous. These poems as well as this anthology explore human suffering and injustice. They are part of what Cary Nelson calls the "fierce humanities"[11] that unsettle readers' self-understanding along with their comprehension of others. Nelson hopes this encounter will haunt us with "a burden of pain" that makes it harder for us to live our lives. Contributor Sheema Khan trusts our discomfort will lead us to speak out and act: "With each fresh revelation about human rights abuses perpetrated by the Canadian government in the name of security, we must heighten our vigilance against abuses of power and demand due process for those who are detained or exiled without charge."

This collection of disparate but related works about Omar Khadr braids together many threads to make sense of an individual history and a nation's transformation. It is structured in five parts, each with reflective pieces that offer a multifaceted understanding of Omar's story.

Part 1 explores the "saga" of Omar Khadr: through essay, memoir, poetic myth, and family and collective history, a public intellectual, a literary critic, a former diplomat, a poet, and a student narrate Omar's story. Writer Sheema Khan analyzes it within a cultural and political framework.

Retired diplomat Gar Pardy offers an insider's perspective as he recollects the history of the Khadr family and the political events that unfolded around them. Child labour activist Craig Kielburger recalls his meeting with a young Canadian boy named Omar. George Elliott Clarke's poem situates Omar Khadr's history within the mythological frame of the American Wild West and the OK Corral where law and order were defined by shoot-outs and the mythological certainties of good and evil, settler and savage. Through twin chronologies, Charles Foran juxtaposes his daughter's life in relation to Omar's from childhood to young adulthood, a telling counterpoint. Hasnain Khan's meditation, "Omar and I," is shaped by a perceptive self-awareness that links the politics of everyday encounters marked by Islamophobic suspicion with the geopolitics that shape contemporary Pakistan and Canada.

Through documents, autobiography, and essays, part 2 investigates Omar's incarceration and torture in US detention centres at Bagram Airforce Base and Guantánamo Bay, Cuba. His official affidavit, "Outlining His Treatment in Captivity," is a disturbing story of torture and mistreatment, and consistent with reports of other detainees and guards. Judith Thompson's one-act play and excerpts from a screenplay by Luc Côté and Patricio Henriquez present dramatic performances of Omar's 2003 interrogation in Guantánamo.[12]

In her meditation on torture, Kim Echlin invites us into the nightmarish rooms of "muffled voices from inside jail cells," both contemporary and historical. Marina Nemat relates her own experience as a sixteen-year-old condemned as "a danger to Iran's national security" to the notorious Evin Prison. She envisions a Canadian democracy that opposes torture.

In part 3, three lawyers, a journalist, and a human rights activist write about the legal case from different perspectives and at various points in time. Omar Khadr's plea bargain document is included here. Legal scholar and lawyer Audrey Macklin worked as a Human Rights Watch witness at Guantánamo and for three years assisted Omar's American attorneys. She writes of "Guantánamo Bay as a metonym for the regime of capture, detention, interrogation and torture applied by the United States and its partners in various locations outside the territorial United States." She confronts the challenge of finding the language and understanding to "do justice to the injustice." American lawyer Richard Wilson writes about the early stages of Omar Khadr's legal defence at Guantánamo. And the Canadian legal case against torture is outlined here by Vancouver lawyer Gail Davidson, whose "Foreign Policy as Torture" speaks to the government's culpability in this travesty of justice.

Journalist Sheila Pratt profiles Dennis Edney and Nathan Whitling, the Canadian legal team who supported Omar Khadr often pro bono over many years. Edney's essay on "the politics of fear" began as a moving speech about the social conditions that haunt the story of Omar Khadr. Maher Arar's piece calls Canada to task for its unmistakable support of the US Military Commission system and its ongoing imprisonment of Omar Khadr.

Part 4 investigates Omar Khadr as a "child soldier." The legal status and relevance of his being a child soldier is interpreted by a military leader, political scientists, a social historian, a legal scholar, activists, and poets. Roméo Dallaire's compelling "How to Unmake a Child Soldier" underscores his advocacy of young people abandoned to violence – sometimes kidnapped into brutal armies, sometimes deserted by their parents who sell or relinquish them to violent exploitation. W. Andy Knight and John McCoy contribute an intricate study of the issue of child soldiers and international law in which they explore the legal context for the discussion of the Khadr family ties.

In her legal study of the child solder, Grace Woo points out that the Supreme Court of Canada ruled the evidence gleaned from Omar Khadr's torture and interrogation inadmissible in a court of law. But the Supreme Court stopped short of demanding his repatriation to Canada. We were to rely instead on the good judgment of our federal government, in the false expectation that Canada would act like all the other nations who felt responsible for repatriating their own citizens.

Western liberal democracies define childhood in specific ways, as social historian Deborah Gorham outlines in her pointedly titled "Canadian Child Soldier." This national shame is taken up by another author: Monia Mazigh shows how Canadian students learn about this issue through African child soldiers but not our own banished citizen Omar Khadr. Lola Tostevin's poem "Delta Force" reminds us how Western popular culture embodies and shapes an increasingly militarized masculinity. Rachel Zolf's collaborative poem "Child Soldier" addresses the limits of policies of toleration that simply regulate our aversion to others who are different from us rather than challenge "what we hate about the neighbour over the fence."[13]

"The story of Omar Khadr touches on who we are," observes lawyer Dennis Edney.[14] The work collected in part 5, "Oh Canada," widens our view to address the alarming changes in Canadian society reflected by the Omar Khadr case, including changes in political attitudes towards Canadians incarcerated abroad, towards multiculturalism, and towards the prison system. This section also considers the stories of others who have been accused or convicted of terrorism. Scholars, writers, and human rights advocates analyze political and social policy and investigate cultural and media representations of the Khadr case.

Yasmin Jawani's exploration of colour-blind racism and the Muslim body concludes that Omar Khadr can be seen as "an exemplar of the profound criminalization, isolation and abandonment of those who are considered deviant, disposable and dispossessed Others." Jawani also investigates the abysmal treatment of another Canadian citizen, Suaad Hagi Mohamud, who after a short visit to Kenya, was denied re-entry into Canada – on the basis of her physical appearance. Robert Diab and Alnoor Gova situate Omar Khadr in the context of the many Muslim Canadians who have been mistreated and exiled to torture regimes.

Nathalie des Rosiers provides us with "the fragile and amorphous legal context" that determines Canada's duty toward citizens incarcerated in other countries. Canada's transfer of prisoner system is being undermined as authority shifts to the arbitrary decisions of politicians and Omar Khadr remains stranded in Guantánamo. Several of the contributors focus on his Canadian citizenship. Jasmin Zine, who contributes "Stolen Youth" to this book, has done many years of research on Muslim youth in Canada who are being transformed "from citizens to outlaws by virtue of their religion, ethnicity, and race." Political philosopher Shadia Drury's essay explores Omar Khadr as a "citizen outsider" for whom "belonging and the guarantee of rights and safety are fragile and uncertain concepts." And Omar remains, in Rick Salutin's words, "a Canadian icon" – a poster boy. For a decade he was a handy stand-in for what was at stake when Canada followed the American call to action post-9/11.

In her afterword, "The Mark of Torture," Sherene Razack notes how the issue of torture surfaces in this anthology again and again. She observes, "When we know that torture is practised in our name ... and we do nothing to put an end to it, we too participate in the torturer's world."

READING BETWEEN THE LINES OF *OMAR KHADR, OH CANADA*: WHAT WE KNEW

On 27 July 2002, Omar Khadr was a fifteen-year-old Canadian citizen when he was taken captive by the US military. His family had moved for years between Afghanistan, Pakistan, and Canada. Early in 2002, his parents allowed him to travel to Afghanistan to translate for visiting Arabs associated with a senior al-Qaeda leader. By June, Omar had begun his "brief summer" of "training"[15] that included bomb-making. In July, while staying in an al-Qaeda safe house, he was captured in a firefight with US soldiers after a four-hour helicopter bombardment. Gravely injured, he was accused of (among other crimes) killing a Delta Force soldier. He was quickly transported for medical treatment and imprisonment to the US Bagram Airforce base detention facility, housed in an unused hanger originally constructed by the Red Army during the Soviet invasion of Afghanistan.[16] We now know that detainees held at Bagram were tortured and even killed. Omar's chief interrogator would later be convicted of murdering other prisoners, including an innocent Afghan taxi driver.[17]

Canadians first heard about Omar Khadr through a truth-telling and a fiction. The truth about his status as child soldier would soon be forgotten or dismissed, but the fiction about his capture would circulate for years. Under international law, he should not have been imprisoned or prosecuted due to his status as a child soldier, but the injustice multiplied as the US military evidence against him changed over time.

It was 9 September 2002 when Canadian Foreign Affairs spoke out about Omar Khadr for the first time and raised the issues of his age and status: "On Aug. 20, [2002,] the Canadian government was contacted by the American authorities seeking information on the nationality of a juvenile, claiming to be a Canadian, whom they had taken into custody ... It is an unfortunate reality that juveniles are too often the victims in military actions and that many groups and countries actively recruit and use them in armed conflicts and in terrorist activities. Canada is working hard to eliminate these practices, but child soldiers still exist, in Afghanistan, and in other parts of the world."[18]

Liberal John Manley was Foreign Affairs minister at the time, and one wonders why the government did not continue to argue for Omar Khadr's release under international law that advocates rehabilitation rather than imprisonment for child soldiers. As Amnesty International campaigner Hilary Homes notes, the problem with Omar is that he grew up.[19] Had he the enduring youth of Peter Pan, the public might have been more repulsed by news of his ongoing imprisonment and torture.

More than a month after Omar was imprisoned at Bagram, US military spokesman Col. Roger King stated that he was "the last surviving enemy in that compound – who is the person that we eventually detained – as his last act at the firefight [he] rose up with a pistol and hand grenade and engaged the coalition forces, threw the grenade ... that resulted in the wounding of a special operations forces medic who, 10 days after the event, died."[20] While the death of US soldier Christopher Speers is a fact, a number of elements in this official statement would prove to be false or misleading. The accidental release of US military documents six years later revealed that Omar Khadr was not alone. He did not "rise up with a pistol and hand grenade": he had been nearly blinded and shot in the back.

THE FIREFIGHT'S CHANGING STORY

As Paul Koring wrote in October 2011, "The U.S. military's version of the firefight has been in dispute for years, not least because the teenager they accused of tossing the grenade that killed Special Forces Sergeant Christopher Speer suffered life-threatening head wounds and had been buried in rubble by an earlier bombing."[21]

For years, the military maintained that Omar Khadr alone remained alive after the battle in the compound and that he aggressively faced the American soldiers. Then, in February 2008, the military inadvertently released a contradictory witness interview with the Delta Force sharpshooter OC-1 who wounded Omar.[22] This accidental revelation of a confidential document key to the trial indicated that military transparency was limited when it came to evidence that failed to support their official story. Until then, they claimed that only Omar survived the four-hour helicopter siege and gunfight, so he was the only possible candidate to lob the grenade. But OC-1 testified how he found two people alive. As he killed one man with a shot to the head, the man's body slumped to reveal Omar Khadr crouching behind. The soldier shot two rounds into Omar's back.

"The dust and angle of the walls prevented him from seeing who threw the grenade," the report reads, but OC-1 believed it was Omar. Yet medical evidence suggests that extensive shrapnel wounds on Omar's face were consistent with the effects of earlier bombing that would have blinded him, making it difficult to throw a grenade. He would never regain the sight in one eye.

At the May 2010 hearing, a US Special Forces commander insisted that when he altered a post-battle report about the firefight, it was "to correct his 'historical' record, not because he had been pressured to do so." However, his first report was consistent with OC-1's, prompting defence lawyers to claim the second report was "manufactured evidence."[23]

In 2009, a *Toronto Star* report by Michelle Shephard provided another turning point in our understanding of what happened that day in Afghanistan. The photographs and written documentation showed Omar under dirt and mud tiles blown off the roof during the American bombing preceding the firefight. A soldier testified that when he entered the compound, he thought he was standing on a trap door. He then realized the cause of his unstable footing was Omar Khadr's wounded body camouflaged beneath him by the dust and sand.

THE REDACTION OF OMAR KHADR

In November 2009, Canadian diplomat Richard Colvin came forward with revelations that point to Canada's complicity in the torture of Afghan prisoners over an extended period. Colvin asserts: "Canada cloaked our extreme practices in extreme secrecy ... Our detainee practices [were] unCanadian, counterproductive and probably illegal."[24]

The redacted memos published in newspapers display how such documents conceal as well as reveal. They show us only a little of the picture. In the absence of full knowledge, we are left with partial truth. And in a democracy, the concealment of information useful to the common good edges us towards the kind of government that Canadians decry as "unCanadian, counterproductive and probably illegal."

For many years after Omar Khadr's capture, we did not see his image except as a portrait from a photograph provided by his family or an official shot of a round-faced boy in orange prison uniform. Then, new court-reporter documentation of the Guantánamo proceedings provided a view of a maturing young man. The two pencil drawings by the artist and poet Heather Spears that precede this introduction are based on his two most widely circulated photographic portraits. Spears's interpretive work animates Omar Khadr, allowing us to imagine a life lived beyond incarceration.

Likewise, over the past decade, we have rarely heard Omar's own words. Usually his legal counsel speaks for him. But in a letter written to his former lawyer Dennis Edney in May 2010, we encounter Omar's voice as he probes what matters to him and a possible future outside of prison: "You always say that I have an obligation to show the world what is going on down here and it seems that we've done every thing but the world doesn't get it, so it might work if the world sees the US sentencing a child to life in prison, it might show the world how unfair and sham this process is ... justice and freedom have a very high cost and value, and history is a good witness to it."[25]

When he writes in the same letter, "I hate being the head of the spear," the metaphor hurts. While a child soldier can act in a lethal way, the thrust of the arm originates elsewhere – in the adults who initiate the child into violence.[26]

THE "WHAT IF?" OF OMAR KHADR

Some detractors condemn Omar Khadr and imagine he has been "let off the hook," even though he spent almost a decade in Bagram and Guantánamo under conditions that have been condemned internationally. The columnist and broadcaster Ezra Levant, author of a recent book about Omar, speaks a rhetoric of vengeance. In a 2010 CBC-TV interview, he concluded that Omar is "not a child soldier" but "a psychopath [who]… should have been killed on the battlefield."[27] The following year he described Omar as "the Paul Bernardo of terror," as if there were a moral equivalence between a boy captured in Afghanistan at the age of fifteen and a serial killer who raped and murdered teenaged girls in southern Ontario.

Others focus on the particulars of the case, Omar's torture and the years he spent imprisoned without trial in Guantánamo. Michelle Shephard's 2008 book, *Guantanamo's Child: The Untold Story of Omar Khadr*,[28] is the only extended investigation of the case. Her *Toronto Star* columns have also offered insightful documentation about ongoing developments.

To Arlette Zinck, dean of arts at King's University College in Edmonton, the story is compelling and horrible because "you can see macro politics played out on the micro level – on the level of human flesh."[29]

Omar Khadr's story can be told in the conditional tense: what would or could have happened if … ? His story would have been different indeed had the standard wartime regulations been in place in Afghanistan. The Bush administration classified him, like other detainees, as "an enemy combatant," not a "prisoner of war." This redesignation meant that Geneva Conventions did not apply. Without an official tribunal, there was "a deliberate lack of adequate screening on capture."[30] Had international law been respected, a Geneva Convention tribunal would have considered Omar Khadr's status as child soldier, and he would have been guaranteed rehabilitation, not torture.[31]

GUANTÁNAMO JUSTICE

Thanks to WikiLeaks, we have access to US cables about a March 2009 meeting between King Abdullah of Saudi Arabia and John Brennan, a senior official in the CIA under George W. Bush and now President Obama's principal counter-terrorism adviser.[32] Among other things, the two men discussed the possible transfer of Yemeni prisoners at Guantánamo to Saudi Arabia. They shared a joke about Guantánamo prisoners: "Abdullah proposed implanting the detainees with electronic chips, as is done 'with horses and falcons.' Brennan said such a proposal would face legal hurdles, noting that 'horses don't have good lawyers.'"[33] The jest embedded in this purloined cable is about living human subjects. To these two powerful men, detainees are not fully human; they can be compared to animals to be mastered. This characterization mimics or symbolizes the degraded treatment of American prisoners in the sometimes lawless zones of Abu Ghraib, Bagram, Guantánamo, or prisons that are "black sites," some still secret, all of them established in the name of security and liberty after September 11, 2001.

To "apprehend" someone, in the philosophical sense, is not the same as to "recognize" that person. As the philosopher Judith Butler states, "Though [a figure] can be apprehended as living, it is not always recognizable as 'a life.'"[34] Through failure to recognize them, human lives have been reduced to the subhuman. Canadian citizens have been abandoned to torture and isolation in prisons beyond the law.

In 2010 Omar Khadr pleaded guilty before a Guantánamo Military Commission, the very existence of which is controversial. He accepted a plea bargain that required him to plead guilty to crimes he had earlier claimed he did not commit. He admitted to murdering Christopher Speer "and to four other charges, including attempted murder, conspiracy, providing material support to terrorists and spying." He apologized to Speer's wife and family.

He was sentenced to forty more years in prison. Lawyer Amir Attaran expressed incredulity at the long sentence: "I was dumbfounded … Even the prosecutor of Omar Khadr hadn't asked for a 40-year sentence. He said no more than 25 years, so ... [the jury,] seven military officers in a military court on a military base ... didn't even recognize their own prosecutor. They went completely off the page … It doesn't suggest discipline on the part of the system, it suggests a system that's really quite out of control."[35]

The plea bargain guaranteed Omar fewer years in prison. But as lawyer Audrey Macklin notes, his life was actually at stake: "Even if acquitted by a military commission, Omar could remain imprisoned at Guantánamo for the rest of his life." According to American lawyer Richard Wilson's contribution to this volume, the Military Commission was engaging in a publicity-seeking piece of "kabuki theatre." It was widely condemned for using evidence obtained under torture.[36]

A key element in the judgment was the determination that Omar would be returned home to Canada after one more year in Guantánamo. Yet Conservative foreign minister Lawrence Cannon insisted Canada would not negotiate with the Americans. At the same time Hillary Clinton reported on a conversation that reached agreement with the Harper government; the signed diplomatic note documenting this was published on the US Secretary of State website. Why did the Canadian government mislead the public? One can conclude once again that political interests trump the truth as the government plays to a partisan law-and-order electorate rather than abide by the Canadian Charter of Rights and Freedoms or by the provisions of international law.

Even after his plea bargain agreement, Omar was returned to Guantánamo for a year. As his ninth year of imprisonment ended, he was eligible to return to Canada to serve seven additional years in prison. However, no one knew how he would be transported: the Canadian government announced it would not pay his airfare from Cuba. And the 2011 US National Defence Authorization Act prohibited the US government from transporting Guantánamo prisoners. This same act required that Canada must be "certified" as a safe country, defined as "a nation not likely to permit him to attack the United States, and one that has control of its prisons."[37] However on 31 December 2011, President Obama signed the 2012 National Defense Authorization Act (NDAA), possibly to accelerate Omar Khadr's transfer. A new exception exempts Khadr's case because there is already a "pre-trial agreement entered in a military commission case."[38]

Omar Khadr is the last foreign national from a Western country still in Guantánamo. Before his planned departure, approximately 604 Guantánamo prisoners had been released. Who were these prisoners? There was much slippage in categorizing the hundreds who landed in Guantánamo. Many innocents and those falsely accused were "swept up through poor intelligence," through which they were turned in to the military for "substantial bounty payments." A second group, "foot soldiers for the Taliban," were "Afghan conscripts" or "Arab recruits, usually drawn to help the Taliban fight the Northern Alliance in what was portrayed as a struggle to establish a pure Islamic state." The third and smallest group were the "few dozen ... genuine terror suspects – those involved with the 9/11 attacks or other acts of international terrorism ... [who] should have been tried in federal court, rather than ... in specially convened military courts that do not have internationally recognized legitimacy."[39]

I reproduce here a complete list of countries that have transferred prisoners from Guantánamo because the range of destinations and their number makes Canada's ten-year reluctance to repatriate Omar Khadr all the more incomprehensible. Since 1992, Guantánamo prisoners have been released to Albania, Algeria, Afghanistan, Australia, Bangladesh, Bahrain, Belgium, Bermuda, Chad, Denmark, Egypt, France, Hungary, Iran, Iraq, Ireland, Italy, Jordan, Kuwait, Libya, Maldives, Mauritania, Morocco, Pakistan, Palau, Portugal, Russia, Saudi Arabia, Spain, Sweden, Switzerland, Sudan, Tajikistan, Turkey, Uganda, United Kingdom, and Yemen.[40]

ON THE KHADR FAMILY

Omar is the son of Ahmed Said Khadr, an Egyptian who moved to Canada in 1977. Ahmed's storied history includes an association with Osama bin Laden, confirmed in interviews with the Khadr family broadcast in a 2004 CBC-TV documentary. Yet details of Ahmed's activities remain confusing.

To many of his supporters, Ahmed Khadr was a charity worker who built a hospital and a school for Afghani girls, while supporting Afghani children orphaned during the Soviet invasion. He was one of thousands of Muslims who travelled to the region to fight to defend the Muslim state of Afghanistan. In Afghanistan and neighbouring Pakistan, he worked for a well-respected Canadian aid organization[41] from 1988 to 1996.

In 1995, Ahmed was charged with complicity and financing a bombing of the Egyptian embassy in Pakistan. He was imprisoned without trial and went on a hunger strike. After an intervention from Canadian Prime Minister Jean Chrétien, he was released in mid-1996; another man was identified as the financier of the embassy bombing. In 1996, Ahmed established his own charity, which was later alleged to have connections with terrorist training camps. According to the testimony of one Khadr son, Abdullah, the family moved to a large compound of houses near Jalalabad, Afghanistan, for a month in 1997.[42] This compound also housed Osama bin Laden and his family. As well, Ahmed knew the man who would replace Osama bin Laden as the leader of al-Qaeda: in 1986 Ayman al-Zawahiri, an Egyptian surgeon, was working as a Red Crescent doctor when he and Ahmed first met in Peshawar, Pakistan.

In 2001, Ahmed Khadr's name was added to the United Nations list of terrorists associated with Osama bin Laden. He would become known as "a leading al-Qaeda member,"[43] though his family and others dispute this claim.[44] DNA tests eventually confirmed that he was killed in an October 2003 Pakistani military helicopter attack on a South Waziristan safe house. Another of his sons, Abdulkareem, was paralyzed in the attack but survived.

It is important to piece together Ahmed Khadr's story from various accounts, because his significant connections with major terrorists make him a person of great interest. However, some commentators simply reduce Omar Khadr's life to that of his father, while they construct all other Khadr family members as an unchanging, undifferentiated entity. Although one can condemn the training in violence they received, and their support of terrorism earlier in their life, it appears that for Omar Khadr's siblings, their lives are unfolding in different directions. In fact, Omar's brother Abdurahman refused to follow his father's directives and may have run away from the al-Qaeda training camps he was sent to as a boy. He apparently became a CIA informant sent undercover to Guantánamo and later to Bosnia.

Omar's sister Zaynab recently married a man who was raised a Mennonite. Her father-in-law is a retired Ontario tax judge.[45]

Another brother, Abdullah, alleged to have been an al-Qaeda gunrunner, had a $500,000 bounty placed on his head in 2004 by the United States. Captured and held without charges for fourteen months in Pakistan, he was denied access to a lawyer and allegedly tortured into confessing, although he maintains his innocence. In 2010 an Ontario court quashed an attempt to extradite him from Canada to the US on terrorism charges,[46] since, according to Dennis Edney, "the United States presented no other evidence than that which had been obtained through Pakistani mistreatment of him."[47]

Another of his lawyers, Nathan Whitling, said that Abdullah was getting married: "He just wants to settle down and live a quiet life."[48]

The recruitment of children into Afghan military or police forces is forbidden by Afghan law, but the Taliban train children for combat. All the Khadr family boys were sent to training camps in Afghanistan – one was as young as twelve or thirteen.[49] Omar's American military lawyer Lt-Col Jon Johnson underscores the irony: "The typical child soldier is ripped from their family fighting to keep them safe in their arms. And here is a situation where the family, the father actually, sent him into the war zone."[50]

But whatever the guilt or innocence of other members of the Khadr family, it is crucial not to take them as representative of all Canadian Muslims, as some of the media have persisted in doing. Omar Khadr, in that sense, has served unwittingly as a useful tool of right-wing forces and for the proliferation of Islamophobia. When I first met Jasmin Zine, who contributes the essay "Stolen Youth" to this book, she wryly pointed out that she only began to receive funding for her work when the word "terrorism" appeared in the body of her research proposals – a sad testament to the way an entire group is constructed and received by public discourses of government, law, and media.

CANADA AND THE "WAR ON TERROR"

We marked the tenth anniversary of Guantánamo in January 2012, five months after the tenth anniversary of 9/11, the beginning of the "War on Terror." Part of the legacy of this "war" in Canada is our ongoing military engagement in Afghanistan. The "War on Terror" has also wrought social injustice in terms of Canada's political, social, and legal response to the tragic events. Refusing to romanticize the anniversary, American economist Paul Krugman writes: "What happened after 9/11 was deeply shameful. [The] atrocity should have been a unifying event, but instead it became a wedge issue. Fake heroes ... raced to cash in on the horror. And then the attack was used to justify an unrelated war the neocons wanted to fight, for all the wrong reasons."[51] Krugman refers here to the American context and the war in Iraq. But there is plenty of shame to share in Canada when we think through the implications of the case of Omar Khadr and that of other Canadian citizens who have been denied their legal rights during our Afghanistan military engagement. Gar Pardy, a former senior Canadian diplomat, writes in his essay in this book of "the inability of our governmental institutions to cope with the tsunami of lies, misdirection, misunderstanding, and failures unleashed in reaction to the attacks ... Unfortunately in the intervening ten years there has been little to show for the thousands who have died and the billions that have been spent."

Omar Khadr is part of our national myth-making about militarization and war. It seems that Canada is governed by the same two-pronged paranoia that Anne McClintock has observed in post-9/11 United States, where "forebodings of perpetual threat" and "phantasms of engulfment" are resolved in "deliriums of absolute power [and] ... inherent superiority." This psychology tends to imagine unlikely wars as solutions to complex problems.[52]

Massive expenditures are realigning Canada with militarized interests. The price of Canada's new military jets is estimated at $29.3 billion.[53] Since 2001, Canada has devoted an additional $92 billion ($69 billion inflation adjusted) to national security spending.[54] Part of the justification for this spending is the invention of national mythologies and "the glorification of the military."[55]

Political philospher Shadia Drury, another contributor to this volume, reminds us that, informed by "a socially conservative agenda inspired by religious fundamentalism, ... Stephen Harper has vowed to transform Canada into a country that his liberal opponents 'will not recognize.'"[56]

Canadian federal policies[57] appear to be mimicking the US investment in prisons as well, expanding the war zone to the domestic sphere where echoes of the war on crime and drugs play out.[58] In her essay, contributor Yasmin Jiwani points to the racialized inequities in Canadian prisons, drawing connections between "the high numbers of indigenous men and women [and] ... black men who are imprisoned ... [and] the growing influence of a law and order agenda by the current Conservative government." Estimates of the Harper government's "Truth in Sentencing Act" suggest that $10 billion to $13 billion in annual funding[59] will be required for expanded jail costs, in spite of declining crime rates[60] and at the expense of social programs.[61]

Canadian analysts draw disturbing conclusions about the cumulative effects of these changes, which add up to an emerging far-right nationalism characterized by an appeal to authoritarianism and the cult of the leader[62] in lieu of democratic policy. By 2011, the *Globe*'s Lawrence Martin saw this trend "brewing not just in terms of the glamorization of the military and the law-and-order regime, but in many other respects – moral certitude on foreign policy [in, for instance, an entirely uncritical support for Israeli policies that is to the right of US policy], information control obsession, anti-intellectualism, less tolerance for multiculturalism, disrespect for democracy, demagogic putdowns of opponents, 'Harper government' nomenclature."[63]

"HARSHER METHODS"

According to the UN Convention against Torture, "torture means any act by which severe pain or suffering, whether physical or mental, is intentionally inflicted on a person for such purposes as obtaining from him or a third person information or a confession ... when such pain or suffering is inflicted by or at the instigation of or with the consent or acquiescence of a public official or other person acting in an official capacity." [64]

Moazzam Begg, a lawyer and human rights activist and Omar Khadr's former Bagram cellmate, recalls that "the guards singled [Omar] out for the worst treatment, payback for allegedly killing one of their own. They would make him perform Sisyphean tasks, such as stacking heavy boxes and crates that the guards would knock over when he had finished and then force him to start again. Each time they walked past his cell they would yell: *Murderer! Killer! Butcher!* It was very, very hard to hear that because it was evident he was just a kid. Not only that, he was terribly wounded."[65]

In February 2003, Omar was treated to the "frequent flyer" sleep deprivation program for three weeks to "soften him up" for a four-day interrogation by Canadian Security Intelligence Service agents. Vincent Warren, executive director of the US Center for Constitutional Rights, condemns this practice as torture: "Things like sleep deprivation are against international law and U.S. domestic law, and all investigators, including those in Congress, need to focus on these issues of programmatic torture."[66]

The pain of torture inspires the victim's interest in giving the interrogators what they want. In Omar's case, the methods used and the frequency of the interrogations indicate that confessions rather than intelligence became the goal. David Keen observes, "Once you start torturing someone, the pressure is on to find them guilty or get a confession. Otherwise you are left torturing an innocent person."[67]

The interrogators were Canadian agents illegally sent by CSIS – an instance of how Canada was "complicit in the torture of Canadian citizens," according to the Supreme Court of Canada ruling. The interrogation included the following exchange:

> CSIS AGENT: If you were bright, Omar, and I want you to think about this for a few minutes. If you're smart, tell me something that can help me, that can show my government that you're willing to help us against the group of people who are bent on doing bad things to us.
> OMAR: You want me to lie?
> CSIS AGENT: I don't want you to lie. I just want you to tell the truth.
> OMAR: That's what I told you, the truth. You don't like the truth.[68]

In a plea to Prime Minister Stephen Harper in February 2010, Robert Holmes of the BC Civil Liberties Association spells out the limitations of Guantánamo law. Omar Khadr was about to appear before a Guantánamo Military Commission. Under new regulations, evidence would be admitted that was obtained by "clean team" interrogators. That is, the prisoner could be brutally tortured by the "bad cop," but should a "good cop" arrive later to interrogate and listen, testimony influenced by earlier torture would be considered reliable evidence:

> While the revised legislation makes significant improvements with respect to eliminating the use of evidence derived from torture or cruel, inhuman or degrading treatment (which, under the Bush administration's military commissions, was admissible as evidence), the Obama administration's legislation still permits the use of *substantive information* originally derived from torture, if that same information was obtained again by a different set of interrogators who did not engage in coercive tactics. This provision is to permit the use of evidence obtained by the FBI's so-called "clean teams" – interrogators who are sent to Guantánamo to re-interrogate detainees who had previously been tortured by the CIA, in order to obtain purportedly "untainted" evidence that could be used in judicial proceedings.[69]

Even former Guantánamo prosecutor Col Morris Davis was sceptical about these procedures: "The question remains whether after you cross the line can you ever walk it back to the right side. Once you ring the torture bell, can you ever un-ring it?"[70]

Torture leads to false testimony according to experts in the field. And false testimony can lead to more torture. In January 2010, an FBI agent testified that during one of his Bagram interrogations Omar Khadr had identified Maher Arar[71] as someone who "looked familiar"[72]: "Khadr initially stated that he did not recognise Arar. Upon cross-examination, Mr. Fuller clarified his testimony saying that at first Mr. Khadr could not identify Mr. Arar. Then after giving him a couple minutes Khadr 'stated he felt he had seen' Maher Arar."[73] This account was later discredited by RCMP surveillance reports that located Arar in North America, not Afghanistan, at the time. Nonetheless it is possible that this torture evidence helped seal Arar's fate. The FBI agent's interrogation of Omar Khadr began on 7 October 2002, the day before Arar's extraordinary rendition from the United States to Syria. For ten months Arar was beaten regularly with shredded cords and then returned to his solitary horror. In his words, "I was buried in my misery ... in a grave, an underground cell ... dark, narrow and damp."[74]

One of Omar Khadr's lawyers, Bill Kuebler, commented: "I think it is very, very likely that Canadian intelligence and U.S. intelligence were working closely together ... It would be truly an amazing coincidence if there weren't some connection between the information the FBI got out of Omar that day and the decision to render Mr. Arar to Syria the next day."[75] Arar was later completely exonerated by a special commission set up to investigate his extraordinary rendition and torture. He was then compensated by the Canadian government.[76]

"WE LOOK LIKE HYPOCRITES"

Omar Khadr's supporters include the former US Chief Prosecutor at Guantánamo, Col. Morris Davis. In 2007 Davis resigned his position, explaining that the Pentagon interfered in his cases; he didn't want to work under a new boss "who had encouraged the use of evidence even if it was gathered through waterboarding – an interrogation method that simulates drowning."[77] He condemned the US military treatment of Omar Khadr: "We look like hypocrites for detaining a 15-year-old in indefinite confinement and subjecting him to this extraordinary process which we would not condone, I would hope, if it was a 15-year-old American being detained by another country."[78]

The Canadian government seems not to have had much difficulty coping with the incarceration of a child soldier, even after accounts of his torture surfaced. Canada has proven itself a dismal failure in defending this young man's human rights. The NDP from early on supported his repatriation and participated in various key lobbying efforts. The Liberals announced his status as a child soldier under international law during the first month of his capture; however, it was years later that various Liberal leaders announced their desire to repatriate him to Canada. The federal Conservatives remained unmoved throughout Omar's imprisonment in Afghanistan and Cuba. Stephen Harper has become renowned internationally for his efforts to keep Omar Khadr in Guantánamo despite Canadian court findings and revelations of his torture. Harper's intransigence runs against the grain even of President Obama's early interest in closing Guantánamo and shipping Omar home in order to avoid what would unfold in the fall of 2010: the trial of a former child soldier by a Guantánamo Military Commission, an event that further undermined the credibility of this improvised legal process outside the conventional American justice system.[79]

Amir Attaran, a University of Ottawa constitutional law expert, has assessed Harper's refusal to repatriate Khadr as motivated by political interests, "a desire to appear tough on the war on terror."[80] For Attaran, the subject of Canadian complicity in torture has multiple trajectories. His Access to Information request brought heavily redacted documents to light in 2007 that revealed the Canadian military was not monitoring detainees who had been transferred from Canadian to Afghan custody.[81]

At that time, Gordon O'Connor, the Canadian minister of defence, announced, "This isn't Somalia. Let's get the scale properly."[82] His reference was to the appalling 1993 torture and murder of the young Somalian Shidane Arone during a Canadian peacekeeping mission – a national scandal. But O'Connor's observation about the difference "in scale" would prove to be misleading, since without monitoring no comparison could be made.

Richard Colvin, a Canadian diplomat in Afghanistan, had been informing top officials at Foreign Affairs and the Canadian Airforce about Afghan detainee torture since 2006.[83] In his November 2009 testimony to a House of Commons Parliamentary Committee, Colvin called our Afghan detainee practices "un-Canadian, counterproductive and probably illegal," even as the federal government attacked and tried to discredit his testimony.[84] He stated: "The likelihood is that all the Afghans we handed over were tortured. For interrogators in Kandahar, it was a standard operating procedure."[85]

These scandalous and widely reported revelations were a key factor in Harper's prorogation of Parliament late in 2009, a tactic to avoid accountability and the release of relevant documents.[86] But by March 2011 when more documentation was unredacted, Attaran substantiated Colvin's claims, announcing that the less censored versions of the documents showed that Canada went even further in intentionally handing over prisoners to torturers. The Harper government did not simply turn "a blind eye to abuse of Afghan detainees," observed Attaran: "It wasn't accidental; it was done for a reason ... It was done so that they could be interrogated using harsher methods."[87] Canada's federal response to the "War on Terror" thus appears to be in concert with the policies laid out in George Bush's unprincipled justification for torture – even though much of the research teaches us that torture often leads to false testimony.[88]

Oblivious to public pressure, CSIS director Jim Judd maintained an unwavering confidence that the Conservative government would refuse to repatriate Omar Khadr. A WikiLeaks document summarizing a memo Judd wrote on 8 July 2008 reveals his contempt for dissenters: "Judd commented that cherry-picked sections of the court-ordered release of a DVD of Guantánamo detainee and Canadian citizen Omar Khadr (ref D) would likely show three (Canadian) adults interrogating a kid who breaks down in tears. He observed that the images would no doubt trigger 'knee-jerk anti-Americanism' and 'paroxysms of moral outrage, a Canadian specialty.'"[89]

MAGICAL THINKING ABOUT OMAR KHADR

The "War on Terror" required, as political scientist Malinda Smith has written, "a conceptual sorcery." It conjured up "an irreducible enemy that could be identified, classified, profiled, targeted, and destroyed in the name of Western civilization."[90] For Americans, Osama bin Laden became the convenient singular face of the enemy, even as al-Qaeda and other organizations proliferated with lethal impact outside Afghanistan and around the world in autonomous terrorist cells.[91] Omar Khadr belongs to us, the baby face of our enemy whose interminable imprisonment helps to justify our presence in Afghanistan. During Stephen Harper's Conservative government era, Omar Khadr stands in for the Muslim terrorist enemy in a Canadian foreign policy hardened in its uncritical support of a far-right Israel. For Canadians, Omar Khadr became an absent presence – the "terrorist" boy exiled to a nightmare prison outside domestic and international law. His abject life in that no-man's-land called Guantánamo helped us maintain our virtuous innocence. We could hear of his torture but hold him at a distance so far away.

In 2009, a confidential cable from the American embassy in Ottawa – a "scenesetter" memo to the US State Department – observed that "Canadians always carry a chip on their shoulder ... Canada is condemned to always play 'Robin' to the U.S. 'Batman.'"[92] While Jean Chrétien's Liberal government refused to participate with the United States in the catastrophic invasion of Iraq post-9/11, we became a kind of sidekick to the Americans participating with other NATO forces in an undeclared war in Afghanistan. There is an uncanny parallel too in the way our nations have imagined the enemy during the "War on Terror" – a duo of masked mastermind and boy sidekick.

British writer Tariq Ali explains how the Canadian government's disinterest in repatriating Omar Khadr underscores our "vassal state relation to American hegemony."[93] Increasingly Canada is being tied ever more closely to the United States through agreements. And our federal government under Stephen Harper has embarked on a campaign to transform Canada into a nation where military history and militarized interests define our value – a convenient transformation when our neighbour to the south has many military preoccupations.

The "Wild West" warfare of this post-9/11 era is dramatized in the poem George Elliott Clarke has written for this anthology. In Clarke's metaphorical landscape, American justice appears to have reverted to an earlier time, when the sharpest shooter ruled – or just like today, when remote-controlled drones roam the world to "take out" the enemy. Eventually the United States got their man: the elusive bin Laden was finally killed in his Pakistan hideout on 2 May 2011, almost ten years after he went on the run; meanwhile we secured our poster-boy enemy Omar Khadr in Guantánamo.

American remote-controlled drones now routinely cross national lines to kill suspected terrorists or innocent civilians – an arms-length warfare with no contact. A drone was authorized to target another alleged terrorist leader, Anwar Awlaki, an American citizen living in Yemen. With no arrest or trial, was the United States murdering its own citizens?[94] Questions fell on deaf ears.

ON SUPPORT FOR OMAR KHADR

The deaths of 158 Canadian soldiers in Afghanistan between 2002 and 2011 have caused understandable grief and pain. Thus, to some, Omar Khadr is an Afghan-based terrorist worthy only of contempt, and anyone who defends him is guilty of treacherous betrayal. One only has to peruse the comment sections in online articles about Omar Khadr to encounter the fury directed at him. The cultural logic of far-right websites leaks into mainstream newspapers that insist this Canadian citizen has no Canadian ties,[95] blame him for his father's crimes, call for his permanent deportation, threaten him with violence, and demonize him as a "barbarian" opposed to the "civilized" Westerners who condemned him to torture.

The Canadian public has often been evenly divided in its attitude towards Omar Khadr. Angus Reid polls over time document how about 40 per cent of Canadians believed his treatment was unfair, another 40 per cent thought he should remain in Guantánamo, and the remaining 20 per cent were undecided or did not express an opinion.[96] A 2008–09 Angus Reid poll noted telling regional differences: "Respondents in Alberta (53 per cent) and Ontario (46 per cent) are more likely to side with leaving Khadr in Guantánamo, while a majority of people in Quebec (53 per cent) demand his repatriation."[97]

OMAR KHADR'S ADVOCATES[98]

In her contribution to this book, Sheema Khan suggests that the question of principles over politics "serves as a backdrop for the unfolding drama of Omar Khadr." Those principles have been defended by Canadian courts and particularly by human rights NGOs, which "play an invaluable role in serving as bulwarks against government abuses of the Canadian Charter."

Through the long years that Omar has lived in Guantánamo, he has sometimes disappeared from view. When he has surfaced in the news, it has usually been thanks to the public advocacy of Amnesty International, Lawyers Against War, Human Rights

Watch, UNICEF,[99] and other NGOs, legal scholars, and organizations committed to human rights. The Canadian Bar Association has also advocated on his behalf, particularly during the latter part of his imprisonment. In spite of this, the response of successive Canadian governments has been unyielding, and Omar remains the last Western prisoner in Guantánamo.[100]

To catalogue briefly the ongoing campaigns of Amnesty International Canada is to encounter some Canadians' unwavering support for Omar Khadr over the years, and to underscore the fixed ideological posturing of the Canadian government in opposition to human rights. Beginning in 2002 when Omar was still held in Bagram, Amnesty Canada's secretary-general, Alex Neve, wrote letters about Omar's case to Prime Minister Chrétien, Foreign Minister Graham, and others. A few smaller NGOs, notably Lawyers' Rights Watch and Lawyers Against War, also became involved. In 2002–03, Amnesty's "Real Security" campaign featured Omar in background materials and postcards about the approximately eighteen children detained at Guantánamo in the early years after 9/11. A separate campaign for Omar was established by 2005, as the Canadian branch successfully lobbied Amnesty's international secretariat to include him among its individual case sheets and campaigns. In the following two years, Amnesty Canada devised a series of protests against the Military Commissions at Guantánamo, and a series of "web actions" focused attention on Omar Khadr's two Military Commission hearings.

By early 2007, several other NGOs had begun to take a serious interest in the case, and the international Child Rights Information Network began an ongoing feature using Amnesty Canada's materials. In June 2007, Neve presented the "eminent persons" letter on Parliament Hill, signed by twenty-five current and former parliamentarians, six human-rights organizations, and 111 lawyers, academics, and activists. The letter reads in part:

> The military commission's dismissal of charges against Khadr confirms our apprehension that the process devised by the United States to try detainees is fundamentally and irreparably flawed. Our concern about the unfairness of this ad hoc regime at Guantánamo Bay is underscored by the fact that the military commission is authorized to try only non-US citizens. If the system is not good enough for Americans, it should not suffice for Canadians either. We do not believe that Canada should remain

silent while the US subjects a Canadian citizen – especially someone who was a minor when first detained – to such a process.[101]

By late 2007, an online email action regularly gave updates about Omar's case. Amnesty continued to organize postcard campaigns and joint letters with other NGOs. They prepared reports for the subcommittee of the Standing Committee on Foreign Affairs that eventually would call for Omar's repatriation. In summer 2008, they co-founded the national NGO Coalition for the Repatriation of Omar Khadr.

In 2009, they presented more than 50,000 postcards and petition signatures to Parliament Hill. They also sought intervenor status at the Federal Court of Appeal. Amnesty continued to develop other online projects, open letters, and lobbying initiatives through 2010 and 2011. A November 2010 open letter after Omar's plea bargain and sentencing requested that the Government of Canada finally resolve outstanding human rights issues in his case. Later Amnesty co-sponsored multiple screenings of the documentary *You Don't Like the Truth*. The consistency of its support over the years has been impressive.

DEBATING CANADIAN MULTICULTURALISM

Threaded through this book is an ongoing discussion about "belonging and banishment,"[102] culture and citizenship. Jasmin Zine describes how Muslim youth are transformed from "citizens to outlaws." Her concern is that "multiculturalism has not provided a guarantee for equality or acceptance and instead serves as a masquerade obscuring the relations of racialized power and privilege that shape the nation." Is Omar Khadr's treatment a sign that multiculturalism can create second-class citizens who are denied access to the rights and privileges of full citizens? Shadia Drury ends her essay in this volume with a warning that "Canadian multiculturalism is perilous to both Canada and its immigrants."

These comments are part of a national conversation. Immigrant connections to their ethnic communities are sometimes thought to inhibit social cohesion to the broader society. But research based on the largest study of ethnic communities in Canada that included 41,666 individual surveys yields fascinating insights into immigrant generations. Sociologist Jeffrey Reitz observes, "There are *consistently positive relations between ethnic involvements and two indicators: sense of belonging in Canada and overall life satisfaction*" (italics in the original).[103] Arguing about multiculturalism, Reitz maintains, can "distract us from addressing the most critical issues."[104]

Some of the critical issues are discrimination and racism. The research of sociologist Irene Bloemraad suggests that Canada's multiculturalism and social supports facilitate Canadian immigrants' integration more easily than the American melting pot. But, Bloemraad notes, "Canadian multiculturalism is falling short to the extent that a central policy goal is ensuring equal opportunity to participate and flourish for all Canadians. Visible minorities hang on to ethnic attachments longer than those of European-origin in part due to a greater perception of discrimination, and they face objective inequalities in the economic system."[105] As Reitz sums up, "white/visible minority differentiation constitutes a significant fault line affecting social cohesion."[106]

Commentary about Omar Khadr and his family circle often develops on the basis of partial evidence and affective hunches sometimes informed by "multicultiphobia," a term coined by Phil Ryan to describe the anxiety and misinformation that can anathematize multiculturalism rather than spur constructive debate.[107]

Some reduce the conundrum of Omar Khadr to Canadian multiculturalism itself. But "to blame Canadian multiculturalism for the fate of Khadr," argues political scientist Yasmeen Abu-Laban, "is, at the very least, an exaggeration." Says Abu-Laban, some people propose "the Khadr family represents a 'culture' that multiculturalism supports" – but she points out that "the Khadr family, reviled as it has been by many Canadians, reflects *itself*, not Canadian multiculturalism policy, and certainly not all immigrants and refugees from the Middle East."

Multiculturalism does not exist in isolation. "Canadian multiculturalism policy operates in the framework of Canadian human rights and Canadian law," Abu-Laban explains. "It is not some carte blanche to murder/oppression/subjugation." Research shows that succeeding generations of immigrants increasingly assimilate. "Canada also stresses a policy of *integration* in relation to immigration. That means immigrants are expected to adapt to the host country, and at the same time the host country adapts to immigrants."[108]

But appeals to multiculturalism can cover over forms of discrimination. In an earlier study, contributor Yasmin Jiwani concluded that the media representation of violence in Canadian society tends to underplay racism in cases where the perpetrators are white: "a cultural explanation is explicitly avoided in order to divert attention from issues of racism and the consequences of racialized difference." On the other hand, in the case of "honour killings," explanations reduce violence against women to cultural factors in visible minority communities.[109]

Contributor Sheema Khan and others have encouraged the Muslim community to "unequivocally condemn imported misogynous practices and attitudes."[110] And Canadian Muslim leaders have publicly addressed practices like "honour killings." During a three-month trial in which three members of the Shafia family of Montreal were convicted of murdering four women,[111] Muslim imams and leaders spoke out across Canada about violence against women. In an interview, Calgary Imam Syed Soharwardy affirmed adherence to the law, religious and secular: "Domestic violence is very un-Islamic. It's a crime in the eyes of the law, it's a crime in the Islamic teaching ... Prophet Mohammed has clearly said in very unambiguous words that women have rights ... and men have an obligation to treat their wife and daughters ... with kindness and courtesy."[112]

By the end of the Shafia trial, experts in child welfare raised questions about whether child-protection services responded adequately to a series of complaints by the young women who were killed. While Nico Trocmé, chair of Social Work at McGill University, "believes the cultural component of the case should be studied, he wonders if the lack of decisive intervention has more to do with breakdowns in the child-protection system."[113] And public debate shifted to include questions about whether domestic violence against women in any family or culture could often be considered "honour killings."[114]

THE STRANGER STRANGER

Omar Khadr's fate provides a space in which to explore the social and cultural construction of the Muslim man in Canadian society, but the way that Muslim women are codified and framed is equally important. To some Canadians, the traditional dress of Omar's sister and mother is as much a sign of foreignness and a target of suspicion as the women's sometimes alienating words of support for terrorism.

Sherene Razack tracks the gendered differences that inform the treatment of "dangerous" Muslim men and "imperilled" Muslim women. Muslim men risk "the camp" and deportation; Muslim women are marked as victims to be rescued or candidates for a transforming makeover without the head coverings, markers of strangeness, secrecy, and suspicion.[115]

Legal scholar Natasha Bakht writes elsewhere about what is at stake in the prohibition of women's religious dress. Objections to the veil in its various forms from the hijab to the niqab are essentially attempts to further marginalize an already targeted religious minority. But "our need for these 'stranger strangers' who refuse to comply with our rules helps us to better comprehend who we are. The real lesson here is that we might be better served by focusing our gaze inward and rigorously questioning our own assessments."[116] Omar Khadr is one of these "stranger strangers" – the face of the enemy, a person rendered invisible and silent behind Guantánamo's veil.

ON THE FUTURE OF OMAR KHADR

Over the years, support for Omar Khadr has developed in many places across Canada. In 2008, King's University College, a small Christian university in Edmonton, began to take up Omar's plight.[117] A series of meetings and rallies at King's, evolving from its advocacy of compassionate Christian ideals, raised the issue of Omar Khadr. By supporting him, King's faced the risk that donors might take their funds elsewhere. But its focus on critical thinking and ethical values, and the commitment of many students along with some faculty, underpinned its dedication to social justice.

Students who researched the story convinced Dean of Arts Arlette Zinck to correspond with him. By January 2009, he was writing in response, "Your letters are like candles very bright in my hardship and darkness."[118]

What will Omar's future bring? To those who have spent time with him since his imprisonment, he appears resilient. On 10 March 2011, Carol Off, host of CBC's *As It Happens*, interviewed Zinck, who with the help of colleagues had prepared for Omar an upgraded curriculum of Canadian literature and mathematics. His last formal studies ended in Grade 8. The curriculum was designed, Zinck told Off, "to engage a very competent adult mind ... Omar Khadr is catching up from missing years in his education ... The challenge is to speak a little comfort to his heart ... He desired above all else an education." She said, "He is an avid reader, and very capable."

While Omar remains in solitary confinement in Guantánamo awaiting his transfer to Canada, he maintains his ongoing program of study. He prepares for his eventual release from prison. At his October 2010 military hearing, he said, "My biggest dream and biggest wish [is] to get out of this place. Because, being in this place, I've really known and understood the wonders and beauties of life I haven't experienced before. I would really like to have a chance to experience these things. The first thing is school and knowledge, [to] have the chance to have true relationships, an experience I've never had in my life ... Education is knowledge ... I just feel it's something beautiful to understand and know and have a sense of everything in life."[119]

NOTES

1 "Omar Khadr's Limbo," *Globe and Mail*, 11 August 2005, A14, *Canadian Periodicals Index Quarterly*, web, 11 September 2011.

2 "Organized oblivion" is the term used by philosopher Hannah Arendt in *The Origins of Totalitarianism* to describe the concentration camp. Sherene Razack explores connections to the contemporary US prison systems including Abu Ghraib and how they are part of what Ruth Wilson Gilmore characterizes "as a 'regime of abandonment' in which surplus and unwanted populations who are mostly of colour are permanently imprisoned and evicted from law." See Sherene Razack, *Casting Out: The Eviction of Muslims from Western Law and Politics* (Toronto: University of Toronto Press, 2008), 60–1.

3 In Nazi Germany, undesirables were subject to new laws that defined "a state of emergency" where some citizens deserved special treatment in a hierarchy of citizen rights. The "state of emergency" was formulated by German Nazi jurist Carl Schmitt. The "state of exception" is discussed by Italian philosopher Giorgio Agamben, who compares Guantánamo Bay to the Nazi camps, both "removed from the law and from judicial oversight." See his *Homo Sacer: Sovereign Power and the Bare Life* (Stanford: Stanford University Press, 1998).

4 Michelle Shephard, "'Khadr Is Rock Star of Gitmo': Psychiatrist," *Toronto Star*, 27 October 2010, http://www.thestar.com/article/881132--khadr-is-rock-star-of-gitmo-psychiatrist-testifies (accessed 20 December 2011).

5 "The Canadian Security Intelligence Service has issued reports that terrorist groups are active in Canada … Those risks could threaten the Canadian economy ... Canada cannot be seen as being an insecure country in the eyes of its major trading partners … Ultimately, it is the biggest concern we have ... in terms of trucking and airports, Harper said." Rick Mofina, "The Arrest of a Canadian Teen Suspected," *CanWest News*, 6 September 2012 (accessed 27 January 2012) CBCA Current Events (document ID351822751).

6 The United States appears eager to return Omar Khadr to Canada. In her 10 January 2012 article, "Analysis: Guantanamo Marks a Decade of Detention," Michelle Shephard notes, "A Pentagon official told me a couple months ago: 'We'd drop him off at the border if we could.'" At http://www.thestar.com/news/world/article/1113578--analysis-guantanamo-marks-a-decade-of-detention.

7 Simone Weil, *Gravity and Grace* (London: Routledge and Kegan Paul, 1992).

8 One entrance into the archive is through Aboriginal work that includes Eden Robinson's novels; Thomas King's *Truth about Stories*, among his other works; the stories and storytelling of Richard Van Camp; and the poems of Marilyn Dumont. Listen to tales of slavery and the effects of continued bigotry in the eloquent works of Afua Cooper, George Elliott Clarke, and Lawrence Hill. Read the intergenerational tales of the Chinese head tax in Fred Wah and Wayson Choy, Larissa Lai, and Rita Wong. In Anita Rau Badami's novel *Can You Hear the Nightbird Call?* and Sharon Pollock's play *The Komagata Maru Incident,* encounter dramatizations of the events in Vancouver Harbour that led to the expulsion of mainly Sikh passengers who would be murdered on their return to Calcutta. Listen to the stories of the World War II internment of Japanese Canadian citizens when knowledge and understanding gave way to fear. Joy Kogawa in her classic *Obasan*, Roy Miki in poems and prose, and other writers interrogate how Canadian citizens came to be seen as enemies of the state during an earlier time of war.

9 Sami al Haj was beaten and sexually abused. He suffered religious persecution and endured a 438-day hunger strike while being force-fed. "'Guantanamo Files': Dozens Held Were Innocent," Al Jazeera website, http://english.aljazeera.net/news/americas/2011/04/201142561524783918.html (accessed 16 October 2011); Robert Fisk, "Six Years in Guantanamo," *The Independent,* 25 September 2008, http://www.independent.co.uk/opinion/commentators/fisk/robert-fisk-six-years-in-guantanamo-941479.html (accessed 3 November 2011).

10 Quoted in Yochi J. Dreaen, "The Prison Poets of Guantanamo Find a Publisher: Military Security Clears 22 after Checking for Code; What's Lost in Translation," *Wall Street Journal*, 20 June 2007, http://online.wsj.com/article/SB118217520339739055.html (accessed 10 October 2011). Marc Falcoff, the editor of the anthology *Poems from Guantánamo: The Detainees Speak (Iowa City: University of Iowa Press, 2007)*, describes the publication process: "It had to be cleared by a Pentagon-appointed censorship team. Or in fact an uncensorship team, as everything is presumptively censored." Quoted in "Poetry and Politics at Guantánamo: An interview with Marc Falkoff, Editor of Poems from Guantánamo: The Detainees Speak," Andy Worthington website, 3 October 2007, http://www.andyworthington.co.uk/2007/10/03/poetry-and-politics-at-guantanamo-an-interview-with-marc-falkoff-editor-of-poems-from-guantanamo-the-detainees-speak/.

11 Cary Nelson, "Keep Your Hands Off the 'Fierce Humanities,'" *Chronicle of Higher Education*, 28 August 2011, http://chronicle.com/article/Keep-Your-Hands-Off-the/128804/(accessed 9 September 2011).

12 Sharon Pollock has published an excellent longer play about Omar Khadr: "Man Out of Joint," in *Sharon Pollock, Collected Works*, vol. 3, ed. Cynthia Zimmerman (Toronto: Playwrights Canada Press, 2008).

13 Zolf's poem is part of "The Tolerance Project" that she writes in response to Wendy Brown's *Regulating Aversion: Tolerance in Age of Identity and Empire* (Princeton: Princeton University Press, 2006). "Brown examines how US government policy notions of tolerance have come to dominate pedagogy and other forums and have shifted discussions from challenging citizens to work on internalized and externalized racism, homophobia, classism, etc., to simply tolerating (or not, in the case of Islamophobia, for example) what we hate about the neighbo(u)r over the fence." See Zolf's essay "The Tolerance Project," *Jacket2*, 20 July 2012, http://jacket2.org/article/tolerance-project#7.

14 Interview with Dennis Edney, August 2010.

15 The episode is captured on video and in photographs. The phrase is journalist Paul Koring's and underscores that Omar Khadr was not the seasoned terrorist that some claimed. See Koring, "U.S. Must 'Certify' Canada before Khadr Can Return," *Globe and Mail*, 21 November 2011, http://www.theglobeandmail.com/news/world/americas/us-must-certify-canada-before-khadr-can-return/article2244046/.

16 Considering the value of winning "hearts and minds" in Afghanistan, this spatial overlap of American torture in what were formerly Soviet

facilities seems an unfortunate historical echo, since the Soviet invasion during the 1980s was so abhorrent to the Afghanis.

17 Michelle Shephard and Tonda MacCharles, "Khadr Linked Arar to Terrorism, Court Hears," *Toronto Star*, 19 January 2009, http://www.thestar.com/news/world/article/573432 (accessed 10 November 2011). Two deaths in Bagram occurred in December 2002 after Omar Khadr's departure, but in 2004, twenty-eight soldiers would be identified by the US Army as possibly involved, and fifteen would be charged. See "Army Completes Investigations of Deaths at Bagram," US Army News Release, Army Public Affairs website, 14 October 2004, http://web.archive.org/web/20071224110128/http://www4.army.mil/ocpa/read.php?story_id_key=6450 (accessed 21 January 2012).

18 "Canadian Teen Held by U.S. Military in Afghanistan Will Get Consular Help," *Canadian Press News Wire*, 6 September 2002, http://www.proquest.com.login.ezproxy.library.ualberta.ca/ (accessed 26 January 2012).

19 Telephone interview, 10 December 2011.

20 Lois Abraham, "Canadian Teen Allegedly Threw Grenade That Killed U.S. Soldier in Afghanistan," *Canadian Press NewsWire*, 9 September 2002, http://www.proquest.com.login.ezproxy.library.ualberta.ca/ (accessed 26 January 2012).

21 Paul Koring, "In Omar Khadr's Legal Saga, a New Chapter Begins," *Globe and Mail*, 26 October 2011, http://www.theglobeandmail.com/news/politics/in-omar-khadrs-legal-saga-a-new-chapter-begins/article2215216/ (accessed 27 October 2011).

22 Michelle Shephard, "Secret Khadr Dossier Issued by Mistake," 5 February 2008, http://www.thestar.com/News/World/article/300470; "OC-1 CITF witness report, 17 March 2004," released Wikisource.org website, http://en.wikisource.org/wiki/OC-1_CITF_witness_report.

23 "Khadr's previous defence lawyer had accused the military of doctoring the report to fit their case – calling it 'manufactured evidence.'" See Michelle Shephard, "At Omar Khadr Hearing, U.S. Officer Explains Changing Battle Report," *Toronto Star*, 1 May 2010, http://www.thestar.com/specialsections/article/803378--at-omar-khadr-hearing-u-s-officer-explains-changing-battle-report (accessed 20 October 2011).

24 Richard J. Brennan and Allan Woods, "Canada Shamed on Afghan Prison Torture," *Toronto Star*, 19 November 2009.

25 This letter is reproduced in "A Letter for Omar Khadr, a Guantanamo Detainee," *Washington Post*, 27 July 2010,

http://voices.washingtonpost.com/checkpoint-washington/2010/07/a_letter_from_omar_khadr_guant.html.

26 Vivian Rakoff, professor emeritus of psychiatry at the University of Toronto, commented about Omar soon after his capture, "Adolescence is a time of separation from the certainty of family, and a time of rebellion. But what [Omar] is accused of doing stops being an act of rebellion and becomes more like filial submission." See Isabel Vincent, "The Good Son," *National Post,* 28 December 2002, http://www.hvk.org/articles/1202/293.html (accessed 10 November 2011).

27 "Connect with Mark Kelley," *CBC-TV*, 26 October 2010, http://www.cbc.ca/connect/2010/10/omar-khadr-rob-ford-sperm-donation.html (accessed 6 October 2011). Levant writes in his blog that Omar Khadr is "clearly not entitled to be treated like a soldier … I call him a murderer. But that implies certain entitlements to due process. I actually don't think he's entitled to even that. Caught illegally marauding in a war zone, I think he's legally entitled to a summary hearing and execution on the spot – not a real trial in Guantánamo Bay, Miami, Toronto or anywhere else … 'Hostis humani generis' – [Omar Khadr is] someone who is literally an enemy of all mankind." See "Let Omar Khadr Rot in Guantanamo Bay," 22 July 2009, http://ezralevant.com/2009/07/let-omar-khadr-rot-in-guantana.html (accessed 2 October 2011). This logic of the "outlaw" was used by John C. Yoo, the Bush administration deputy assistant attorney general, who composed what came to be known as "the torture memorandum," a 2003 document officially titled "Re: Military Interrogation of Alien Unlawful Combatants Held Outside the United States." Sceptical of international law, this text justified torture *in particular spaces*, like Bagram and Gitmo, US military bases outside of the United States. It sanctioned torture *for particular people*, like the Taliban and al-Qaeda, who were considered to be what the Romans would have called "homo sacer" – non-citizens outside the law in a state of exception where the usual laws of war including the Geneva Convention do not apply. See American Civil Liberties Union website, http://www.aclu.org/pdfs/safefree/yoo_army_torture_memo.pdf (accessed 20 December 2011). Ezra Levant's book *The Enemy Within: Terror, Lies and the Whitewashing of Omar Khadr* was scheduled for publication in March 2012.

28 Michelle Shephard, *Guantanamo's Child: The Untold Story of Omar Khadr* (Toronto: John Wiley 2008).

29 Personal interview, Edmonton, 30 September 2011.

30 Andy Worthington in an interview with Saurabh Kumar Shahi, "An Interview with Andy Worthington, Investigative Journalist and Author of 'The Guantánamo Files,' for *The Sunday Indian Times*," Andy Worthington website, 26 October 2011, http://www.andyworthington.co.uk/2011/10/26/an-interview-with-andy-worthington-investigative-journalist-and-author-of-the-guantanamo-files-for-the-sunday-indian/. See his book *The Guantánamo Files: The Stories of the 774 Detainees in America's Illegal Prison* (London: Pluto Press, 2007).

31 Roméo Dallaire reminds us how "children are vulnerable and easy to catch, just like minnows in a pond." See *They Fight Like Soldiers, The Die Like Children: The Global Quest to Eradicate the Use of Children* (Toronto: Random House, 2010), 3.

32 Brennan was Obama's initial choice as CIA director, but he withdrew himself from consideration because of public criticism of his CIA work under George Bush and his support of the rendition of prisoners to countries where they were tortured. His position in the Obama administration as deputy national security advisor for Homeland Security and assistant to the president did not require Senate confirmation.

33 "WikiLeaks's Release Shows Struggle to Relocate Guantanamo Detainees," *Washington Post*, 28 November 2010, http://www.washingtonpost.com/wp-dyn/content/article/2010/11/28/AR2010112804659.html.

34 Judith Butler, "Precarious Life, Grievable Life," in *Frames of War: When Is Life Grievable?* (Brooklyn: Verso, 2009).

35 *Canada AM* Interview with Amir Attaran, "Canada Will Repatriate Khadr, Cannon Says," 1 November 2010, *CTV News*, http://www.ctv.ca/CTVNews/TopStories/20101101/khadr-documents-101101/ (accessed 12 September 2011).

36 The American Civil Liberties Union notes that, even after changes, the Military Commissions Act of 2009 "still contains unconstitutional provisions": "The military commissions were created to circumvent the Constitution and result in quick convictions, not to achieve real justice." See "House Passes Amendments to Military Commissions Act," *Jurist*, 9 October 2009, http://jurist.law.pitt.edu/paperchase/2009/10/house-passes-amendments-to-military.php .

37 Paul Koring, "U.S. Must 'Certify' Canada before Khadr Can Return," *Globe and Mail*, 21 November 2011, http://www.theglobeandmail.com/news/world/americas/us-must-certify-canada-before-khadr-can-return/article2244046/.

38 For an outline of related issues, see: Daniel Schwartz, "Khadr Still in Limbo 10 Years after Opening of Guantanamo," 11 January 2012, CBC *News*, http://www.cbc.ca/news/canada/story/2010/11/10/f-omar-khadr-returns-faq.html.

39 Saurabh Kumar Shahi, "An Interview with Andy Worthington."

40 CNN *Wire*, 19 July 2010, http://articles.cnn.com/keyword/palau/featured/2.

41 The history and status of Human Concern International is described by Faisal Kutty in an article reproduced on his website: "Canada Calling – Canadian Charity Claims Religious Discrimination," *Washington Report*, July/August 1999, 52, 137, http://faisalkutty.com/publications/washington-report/canada-calling-canadian-charity-claims-religious-discrimination/ (accessed 26 December 2010).

42 According to an FBI interview with Omar's brother Abdullah Khadr, their father "last saw Bin Laden in 1999 when Bin Laden met with Ahmed Said to discuss Ahmed Said's efforts to reconcile differences among Bin Laden, the Taliban, and Afghan warlord." See "Affidavit of Gregory T. Hughes (2005)," Wikisource, http://en.wikisource.org/wiki/Affidavit_of_Gregory_T._Hughes.

43 Koring, "U.S. Must 'Certify' Canada."

44 The most extensive documentation is in the Wikipedia article "Ahmed Khadr," which references 100 articles to piece together his history and notes that lawyer Dennis Edney and Ahmed's imam in Toronto were unconvinced of his "senior" position in al-Qaeda. His family said he "maintained the contacts with al-Qaeda leaders in order to support his charity work" (*Wikipedia,* accessed 21 November 2011). The "Stipulation of Fact" document for Omar Khadr's plea bargain, 10 October 2010, states that "Ahmad Khadr was a trusted senior member of al Qaeda who had direct and continuous interactions with other al Qaeda."

45 Michelle Shephard, "A Break-In, a Slaying, a Khadr Marriage Mystery," 1 April 2009, http://www.thestar.com/news/canada/article/612188 (accessed 25 December 2010). Elsewhere the husband is characterized as having been raised a Christian. He defends his wife from those who vilify her on the basis of her 2004 *CBC-TV* interview: "If you take any person and the worst statement they've made at a difficult time and you repeat it ad nauseam in the press, anybody can look like a super-villain."

46 Linda Nguyen, "Court Frees Abdullah Khadr, Turns Down U.S. Extradition Request," *National Post,* 24 August 2010, http://www.

nationalpost.com/news/Court+frees+Abdullah+Khadr+turns+down+extradition+request/3358679/story.html (accessed 21 October 2011).

47 Randall Palmer, "Supreme Court Blocks Khadr Extradition to U.S.," Reuters Canada, 3 November 2011, http://ca.reuters.com/article/topNews/idCATRE7A24PG20111103.

48 Linda Nguyen, "Court Frees Abdullah Khadr."

49 The use of children in fighting by the Taliban and others is documented elsewhere. A child rights adviser with the UN Assistance Mission in Afghanistan (UNAMA) said, "We have evidence that the Taliban have been recruiting children aged 11–17 to carry out a range of activities – from armed combat to smuggling of weapons across the Pakistan-Afghan border and planting IEDs [improvised explosive devices]." See "Afghanistan: Taliban Deny Children Being Used as Suicide Bombers," 23 May 2011, IRIN Humanitarian News and Analysis, http://www.irinnews.org/report.aspx?ReportId=92790 (accessed 21 December 2011).

50 Interview with Carol Off, CBC-Radio's *As It Happens*, 10 March 2011.

51 "The Years of Shame," in "The Conscience of a Liberal," *New York Times* blog, 11 September 2011, http://krugman.blogs.nytimes.com/2011/09/11/the-years-of-shame/.

52 Anne McClintock, "Paranoid Empire: Specters from Guantanamo and Abu Ghraib," *Small Axe* 13, no. 28 (March 2009): 53–4.

53 "Comparing PBO and DND Cost Estimates on Canada's Proposed Acquisition of the F-35 Joint Strike Fighter: Some Preliminary Questions and Answers on Key Issues," Office of the Parliamentary Budget Officer, 23 March 2011, http://www.parl.gc.ca/PBO-DPB/documents/F35_QA_EN.pdf.

54 This spending has created a new "national security establishment" that includes the departments of National Defence, Foreign Affairs and International Trade, Public Safety, Justice, and related organizations such as the RCMP, CSIS, and the CBSA. See David MacDonald, "The Cost of 9/11 – Tracking the Creation of a National Security Establishment in Canada," Rideau Institute, September 2011, http://www.rideauinstitute.ca/file-library/cost-of-9-11.pdf. MacDonald asks how this money might have transformed public transit in Canadian cities, established a national daycare program, or "eliminated all payments for prescription medication" (6). He questions "whether Canada should spend another $100 billion or more over the coming decade on another national security establishment."

55 Lawrence Martin, "The Rise – in Canada of All Places – of Right-Wing Nationalism," 2 December 2011, http://www.ipolitics.ca/2011/12/02/lawrence-martin-the-rise-in-canada-of-all-places-of-right-wing-nationalism/.

56 The American Republican-style ideology and policies of the current Canadian leadership have a fascinating geneology. Contributor Shadia Drury once labelled Stephen Harper a "product" of the "Calgary School" – saying the University of Calgary political science department where Harper studied is home to "Canadian appropriation of American neo-conservatism." Drury warned that "members in the Calgary School want to replace the rule of law with the populism of the majority." She has attributed this in part to its philosophy informed by Leo Strauss's notion of "the noble lie" that represents "a huge contempt for democracy." See John Ibbitson, "Educating Stephen," *Globe and Mail,* 26 June 2004 (updated 8 April 2009), http://www.theglobeandmail.com/archives/educating-stephen/article931875/singlepage/#articlecontent. Marci MacDonald explores the Calgary School philosophy in "The Man behind Stephen Harper," *The Walrus* (October 2004).

57 For the significance of the Canadian government budgetary cost information in our analysis of Canadian policy, see David R. Boyd, "Courage and Public Policy: Twenty-First Century Challenges," Fedcan blog, "Equity Matters," 28 June 2011, http://blog.fedcan.ca/2011/06/28/courage-and-public-policy-21st-century-challenges/.

58 Canada mimics American-style prisons at the very moment the United States is crushed by the costs of the largest prison system in the world and releasing one-third of the prisoners in order to relieve the financial burden. Efforts to privatize Canadian health care also track this same trajectory of working towards failed American systems.

59 "The Funding Requirement and Impact of the "Truth in Sentencing Act," Office of the Parliamentary Budget Officer, 22 June 2010, http://www.parl.gc.ca/PBO-DPB/documents/TISA_C-25.pdf.

60 The response of the Canadian Ministry of Justice office – "We don't use these statistics as an excuse not to get tough on criminals" – proved absurd enough to qualify as part of the Calgary School "noble lie" rationale. See "Crime Rate Continues to Drop across Canada," *National Post,* 21 July 2011 http://news.nationalpost.com/2011/07/21/crime-rate-down-across-canada.

61 In the context of this US-style approach to crime and punishment, the Harper government's ongoing refusal to repatriate Omar Khadr is

unsurprising. In his study of child soldiers, anthropologist David Rosen notes that since the 1970s child soldiers have been "immunized from prosecution" by various "legal and social changes." But simultaneously there is a shift in how children are being criminalized: "especially in U.S. law ... there is a tendency to treat children like adults ... [and] in Western legal systems, especially in the United States, reclassifying children is rarely to their benefit." David M. Rosen, *Armies of the Young: Child Soldiers in War and Terrorism* (Chapel Hill, NC: Rutgers University Press, 2005), 136.

62 Instructions were given to public servants that "Government of Canada" in federal communications should be replaced by the words "Harper Government": Bruce Cheadle, "Tories Re-Brand Government in Stephen Harper's Name," *Globe and Mail,* 3 May 2011, http://www.theglobeandmail.com/news/politics/tories-re-brand-government-in-stephen-harpers-name/article1929175/ (accessed 2 December 2011).

63 Lawrence Martin, "Don't Expect a Border Pact Backlash," *Globe and Mail,* 6 December 2011, A15. Martin's claim about right-wing nationalism seems increasingly fitting as critique. The cult of the leader plays a role in this far-right nationalist ideology.

64 "[UN] Convention against Torture and Other Cruel, Inhuman or Degrading Treatment or Punishment," Human Rights Web, http://www.hrweb.org/legal/cat.html (accessed 18 November 2011).

65 Michelle Shephard, *Guantanamo's Child,* 90.

66 Josh White, "Tactic Used after It Was Banned," *Washington Post,* 8 August 2008, http://www.washingtonpost.com/wp-dyn/content/article/2008/08/07/AR2008080703004_pf.html (accessed 17 November 2011).

67 David Keen, *Endless War: Hidden Functions of the "War on Terror"* (London: Pluto, 2006), 242.

68 Omar's words provides the title for the documentary *You Don't Like the Truth: 4 Days inside Guantánamo.* See excerpts from the screenplay in this book.

69 Robert Holmes, BC Civil Liberties Association, letter to Stephen Harper, 17 February 2010, http://www.bccla.org/pressreleases/Letter_PM_Harper_Khadr.pdf (accessed 1 November 2011).

70 Morris Davis, "The Government's Narrative Was a Lie," *Der Spiegel,* 2 May 2011, http://www.spiegel.de/international/world/0,1518,760142,00.html (accessed 1 November 2011).

71 Arar, a Canadian citizen on a New York City stopover in transit from a family vacation, was detained in the United States in September 2002

and then deported for thirteen months to Syria – where his torture could be anticipated because it was a well-known Syrian prison practice.

72 "Khadr Only Said Arar 'Looked Familiar': FBI Notes," *Ottawa Citizen,* 21 January 2009, http://www.canada.com/ottawacitizen/news/story.html?id=34ee0fd3-bdd9-4bbc-80a8-97b1135a2ba5 (accessed 20 November 2011).

73 Ibid.

74 Monia Mazigh, *Hope and Despair: My Struggle to Free My Husband, Maher Arar,* trans. Patricia Claxton and Fred A. Reed (Toronto: McClelland & Stewart, 2008).

75 "Khadr Only Said Arar 'Looked Familiar.'"

76 In an analysis of the way Maher Arar's story "may be mapped in different ways," scholars Yasmeen Abu-Laban and Nisha Nath write: "The dominant Canadian narrative posits Arar's case as a simple tale of guilt versus innocence, in which the federal government's commission ultimately determined that an innocent man was wrongfully accused. Yet, through a more critical reading of the statements made by public officials, we identify two other dualistic discourses lurking below and working in tandem with that of guilt/innocence. The first dualism spins around Arar's status as a Syrian citizen (foreigner) and his status as a Canadian citizen and full member of Canada's immigrant-receiving and multicultural polity. The second dualism spins around a tension between the force of law (where coercive power allows that racialized violence is possible) and the rule of law (where the Canadian government's commitment to human rights, both nationally and domestically, limits the force, or at least legitimacy, of repression)." A similar analysis can be brought to bear on Omar Khadr with the ongoing refusal to recognize his citizenship and legal status. The title of Audrey Macklin's essay in this volume echoes this counterpoint between the force and rule of law in relation to the Khadr case.

77 Michael Melia, "Ex-Gitmo Prosecutor Charges Pentagon Interference," *Toronto Star,* 29 April 2008, http://www.thestar.com/News/World/article/419384 (accessed 13 November 2011).

78 Morris Davis, "The Guantanamo Paradox," Crimes of War website, http://www.crimesofwar.org/commentary/the-guantanamo-paradox/ (accessed 6 November 2011).

79 Commentator Norman Spector quotes from an *Ottawa Citizen* story, "U.S. Has No 'Stomach' to Try Omar Khadr," that "officials [probably in the Secretary of State's offices] are quietly seeking a way to

repatriate [the] Canadian-born terror suspect," in Spector's "Second Reading" blog post "Harper Should Call Obama Re: Omar Khadr," *Globe and Mail* website, 8 March 2010, http://www.theglobeandmail.com/news/politics/second-reading/spector-vision/harper-should-call-obama-re-omar-khadr/article1493491/ (accessed 12 September 2011).

80 CANADA AM interview with Amir Attaran, "Canada Will Repatriate Khadr, Cannon Says."

81 Attaran noted that chief of defence staff Gen. Rick Hillier "signed an agreement in December 2005 that allowed for the transfers, but didn't include a clause giving the Canadian military the right to inspect detainees after transfers have taken place. He said European countries that have transfer agreements have included this clause, which is crucial. [Attaran said,] "If we hand detainees over to known torturers ... and we tell them, 'nudge, nudge, wink, wink, we will not be back to inspect them,' that gives them a lot of latitude." "Latest Afghan Abuse Claims Spark Cries for O'Connor to Resign," *CBC News*, 23 April 2007, http://www.cbc.ca/news/canada/story/2007/04/23/afghan-torture.html.

82 "Military Probes Abuse Allegations in Afghanistan," *CBC News*, 6 February 2007, http://www.cbc.ca/news/canada/story/2007/02/06/military-probe.html (accessed 10 November 2011).

83 "All Afghan Detainees Likely Tortured: Diplomat," *CBC News*, 18 November 2009, http://www.cbc.ca/news/canada/story/2009/11/18/diplomat-afghan-detainees.html (accessed 10 November 2011).

84 Discrediting critics is part of a larger government campaign, according to Amir Attaran and other university faculty members critical of the Harper government. Reporters Susan Delacourt and Bruce Campion-Smith write of "an academic witch hunt by the governing party – part of a wider campaign to silence university voices that may be critical of the Conservatives. This hyperpartisan chill descended on the federal bureaucracy years ago – now the concern is that it's stretching into academia as well." "Tories Accused of Digging up Dirt on 'Liberal' Profs," *Toronto Star*, 11 February 2011, http://www.thestar.com/news/canada/article/936704--tories-accused-of-digging-up-dirt-on-liberal-profs#article (accessed 3 October 2011).

85 "All Afghan Detainees Likely Tortured: Diplomat."

86 Lawrence Martin writes, "The detainees imbroglio saw the government attempt to discredit a respected diplomat, Richard Colvin, for having the courage to come forward and challenge its story. It prompted Mr. Harper to try and deny Parliament its historic right of

access to documents. It was a catalyst in the Prime Minister's decision to prorogue Parliament 15 months ago, which touched off a national protest. It led to the Speaker's historic ruling condemning Mr. Harper's government." See "Tories Desperate to Deep-Six the Detainees File," *Globe and Mail*, 15 April 2011.

87 "Canada Wanted Afghan Prisoners Tortured: Lawyer," CBC *News*, 5 March 2010, http://www.cbc.ca/news/canada/story/2010/03/05/afghan-attaran005.html (accessed 4 October 2011).

88 "What torture has proven is exactly what experienced interrogators have said all along: First, when tortured, detainees will give only the minimum amount of information necessary to stop the pain. No interrogator should ever be hoping to extract the least amount of information. Second, under coercion, detainees give misleading information that wastes time and resources – a false nickname, for example. Finally, it's impossible to know what information the detainee would have disclosed under non-coercive interrogations." Matthew Alexander, "Tortured Logic," *Foreign Policy Review*, 4 May 2011, http://www.foreignpolicy.com/articles/2011/05/04/tortured_logic (accessed 3 November 2011).

89 "US Embassy Cables: Terror Suspects, Canada and the Law," *The Guardian,* 14 December 2010, http://www.guardian.co.uk/world/us-embassy-cables-documents/161421.

90 Smith, "Preface Post-9-11: Thinking Critically, Thinking Dangerously," in *Securing Africa: Post-9/11 Discourses on Terrorism* (Aldershot: Ashgate, 2010), xii. David Keen notes that the terrorist often performs a disappearing suicide act: "highly mobile, un-uniformed and often drawing sustenance from a criminal underworld, the terrorist is elusive even in death: on the whole the perpetrators of the worst atrocities can neither be interrogated or punished because they have committed suicide in the course of the crime." See David Keen, "War without End? Magic, Propaganda and the Hidden Functions of Counter-Terrorism," *Journal of International Development* 18 (2006): 87, 93–7.

91 Keen, like other commentators, describes how the "War on Terror" can actually enhance terrorist forces: counter-insurgency as practised by NATO and US forces in Afghanistan "profoundly shapes patterns of violence and terror, often by attracting new recruits to an otherwise-weak rebellion ("War without End?," 88).

92 Embassy Canada, Ottawa, "Scenesetter for the Secretary's Meeting with Canadian MF Cannon," 9 June 2009, WikiLeaks, http://wikileaks.

org/cable/2009/06/09OTTAWA448.html. See also Charlie Savage, "U.S. Diplomats Noted Canadian Distrust," *New York Times*, 1 December 2010, http://www.nytimes.com/2010/12/02/world/americas/02wikileaks-canada.html.

93 Tariq Ali, keynote address, International Week, University of Alberta, 30 January 2012.

94 These drone attacks are called a "targeted killing program" by the American Civil Liberties Union, and this program has been expanded by Obama.

95 For the first extended account of Omar Khadr's Canadian childhood, see Vincent, "The Good Son."

96 For instance, in August 2009, 42 per cent wanted Omar Khadr's repatriation while 19 per cent were undecided and 40 per cent recommended he be tried in Guantánamo. This had changed little from November 2008 when 37 per cent preferred Guantánamo-style justice. By 14 July 2010, 36 per cent preferred repatriation while 43 per cent wanted Guantánamo – a rise of six points in the two years leading up to the Military Commissions trial in Guantánamo in October 2010. See "As Trial Looms, Little Change in How Canadians Feel about Omar Khadr," 14 July 2010, Angus Reid, http://www.angus-reid.com/polls/43136/as-trial-looms-little-change-in-how-canadians-feel-about-omar-khadr/ (accessed 22 November 2011).

97 "Canadians Evenly Divided on Omar Khadr," Angus Reid, 2 September 2009, http://www.angus-reid.com/polls/40317/canadians-evenly-divided-on-how-to-deal-with-omar-khadr/ (accessed 20 November 2011).

98 This paragraph was written from notes provided by Hilary Holmes, campaigner for International Justice, Security and Human Rights, Amnesty International Canada, email correspondence, 21 October 2011.

99 "UNICEF Defends the Rights of a Child Soldier Held in Guantanamo," 5 February 2008, UNICEF, http://www.unmultimedia.org/radio/english/detail/37852.html.

100 Skype interview with Gail Davidson, Lawyers Rights Watch Canada, 4 October 2011.

101 Lloyd Axworthy et al. to Stephen Harper, 4 June 2007, Omar Khadr Case website, University of Toronto Faculty of Law, http://www.law.utoronto.ca/documents/Mackin/Khadr_OpenLetter.pdf (accessed 15 November 2011).

102 For more on this, see Natasha Bakht, ed., *Belonging and Banishment: Being Muslim in Canada* (Toronto: TSAR Publications, 2008).

103 Jeffrey Reitz, "Assessing Multiculturalism as a Behavioural Theory," *Multiculturalism and Social Cohesion,* 38. "Ethnic community attachments are not necessarily the most powerful determinants of social integration or vice versa. Other factors must be considered including the extent of equality and economic opportunity experienced by minority groups. And as well access to participation in the institutions of mainstream society. These in turn may be affected by broader aspects of society including labour market structures, the educational system, and availability of social services" (43).

104 Ibid.

105 Irene Bloemraad, "Canada: Multicultural Model or Cautionary Tale?," *Canadian Journal of Sociology* 35, no. 2 (2010): 311–12. See also her comparative study, *Becoming a Citizen: Incorporating Immigrants and Refugees in the United States and Canada* (Berkeley: University of California Press, 2006).

106 Jeffrey Reitz, "Assessing Multiculturalism as a Behavioural Theory," *Multiculturalism and Social Cohesion.*

107 See Phil Ryan, *Multicultiphobia* (Toronto: University of Toronto Press, 2010). Elsewhere Ryan argues against "an endless discussion about whether immigrants must adapt to 'Canadian ways,' we need to become more aware of what those Canadian ways truly are, and we all need to talk about just what we want them to be." See "Canada's Great National Itch: Debating Multiculturalism," Fedcan blog, 28 February 2011.

108 Personal correspondence, 13 and 23 January 2012. I am especially grateful for Yasmeen Abu-Laban's insights into key research, along with her numerous essays about debates in multiculturalism.

109 Jiwani observes that the 1998 Reena Virk murder in Victoria was widely reported as an event "emerging from girl violence and bullying" in spite of the fact that Virk was South Asian and her attackers were white. (Later the only male perpetrator would discover his Métis heritage.) In analyzing the media representation of an "honour killing" that occurred in nearby Vernon, BC, "the cultural signifiers used throughout the reportage clearly position the murders as arising from a cultural practice of arranged marriages and women's supposedly subordinate status." Yasmin Jiwani, *Discourses of Denial: Mediations of Race, Gender, and Violence* (Vancouver: UBC Press, 2006), xx. I am grateful for Yasmeen Abu-Laban for reminding me of

this text. During the writing of this introduction, another "honour killing" was in court, and the way the cultural issues played out in the media clearly defined how culture is framed by the law of the land.

110 Sheema Khan continues, "They should deal with the root causes of gender-based violence head on, rather than blaming the media for image problems. It's time for a critical examination of violence rooted in religious and cultural tradition." See "The Shame of Honour Crimes," *Globe and Mail,* 21 June 2010, http://www.theglobeandmail.com/news/opinions/the-shame-of-honour-crimes/article1612108/.

111 In 2009, a Montreal father, son, and second wife were charged with the murder of three daughters and the first wife, who were found submerged in a car near Kingston, Ontario. Testimony suggests the deaths were planned after one daughter's flight to a women's shelter to escape persecution by her family for her "immoral" behaviour that involved disobeying her father and having a boyfriend. At the sentencing hearing, the trial judge, Mr Justice Robert Maranger, said, "It is difficult to conceive of a more despicable, more heinous crime. The apparent reason behind these cold-blooded, shameful murders was that the four completely innocent victims offended your completely twisted concept of honour, a notion of honour that is founded upon the domination and control of women." Timothy Appleby, "Shafia Family Guilty of Murder; Judge Condemns 'Sick Notion of Honour,'" 29 January 2011, http://www.theglobeandmail.com/news/national/shafia-family-guilty-of-murder- judge-condemns-sick-notion-of-honour/article2318731/.

112 Myths about Islam were also publicly addressed by Queen's University Muslim scholar Ariel Salzmann, who described the Qu'ran as "an incredibly progressive document" for its time. Salzmann said the Qu'ran, while it maintains strongly patriarchal elements common to most religious texts, also "enshrines female rights and economic freedoms not seen in Christianity or Judaism." Michelle McQuigge, "Canada's Muslim Clerics Band Together to Denounce So-Called 'Honour Killings,'" *Winnipeg Free Press,* 9 December 2011, http://www.winnipegfreepress.com/breakingnews/canadas-muslim-clerics-band-together-to-denounce-so-called-honour-killings-135335613.html.

113 John Allemang, "Could Quebec Child Services Have Stopped the Shafia Deaths," *Globe and Mail,* 28 January 2012, http://www.theglobeandmail.com/news/national/could-quebec-child-services-have-stopped-the-shafia-deaths/article2318277/.

114 "According to the 2006 census, there are 48,090 Canadians with Afghan ancestry. Yet the media have unearthed only this one

high-profile case of multiple familial homicides. If the phenomenon of "honour killing" is reflective of cultural practices or religious traditions, why is the number of incidents not higher?" Yasmin Jiwani and Homa Hoodfar, "Should We Call It 'Honour Killing'?," 31 January 2012, *Montreal Gazette*, http://www.montrealgazette.com/news/Should+call+honour+killing/6075589/story.html. Questions about domestic violence in relation to honour killing were also raised earlier by Gerald Kaplan, "Honour Killings in Canada Even Worse Than We Believe," 23 July 2010, updated 15 November 2010, http://www.theglobeandmail.com/news/politics/honour-killings-in-canada-even-worse-than-we-believe/article1650228/.

115 Sherene Razack, *Casting Out*, 108.

116 Natasha Bakht, "Veiled Objections: Facing Public Opposition to the Niqab," in *Defining Reasonable Accommodation,* edited by Lori Beaman (Vancouver: UBC Press, 2010), 20.

117 "Statement of Faith," http://www.kingsu.ca/about-us/stmt_faith.html.

118 Sheila Pratt, "From Khadr, with Love: Professor Exchanged Letters with Accused Terrorist for Two Years," 30 October 2010, *Edmonton Journal,* http://www.canada.com/news/From+Khadr+with+love+Professor+exchanged+letters+with+accused+terrorist+years/3752425/story.html.

119 "Omar Apologizes to Widow," 29 October 2010, *CBC News*, http://www.cbc.ca/news/world/story/2010/10/28/omar-khadr-sentencing-hearing.html.

PART ONE

The Saga of Omar Khadr

Politics over Principles: The Case of Omar Khadr

SHEEMA KHAN

The saga of Omar Khadr has yet to reach a conclusive end. Yet the tortuous journey of this young man will continue to have reverberations in many ways for years to come – in the fields of law, human rights, and politics and, more importantly, for what his case has to say about the value of Canadian citizenship.

While successive federal regimes have acquiesced to the gulag that is Guantánamo Bay, public disclosure of Omar Khadr's's plight has moved both our courts and the wider public to demand just treatment of a fellow human being. The fact that the Canadian government has failed to stand up for the human rights of one of its citizens – a Muslim – has not been lost on the nation's Muslim population.

The treatment of Omar Khadr follows a disturbing pattern of human rights abuses of Muslims in Canada in the wake of the terrorist attacks on American soil in 2001. These include government complicity with the notorious American practice of extraordinary rendition (Maher Arar); collusion with foreign security services in the detention and torture of Canadians travelling abroad (Abdullah Almalki, Ahmad El Maati, and Muayyed Nureddin); and the use of secret evidence to detain immigrants (Hassan Almrei, Adil Charkaoui, Mohamed Harkat, Mahmoud Jaballah, and Mohamed Zeki Mahjoub).

In the spring of 2008, Canadians learned of the case of Abousfian Abdelrazik, a forty-six-year-old Canadian of Sudanese origin who had been stranded in Sudan for nearly five years as successive Canadian governments thwarted efforts to bring him home to his family in Montreal. According to federal government documents, he had been imprisoned in Khartoum at our own government's request. When he was eventually released, the government denied him a passport to return home to Canada. While the Harper government accused him of links to al-Qaeda, Abdelrazik has never been charged with any crime. Subsequent investigations by the RCMP and CSIS cleared him of any wrongdoing. In trying to find an explanation for why the government refused to bring him home, Abdelrazik told the *Globe and Mail* on Canada Day in 2008, "The Canadian government has a racist mind. It is because I am black and Muslim."[1]

In addition, government documents from April 2008 reveal that fear of displeasing the Bush administration has played a significant role in its refusal to return Abdelrazik to Canada: "Senior government of Canada officials should be mindful of the potential reaction of our US counterparts to Abdelrazik's return to Canada as he is on the US no-fly list ... Continued cooperation between Canada and the US in the matters of security is essential."[2]

In June 2009 the Federal Court ordered the Harper government to bring Abdelrazik back to Canada, since his citizenship rights had been violated. Abdelrazik had been on the United Nations Security Council blacklist, which included an asset freeze and travel ban, until November 2011. He has launched a multi-million dollar lawsuit against the government.

The now-infamous case of Maher Arar was the subject of an in-depth inquiry by Justice Dennis O'Connor that resulted in a multi-million dollar payout for Mr Arar from the Canadian government, and a slew of recommended changes to RCMP and CSIS practices. (A number of these recommendations remain unfulfilled as of 2012. The Harper government has given the go-ahead to CSIS to share information with foreign agencies even when there is a "substantial risk" it will lead to torture, contrary to Justice O'Connor's recommendation.)

Much of the Iacobucci inquiry into the events surrounding the detention and torture of Almalki, El Maati, and Nureddin has been held behind closed doors. The findings, published in October 2008, vindicated the three Muslim men at the heart of the inquiry. Nonetheless, the government admitted in January 2008 that Canada was justified in working with countries accused of engaging in torture, saying that the United Nations Convention against Torture was not a factor in deciding whether to send information to countries such as Syria and Egypt about Canadians detained there. However, as author Erna Paris notes, signatories to the UN Convention against Torture (which includes Canada) are prohibited from transporting any individual to a country that practises torture.

Finally, the Supreme Court of Canada deemed portions of the security certificate legislation unconstitutional. Those held under a security certificate now have the right to security-cleared counsel, who will have access to the evidence against the accused. The new process will still involve some court hearings that the suspects will not be permitted to attend.

These examples of injustice towards Canadian Muslims suggest that in a post-9/11 era, political, and security considerations take precedence over basic human rights. However, Canadian courts and human rights NGOs play an invaluable role in serving as bulwarks against government abuses of the Canadian Charter. It is this essential tension – between politics and principles – that serves as a backdrop for the unfolding drama of Omar Khadr.

THE "KHADR EFFECT"

In order to discuss the predicament of Omar Khadr in proper context, one must first look at the history of the Khadr family and the incidents leading to Omar Khadr's detention. Michelle Shephard, author of *Guantanamo's Child: The Untold Story of Omar Khadr*, provides an excellent in-depth analysis of Omar's story.[3]

The family patriarch was Ahmed Said Khadr, an engineer who moved to Canada from Egypt in 1977 and shortly thereafter married an Egyptian Palestinian refugee, Maha Elsamnah. In 1985, at the height of the Soviet occupation of Afghanistan, the family moved to Peshawar, Pakistan, where Khadr was put in charge of the office of Human Concern International (HCI), an Ottawa-based charity that provided relief to Afghan refugees. The Khadr family shuttled between Pakistan and Canada; Omar was born on 19 September 1986 in Scarborough, Ontario. Then, in 1995, Pakistani police charged Ahmed in connection with the bombing of the Egyptian embassy in Islamabad and imprisoned him. Protesting his innocence, he went on a hunger strike and was hospitalized. During that very period, then Prime Minister Jean Chrétien was on a state visit to Pakistan. Maha Elsamnah used the occasion to plead with Chrétien to secure her husband's release. During talks with Pakistani Prime Minister Benazir Bhutto, Chrétien asked that Mr Khadr be treated fairly. A few weeks later, the charges were dropped and Khadr was released. Subsequently, HCI fired him, and he went on to run his own relief organization.

By 1998, Pakistani security agencies were after Khadr again for alleged ties with Osama bin Laden. The Khadr household – consisting of the parents and six children – was based in Jalalabad, Afghanistan. According to accounts provided by Zaynab Khadr in Lawrence Wright's book *The Looming Tower*, the Khadr clan shared a large family compound with the bin Ladens in Jalalabad. Following 9/11, Ahmed Said Khadr's name was placed on an international list of terror suspects.

Chrétien's intervention in Khadr's case, and the subsequent link to bin Laden, would later be known as the "Khadr effect" in Ottawa, and would play a significant role in the handling of Omar Khadr's affairs by both the Liberal and Conservative governments. Basically, this moniker signified the risk of prime ministerial intervention on behalf of those accused of terrorism.

It should be understood that all the Khadr children had been indoctrinated with the al-Qaeda ideology from an early age.

OMAR KHADR'S STORY: PAYING FOR THE SINS OF HIS FAMILY

Born in Ontario, Omar Khadr moved with his family to Afghanistan permanently when he was eleven years of age. On 17 July 2002, then aged fifteen, he was seriously wounded in a firefight with US soldiers in Afghanistan. He was accused of killing a medic, US Sgt Christopher James Speer, during that fight, and was detained at the notorious Bagram Air Base for two months. One of his interrogators at Bagram prison was later courtmartialled for brutality and for the murder of a prisoner. Foreign Affairs was notified of the arrest on 20 August 2002. Even at that time the government had concerns about the possible transfer of Omar to Guantánamo Bay; Canadian officials asked that his age be taken into account. In 2008 it was revealed that the Canadian government had asked the United States not to send Omar to Guantánamo. However, Stephen Harper, then head of the Canadian Alliance Party, told the media that his immediate concern was not that the fifteen-year-old be returned to Canada. Rather, the Canadian Alliance was more preoccupied "about Canada being a platform for activities that are dangerous to the Western Alliance."[4]

In late October 2002, Omar was transferred to Guantánamo Bay. He was not permitted to see a lawyer and was subject to torture by American authorities. A few months later, in February 2003, Foreign Affairs announced that Canadian officials had met with Omar, and that "he seem[ed] well."[5] As Canadians later learned, this meeting actually consisted of an interrogation by a CSIS official after Omar had been "softened up" by sleep deprivation techniques applied by the Americans. In 2009 the Security Intelligence Review Committee, the watchdog for CSIS, would reprimand the spy agency for ignoring human rights concerns in deciding to interview Omar at Guantánamo. A video of the event, released to the public by court order in 2008, did not show that the teen seemed "well," but rather, that he was in obvious mental and physical distress. This was not the first time that the Canadian government would be disingenuous about the state of Omar Khadr.

By the spring of 2004, the governments of Australia and Britain were actively trying to have their nationals removed from Guantánamo. Yet the Canadian government remained silent regarding the status of Omar Khadr. Dennis Edney, a Winnipeg-based lawyer, decided to act on Omar's behalf since Ottawa would not do so. He filed a legal brief challenging the legality of Omar's detention since he had been denied access to a lawyer for more than one and a half years, and he underlined the importance of protecting children's rights.

Any hope of garnering public sympathy for Omar's plight were soon sabotaged by a controversial interview given to the CBC in 2004 by Omar's mother, Maha Elsamnah, and sister, Zaynab Khadr. Both women lambasted Canadian liberalism and its societal mores and boasted of their friendship with Osama bin Laden, as they prepared to use the Canadian health care system for the rehabilitation of the youngest Khadr child, Karim, shot in the back outside the home where his father had been killed during combat. The response by Canadians was swift; almost ten thousand people signed an online petition demanding that the family be expelled from the country, while MP Stockwell Day suggested that they be barred from returning to Canada and a Liberal MP demanded that Ms Elsamnah be charged under the Anti-Terrorism Act.

Given the huge unpopularity of the Khadr name, few politicians dared to speak up on behalf of Omar, who was essentially paying the price for the sins of his family. According to three former Guantánamo Bay detainees, he was "in constant pain" and was prevented from getting proper medical treatment – in direct contradiction to statements given by Canadian government officials. Yet in 2004 the story remained under the radar for most Canadians, due in part to the unpopularity of the Khadr family.

Meanwhile, Canadian intelligence agents continued to travel to Guantánamo to interrogate Omar, while he remained in the legal black hole of Guantánamo where he had no impartial tribunal before which he could either clear his name or be given a defined punishment. Nor could he argue that as a minor, he bore a diminished responsibility for his actions. Canada's domestic spy agency, CSIS, took full advantage of the situation to gather information that was then passed on to both the RCMP and American authorities. Canadian government authorities, unlike their British and Australian counterparts, did not press the American administration for due process. The best that Foreign Affairs Minister Pierre Pettigrew could muster was to unsuccessfully seek reassurances from the United States that Omar Khadr would not be executed. The timidity and complicity of the Liberal government was shameful. Thankfully, the Canadian judicial system would not let politics get in the way of justice. In August 2005 the Federal Court ordered a temporary stop to these interrogations, pending a fuller hearing of Omar's Charter rights as a Canadian.

CALLS FOR JUSTICE

By early 2006 a chorus of world leaders had voiced unanimous objection to the existence of the military tribunals at Guantánamo Bay. A damning UN report found the prison falling far short of meeting international standards of justice, prompting British, French, German, and Italian leaders to demand its closing. Not only did Canada remain conspicuously silent but it went so far as to justify the need for Guantánamo – in step with the views of Donald Rumsfeld. While the Liberals had maintained a shameful silence, the new Conservative government unabashedly toed the Bush administration's line. In fact, at the time, Canada's special forces units in Afghanistan continued to hand terrorism suspects over to US forces who shipped at least some of them to Guantánamo.

Two years after arriving at Guantánamo, Omar Khadr finally had access to a lawyer, Muneer Ahmad. After the publication of the UN report, Ahmad criticized Ottawa for failing to stand up for the human rights of one of its citizens – a minor – while other Western allies had successfully lobbied the Bush administration to have their nationals returned. A year later, Omar was permitted to call his family – almost five years after arriving at Guantánamo.

While it seemed that Omar's case was on the verge of fading into oblivion, six former Canadian foreign ministers wrote an open letter to Prime Minister Harper on 1 February 2007 (the fifth anniversary of the opening of Guantánamo) to take action and demand that it be closed down. Arguing that the detention centre "flagrantly violates human rights, undermines the rule of law, and sends a signal to other governments that it is acceptable to abuse the rights of their citizens,"[6] Joe Clark, Lloyd Axworthy, Flora MacDonald, Bill Graham, John Manley, and Pierre Pettigrew made a number of demands to the Harper government: it should press Washington to release the detainees immediately, unless they were to be charged and tried under recognized international standards of justice; it should not send detainees to countries where they might face human rights abuses; it should ensure that the ill treatment and torture of the detainees stop immediately; it should forbid the use of evidence obtained under torture or ill- treatment; and it should permit UN and other international human rights experts full and private access to the detainees.

However, even this call did not move the Conservative government. Its silence remained inexplicable, even contradictory, to a statement made one week earlier by Prime Minister Harper after the settlement of the Arar affair: "Canada fully understands and appreciates and shares the United States' concerns with regard to security ... However, the Canadian government has every right to go to bat when it believes one of its citizens has been treated unfairly by another government."[7] Taking this statement at face value, in combination with the inaction on the Khadr file, implies that the Canadian government either believed that Omar was being treated fairly by the US government (in spite of ample evidence to the contrary) or believed in a second-tiered citizenship for Omar.

Pressure mounted further still when Australia successfully fought for the repatriation of one of its nationals, David Hicks, who struck a plea bargain and returned to Australia to serve nine months. Furthermore, as Omar's lawyer, Muneer Ahmad, pointed out, Omar was the first juvenile in modern history to be charged with war crimes; people of that age were not charged in Rwanda, Sierra Leone, or in the former Yugoslavia. When the military commission at Guantánamo dismissed the charges against Omar in June 2007 (on a technicality), the Canadian government could have lobbied to repatriate him, especially in face of the Kafka-like scenario in which the US government promised to appeal the decision to an appeals court that had yet to be created. From the get-go, the American administration was making up the rules on the fly, and Canadian officials were shirking their responsibilities towards a citizen.

The Canadian legal community began to find its voice after four years of silence. A University of Ottawa associate professor and scholar of international law, Craig Forcese, supported the call for Omar's release, saying his detention had no basis in international law. At its annual convention in August 2007, the Canadian Bar Association (CBA) announced that it would pressure the federal government for his release. Members of the CBA were moved to action after hearing the US military lawyer assigned to represent Omar, Lt-Cmdr William Kuebler, speak about the travesty of justice in Guantánamo and Omar's deteriorating mental condition. In trying to explain the reason for government silence, lawyer Lorne Waldman (one of Maher Arar's lawyers) pointed to the "Khadr effect" – that the media and the government shied away from speaking on behalf of Omar due to his family's notorious links to al-Qaeda. In fact, the *Globe and Mail* reported that then Foreign Affairs Minister Peter MacKay had scripted answers in response to possible media queries about the fate of Omar, which included deference to the highly flawed legal process.

Soon after the call by the CBA, legal experts began to question the feasibility of trying Omar in Canadian courts. The primary difficulty would lie in presenting evidence before the courts, and what evidence a Canadian judge would accept as untainted. The Americans would have to agree to hand over their evidence, and courts would have to be satisfied that neither the Canadian nor US government was claiming too much secrecy. Also, lawyers for Omar could argue that self-incriminating statements ought to be inadmissible as he was physically abused and denied medical treatment. There is also the likelihood that Canadian judges would be much more accepting of arguments that Omar Khadr was a child soldier acting in self-defence during wartime.

Soon after the CBA convention, opposition leader Stéphane Dion threw the "Khadr effect" to the wind, announcing his intention to meet with Omar's lawyers and press for his repatriation. "It's not a matter of polls, it's not a matter of public opinion, it's a matter of rights,"[8] explained Dion about the reasons for his personal involvement in the affair. A year later, former Prime Minister Paul Martin forcefully argued for repatriation: "If we had known then what we know now, then we would have taken strenuous steps to repatriate Mr. Khadr to Canada."[9] Martin had served as prime minister between 2003 and 2006.

In addition to an increase in domestic activism on the Khadr file, Britain's law societies called on Canada to defend Omar's rights in late 2007, pointing out the obvious – a fifteen-year-old Canadian citizen had been detained for five years and subjected to torture and interrogations without the right to silence or legal advice, and was facing a war crimes trial before a US military commission whose rules were stacked in favour of a guilty verdict. While the US Supreme Court had ruled that juveniles could no longer face the death penalty, the American government declared that even if Omar was not found guilty, it might continue to hold him indefinitely. International law experts pointed out that he would be the first child soldier to face a trial in the West.

In a joint letter to Prime Minister Harper, Britain's General Council of the Bar, the Law Society, the Criminal Bar Association, the Commonwealth Lawyers' Association, and the Bar Human Rights Committee wrote, "The lengthy detention, and putting on trial for war crimes, of someone who appears to be a 'child soldier' is contrary to the special protection to which Khadr is entitled."[10]

While the Harper government maintained a steely silence, it was faced with the embarrassing disclosure that an internal Foreign Affairs document placed the United States on a list of countries suspected of torturing prisoners – based on the prison at Guantánamo Bay where Omar was being held. Not surprisingly, US Ambassador David Wilkins was indignant, demanding immediate removal of this reference.

Further international calls for Omar's repatriation came in February 2008 when Human Rights Watch, Amnesty International, the Coalition to Stop the Use of Child Soldiers, and Human Rights First asked Harper to formally request that the United States either try Omar under juvenile justice rules or send him back to Canada. In addition, leaders of bar associations in Canada, the United Kingdom, and France pointed out that the US Military Commissions Act of 2006 wrongly subjects individuals to trial by military commission solely on the basis of their status as aliens, noting that US citizens are not subject to its provisions.

That same month another bombshell emerged in Omar's case. The military prosecutor inadvertently revealed that a key eyewitness to the murder of Lieutenant Speer did not actually see Omar throw a grenade at the medic. Rather, the eyewitness felt that an older fighter present in the vicinity threw the grenade. For years, the official American story was that Omar was the only combatant alive in the compound at the time of the medic's death, and that his suspension of rights was justified based on his alleged battlefield actions. This official version was now fully in doubt and fuelled further calls for repatriation.

Still the Harper government continued to insist that the process should be allowed to continue – a process that was never fair to begin with, where a minor citizen of Canada was being degraded through a long, painful incarceration during which his basic human rights were suspended.

This strident approach flew in the face of many legal opinions. Omar was a "child" under the terms of the UN Convention on the Rights of the Child and his trial was prohibited under international humanitarian law, which regards a child soldier as a victim to be rehabilitated rather than a perpetrator to be prosecuted. Senator Roméo Dallaire later publicly reiterated this point. Moreover, Omar's trial would constitute a violation of the fundamental principles of law, including arbitrary and illegal detention; denial of procedural due process; the absence of the presumption of innocence; denial of the right to counsel; denial of the right to trial within a reasonable time before a fair and impartial tribunal; coerced interrogation; and cruel and unusual punishment in detention.

Irwin Cotler, a justice minister during Omar's detention, broke his silence in 2008 by pointing out that the US Military Commissions Act of 2006 criminalizes certain conduct for the first time and applies the law retroactively; it fails to meet the requirements of the Geneva Convention Relative to the Treatment of Prisoners of War; it permits military commissions to consider coerced statements; and it denies defence counsel access to evidence, which may be essential to a proper defence on the basis of national security.

Canadian politicians finally mustered enough courage to intervene. At a news conference in late February 2008, MPs from the Liberal Party, the NDP, and the Bloc Québécois joined Omar's US military lawyer, Lt-Cmdr Bill Kuebler, to demand Omar's return. Admitting that they had previously failed to protect his rights, and fully aware of the unpopularity of the Khadr name, the MPs made it clear that the issue at hand was a restoration of basic human rights and a fair, judicial process for the young man.

Throughout the spring of 2008, calls grew louder for the return of Omar to Canada. The growing clamour was punctuated by the March 2008 revelation by the Guantánamo military commission that suggested evidence tampering by US government officials during the initial period of Omar's imprisonment. One day after the fateful battle on 27 July 2002, a US commander at the scene wrote in a report that the assailant of Sgt Speer had been killed; in another version of the report written several months later, someone had changed the word "killed" to "engaged." If the assailant had been killed, then Omar could in no way be charged with murder. Despite this latest revelation, the Harper government insisted on letting the Guantánamo "justice" system take its course.

In May 2008 a US military judge denied a defence motion to dismiss charges against Omar because of his age at the time of his alleged offences.

Then, in a stunning judgment in June 2008, the US Supreme Court ruled that terrorist suspects imprisoned at Guantánamo were allowed to fight for their rights in the United States. This position was a direct rebuke to President George Bush who had announced the nature of the military tribunal on 13 November 2001 in these terms: "It is not practicable to apply the principles of law and the rules of evidence generally recognized in the trial of criminal cases in the United States district courts."[11]

Another key turning point in the battle of public opinion occurred in July 2008, when videotapes of Omar's interrogation in 2003 by CSIS agents were released – by order of the Canadian Supreme Court. The release followed a 9–0 ruling by the Supreme Court that the Canadian Charter of Rights and Freedoms may apply when Canada is complicit in human rights violations affecting a Canadian abroad.

Let us also remember that the US Supreme Court has ruled on three separate occasions that Guantánamo detentions violate the US Constitution. United Nations human rights experts have said the same with respect to international legal standards. In 2008, President-elect Barack Obama, Hillary Clinton, and John McCain all called for Guantánamo to be shut down.

In 2005, a Canadian federal court concluded that the "conditions at Guantánamo Bay do not meet Charter standards."[12] The legal fight on behalf of Omar continued when his Canadian lawyers filed a lawsuit against Prime Minister Harper in August 2008, arguing that the government had ignored its obligation to rehabilitate and reintegrate a child soldier. The suit sought to impel the government to repatriate Omar.

In April 2009 the Federal Court ruled in Omar's favour. This decision was appealed by the government and later affirmed by the Federal Court of Appeals. It was then appealed to the Supreme Court of Canada, which unanimously refused to order the Canadian government to repatriate Omar. However, it did assert that the Omar's Charter rights had been violated and strongly recommended the government to provide redress.

In spite of the Supreme Court's refusal to order the government to repatriate Omar, many urged the government to do the "right thing." Yet again the government steadfastly refused, arguing for the US military tribunal to run its course. Yet this very tribunal seemed to ignore basic precepts of the admissibility of evidence.

As Omar's trial final began in 2010, the presiding judge ruled admissible evidence that was obtained under duress, in spite of an affidavit in which Omar alleged that US military interrogators at Bagram threatened him with rape and treated him harshly, thereby forcing him to make false statements. The judge's ruling also flew in the face of a diplomatic note sent by Canada to the United States, requesting that information gleaned from CSIS interviews in 2003 not be used against Omar since the Supreme Court of Canada had ruled his Charter rights had been violated.

Finally, in October 2010, Omar agreed to a plea bargain, pleading guilty to murder and terrorism charges. According to his Canadian lawyer, Dennis Edney, the plea deal was a means to avoid an unfair trial based on tainted evidence, adding that his client "would have confessed to anything, including the killing of John F. Kennedy, just to get out of this hellhole."[13]

The terms of the deal were that Omar would serve one year in Guantánamo and seven in Canada. The Canadian government indicated to the US Secretary of State, Hillary Clinton, that it would "favorably consider" Omar's repatriation application after one year of serving his sentence. Following the plea bargain, the US military jury deliberated and sentenced Omar to forty years in prison. During sentencing proceedings, Omar apologized to the wife of Sgt Christopher Speer.

Unofficial reports indicate that the US Administration was keen to resolve Omar's case before trial, due in large measure to fact that his alleged crimes were committed when he was a minor. The prospect of a military trial of a child soldier, held for almost one-third of his life at Guantánamo Bay, did not sit well with many.

In early March 2011, international headlines announced Obama's about-face on Guantánamo. An article by *The Guardian*'s Karen Greenberg expressed a sense of betrayal: "Guantánamo: no closure for Obama. The White House insists it's making the best of a bad lot. But technocratic tinkering fails to address the basic moral anomaly":[14]

> In the nine years since the opening of the Guantánamo Bay detention facility, the country has moved incrementally towards institutionalising the existence of the facility. On [8 March], the Obama administration took the process of institutionalisation one step further, issuing both an executive order on detention – the first since the pathbreaking executive order that began his presidency, calling for the closure of Guantánamo and promising a rethink on the detention policy – and the revocation of the ban on military tribunals there.
>
> In contrast to its predecessor, yesterday's executive order was anything but pathbreaking. It tacitly acknowledged that the premises of detention in the "war on terror" begun by the Bush administration in the fall of 2001 still hold. More tellingly still, it demonstrated that the Obama administration now not only accepts the fact of Guantánamo's existence as a given, but has also abandoned any debate over whether or not indefinite detention should be the policy of the land.

All experts agreed that regardless of the outcome of this case, it would be precedent setting. But would the Guantánamo regime endure?

QUESTIONS FOR THE FUTURE

So, what are we to make of government complicity in a process that is widely recognized as a travesty of justice? Is it simply a combination of racism and Islamophobia, as some suggest? The evidence indeed indicates that suspicion of the "other" has played a role in the suspension of civil liberties of Muslim and Arab men by Canadian security, intelligence, and political officials.

If we look to history, we do see a disturbing pattern, wherein the collective rights of an identifiable group were trampled in the name of security. During both world wars, Canadian government policymakers did not hesitate to intern Canadians of diverse ethnicities, including Japanese, German, and Ukrainian Canadians. Lives were destroyed in the name of security. Similarly, with the operation of the War Measures Act, hundreds of innocent Quebecers were rounded up and imprisoned on suspicion of *indépendentiste* leanings.

And since the events of 9/11, Muslims and Arabs have also come under suspicion – especially if they speak out against American or Canadian foreign policy. And while there are no blanket internment policies this time, it is clear that the creation and maintenance of Guantánamo and other security and intelligence strategies operate as a form of severe internment that disregards the basic human rights of many Muslims. Recall that senior RCMP intelligence agents assigned to monitor Arar told the O'Connor inquiry that "all caveats were down"[15] – meaning that safeguards were cast aside in the pursuit of terrorism suspects.

While Prime Minister Jean Chrétien showed true leadership in keeping Canada out of the immoral Iraq invasion of 2003, the silence and complicity of the ruling Liberal government in the affairs of Maher Arar, Abdullah Almalki, Ahmad El Maati, Muayyed Nureddin, and Omar Khadr are shameful.

The current Conservative regime – with its tough stance as a law-and-order party – has decided that security trumps human rights. It is safe to say that the new Conservative Party is the ideological cousin of the former Republican administration of George W. Bush. And the Conservatives know full well how to exploit the politics of fear, especially when it comes to Muslims. Prime Minister Harper appealed to the fear factor of the Quebec electorate when he waded into the manufactured veiled vote brouhaha during by-elections in Quebec in 2007. In December 2011, Immigration Minister Jason Kenney banned the wearing of the niqab at Citizenship ceremonies. A charter challenge is expected. Just prior to the tenth anniversary of the 9/11 terrorist attacks, he told the CBC that the greatest threat to Canada was "Islamicism" (a term never used before), without mentioning that the vast majority of Muslims in Canada have nothing to do with extremism.

The web of deceit surrounding Omar's case has been woven with many strands, including Islamophobia and racism. However, it seems that the strongest impetus by successive Liberal and

Conservative governments to keep a child soldier imprisoned in Guantánamo has been the desire to acquiesce to American demands about security. Our sovereignty has been compromised by political considerations, thus leading many to ask: "What is the value of my Canadian citizenship?"

And what has been the reaction of Canadian Muslims to these events? Initially, there was fear of speaking out against injustice lest one be labelled a terrorist sympathizer. We must remember that a large portion of the Canadian Muslim community are immigrants and are acutely aware of possible reprisals by the governments of both their countries of origin and Canada. Also, many do not know how to navigate the Canadian legal and political systems. While a few national Muslim community institutions have emerged within the last ten years, many are still experiencing growing pains. Nonetheless, Muslims need to stand up for justice in a balanced way that protects human rights and security.

It is civil society that has shown true strength of character during these troubled times. NGOs, human rights groups, journalists, and the courts have slowly, but surely, fought for justice for those wrongly treated. We cannot take the freedoms and rights that we have for granted, for these have been established through hard work and sacrifice by many Canadians who preceded us. In one aspect, Canada is a compassionate meritocracy woven by the efforts of countless women and men. We must join together to uphold values that we cherish, such as freedom, genuine respect, and fairness.

In looking back through Canadian history, we see that dark episodes of ethnic profiling have been punctuated by the enlightened efforts of those who fought back, leading to the evolution of social justice and law for the benefit of future generations. In the process, each discriminated group became further entrenched within the Canadian mosaic. At this point in Canadian history, Canadian Muslims and Arabs face the pernicious spectre of ethnoreligious profiling and a devaluation of their citizenship. If we are to learn anything from history, it is that abuses of government power cannot be left unchallenged. Canadians of good conscience must join to fight for the basic human dignity of their fellow citizens. With each fresh revelation about human rights abuses perpetrated by the Canadian government in the name of security, we must heighten our vigilance against abuses of power and demand due process for those who are detained or exiled without charge. Let's take on this responsibility with confidence, tenacity, and courage, remembering the Qur'anic verse: God does not place a burden on anyone heavier than one can bear.

NOTES

1 Heba Aly, "Canadian Languishes in Embassy in Sudan," *Globe and Mail,* 1 July 2008, A10.
2 Paul Koring, "Canada Feared US Backlash over Man Trapped in Sudan," *Globe and Mail,* 24 July 2008.
3 Michelle Shephard, *Guantanamo's Child: The Untold Story of Omar Khadr* (Mississagua: John Wiley, 2008).
4 Allison Dunfield, "Khadr's Arrest Raises Serious Questions, Harper Says," *Globe and Mail,* 2 September 2002; Clifford Krauss, "Canadian Teenager Held by US in Afghanistan in Killing of American Medic," *New York Times,* 14 September 2002.
5 "Canadian Officials Visited Teen Held by United States," *Globe and Mail,* 22 February 2003, A7.
6 Joe Clark, Lloyd Axworthy, Flora MacDonald, Bill Graham, John Manley, and Pierre Pettigrew, "Speak Up, Mr Harper – Guantanamo Is a Disgrace," *Globe and Mail,* 1 February 2007.
7 Ian Austen, "Canada Reaches Settlement with Torture Victim," *New York Times*, 26 January 2007. See also Gloria Galloway, "Harper Apologizes to Arar for Torture in Syria," *Globe and Mail,* 26 January 2007.
8 Colin Freeze, "Khadr Should Face Justice in Civilian Court, Dion Says," *Globe and Mail,* 19 September 2007.
9 Colin Freeze, "Bring back Khadr, Former PM Says," *Globe and Mail,* 20 July 2008.
10 "Our Deafening Silence," editorial, *Globe and Mail,* 2 January 2008.
11 "President Issues Military Order," White House press release, 13 November 2001 [Presidential Order, Section 1(f)].
12 *Khadr v. Canada,* [2006], 2 FCR 506.
13 "Khadr to Return to Canada: Lawyer," 25 October 2010; *CBC News*, http://www.cbc.ca/news/world/story/2010/10/25/omar-khadr-trial-resumes.html (accessed 11 September 2011).
14 Karen Greenberg, *The Guardian*, 3 March 2011.
15 "Report of the Events Relating to Maher Arar: Analysis and Recommendations," Commission of Inquiry into the Actions of Canadian Official in Relation to Maher Arar, 23, 108, 110, and 147.

The Long Way Home: The Saga of Omar Khadr

GAR PARDY

Ahmed Said Khadr was one of the best-known fathers in Canada but certainly not the best. He and his wife, Maha Elsamnah, the parents of Omar Khadr, have been controversial figures since late 1995 when Ahmed was detained by the Pakistani authorities. The detention was on suspicion of funding the group that successfully bombed the Egyptian embassy in Islamabad on 19 November 1995, killing sixteen and injuring sixty. Responsibility for the attack focused on Ayman al-Zawahiri, an Egyptian medical doctor and a senior leader of Islamic Jihad. For Canadians, there has been little interest in the background of Ahmed Khadr and Maha Elsamnah before their arrival in Canada. For most, their antecedents were not important, and the rush to large conclusions has characterized the nation's view of this "first family of terrorism." There is, however, another dimension. As a famed Canadian novelist wrote, what is "bred in the bone will come out in the flesh." This proverb is an apt description of the Khadr family's background and is important in understanding their actions. The description worked for the Cornish family of the Ottawa Valley, and it has value as well for those born into the cauldron that has characterized the Middle East since 1945.

Maha was seventeen when she arrived in Canada on 1 August 1974; Ahmed was twenty-nine when he arrived early in 1975. Both were formed by the conflict-driven environment of the Middle East they left behind in those fateful days of the mid-1970s. The initial victory of Egypt in the 1973 war with Israel gave promise of possibly greater victories in the future. Then the decision of Anwar Sadat, the president of Egypt, to sign a peace agreement with Israel in 1975 was seen as a betrayal of the Palestinian cause. These events along with the Soviet invasion of Afghanistan in December 1979 were part of the "bone" for many Muslims in the Middle East and the millions spread around the world including in Toronto and Ottawa. It is to the Middle East context that Canadians must look if we are to have an understanding of the hundreds of thousands of our fellow citizens for whom the Middle East remains a plane ride away and whose politics influence their daily lives.

Canadians first saw Omar Ahmed Khadr as a ten-year-old sitting at the end of his father's hospital bed at the Institute of Medical Sciences in Islamabad in mid-January 1996. Born in Toronto on 19 September 1986, he had moved along with his five brothers and sister to Pakistan in 1987 where his father was involved with humanitarian organizations helping Afghan refugees including as a volunteer in the field office of Human Concern International (HCI). Eric Magolis, a well-known writer and commentator on events in South Asia, remembers meeting Ahmed at the time; he later described him as a "man of respect" who was "entirely humanitarian and not ideological at all." In 1992 Ahmed had been severely injured by a landmine explosion and was initially treated in Pakistan and subsequently in Canada. The treatment was successful in saving his arm, but he walked with a serious limp for the rest of his life.

At the time when Canadians first became aware of Omar, Ahmed had been detained by the Pakistani authorities for providing funds for the two-person suicide bombing attack on the Egyptian embassy in Islamabad. Al-Gama'a al-Islamiya, a militant Egyptian group, claimed responsibility, but more likely the bombing was the work of Islamic Jihad, another Egyptian group under the control of Ayman al-Zawahiri, who has been described as the "man behind bin Laden."

In the aftermath of the bombing, there were allegations that Ahmed Khadr was using the HCI office and its money as a mechanism to fund terrorism. Clearly, the Pakistani authorities had their suspicions, and this led to Ahmed's detention on 3 December 1995. He was questioned vigorously by the Pakistani authorities; his wife and family complained to the Canadian authorities and to the media that he was tortured. He began a hunger strike. Eventually, he was transferred to the Institute of Medical Sciences for treatment and, serendipitously, this coincided with a visit to Islamabad in mid-January 1996 by then Prime Minister Jean Chrétien.

Before leaving Ottawa, officials in Mr Chrétien's office were approached by friends of Ahmed Khadr, including representatives from the Canadian Arab Federation and the Jewish Civil Rights Educational Foundation of Canada. The foundation also wrote to the Pakistani government and asked for a fair trial, expressing concern about the "unfair and unnecessary hardship placed on individuals like Khadr." The Canadian-Muslim Civil Liberties Association circulated a petition in his support. The executive director for HCI also spoke publicly in his defence and stated that "politics was not his cup of tea." These expressions of support led Prime Minister Chrétien's officials to recommend that he raise the matter during his planned meeting with Pakistani Prime Minister Benazir Bhutto. Before Chrétien's arrival in Islamabad, the story of Khadr's detention and alleged mistreatment were on the front pages in Canada, and many visiting Canadians were able to visit Khadr in the hospital.

Prime Minister Chrétien raised Khadr's detention with Prime Minister Bhutto, asking that he be treated fairly and given a fair trial. In subsequent weeks Khadr was charged under Pakistan's explosives laws and returned to prison. In the meantime, the three youngest children, including Omar, went back to Toronto to live with Maha Elsamnah's mother, Fatmah Elsamnah. In late March Ahmed Khadr was released when the presiding judge decided there was insufficient evidence for the case to proceed. He and the rest of the family returned to Canada.

In the fifteen years since these events in 1996, the effect of Mr Chrétien's representations on Khadr's behalf have taken on mythical proportions in the minds of many Canadians and the media. After 9/11, Chrétien's action was often interpreted as contributing to terrorism, giving the "Khadr effect" to the politics of the nation. In the minds of many, the world is far simpler than it is for those who drive the world's efforts to bring peace, security, and prosperity to its far corners. The simple act of mentioning Mr Khadr to Prime Minister Bhutto is now seen as exceptional and unworthy of the Canadian prime minister. Of course, this ignores a basic tenet of Canadian politics that when a Canadian is in difficulty abroad, everyone in government from the prime minister downwards should contribute to resolving the matter. Even the government of Prime Minister Harper, which has a harder nose than most on these matters, could not ignore the pleas of Brenda Martin as she whiled away time in a Mexican prison.

Prime Minister Chrétien's intervention is a common occurrence in the world of international politics. It is understood by those involved for what it is – a needed gesture on the part of the demander but one that does not require action by the recipient. Benazir Bhutto, given the tragic history of her family, understood the game better than most, and for Canadians to believe that she took specific action to help Ahmed Khadr strains credulity. It also ignores the interests that parts of the Pakistani government had in supporting Khadr's work, which indirectly was helpful to the Pakistani proxy, the Taliban, in the Afghan civil war that was just coming to a close.

It ignores, as well, Pakistan's relationship with Egypt, whose bombed embassy was at the centre of Khadr's detention. Pakistan's relationship with Egypt is a close one, and to believe that Pakistani authorities would ignore it as they made decisions affecting an individual who might have been involved in the bombing of its embassy is just as fanciful as believing in the international influence of the Canadian prime minister. If there was any substantive evidence of Mr Khadr's involvement in the bombing, then he would have been in Cairo without any second thoughts on the part of Pakistani courts or officials. There he would have encountered rigorous treatment similar to that of Ahmad El Maati.

Craig Kielburger, the co-founder of Free the Children organization, provides a personal account of those January 1996 days in Islamabad in an article reprinted in this volume. Mr Kielburger and his organization are justly well known to Canadians for their work in promoting an end to child labour, which is endemic to Pakistan. As he reminisced in his article, he had little reason to recall the encounter some fifteen years earlier, but with the publicity now associated with Omar Khadr, he commented that he and Omar were the "products of our environments. Omar is just being punished for his."

A sad side issue to the matter was its effect on the work of Human Concern International, which was often described in the media as the vehicle or cover through which Ahmed Khadr carried out his terrorist activities. In the aftermath of his detention, CIDA and Canadians cancelled their support for HCI, and ever since it has fought in the courts and elsewhere to demonstrate that it was in no way involved in the violent activities attributed to Mr Khadr.

The Canadian Security and Intelligence Service was involved in these matters from the beginning – and even earlier, according to one of its senior officers, who suggested that Ahmed Khadr had been in their sight for some time. In providing information to the Federal Court of Canada via the ministers of public safety and citizenship and immigration, HCI charged that CSIS made a false statement to the effect that Khadr had used HCI in order to funnel money for terrorist purposes. HCI complained to the Security Intelligence Review Committee and in its 2006–07 annual report to Parliament, SIRC reported that CSIS had made an "unsubstantiated statement" about HCI that "could lead to injury or loss of support and funding." SIRC recommended that CSIS formally retract the unsubstantiated statement

The *National Post*, which had included the CSIS information in an editorial on 6 March 2004, published an apology on 26 April: "The National Post has no reason to believe that there is evidence of any misuse of HCI funds to support terrorism. HCI itself has never been accused of terrorism or of supporting terrorism. The Post has no reason to believe that any of its other volunteers or staff has been accused of terrorism or of supporting terrorism ... The National Post apologizes to HCI, its board of directors, volunteers and donors for any harm or embarrassment its errors may have caused."

Ahmed Khadr first went to Pakistan in the summer of 1984. At the time he was teaching at the Gulf Polytechnique University in Bahrain following a master's degree in computer science from the University of Ottawa. The year was important. The Soviets had invaded Afghanistan in late December 1979, and in the intervening years there was a widespread perception that the world had failed to respond to the invasion. For the countries of the region and beyond, it was a sharp reminder of the fragility of the international system, leading US President Jimmy Carter to state it was "the most serious threat to peace since the Second World War." In the same period, Egypt and Israel had signed a peace agreement, ending the broad Arab coalition in support of the Palestinians; there was also a revolution in Iran and months of detention for American diplomats.

Foreign ministers from Islamic countries protested the Soviet invasion, and the UN General Assembly passed a condemnatory resolution. A few months later in 1980, the United States and other western countries refused to participate in the 1980 Olympic Games in Moscow, and in 1984 the Soviet Union and its allies boycotted the games in Los Angeles. Behind the scenes, the United States, Saudi Arabia, and Pakistan, along with China and the United Kingdom, began covert actions to arm the Afghan opposition, which became known as the Mujahedeen. In the following decade of war, Afghanistan was destroyed. More than five million refugees went to Pakistan; two million Afghans were killed or maimed. The country's infrastructure was destroyed, and economic life was eliminated, except for the poppy.

By 1984 the humanitarian disaster was well known, and thousands of outsiders went to Pakistan to help. The majority of them came from the world of Islam, which saw the struggle as a holy war. Ahmed Khadr was one of these and, in the calculus of the time he was one of the "good guys." It is from this period that others who have become well known in the aftermath of 9/11 went to Pakistan and Afghanistan and were part of the effort to force the Soviets out of Afghanistan. These included Osama bin Laden and Ayman al-Zawahiri; the latter continues to direct al-Qaeda from the mountains of the region they came to know well during the Soviet occupation. In historical terms, they were companions to the thousands who flocked to Spain in the mid-1930s to fight fascism.

The defeat of the Soviet Union and its complete withdrawal from Afghanistan by mid-1989 is now well known and was recently popularized through the book *Charlie Wilson's War* by George Crile and Mike Nichols film of the same name. Unfortunately, as in Crile's book, the story of Afghanistan is deemed to have ended with the Soviet withdrawal. The unjustified euphoria was masked to some extent by the collapse of the Soviet Union, and while the rest of the world moved on, for the Afghans and their Pakistani neighbours the humanitarian disaster continued. The legacy Afghan government under President Mohammad Najibullah in power when the Soviets left soon resigned and died, figuratively and literally, in the Taliban victory. The struggle for a stable, legitimate Afghan government continues to this day.

Ahmed Khadr is a product of this period, and his humanitarian efforts in Pakistan and Afghanistan, like those of so many others, fell victim to the region's politics. His early friends and allies understood and supported his efforts to bring safety, health, and education to Afghan refugees. His work was part of a legitimate worldwide effort to counter the nasty effects of the Soviet invasion. The Soviet withdrawal and the withdrawal of the rest of the world from its consequences were equal tragedies. Countries can ignore their large mistakes, but for individuals like Ahmed Khadr, who continue to deal with these consequences at the humanitarian level, it is easy to take wrong roads and make mistakes. Unfortunately, Khadr's mistakes remain seminal events in the lives of his family, especially for his second-youngest son, Omar.

In *Charlie Wilson's War*, George Crile includes an epilogue called "Unintended Consequences." Written in 2003 while the fires of 9/11 were still hot, Crile's epilogue conveyed what Charlie Wilson hoped would be history's judgment on what he and others had achieved:

> It's not what Charlie Wilson had in mind when he took up the cause of the Afghans. Nevertheless, in spite of 9/11 and all the horrors that have flowed down from it, he steadfastly maintains that it was all worth it and that nothing can diminish what the Afghans accomplished for America and world with their defeat of the Red Army:
>
> They removed the threat we all went to sleep with every night, of World War III breaking out. The countries that used to be in the Warsaw Pack are now in NATO. These were truly changes of biblical proportion, and the effect the jihad had in accelerating these events is nothing short of miraculous.
>
> These things happened. They were glorious and they changed the world. And the people [Afghans] who deserved the credit are the ones who make sacrifice.

Then Charlie Wilson in his inimical style summed it up: "And then we fucked up the endgame."

Shortly after the events of 1995 and 1996 in Pakistan, all members of the Khadr family were back in Toronto. In addition to Ahmed and Maha, the family included Zaynab (1978) and Abdullah (1981), both born in Ottawa; Abdurahman (1982), born in Bahrain; Omar (1986), born in Toronto; Abdul Kareen (1989), born in Pakistan; and the youngest, Maryam (1991), born in Toronto. The family was peripatetic, moving frequently between Pakistan and Toronto, often for Maha to give birth – Omar, Ibrahim (who died early of a congenital heart defect), and Maryam were born in Toronto, where Ahmed returned frequently to maintain and expand his support network. Organized schooling for the children was episodic. Sometimes they attended private schools in Pakistan; sometimes it was private tutoring or (infrequently) public schools in Toronto.

HCI severed its ties with Ahmed following the allegations that he had played a role in funding the bombing of the Egyptian embassy.

Ahmed responded by forming his own organization, Health and Education Projects International, with the Salahedin Mosque in Toronto as a partner. He returned to Pakistan in the fall of 1996 without hindrance from the Pakistani authorities. In mid-1997 he and his family moved to Afghanistan and headquartered his new organization in the Kari-e-Parwan area of Kabul. Throughout this period, he was a well-known and respected figure in the region and there was recognition of his dedication in helping Afghans. Funding did not appear to be a problem as he made frequent trips to Canada and the United States, where he made the plight of the Afghans, and the need for the world not to forget, central topics of his speeches.

But the world had moved on, and for Ahmed it was lonely and frustrating work. His leg injuries from 1992 limited his mobility, and there were even troubles with the new Taliban government over the inclusion of girls in his schools. Nearly everyone who met him during this period speaks of his dedication and zeal for his work, and while the metaphors were understandably Islamic, there is no evidence to suggest that he was a convert to worldwide jihad. His anti-western comments were made more in sorrow than in anger as he believed that the West still had a moral obligation to help Afghans. His zeal was for charity. His family was now with him in Kabul, and for the first time in many years there was some stability.

Afghanistan, however, was not a place of peace or of tranquillity. The Taliban had recently emerged as the dominant force in the country, but its writ was still being tested in the north and central Afghanistan. Leaders were insecure and used their power to assassinate opponents and enforce a very harsh interpretation of Islam. A reign of terror prevailed. There were many outsiders, generally referred to as "Arabs," who stayed behind after the Soviet defeat and saw Afghanistan as the base for their larger worldwide fight to create fundamentalist Islamic governments.

The extent of bin Laden's activities in Afghanistan during this period is not well known. After the Soviet defeat, he tried to interest the Saudi government in using his followers in the first Gulf War, but his overture was rejected. He then went to the Sudan, where he remained until early 1996 when, following American pressure, he and his supporters decided to re-establish in eastern Afghanistan in Jalalabad. It was during this period that al-Zawahiri and bin Laden united, and al-Qaeda became a name known around the world.

Schooling for the Khadr children was now at a private school in Kabul, although there were frequent visits back to Canada to stay with Maha's parents in Toronto. Zaynad, Abdullah, and Abdurahman became adults, and Zaynab was promised in marriage to an Egyptian friend of her father's, although there was not much enthusiasm on her part for the arrangement. The marriage lasted less than six months. Sibling rivalry between Abdullah and Abdurahman was often conflictive and resulted in loud arguments and threats of violence. Ahmed made arrangements for Abdullah to live with other Arab families or to go to insurgent training bases. Omar was the favourite of the family, and his relationship with Zaynab was close.

Ahmed was rarely present, devoting his time and energy to humanitarian activities. There were suggestions he was not completely trusted by those around bin Laden because of his frequent travels to Canada and his relative independence. From post-9/11 interviews with members of the family by Michelle Shephard, it was during this period that the bin Laden and Khadr families associated, and there were often times they lived close to each other near Jalalabad. (See Michelle Shephard's excellent book, *Guantanamo's Child: The Untold Story of Omar Khadr*, for more details on these aspects of the Khadr family.) There were plans for the Khadrs to live in the bin Laden compound in Jalalabad in 1997, but bin Laden and his group moved nearer to Kandahar for security reasons, leaving the Khadr family on their own. In January 2001, the United Nations added Ahmed Khadr to its 1269 Resolution List as a person associated with the Taliban and al-Qaeda.

During this period the planning and preparations began for the 1998 attacks on the American embassies in Nairobi and Dar es Salaam and 11 September 2001 attack on the United States. There is no evidence available to support allegations that Ahmed Khadr was involved or knew of this work. As far as can be determined, he continued his humanitarian work, although he and other members of his family, along with millions of Muslims elsewhere, cheered the attacks. In the aftermath of the 9/11 attacks, they, along with most others, were unprepared for the speed and the intensity of the American reaction, especially the direct attack on Afghanistan, first by bombers and then troops allied with the forces of the Northern Alliance.

Even in Ottawa there was little awareness of American intentions, although there was understanding that retaliation was in the works.

On a Sunday afternoon, 7 October 2001, the deputy minister of Foreign Affairs summoned a group to the Pearson Building to inform staff that President Bush had advised Prime Minister Chrétien that attacks on Afghanistan were underway. Work began immediately to make Canadian policy fully in support of the Americans, and within weeks Canadian troops, mainly the special forces unit JTF2, were in Afghanistan fighting alongside the Americans.

The response, and especially the speed with which Western troops arrived in Kabul – Kabul fell on 11 November – found the Khadr family separated and unprepared. They were in the process of moving to Logar Province, where Ahmed was running an orphanage. Ahmed and Elsamnah were in Kabul, and Omar was in Logar along with Zaynab, Abdul Kareem, and Maryam. Abdurahman was returning to Kabul from Logar and was subsequently detained by troops of the Northern Alliance. He was turned over to the Americans and sent to Guantánamo. Zaynab had remarried, again with great reluctance, in 1999, to a Yemeni, had a child, Safia, in Toronto in 2000, and then returned to Afghanistan. As with her first marriage the second one did not last beyond a few months. Ahmed and Elsamnah left Kabul just ahead of the surging Northern Alliance troops and went to Logar. According to Michelle Shephard, Ahmed tried to convince Elsamnah to return to Canada with the children, but she refused.

By February 2002 Elsamnah and most of the children were in Pakistan seeking medical attention for Safia and Abdullah and hiding from both Pakistani and American forces. Omar at fifteen was eager to join his father and older brother, Abdurahman, who were in Afghanistan and infrequently visiting the rest of the family in Pakistan. His father agreed, and by July, Omar was with friends of Ahmed in Khost. According to American military reports from the period, Omar was trained by al-Qaeda "in the use of rocket-propelled grenades, rifles, pistols, grenades and explosives," and later on "he joined a team of other al-Qaeda operatives and converted landmines into remotely detonated improvised explosive devices," planting them where they could be triggered by American forces. On 27 July, American military units attacked the compound where Omar was staying. He was severely wounded and, following emergency battlefield treatment, flown to the massive American base at Bagram to the north of Kabul.

More than a year later on 3 October 2003, Ahmed along with his youngest son, Kareem, were in South Waziristan when the Pakistani army attacked, killing Ahmed and severely wounding Kareem. On 15 October 2004, Abdullah was captured by Pakistani forces after the Americans posted a $500,000 reward; in late November he was released, and on 2 December 2005 returned to Canada, escorted by two officials, including one from CSIS. Clearly in a prearrangement, the US government within a few weeks requested his extradition on the basis of his involvement in terrorism. Abdullah was detained and spent the following four years in prison in Toronto.

Justice Speyer of the Superior Court of Justice for Ontario heard the arguments concerning Abdullah's extradition. The attorney general of Canada represented the United States and argued that the extradition should be granted, as not to do so would be unprecedented and not in the interests of Canada. On the other side, Abdullah was represented by Dennis Edney and Nathan J. Whitling, the two Calgary lawyers who, from the early days of Omar's imprisonment at Guantánamo, had represented him before the Canadian courts.

Edney and Whitling were equal to the task on Abdullah's behalf, and on 4 August 2010 Justice Speyer ruled that the request for extraction should be "stayed." In doing so, he wrote, "A stay in proceedings is granted rarely. It is a remedy of last resort that must meet the 'clearest of cases' standards. It is an exceptional remedy because its effect is to deprive society of adjudication on the merits." Justice Speyer further explained his extraordinary ruling that the central issue in this "extradition proceeding is whether the applicant, Abdullah Khadr ... has established *misconduct attributable to the Requesting State, the United States of America, on a level so serious that it would violate those fundamental principles of justice which underlie the community's sense of fair play and decency*" (emphasis added). Justice Speyer answered his own question resoundingly in the affirmative, and today Abdullah and Canadians can appreciate the safety that Canadian courts provide for citizens when nefarious actions are taken by governments.

By 2005 all of the remaining members of the Khadr family were back in Canada. Elsamnah, Kareem, and Maryam had returned shortly after Kareem had been wounded at the time Ahmed had been killed. Abdurahman was captured in November 2001 and was initially sent to Guantánamo but there he agreed to work for the Americans and was used in counter-terrorism efforts in Eastern Europe. When he returned to Canada in 2003, he lied about his activities but inconsistencies in his story eventually resulted in the true story becoming known. Zaynab and her child, Safia, did not return to Canada until 2004. She had since married a third time. The family was now united, except for Ahmed, who was confirmed dead in Pakistan, and Omar, a prisoner of the Americans in Guantánamo.

The saga of the Khadr family had come full circle. The mother and father came to Canada from the Middle East to escape the wars and insurgencies of the region and to create a new life. Seven children later, the Soviet war in Afghanistan, the emergence of the Taliban government, the arrival of the bin Laden and his followers, 9/11 and the Western invasion all provided an environment where the Khadrs and thousands of others made the choice that this was where the battle between Islam and the West would be fought. They had arrived in the region when fighting the Soviet invaders was a noble and lauded struggle; they left the region as enemies of their fellow citizens. There will come a time when greater perspective and charity may alter the judgment of their fellow citizens. In the meantime, the opprobrium and unforgivingness of Canadians were unloaded onto the shoulders of their fifth child, Omar Ahmed Khadr, who at fifteen entered the dark world of American justice circa 2002 at Guantánamo.

Evil repeated becomes normal. The decisions of the American government in the aftermath of 9/11 overshadowed and largely eliminated the attending global wave of support. The decision to overthrow the Taliban government of Afghanistan was understandable and widely supported. Beyond that decision, the American government descended into a paroxysm of self-defeating actions that today has left American policy and influence in serious decline and needing concentrated intelligent effort for recovery. Nowhere were those decisions more self-defeating than those associated with Omar Khadr and the treatment of other prisoners taken in Afghanistan, Iraq, and numerous other battlefields of the war on terror. In a policy initiated by Vice-President Dick Cheney and supported by the president and a cadre of ideological lawyers, the thin fabric of international protections that governed war were torn, ignored, or egregiously manipulated to give a veneer of legitimacy to large violations of international human rights norms. Bagram, Abu Ghraib, Guantánamo, black prison sites, extraordinary renditions, "torture memos," warrantless surveillance, illegal enemy combatants, and determination that the Geneva Conventions were obsolete became the face of American foreign policy.

There were thousands of victims of American aberrations. Canadians have had front row seats. Numerous Canadians – Maher Arar, Ahmad El Maati, Abdullah Almalki, Muayyed Nureddin are the best known – were snared into the traps represented by American policy, and as we have come to know, there was little difference between those who might have been guilty and those who were accidental victims caught in the tentacles of a system that carried its own justification and was self-fulfilling. Victimization and the urge for revenge are not admirable characteristics in individuals; when carried out at a national level, they are disastrous and, more likely than not, will add to the hurt.

Omar Khadr has emerged as the symbol of the evils of this system. And sadly, responsibility for this evil can be shared by the government of Canada. The law, as we have come to know, can be "an ass," as Mr Bumble noted some 170 years ago. At the same time it is the most ennobling feature of our liberal democracies. One of the more hopeful signs of our liberal democracies has been the web of laws that take into account the vulnerability of children and the need for our justice systems to provide special adjudication, lessened sentences and special efforts at rehabilitation and reintegration. These national advances have been reflected within the international system where treaties, law, and standards have been almost universally agreed upon. Omar was not the only juvenile captured by American forces and jailed in Bagram and Guantánamo. He was, however, the only one charged, tried, and convicted of crimes that were not even crimes under American law when he was captured in late July 2002.

Bagram was especially evil, even by the standards of the period. Fifteen-year-old Omar, badly wounded, was still on his evacuation stretcher when the harsh interrogations began. In the testimony of others, including interrogators, little attention was given to his medical condition, and no attention was given to his age. The objective was to obtain "operational intelligence" quickly that would help in providing protection to American and allied troops on the battlefield and, hopefully, the "homeland" – the eponymous word that has come to represent the United States. (Ironically, it was the same word used by apartheid South Africa when it tried to create geographic separation for its black population.) The "ticking time bomb" scenario was a favourite in both Washington and television dramas. Little distinction was made between harsh conditions, prisoner abuse, and torture. They were all on the same scale and while efforts continue to be made to increase the distance between them, in reality, for prisoners like Omar, they were part of a short continuum. Omar for three months at Bagram was subject to these conditions, and sadly, when his trial was concluding some eight years later at Guantánamo, his words from this period were used in his persecution and prosecution.

The Canadian government was indirectly informed by the American military of the capture of a "Canadian" in mid-August 2002. Efforts were taken to identify the prisoner, and before the end of the month Omar was identified. A request for access by Canadian consular officials was sent to the US State Department on 29 August 2002, but officials were told such access would not be granted and most likely Omar would be transferred to Guantánamo. Two weeks later, on 13 September 2002, Foreign Affairs sent another diplomatic note to the US State department. The note made three points: there was "ambiguity as to the role that Mr Khadr may have played" in the battle on 27 July 2002; Guantánamo Bay "would not be an appropriate place for Mr Omar Khadr to be detained," since "under various laws of Canada and the United States," his age "provides for special treatment of such persons with respect to legal or judicial processes;" the diplomatic note went on to ask for "discussions between appropriate officials on Mr Khadr prior to any decisions being taken with respect to his future status and detention."

Five weeks later, on 28 October 2002, Omar was a prisoner at Guantánamo. Canada was officially informed of this the following day, but in discussions between American officials at their embassy in Ottawa and Foreign Affairs, it became clear that prisoners at Guantánamo were beyond the reach of all long-standing and normal international law and practices. Canadian consular officials would not be allowed to visit Omar, and while officials of the International Committee of the Red Cross would be allowed to meet with the prisoners, they would not provide Canada with information on such visits and specifically not on Omar Khadr.

Eventually the Americans indicated that Canadian security officials would be allowed to visit Guantánamo and interrogate prisoners for security purposes. At the same time, media reporting and the photographs of prisoners at Guantánamo gave early warning that it was not a normal prison in any sense of the word. The camp commander and senior officials from the Bush administration all spoke to a single script – this was a place where information was going to be extracted, and there were few if any limits on how it would be done.

In the face of American intransigence, indirect reports of Omar's medical condition, and no expectation for consular visits, Canadian officials decided to take advantage of the agreement for security visits and have an official from Foreign Affairs go to Guantánamo and visit Omar. Accordingly, an experienced Foreign Service officer and a member of the department's Security and Intelligence Bureau, Jim Gould, was selected to meet with Omar and report on his condition and treatment. In subsequent years, the Security and Intelligence Bureau has been depicted as a super-secret organization bent on nefarious and unreported actions inimical to the interests of Canadians. The reports of Commissioners O'Connor and Iacobucci have stripped away these misleading views and show the bureau as carrying out a legitimate function of government.

Unfortunately, Mr Gould did not visit Guantánamo independently but was included as part of a visit by a member of CSIS in late February 2003. Officials in the Consular Affairs Bureau of Foreign Affairs were not aware of this arrangement prior to the visit, and as we have now come to learn, Mr Gould's work was distorted by the overlay of the visit by a CSIS official. The interviews with Omar were filmed, and as the result of a court order in 2008, the video records were released. Two Canadian filmmakers, Luc Côté and Patricio Henriquez, decided the released video should be brought to the attention of a wide audience and in 2010 released the film *You Don't Like the Truth: 4 Days inside Guantánamo*. The film provides a stark and realistic portrait of Omar as he was in early 2003. As well, it gives an unvarnished view of the interrogation methods of CSIS officials and perhaps an understanding of why there is such animosity between the Canadian Islamic community and Canadian security officials. Mr Gould did provide consular officials with a detailed report of his observations and views on Omar's condition, and this was the first independent report on conditions inside the prison at Guantánamo and how they were affecting a sixteen-year-old Canadian.

Over the intervening years there have been numerous reports on conditions inside Guantánamo, many from released prisoners and others from guards and interrogators. The early reports were accurate, and it was evident that Guantánamo was a prison beyond the rule of law other than that proscribed by the American president.

As well, it was evidently a place where intimidation, abuse, and torture were routine, and there were few signs that international pressure had any effect. It was only when the American courts began to exercise their authority under the American Constitution that the legal fiction surrounding Guantánamo began to unravel.

In 2004 the American Supreme Court in two landmark decisions (*Hamdi v. Rumsfeld* and *Rasul v. Bush*) ruled (in *Hamdi*) that American citizens must have the ability to challenge their enemy combatant status before an impartial judge. It was a partial victory in that it only applied to the rare American citizen imprisoned at Guantánamo or elsewhere in other American gulags. The ruling recognized the power of the American government to imprison enemy combatants. However, in the *Rasul* decision, the Supreme Court went much further and ruled that American courts have jurisdiction to hear habeas corpus petitions filed by foreign detainees at Guantánamo. The *Rasul* decision relied extensively on the Geneva Conventions and other international instruments relating to the conduct of war, casting doubts on earlier administration attempts to avoid the application of law to prisoners in such places as Guantánamo.

Initial attempts by the Canadian government to provide consular assistance to Omar Khadr faded quickly in Ottawa. The increasing involvement of Canadian troops in Afghanistan, the casualties, and the growing awareness of activities of Khadr family members cemented in the minds of many that these were Canadians antithetically opposed to the views of the country and that their citizenship was being misused. Shortly after the diplomatic note of 13 September 2002 to the Americans, the legal adviser at Foreign Affairs intervened stating that in dealing with Omar, Canada should "claw back on the fact that [Omar] is a minor."

Those few words of the legal adviser became the policy of successive Canadian governments, and it has survived intact in the face of numerous court decisions and overwhelming evidence that the adjudication process associated with Guantánamo was fundamentally flawed. As Omar's lawyers have demonstrated in several cases before Canadian courts, governments of Canada have been negligent and, except for a concluding decision by the Supreme Court, acted illegally. Successive Canadian governments have given Omar the cold shoulder and hidden behind the fiction that there was a "legal" process underway at Guantánamo. This was argued before the public and before the courts and provided the veneer for the legal fiction that it was inappropriate for the Canadian government to intervene before the conclusion of that process.

Throughout the months and years of Omar's imprisonment at Guantánamo, the American judicial system slowly eviscerated the carefully crafted legal basis placing it supposedly beyond the legal and constitutional protections available to persons within the boundaries of the American union. Extraterritoriality has never been foreign to American lawmakers and its courts, and "American Exceptionalism" was at full flower during this period. But this was extraterritoriality at its worst as Guantánamo became a euphemism for torture and the denial of over 800 years of legal protections going back to the days of Magna Carta. These protections – namely habeas corpus and public trials – have been at the centre of our fundamental protection against overreaching governments who use temporal difficulties to justify egregious and illegal actions.

The American Congress went along with the legal fiction associated with Guantánamo, but the American courts, as noted above, did not, and by 2006 had decided in several decisions that the initial law giving authority for Guantánamo was unconstitutional. By June 2008 the legal fiction associated with Guantánamo was eliminated when the US Supreme Court ruled (in *Boumediene v. Bush*, 12 June 2008) that foreign terrorism suspects held at Guantánamo have constitutional rights to challenge their detention in American courts.

Indirectly, these legal developments were of some assistance to Omar, but as the endgame illustrates, not much. Apart from the visits by Canadian security officials in 2003 and 2004, it was not until 2005 that he was visited by Canadian consular officials who were specifically concerned with his welfare and well-being. These visits were classified as "social" ones, and the resulting reports were shared with Omar's Canadian lawyers. The visits provided the first significant first-hand details of his condition. The report for 12 and 13 March illustrates the insights gained:

> The overarching theme of much of our discussions focused on his desire to get out of Guantánamo, to return to Canada, to fix his health, educate himself, to have a family, and to eventually find a job satisfying his personal commitment to help those in need. By contrast, he also expressed a hyper-awareness of the challenges that he would face but demonstrated no bitterness or anger, emphasizing instead a desire to move forward in life.

> The trusting relationships he has built with CNO/Collins and JLH/Nolke [previous visitors], which are clearly important to him, and the very positive visit we shared, seem to have put a face on the Canadian Government in his eyes, and he appeared hopeful that Canada is aware of him, cares about him, and will help him.

According to the terms of his 2010 plea bargain, Omar Khadr would be twenty-five years old when he was to arrive back in Canada in the fall of 2011. His is a story few can understand, carrying with it extremes of behaviour little understood or appreciated by many Canadians. He is not alone in experiencing the inability of our governmental institutions to cope with the tsunami of lies, misdirection, misunderstanding, and failures unleashed in reaction to the attacks in the United States on 11 September 2001. Unfortunately in the intervening ten years there has been little to show for the thousands who have died and the billions that have been spent. The winding-down of some of those actions is underway, but there is little success that can be claimed in our hysterical expectation for greater security or the expansion of peace or improvements in the quality of life for many in distant countries. It is a game played out in the real world where both sides have less today than when they started. As one aphorism would have it, if you only carry hammers, you will always finds nails.

Few clues are available to us that might offer understanding of Omar Khadr's life beyond Guantánamo. The black hole of Guantánamo provided few opportunities where Omar could offer his own views on what has happened or when reasoned assessments could be made. Nevertheless there is some support for the view that he is not irredeemably lost as a result of the injuries and injustices that have surrounded his life so far. The decision to accept the plea agreement offered by the Americans late in the process suggests he fully understood the futility of trying to win in a system so completely stacked against him. It offered a relatively early escape from the system that his own lawyer described as a fraud. A further clue can be found in Omar's conversations with Canadian officials during their "social visits." In the March 2008 visit, the Canadian visitors quoted the American guards as saying that Omar is "salvageable," "non-radicalized," and "a good kid," who is well liked both within the Camp and by JTF staff. The visitor also writes that "he nevertheless demonstrated remarkable insight and self-awareness." Muneer Ahmad was for a time one of Omar's Canadian lawyers. In the book *The Guantanamo Lawyers*, Muneer is quoted:

> It would be a mistake to say that Omar was concerned merely with short-term relief ... while we were concerned with the long-term goal of his release. The difference between us was rather more profound and concerned competing judgments about how best to achieve the long-term goal. In the beginning of our relationship, Omar gave law and us, the benefit of the doubt. But over time, he ... came to see law as the government's tool of oppression rather than his and the other detainees' instrument for liberation.

The prison of Guantánamo will be with us for some time to come. The American political system of counterbalance and check will not permit elimination of Guantánamo and the evil it represents. There have been improvements; over six hundred detainees have been released, but this was more of an indication of just how loose was the standard in the filling of its cells than the exercise of mercy. Abu Ghraib represented a paroxysm of sadism encouraged by American leaders who assumed their injury was greater than that of anyone else. Guantánamo represents a corruption of the American political and legal system where there is no willingness for accounting or for responsibility. One young Canadian may be about to escape its clutches but we should not forget that there are still over a hundred that have little hope of doing so.

My Encounter with Omar

CRAIG KIELBURGER

The day I met Omar Khadr was the most terrifying of my life.

I was sitting in a meeting room in Islamabad, shaking. Omar's presence was oddly comforting. It was January 1996 and the two of us were waiting in a five-star hotel for then Prime Minister Jean Chrétien to appear. I had just turned thirteen. I was travelling through South Asia learning first hand about child labour. The prime minister was also in the region. A week earlier I had said at a press conference that he had a moral responsibility to do something about child labour.

He heard about it. Then he pencilled me into his schedule in Islamabad.

I was terrified. Looking back, it was actually kind of comical. Here I was, nervous about meeting with the Shawinigan Strangler when I was sitting next to Canada's first family of terrorism.

That morning I walked into the hotel lobby and was immediately surrounded by reporters. It was my first scrum, and it did nothing to calm my nerves. When the Khadr family walked in and the reporters shouted their name, I didn't know who they were but was thankful they had taken the attention away from me.

We made our way to a waiting room – me, my mentor, Alam, Mrs Khadr, and her brood of kids, including nine-year-old Omar.

Mrs Khadr was pleading the case of her husband, Ahmed Said Khadr, imprisoned in Pakistan for his role in the car bombing at the Egyptian embassy that killed seventeen people. She claimed he was wrongly accused and was being tortured. I felt sympathy, looking into the faces of her worried children.

Omar and I smiled at each other. It was comforting sitting with a kid so close to my own age. We exchanged a few words, and I learned we were from nearby neighbourhoods in Toronto. I breathed a bit easier as we reminisced about our hometown.

An aide then told me it was my turn. I said goodbye as the kids were given some candy to ease their nerves.

In our fifteen-minute meeting, Chrétien talked a lot about trade laws before sighing and promising to bring up child labour with Pakistan's Prime Minister Benazir Bhutto. My last thought of the Khadr family was wondering if they were able to make any more headway.

Weeks later, I returned home to a firestorm of media attention. Many asked how I had accomplished so much at such a young age. Years later, when I learned that the boy I met in Pakistan allegedly killed an American soldier in a firefight in Afghanistan, I wondered if anyone asked him that question.

It dawned on me that people thought my thirteen-year-old self did something kids shouldn't be capable of doing. But when Omar was pushed into weapons training at ten, apparently he should have known better.

Really, though, the two of us are products our environment. Omar is just being punished for his.

Omar and I were born in the same city, but we come from very different places. My parents never considered themselves activists per se, but my mom worked with a street youth drop-in centre, and my dad volunteered with mentally challenged individuals. They found fulfillment in these experiences, and they encouraged my brother and me to find our own.

That influence ultimately led me to Pakistan in 1996. I didn't realize it at the time, but while I had made the choice to be there, Omar had not.

Growing up in Toronto, Omar liked comics, and his siblings described an impression he used to do of Captain Haddock from the comic *Tintin*. His teachers described him as smart and eager to learn. Of course, they didn't see the enormous pressure his father applied. Whereas most kids are encouraged to become doctors or lawyers, the Khadr boys grew up holding suicide bombers in the highest admiration. Their father threatened death if they ever betrayed Islam. Omar, said to be the closest to Ahmed, didn't want to disappoint.

That explained the apparent worry on Omar's face in Pakistan. He had seen his father in trouble before. A few years earlier, he had refused to leave Ahmed's bedside while he recuperated from near-deadly injuries after stepping on a landmine in Afghanistan. This childhood defined by fear, family loyalty, and intense pressure led him to that Islamabad hotel. When his childhood led him to battle, it would come back to haunt him.

Mrs Khadr and her kids got a lot of sympathy that day as many questioned why the prime minister was unwilling to help her husband, a Canadian citizen. Chrétien was as good as his word, though. He brought up both of our issues with Bhutto. I'm not sure what she said about child labour, but she did assure him that Khadr would receive a fair trial.

Weeks later, his charges were dropped. Most Canadians, myself included, forgot about the incident. Then, after September 11th, the Khadr name resurfaced – this time linked to Osama bin Laden.

As it turned out, that meeting with Chrétien had a major impact on both Omar's life and my own. For me, the increased media attention had allowed Free the Children to gain a foothold. We were growing quickly. The boy whose mother led him by the hand through a scrum of reporters saw his father released from prison. Just months later, that father had him learning to make bombs and to wield an assault rifle in weapons training. That one fateful moment changed the course of both of our lives – so much so that when fifteen-year-old Omar turned up nearly dead at the Bagram Detention Centre, he had spent his childhood training as a child soldier.

For years the Canadian government has been unwilling to risk his repatriation after his father's betrayal. His mother only worsened the sentiment by appearing on television to denounce Western democracy.

The twenty-four-year-old Omar we see in the news today bears little resemblance to the nervous nine-year-old I saw accepting candy from Chrétien's political aide. Instead he looks more like his father. It's unfair for any kids to have to live up to their parents. It's especially so when you're a Khadr.

Today, Omar's legal battles are seemingly drawing to a close. But the boy I met in Pakistan was dealt a sentence through his family name.

Reflections

Re: That Gunfight at the O.K. Corral

GEORGE ELLIOTT CLARKE

I

Gitmo is the X-ray[1] Spandau,[2]
and you, O.K. –
though you prefer dynamite to architecture –
are still posed as the kiddy Albert Speer[3]
a stand-up stand-in for the once unkillable
Osama bin Hitler,
our ex-ally,
who loved to martyr all but himself.

To us, you're the kid with the viper backbone,
who could glide through grass,
amid unnerving shadows,
a night theatre of skeletons,
when stars looked arrows,
even though our cannon were pluggin every cavern
amid them labyrinthine plots

round Ayub Kheyl,[4]
the Afghan O.K. Corral.[5]

Did you set out to whack us –
to behead us "alcoholics and adulterers,"
or to try not to be exploded
or decapitated?

Answer yes, either way.
(Blame is sticky:
A Tar Baby.)[6]

In your defence, you could complain
our delegates were soaring, targeting,
and blasting your buddies
into puzzling pretzel pieces.
(Yes, sometimes, we even slay our pals,
but friend or foe is hard to distinguish
from a God's-eye view.)
Our cluster bombs were also ripping apart
curious children
like so many cheap dolls.[7]
(But that's war: No hard feelings ...)

You testify you were tryin to skedaddle,
to treasure life's beauties,
but our *lawful* troops had you cross-haired
(our firepower be awful, "awesome"),
so you had to wing a grenade,
and triggered a lasting *murder*.

To swim among corpses,
a pool of skulls,
biblical remains
(so many
that the Grim Reaper is Santa),
that's no picnic, you recall.

(Sides, all the ranked dead –
Christian, Muslim, Jew, etc. –
are crafted corpses:
Trash
no tears can polish.)

So why should your heart vomit
at news an "enemy combatant"[8]
got his noggin smacked open?

II

Let's say,
honestly, they're false –
those reports (guns, grenades, *guilt*) …

Yet, while our amigos were strafing your hideout,
Kid Omar
(and our witnesses swear you swore martyrdom),
shrapnel brained our brave Kit Speer.[9]

Clearly, you misunderstood facts.

Our job is to kayo
your type, okay?

(You ain't no Omar Khayyam!)[10]

Don't you understand
we were – are – powerless against opium,[11]
although our detonations
reverse night and day,
day and night,
in enveloping chiaroscuro?

Too, the Taliban
(as if boozed on Ballantine)
keep on comin,
mockin
every demonic instrument and demented punishment:
They're like those blow-up Bozos
that bob back
no matter how hard they're swatted!
Christ!

So, once you was netted, nailed,
twas *necessary* for us to test out torture.
(Yessuh, boy, nothin's as fundamental
as your ass!)

Damn it! Taliban killin our Coalition Club
like we were – are – maggots.
But them greasy toads, them grisly fanatics,
who blew up millennia-old, Buddhist statues[12]
(humanity's divinity),
merit mass murder,
cos they chuckled when al-Qaeda's kamikaze
toppled Wall Street's twin totems
(a decade before jet-set fraudsters could).

III

O.K., because you outlived our explosives,
you're now a prize catch, kiddo.

Who'd we really want?

That crusty, untrustworthy engineer –
Osama –
with his trusty, dustless Qu'ran
and AK-47,
that gold toothache,
that billionaire bandit,
crabbing through caves,
then hunkered down in a Pakistan villa/bunker,
who had us pursuers –
usurpers –
chrome cockroaches in dark depths –
insisting on his sentimental sacrifice.
(So he stuttered scripture after scripture:
We served him Saddam's fatal rapture.)

IV

Let's say your childhood was cold:
Some bad smell of blood
outta your Dad's hospitals and orphanages;
or say your kitchen table was slashed with knife marks,
and there were bite marks on the table legs;
or say you never read *Archie* and lusted after Betty;

or say your crib never had anything gooey or sugary;
or say that your Dad ordained a wise-guy persona;
or say that, while neighbourhood kids shot pucks,
your Dad drilled you to shoot "gross infidels";
and showed you how a razor
castrates a dog
or sticks a hog.

But a guerilla camp
got no room for gilded respectability.

Yep, your Pops, Ahmed, was a gimp
with a limp.
Looks like he had a punched in
and kicked about face.
He was a prizefighter poet,
his mouth all twisted up,
snarling verse.
Hasty, stringent, cryptically arrogant,
a chap capital at political bullying,
that ostentatious dude couldn't shoot straight
shit …
He had
to hustle and muscle his way into the *jihad*, eh?

Good: Pakistani S.S. bushwhacked him
in goddamn, shifty-sand Afghanistan.

Your Dad – disloyal Canuck (we say) – died,
snacking on bullets.
You bawled, you bawled, you bawled!
That's crappy.

But, hey, even "giants" find graves
that fit them to a T.

V

In archives seething with teeth,
drab bards,

their eyes gone,
tattle teetering tongues,
to chisel an epic
about that continent of discontent –
The Middle East –
and brand you
the poster child
of insidious assassination.

It's easy enough.
Newsprint authors follow the lead
of a spooky kook,
Prez Bush II,
a shabby brain, much sloppy speech,
sly lies,
such Texas-explicit vulgarity
(even we Habs[13] giggle at his terms).

But Bush was belligerent and repugnant,
a born monster,
always blank-faced, free of emotions
(and most thought),
with a coward's prowess in deceit;
his tears were clear piss.

And our lawn-jockey[14] PM is Quisling.[15]

So, even if we agree
it was a dirty, nasty, ugly, evil thing –
that lethal grenade you could've thrown –
free citizens gotta spy bottom-lines, not just headlines.

VI

Thus, the true nature of disgrace is
US –
who dispatch flying squads
of death-bringers,
blindly bombing,
blithely bombing,
mosque and kindergarten,[16]

and shackling down babies,
in wars we got no guts to declare,
and then sobbing, "Unfair,"
when one of our drones is downed
or one of our heroes gets crowned
by lead fragments or flame.

It is our irreversible damnation
that we deem our injuries
innocence,
so that we slaughter innocents
in the name of what might-makes-right
(i.e., our right to feed and fatten on fossil fuels),
and then shout surprise
when the survivors among our victims –
totin their holy books and squawkin their big mouths –
hasten to strike back and strike down
our innocents.

Okay,
it's not okay.

Even if we judge you're O.K.

EDITOR'S NOTES

1 Camp X-Ray was the temporary prison established for three months in 11 January 2002 at the US Naval Base in Guantánamo, Cuba, to house the first twenty prisoners. It had been replaced by Camp Delta, Guantánamo (nicknamed Gitmo), when Omar Khadr arrived on 29 or 30 October 2002.

2 Spandau Prison, located in West Berlin, was destroyed in 1987 after the last of the seven Nazi war criminals convicted at Nuremburg was no longer housed there.

3 Albert Speer (1905–81) was Hitler's highly trained chief architect and later minister of Armaments and War Productions for the Third Reich. After accepting "collective responsibility" for the Third Reich's war crimes at the Nuremburg trials, he was imprisoned at Spandau Prison from 1949 to 1966. Speer wrote drafts of a distinguished memoir and history in prison. Although he served out his

full sentence, many around the world, including heads of state, called earlier for his release.

4 The Afghan village where Omar Khadr was captured.

5 The O.K. Corral thirty-second gunfight took place in Tombstone, Arizona, in 1891, but became mythologized in a fictional biography of lawman Wyatt Earp and in two American Western films, John Ford's *My Darling Clementine* (1946) and John Sturges's *Gunfight at the O.K. Corral* (1957).

6 "Tar baby" originates in African folklore and later in the Uncle Remus early American stories as a doll made up of turpentine and tar – the more Uncle Remus fights with him, the more he is entangled with the doll. The term has been associated with racist connotations in the United States and Canada. Liberal MP Ralph Goodale raised this association in a parliamentary point of order question when he addressed Conservative member Pierre Poilievre, secretary to the prime minister, and asked him to apologize for the use of this term. Goodale explains: "In addition to being a pejorative term, which might well prove to be unparliamentary ... many authorities in this country and in many others ... consider the term racist." Poilievre replied that he referred to "issues that stick to one." NDP MP Paul Dewar pointed out that "tar baby" "has been interpreted by many African Americans and others ... [as] a term that should not be used." Goodale noted that both former US Governor Mitt Romney and Senator John McCain have apologized in the US Senate for using this term (*Parliamentary Debates,* House of Commons, 29 May 2009).

7 In 1986, Ahmed Khadr, Omar's father, condemned Russia's use of cluster bombs that explode into "bomblets" shaped like "pretty toys" attractive to young children. The unexploded ordinance of cluster bombs can be especially lethal to civilians. In Afghanistan, US forces dropped humanitarian rations coloured the same yellow as cluster bombs. The packaging of rations were later changed to blue and then to clear to avoid this deadly confusion.

8 Historically this term refers to "Any person in an armed conflict who could be properly detained under the laws and customs of war." On 14 September 2001, US Congress passed a law defining "enemy combatant" as anyone associated with al-Qaeda or the Taliban. These prisoners are ruled not subject to the prisoner-of-war status of the Geneva Convention: this exceptional category of persons beyond the laws of war has been condemned by human rights organizations and others.

9 Christopher Speer is the US Delta Force soldier killed by a grenade. Omar Kadar was convicted of his death in a US Military Commission that relied on disputed evidence.

10 Renowned as a great Persian mathematician, astronomer, philosopher, and scientist in Iran during his time (1048–1131), Khayyam is remembered today for his poetry including his thousand-verse epic, *The Rubaiyat of Omar Khayyam*.

11 Opium production was reduced by 91 per cent after the Taliban declared the drug un-Islamic in 2000 – a most effective drug eradication program. Post-fall of the Taliban, production climbed. By 2007, 94 per cent of opiates in the world came from Afghanistan, amounting to an economy of $64 billion.

12 In March 2001, Taliban who ruled Afghanistan destroyed two magnificent towering sixth-century Buddhist statues carved into sandstone cliffs and covered with stucco, mud, and straw. Located in Bemiyan, Afghanistan, this site had once been a part of the Silk Road and was a thriving Buddhist spiritual centre between the second and eight centuries. This destruction appalled many in Afghanistan and around the world.

13 Fans of the Montreal Canadiens hockey team cheer for the Habs. From the seventeenth to the twentieth century, *habitans* and later *habitants* referred to the French who lived and settled along the St Lawrence River in what became the province of Quebec.

14 Traditionally depicted as black, this lawn ornament is often considered racially insensitive and racist.

15 This term was popularized by Winston Churchill's description of Nazi collaborationists in a 1949 speech to the US Congress: "Still more fiercely burn the fires of hatred and contempt for the filthy Quislings." Norwegian Vidkun Quisling led Norway's Nazi collaborationist government which he helped install.

16 German origins meaning "garden of children."

Our Kids

CHARLES FORAN

THINGS THAT HAPPEN TO OMAR KHADR[1] BEFORE HE TURNS EIGHTEEN

1 He is born in Toronto.
2 He is taught to speak English, Arabic, Pashto, and Dari. Also some French.
3 His father, a terrorist, takes him, his mother, and his siblings to Pakistan and then Afghanistan, to plot and make jihad. Omar learns to fire rocket-propelled grenades and assault rifles. Also to build and plant IEDs (improvised explosive devices).
4 He turns fifteen on 18 September 2001 in Afghanistan.
5 His father assigns him to work as a translator for the Libyan Islamic Fighting Group. Does undercover reconnaissance among American troops.
6 He finds himself pinned down inside a mud compound. Refuses to leave with women and children, or to surrender. US war planes bomb the site, and Delta Force commanders enter. Omar, hiding behind a wall, tosses a grenade at a soldier ("like in the movies," he later admits). He is shot twice in the back.
7 The US soldier, Sgt Speer, dies ten days later. Omar survives multiple surgeries, including on his right eye, hit by shrapnel. He loses sight in it.
8 Spends three months in military hospital in Afghanistan. Is interrogated forty times. Claims he is hung by his wrists and soaked in water, a hood over his head.
9 He turns sixteen. In isolation cell in Guantánamo Bay, Cuba. Claims he is spat upon and shackled to ground for hours. Weeps during taped confession and cries out for his mother.

10 His father is killed in shootout with Pakistani authorities.
11 During interrogation with Canadian foreign affairs officials in Guantánamo, he urinates on photo of his family. Twice. Then he lies next to photo in "affectionate manner."
12 His younger brother, also fighting at his father's behest, is caught in crossfire with US troops. Kareem Khadr is paralyzed from waist down.
13 While still in solitary cell inside Camp 5, Omar is visited by lawyer, who embraces him. "No one had touched him in years," the lawyer says.

THINGS THAT HAPPEN TO ANNA FORAN BEFORE SHE TURNS EIGHTEEN

1 She is born in Montreal.
2 She is taught to speak English, French, and later some Mandarin.
3 Her parents, a writer and a teacher, relocate her and her younger sister, Claire, to Peterborough, Ontario, to be near their Canadian grandparents. Girls watch *The Lion King* obsessively during move into new house. Meet neighbouring girls, the Bartleys, on first day. Recreate scenes involving Simba and Mufasa in backyard fort, singing "Circle of Life." No one wants to play the evil lion Scar.
4 Participates in family written and performed plays inside barn on grandparents' farm. A friend videos one show, titled "The Play Is the Thing."
5 Parents decide to relocate again to Hong Kong for three years. Anna and Claire are enrolled in Canadian International School, where they learn to say "Give me a break!" in Cantonese and sing "Frere Jacques," now about a tiger, in Mandarin. Christmases and vacations in Bali, China, Malaysia, and Thailand.
6 On TV in apartment on Hong Kong island, Anna watches Twin Towers fall. "Today, the world changed," her father says (pompously). He still reads her a chapter of *Harry Potter and the Prisoner of Azkaban* before bed that night, despite his misgivings about J.K. Rowling's prose.
7 Back in Canada, she takes piano lessons on piano in living room. Makes her high-school basketball team and helps organize movie-themed school dances, *Grease* being especially popular.

8 Turns sixteen on 19 January 2007 in Peterborough. Requests Indian dinner for a dozen friends, all girls, who paint henna tattoos over each other's arms and watch the video of the family barn play. "You were SOOOO cute!" the friends say.
9 Develops obsession with BBC adaptation of *Pride and Prejudice*. Possibly a Daddy crush on actor Colin Firth.
10 Divides summers between visiting other grandparents in Milwaukee and attending Camp Kawartha on Clear Lake. While at camp, turns wild-eyed and feral, skin deeply tanned.
11 Joins high school model UN trip to The Hague and Barcelona. First time away from family. Many hugs – mother/daughter, father/daughter, sister/sister, father/mother/sister/sister – upon departure. Some tears.
12 Attends tea party in backyard of family house before Grade 12 formal. Has first boyfriend. He does not accompany her to dance.
13 Is accepted by McGill University. Parents full of general worries about train derailments, dark alleys, biting cold. Very proud of their girl.

THINGS THAT HAPPEN TO OMAR KHADR BEFORE HE TURNS TWENTY-FOUR

1 He is charged with murder. Ordered to stand trial before military commission. Claims his confession of throwing grenade at Sgt Speers was coerced.
2 Is kept in solitary for a sixth year. Has not seen any parents since he went to Afghanistan, on his (dead) father's orders. Has not seen his siblings (one paralyzed from waist down) since then either. Has not seen Toronto since his parents took him away from the country of his birth, so they could make jihad and, by the by, destroy their children.
3 He continues to go largely unhugged by any adult. He continues not to attend high school dances or summer camp.
4 He turns twenty-two. Is finally transferred to Camp 4 at Guantánamo, a communal section, where he can mingle with fellow prisoners. Spends days drawing pictures with crayons and reading. Likes the Harry Potter books (early high school level), *Great Expectations* (standard Grade 11 text) and *Huckleberry Finn* (Grade 11 or 12). Also, novels by John Grisham.

5 His oldest brother, Abdullah, is charged with gun-smuggling in US. His sister, Zaynab, is under investigation by RCMP. His mother declares public support for suicide bombers while also saying, "Omar has been branded by the family." Media call the Khadrs "Canada's first family of terrorism."

6 He is visited by a psychiatrist, a retired US army brigadier-general. "He is a very decent, kind young man – and he has faith," Stephen Xenekis reports of his one hundred hours with Omar. "I don't think it has radicalized him," he adds of prison. "There is no hard edge to him at all, and there is no sense of vengeance."

7 Is passed smuggled notes from a professor in Edmonton. "Your letters are like candles very bright in my hardship and darkness," he writes back.

8 He reads *A Long Way Gone: Memoirs of a Boy Soldier* by Ishmael Beah, concerning a thirteen-year-old forced into Sierra Leone army. Afterwards, writes to Edmonton supporter, "Children's hearts are like a sponge that will absorb what is around it, like wet cement, soft until it is sculptured in a certain way."

9 He spends his three-thousandth day and night in prison. One-third of his life. All of his adulthood. Most of his teenage years.

10 He is put on trial for war crimes. Signs a plea deal, confessing to throwing grenade at age fifteen while trying to please his father, to be a good, dutiful son, a worthy (extremist) Muslim, in exchange for another eight years of incarceration. "He's a murderer in my eyes and always will be," says the widow of Sgt Speer. "My children are the victims."

11 He waits to return to a home that does not want him. He waits for his life to stop being about parents' fanaticism and mistakes, bequeathed to their jihadi boy soldier, their precious, beloved son.

THINGS ANNA FORAN DOES BEFORE SHE TURNS TWENTY

1 Gets a cell phone. Calls her Mom and Dad most days or is called by them. Prefers to text message or Skype her sister.

2 Spends her first year in university residence, single (monastic) room, with meal plan. Noisy neighbours, food not so great.

Room often needs tidying. Accepts invitations from friends of family who offer to cook or take her to dinner.

3 Rides overnight bus to New York for long weekend with classmates. Remembers to bring passport. Her parents worry when she does not call on arrival.

4 Enrols in first-year Arts Legacy program. "Moving from ancient societies to modern time and focusing on Western and non-Western traditions alike," the website says, " the Arts Legacy curriculum gives you the opportunity to establish a foundation of knowledge on which to build your university career. " Anna attends art exhibits, hears a speech by the Dali Lama, goes for drinks with professors. Loves every minute.

5 Struggles to write essay on Islamic and Christian religious iconography. Writes a good paper, regardless.

6 Misses family wedding in Georgia, and chance to see her American grandparents, due to spring exams. Sees her Canadian grandparents regularly once school is finished.

7 WWOOFS with her childhood friend Ingrid on farm near Uxbridge in May. Parents inquire about the acronym, which stands for "World Wide Organization of Organic Farms." Plants seeds, clears fields, takes photos of animals. Loves every minute. Works for rest of summer at a local daycare.

8 Rents a Montreal apartment with two other girls, one from Vancouver, the other Brooklyn. Funky Plateau neighbourhood, charming flat. Also rundown and overpriced. Excellent life-learning experience.

9 She meets boys. Boys meet her.

10 Signs up for weekend painting class. Can't decide on major: art history or maybe English. Loves to make collages, to read about art, to think about art, but also to study literature. (*Gulliver's Travels* is a major discovery of fall semester. "Nothing is great or little otherwise than by comparison," Jonathan Swift writes of perceptual irony of one group appearing grotesque simply because their dimensions magnify what are otherwise ordinary human flaws.) Loves every minute of her life in Montreal, at McGill.

11 Returns home for Christmas holidays. Parents feed her, do her laundry, encourage her to sleep in. Very proud of her, and her sister. She can't wait for second semester to begin, for spring travel plans to unfold, for the summer ahead. She can't wait.

NOTE

1 All but a handful of these details about Omar Khadr have been taken from the *Maclean's* cover story for 15 November 2010, "Who Is the Real Omar Khadr?"

Omar and I: Stability and Democracy

HASNAIN KHAN

Summer 2009. In one of the several bookstores that dot Edmonton's Whyte Avenue, I was taking a break from studying to browse the politics section of the bookstore. A short, bulky gentleman in the same section initiated a conversation with me. In less than two minutes Omar Khadr became the subject of *his* conversation – I was doing most of the listening. The words he used for Omar are not worth repeating. To call them xenophobic is an understatement.

I didn't say much other than the occasional "yeah" to indicate I was still listening. He must have sensed my growing discomfort with the conversation. So the topic shifted – from extremists and terrorists amongst *my people* to Sikh terrorists. Then he threw in the Tamil Tigers for good measure. Maybe this was his way of saying that he was no Islamphobe, just a "freedom-loving" Canadian.

I was born in Pakistan. The year of my birth: 1988. That same year, many Pakistanis sighed with relief – while some wept with grief for Mohammad Zia-ul-Haq, the dictator supported by the West, who crashed to his death in an airplane accident that remains a mystery to this day. That date makes me about a year and a half younger than Omar Khadr. It also makes me a member of what has come to be known as the Zia generation: the generation born during or close to the eleven-year dark reign of General Zia.

The Zia generation bore the brunt of Zia's Islamization of the country. He overthrew an elected government and installed himself in power. He called himself a "Soldier of Islam" in his very first speech to the Pakistani nation. Today, there is little doubt that it was his goal to turn all of Pakistan, especially its youth, into Soldiers of

Islam – his Islam, a puritanical Islam with little space for dissent, for culture, for women, for justice, for tolerance, even for truth.

One of the lasting legacies of his project of Islamization has been the destruction of the Pakistani education system. Pakistani children were taught blatant lies – about ourselves and about others. All this while Zia continued to be perceived in the West as a loyal friend leading the fight against the Godless Communists. Billions of dollars of Western, particularly American, aid destined for Afghanistan entered Pakistan and never reached the intended destination.

Once Afghanistan had been liberated, it was time to liberate Kashmir. The liberation of Kashmir was instilled in the pupils of the Pakistani state's education system as a religious and a national duty. After the Soviets left, so did the Western spies. They left behind caches of weapons along with many trigger-happy, radicalized mercenaries who had been told that their purpose in life was to liberate Muslims and protect Islam.

Had I remained in Pakistan, it's quite possible that I would today be among the hoards of young angry men burning American and Israeli flags. But I didn't stay. I was fortunate enough to immigrate to Canada at the age of twelve, where I had access to a decent education and to knowledge that was previously unavailable to me.

My earliest memory of Omar Khadr is from a letter, probably the first, that he sent to his family from Guantánamo Bay. It was published in a newspaper that I used to read every day when I worked at my parents' convenience store. What struck me then – and I still haven't forgotten it – was Omar's spelling. The letter was from a teenage Omar, but it may as well have been written by a second grader.

At fifteen years of age, Omar found himself in Guantánamo, badly hurt and alone. At the age he was captured, I would have been reading Harper Lee's *To Kill a Mockingbird*. At the age he was transferred to Guantánamo Bay, I had likely just cracked open George Orwell's *1984*.

I was disturbed by Omar's letter. I asked myself: How could anyone justify the treatment being meted out to Omar?

Sadly, all I did was ask this question.

Days and nights passed, and Omar Khadr became just another issue among many. I had assignments to hand in, books to read, projects to complete, movies to watch, my daily shifts at the store, and – of course – more newspapers to read to learn more about disturbing issues that I could then object to and complain about and stash away in some forgotten part of my mind.

It was not until the second year of my studies at the University of Alberta that I heard Dennis Edney, Omar's defence attorney, speak at a charity dinner. His description of Omar's time in prison, particularly his interrogations, was heart wrenching. It moved me and some friends sufficiently to participate in several events meant to raise awareness of Omar's plight.

But to my discredit, that's all I did. In a sea of ignorance about Omar, my contribution was an insignificant droplet. Instead of changing the tide, this droplet became a part of the sea.

I could have said many things to that gentleman at the bookstore to explain to him that Omar wasn't just a psychopath who had woken up one day and decided to kill Americans, that there was more to the story than just hate for America and the West or a twisted religious ideology.

For instance, as Tariq Ali explains in one of his books, the jihadi manuals circulated among the mujahideen fighting the Soviet invaders and in Afghan refugee camps were produced at the University of Nebraska–Omaha.[1] The same manuals are in use today.

I could have pointed out how the United States and Canada unabashedly supported the thirty-year dictatorial rule of Hosni Mubarak in Egypt – the country of Omar's parents – even as they continued to harp about democracy and human rights in Iran and other countries.

I could have asked him if liberating the women of Afghanistan, despite their vehement opposition to such liberation,[2] was in fact the objective of our mission, then why not liberate Saudi women who have suffered far worse and for much longer?

I could have asked about the tens of billions of dollars in military aid that United States has given to both Egypt and Pakistan, among many other countries.

I could have asked why, when pressed to choose between democracy and stability, the United States and its allies preferred stability over the aspirations of the people. I could have asked why it took the United States so long to support the thousands of Egyptians who gathered in Tahrir Square to protest against Hosni Mubarak's stifling thirty-year rule.

I could have asked why the United States, Canada, and Europe saw fit to enforce a no-fly zone in Libya against Muammar Gaddafi, but all they could do for the thousands of peaceful demonstrators being brutally crushed in Bahrain, Yemen, and Saudi Arabia amounted to muzzled messages of restraint.

I could have broken my silence in that bookstore and told that gentleman about my life in the 1990s in Pakistan as a member of the Shia Muslim minority. After the mujahideen and other extremist groups had finished "liberating" Afghanistan, they turned to saving Islam from those they considered non-Muslims: Shias, Ahmadis, Christians, Hindus, etc. I want to ask him where his disgust and anger with extremism and terrorism were when ordinary civilians were being killed by the weapons and mercenaries that America had left behind.

Today Omar is paying the price of flawed policies. Is he any different from a Rwandan boy given guns instead of books? Is he any different from an underaged prostitute caught in the streets of Edmonton? How can we accuse him of malicious intent when the circumstances in which he grew up never gave him a choice?

I said none of this and asked no questions of the man at the bookstore. For where was I when Omar Khadr was made to spend his youth in a cell at Guantánamo? I will always be ashamed of both instances of my silence – silence in the face of Omar's immoral and unethical imprisonment and silence in the face of an ignorant man who epitomized the worst of the prejudice and stereotypes prevalent in Canadian society. I knew better, yet I still did nothing.

NOTES

1 Tariq Ali in his book *The Duel: Pakistan on the Flight Path of American Power* explains that these manuals were later used in the Afghani state school system by the Taliban and continue to be used to train those fighting NATO forces.

2 The Revolutionary Association of the Women of Afghanistan condemned the 9/11 attacks as well as the imminent American invasion of Afghanistan. Their statements, reminding the United States and the West in general of their support for the mujahideen including Osama bin Laden, are available online at http://www.rawa.org/ny-press.htm.

PART TWO

Omar Khadr in Guantánamo: Architecture Is Not Justice

Some Images of the Unseen: On the Making of the Film *You Don't Like the Truth: 4 Days inside Guantánamo*

PATRICIO HENRIQUEZ

Translated by Mark Abley

In their permanent quest to capture the real, one of the most important barriers that documentary filmmakers confront is the invisibility of things. Which part of reality can be filmed by documentary cameras? It's difficult to respond to that question with precision, but many of us suspect that what escapes our filming eyes is in truth greater, and perhaps more essential, than what is visible to us.

So it was with understandable excitement that I rushed to my computer on the afternoon of 15 July 2008. It had been announced on the radio that Dennis Edney and Nathan Whitling – the Canadian lawyers of Omar Khadr – had just posted an online video containing excerpts of the interrogation carried out by CSIS agents at Guantánamo Bay in February 2003. These excerpts formed part of a total of nearly eight hours of recordings whose public release had been ordered by the Supreme Court of Canada.

I was aware of the fate of Omar Khadr, abandoned at the age of fifteen by successive Canadian governments since 2002 at Bagram and Guantánamo, two of the most despicable places on the planet. And now I was deeply moved to see this child on television and on the Internet, cracking under the unbearable psychological pressure that Canadian secret agents applied to him. Yet at the same time – is this a habit that comes from my job? – I was fascinated: this was an undeniable scoop. Despite the poor technical quality of the video, it was finally bringing us images captured in the heart of the unseen: the dark side of Guantánamo, which the Pentagon was excluding from the sightseeing tours it organizes for the many journalists invited to visit this American military base on Cuban soil.

But we still don't understand how – in the digital age, and at a moment when the United States and its allies were spending tens of billions of dollars on the war in Afghanistan – the words spoken by "the worst terrorists in the world" had been recorded on VHS! One begins to question the "professionalism" of these information specialists on listening to very long passages in which the sound is completely inaudible. If the information they obtained had such a high value for our own security, as CSIS claimed it did, why did they not make sure to obtain a soundtrack that would have allowed for a faithful transcription?

After having watched the video many times, with a mixture of excitement and indignation, I called my friend and colleague Luc Côté with the idea of processing this material as fast as possible on web platforms. Luc replied with enthusiasm, and together we gathered a small team of volunteers with whom we produced two short films, each seven minutes in length.

Some journalist friends later sent us the nearly eight hours of video that CSIS had been forced to release in conformity with the Supreme Court of Canada's ruling. We spent weeks in dissecting the content of these recordings, and the more we advanced in our work, the more our fascination grew. The Canadian agents played their roles with an authenticity guaranteed by the absolute certainty that the recordings would never be brought to public knowledge. As for Omar, either he knew nothing of the cameras installed outside the interrogation room or, more likely, they were the least of his worries.

In this interrogation, we found human nature expressed in all its dissonance. It revealed the old dialectic between the one who holds power and the one who suffers the consequences.

CSIS AGENT: Right now Omar, it doesn't get any worse, you know. It's never gonna get any worse for you now. But –
OMAR: It may get worse.
CSIS AGENT: In what sense?
OMAR: More torturing. Put in an isolated room, with no stuff.

CSIS AGENT: Get put in an isolated room with no stuff? I wouldn't consider that to be torture.
OMAR: I don't think you can handle that for one night.
CSIS AGENT: No? Well, I mean, fortunately, I'm not in a position where that has to be something I have to worry about. I'm not here to change positions with you and I'm not here to tell you what your life is about right now, because, you know, quite honestly that doesn't apply to me and, and it's a stupid game to get into anyway.

So there you have agents in search of the truth. (But which one?) And of the lie. (But which one?) The interrogation dances between threat and blackmail, hope and despair. And finally it reaches a wall of non-communication, one that these unequal speakers cannot overcome. Failure. How could it be otherwise in this forced dialogue? The fact remains that Omar Khadr, who was only sixteen years old at the time, demonstrated a tremendous intellectual resistance, the only one possible in his position. The interrogator almost implores him:

CSIS AGENT: If you were bright, Omar, and I want you to think about this for a few minutes. If you're smart, tell me something that can help me – that can show my government that you're willing to help us against the group of people who are bent on doing bad things to us.
OMAR: You want me to lie?
CSIS AGENT: I don't want you to lie. I just want you to tell the truth.
OMAR: That's what I told you, the truth. You don't like the truth.

For documentary filmmakers, the chronological order of a film shoot does not always produce a dramatic structure. But with the surveillance video, we didn't have to betray this order, so much did it seem the work of a scriptwriter. We identified each day by a title, a single word, which depicted it perfectly. Day 1: Hope. Day 2: Breakdown. Day 3: Blackmail. Day 4: Failure.

In making *You Don't Like the Truth: 4 Days inside Guantánamo*, the film's editor Andrea Henriquez, Luc Côté, and I showed a first rough cut of the material in this order, and then (with the cooperation of Pascale Bilodeau) set out to do further research. We wanted to find people – eyewitnesses, experts, decision-makers, privileged observers – who could contextualize and better explain the interrogation of Omar Khadr. To everybody who gave us their interviews and their trust, we owe our sincere and grateful thanks. As one of our colleagues rightly said, they filled with their humanity the cold cell where Omar Khadr was interrogated.

EPILOGUE

On 2 July 2008, a secret meeting was held in Ottawa between Jim Judd, then the director of CSIS, and Eliot Cohen, counsellor to the US State Department and a prominent neo-conservative. Among the matters they discussed were Omar Khadr, the video of his interrogation, the Supreme Court of Canada's decision to order its release, and the potential consequences of this decision.

In the memorandum of this meeting drawn up by the State Department on 9 July 2008, we can read: "Director Judd discussed domestic and foreign terror threats with Counselor of the State Department Cohen in Ottawa on July 2. Judd admitted that CSIS was increasingly distracted from its mission by legal challenges that could endanger foreign intelligence-sharing with Canadian agencies. He predicted that the upcoming release of a DVD of Guantánamo detainee and Canadian citizen Omar Khadr's interrogation by Canadian officials would lead to heightened pressure on the government to press for his return to Canada, which the government would continue to resist."

The memorandum adds, "Judd commented that cherry-picked sections of the court-ordered release of a DVD of Guantánamo detainee and Canadian citizen Omar Khadr (ref. D) would likely show three (Canadian) adults interrogating a kid who breaks down in tears. He observed that the images would no doubt trigger "knee-jerk anti-Americanism" and "paroxysms of moral outrage, a Canadian specialty," as well as lead to a new round of heightened pressure on the government to press for Khadr's return to Canada. He predicted that Prime Minister Harper's government would nonetheless continue to resist this pressure."

Judd, who seemed more worried about preserving a good image of the United States than about the fate of a Canadian child tortured by American agents, complained to Cohen about the obstacles that

Canada's judicial system raised for CSIS. Director Judd ascribed an "Alice in Wonderland" worldview to Canadians and their courts, whose judges, he said, have tied CSIS "in knots."

If Judd was speaking so confidently at this meeting, it is because – like his agents at Guantánamo – he never thought that one day his words would be published. We owe this publication to WikiLeaks. It is the kind of truth that Judd surely dislikes.

Nonetheless, we must recognize that Judd was correct in his predictions. The release of the video of Omar Khadr's interrogation provoked, and continues to provoke, revolt not just in Canada but everywhere in the world where people have been able to see it. And yes, Prime Minister Harper has kept the word given by his secret agents: he has done nothing for Omar Khadr.

Excerpts from the Screenplay *You Don't Like the Truth: 4 Days inside Guantánamo*

LUC CÔTÉ AND PATRICIO HENRIQUEZ

In July 2008, the Supreme Court of Canada authorized the disclosure of a seven-hour video that had been classified as top secret. The video was recorded over a period of four days in February 2003 at the Guantánamo Bay prison. It contains the interrogation of sixteen-year-old Canadian Omar Khadr. Agents from CSIS, the Canadian Security Intelligence Service, conducted the interrogation.

DAY 1: HOPE

INTERROGATOR: How's your English?
OMAR KHADR: Good.
INTERROGATOR: It is good?
OMAR: Yeah.
INTERROGATOR: Look, the reason we're down here, we wanted to talk to you for a couple of days, talk to you about a bunch of things.
OMAR: No problem.
INTERROGATOR: You're good with that?
OMAR: Yes.
INTERROGATOR: So I guess we're the first Canadians you've seen in a while?
OMAR: Canadians?
INTERROGATOR: Yeah.
OMAR: Finally!
INTERROGATOR: Yeah.
OMAR: Can I have my cuffs off or – no?

INTERROGATOR: Pardon me?
OMAR: Cuffs, handcuffs.
INTERROGATOR: You know, I don't see any reason why not.
SECOND INTERROGATOR: Want to offer him a sandwich?
INTERROGATOR: Are you hungry right now? Have you eaten?
OMAR: No.
INTERROGATOR: No. You want some Subway?
OMAR: Yeah.
INTERROGATOR: All right. We might as well feed you before. Ask them to take the cuffs off when you see them.
OMAR: We're requesting the Canadian government for a long time now.
INTERROGATOR: Is that right?
OMAR: Yeah.
INTERROGATOR: It's not as easy as it can be, you know.
OMAR: I'm actually very happy and excited.

DR RAUL BERDICHEVSKY (psychiatrist, University of Toronto): I think the first element that comes out that is probably very important is to find out that he was so excited, so hopeful, even in his body language, when he hears about Canadians. And I think Omar probably is under the impression that these are people from the diplomatic corps of Canada, and they're there to find out about his situation and to help him. So it's perfectly legitimate that he would feel so happy and so excited about it.

MOAZZAM BEGG (Omar Khadr's cellmate): One of the worst things with being held as a prisoner in Guantánamo is that you become sometimes so isolated, so frustrated, so separated, that you become trusting, and trust in your interrogators. And when they happen to come from your country, you have a feeling of elation that finally somebody is going to come along and advocate on your behalf.

INTERROGATOR: Do you want a Coke, Omar?
OMAR: Yeah.
INTERROGATOR: I got you a turkey sub there.
OMAR: Thanks.
INTERROGATOR: All right. You're probably aware of the kind of things we're interested in, but mostly we'd like you to just start telling us, from the very beginning, from your earliest memory

about your life. And probably stuff you've been over a hundred times before, but you haven't been over it with us and so we'd like to hear.

We're very interested in anything new. We're very interested in your life.

Invoking security reasons, CSIS *requested and obtained from the court the right to erase some audio from the video released to the public.*

INTERROGATOR: So, do you want to eat first?
SECOND INTERROGATOR: Yeah, why don't you have something to eat first.

GAR PARDY (Canadian Foreign Service, retired): I was director-general of what is known as Consular Affairs, and that's the group of people in Foreign Affairs that look after Canadians who are in difficulty in foreign countries. On September 9th, 2002, the American government sent us notice that they had captured a Canadian in Afghanistan. They didn't identify him in their communication. And from other sources, I guess, we assumed this was Omar that had been captured by the American forces.

And so when we got that information, I think two or three days later, I sat down and instructed our embassy in Washington to go in to the American authorities and seek additional information on this. We never did receive a written reply. The next we heard was that Omar was at Guantánamo, which would have been early October, I think it was.

BILL GRAHAM (Canadian Minister of Foreign Affairs, 2001–03): At that time I had a meeting with Mr Powell, who was coming up to Ottawa. That was a big issue in the fall of 2002. So basically my plea with Mr Powell was: "Is he getting proper treatment? Is he going to get proper legal representation? Are you recognizing the fact that he was a minor, as in covered by the international convention that deals with youths? And would we be able to get access to him?"

The answer of Mr Powell's was: "Look, he killed a fine young American, he's gone to Guantánamo Bay, he'll be treated by the justice system with the proper American justice – and that's all I am prepared to talk about it."

GAR PARDY: The Americans at that point were not allowing any consular visits whatsoever to any government who had nationals in Guantánamo, the Brits or the Saudis or the Swedes or anybody.

BILL GRAHAM: If a Canadian was incarcerated in jail in Texas, there's no question we would have a right to access that person. But they said, "No, no, Guantánamo's not part of the United States, it's under different rules. And no, you can't have access."

GAR PARDY: But over time the Americans said they would allow non-consular foreign officials to go in.

INTERROGATOR: So, why don't you just start at the very beginning and we'll get all your bio data out of the way first. That means your full name.
OMAR (*eating*): Omar Ahmed Khadr.

MICHELLE SHEPHARD (National Security reporter, *Toronto Star*): In February 2003, the first delegation of Canadians went down to visit Omar, and part of that delegation was a senior agent with Canada's spy service, CSIS. He had been following the Khadr family for years. Jim Gould, a Foreign Affairs representative in the intelligence section went down.

INTERROGATOR: Sorry, you pronounce your last name "Kidder"?
OMAR: Khadr.
INTERROGATOR: Khadr, OK. We got it. Khadr, thank you. Date of birth?
OMAR: September 1986, 19 of September.

MICHELLE SHEPHARD: And there was a third person, a woman with the CIA who was a liaison officer, and before they went on their trip, they were taken to CIA headquarters and given instructions on what they could and couldn't do. And she accompanied them, as a sort of escort, I guess.

LT-CMDR WILLIAM KUEBLER (Omar Khadr's former US Military lawyer): This was Canadian agents participating in basically a joint venture, to exploit this young man as a source of intelligence with the US government.

NATHAN WHITLING (one of Omar Khadr's two Canadian lawyers): The bottom line is, they're breaking the law in this video. At the time, as everyone understood, these detainees were in a legal black hole, as the English court of appeal had put it. They had no ability to speak with a lawyer, they had no right to appear before a court, they couldn't bring a habeas corpus application, they hadn't been charged with anything, much less tried for anything – and it was obvious to everyone who looked at the situation, including the United Nations and by then some American courts, that this was unlawful.

INTERROGATOR: And you were born in...?
OMAR: Toronto, Canada.
INTERROGATOR: OK. Do you remember, you don't remember, but did they ever tell you what hospital?
OMAR: Actually I didn't know I was born in Scarborough until I came here.
INTERROGATOR: So, tell me about what you first remember and how you first found yourself living in Canada.
OMAR: First thing I remember in Canada was first grade. We went because of my father's injury. So it was a vacation in Canada.

MICHELLE SHEPHARD: Omar's father, Ahmed Said Khadr, was an Egyptian student who came to Ottawa to study for his master's and became a Canadian citizen. During the Soviet occupation of Afghanistan, he decided to go there as a charity worker. He set up various charities for orphans, some for women – at that point Omar was very young – and he would bring his family back and forth between Afghanistan, Pakistan and Canada. They had this bizarre upbringing where they'd go back and forth.

INTERROGATOR: And he met your mother while he was in Canada, studying?
OMAR: Yes.
INTERROGATOR: And your mother, the Elsamnah family, are Palestinians?
OMAR: Yes.
INTERROGATOR: But from Egypt.
OMAR: My grandmother is from Egypt. My grandfather is from Palestine.
INTERROGATOR: And your father is an engineer?

OMAR: Yes.
INTERROGATOR: But how did your father come to get into the relief business, the aid business?

MICHELLE SHEPHARD: Once the Soviets withdrew, Ahmed Said Khadr stayed in Afghanistan. He had met Osama bin Laden and other members of those who would eventually become al-Qaeda's elite. And he then continued his charity work. But in the early 90s, there were allegations that he also was starting to finance al-Qaeda.

INTERROGATOR: And how many orphans were being helped out at that time, any idea?
OMAR: In Peshawar there was maybe, there was lots of kids, maybe five hundred or something.

GAR PARDY: I guess November of 1995, there had been a bombing of the Egyptian embassy in Islamabad, and people were killed. And shortly after that, the Pakistani authorities arrested Ahmed Khadr and claimed that he had some responsibility for organizing that particular bombing. Shortly thereafter the Pakistanis released Ahmed and he came back to Canada. And I think Ahmed spent some time in Toronto raising money, and then went back to Afghanistan.

INTERROGATOR: When you were growing up, what did you think about your father? Did you think he was a very important guy?
OMAR: I don't know.
INTERROGATOR: But a lot of people around him thought he was an important character, right?
OMAR: To the Arabs or to the Americans?
INTERROGATOR: Oh, to the Arabs.
OMAR: I don't think so.
INTERROGATOR: No? You think the Americans think he's an important guy?
OMAR: Yeah.
INTERROGATOR: Why do you think that is?
OMAR: They say that he gives money to the training camps.
INTERROGATOR: What do you think about that?
OMAR: No.
INTERROGATOR: You don't think so?
OMAR: No.

INTERROGATOR: How did your father get along with the Taliban?
OMAR: He doesn't have any problem with the Taliban.
INTERROGATOR: He didn't?
OMAR: He was doing only projects.
INTERROGATOR: Your father had been involved with Afghanis before though, eh?
OMAR: Yes.
INTERROGATOR: And he was there during the jihad against the Russians?
OMAR: Yeah.
INTERROGATOR: And at that time who was his main contact, did he ever talk about that? With the Afghans?
OMAR: No.
INTERROGATOR: Did he ever mention about Gulbuddin Hekmatyar?
OMAR: No.
INTERROGATOR: Or the Hezbi Islami guys?
OMAR: No.
INTERROGATOR: Never brought those guys up?
OMAR: No. He didn't do anything with them at that time.
INTERROGATOR: He didn't do anything with them at that time? So at that time he was just basically, he had moved ...
Audio erased by CSIS

Gulbuddin Hekmatyar is leader of Hezbi Islami Gulbuddin, one of the most powerful and radical Islamic groups in Afghanistan. In the 1980s he waged war against the Soviets, with the support of millions of dollars provided by the US. Since the American invasion of Afghanistan in 2001, Hekmatyar has been fighting coalition forces. He is now on the US list of the most wanted terrorists in the world.

INTERROGATOR: OK. So you went to spend Eid in – can you say that again for me?
OMAR: We spent Eid there, I think so. It was before Eid for two days. We went to Kandahar. We were there at Eid celebration in Kandahar and there was Osama.
INTERROGATOR: With whom?
OMAR: Osama.
INTERROGATOR: Osama?
OMAR: And ...

INTERROGATOR: So this was in 1997, and you spent the Ramadan Eid celebrations in Kandahar with – and we're talking about Osama bin Laden. Your father with his – inside his camp. Was that at the farm? The compound?
OMAR: Yes.
INTERROGATOR: What was the relationship, did you know, between him and your father?
OMAR: Friends.
INTERROGATOR: They were friends? Now, when your father used to meet people, were you there? Were you invited into the meetings or did he just like to talk to people by themselves?
OMAR: All of the meetings were dinner and lunch.
INTERROGATOR: OK, and they would just talk about things? Did you ever listen in on what they were talking about?
OMAR: War stories, front line, and stuff in Kabul.
INTERROGATOR: Yeah? Now by front line –
Audio erased by CSIS
INTERROGATOR: When we talk about the word al-Qaeda, that name – what does that mean to you?
OMAR: It's an organization ... Islamic ...
INTERROGATOR: What kind of organization?
OMAR: A terrorist organization.
INTERROGATOR: Did you use that word ever in Afghanistan, or did you just start using it when you came here?
OMAR: Just when I came here.
INTERROGATOR: Now, after the events of September the 11th, in 1991, 2001, sorry, your father decided to keep his family inside Afghanistan, is that true?
OMAR: Yes.
INTERROGATOR: In Kabul?
OMAR: Actually I went to Logar.
INTERROGATOR: You went to Logar Province? You know what, I think I've asked enough questions for today if that's OK with you folks.
OMAR: Yeah, I'm fine.
INTERROGATOR: We've got all day tomorrow. And on a more important matter, if we're gonna pick you something to eat tomorrow, what would you like, McDonald's or Subway?
OMAR: Anything, I'll take anything.
SECOND INTERROGATOR: Do you want a milkshake or something?

INTERROGATOR: All right, we'll pick up something, and then how about we get together tomorrow for a talk?
OMAR: No problem.
INTERROGATOR: All right?
OMAR: I'm very happy to see you.
INTERROGATOR: Yeah, it's good to see you. But you know what, I'm tired and I'm sweaty now.
SECOND INTERROGATOR: He can't take the heat, it's terrible.
INTERROGATOR: All right man, I'll see you tomorrow, all right?

DAY 2: FALLOUT

INTERROGATOR: You look tired. OK, so I brought you a burger. It's very hot, though. What's happening? Pardon me?
OMAR: I want to say something very important but I'm scared to say it.
INTERROGATOR: Take your time. Can you do me a favour today while we're talking? Just make sure you talk nice and loud, so that I can keep that air conditioning on so we're cool.
OMAR: There's something that I'm scared to say.
SECOND INTERROGATOR: You don't have to be scared about anything from us.

LT-CMDR WILLIAM KUEBLER: You see on day one that Omar is elated to see the Canadian officials. And if he cooperates, and tells him what they want to hear, he's going to be able to leave Guantánamo. Day two, he realizes that's not true. And you see the effect on Omar of that sudden realization: they are not there to help him.

INTERROGATOR: What are you scared to say?
OMAR: Promise me that you're gonna protect me.
INTERROGATOR: Why don't you just tell us what it is you have to say?
OMAR: Promise me you're gonna protect me from the Americans.
INTERROGATOR: From the Americans?
OMAR: Yes.
INTERROGATOR: OK, what's going on with the Americans?
OMAR: Promise me that you're gonna protect me if I tell you.

INTERROGATOR: Well we can't protect you if we don't know what it is you have to say directly.
OMAR: Promise me you're gonna protect me if I tell you.
INTERROGATOR: Well, the only thing I'll promise you is that I'll listen to you and I'll talk to the Americans for you, here.
OMAR: And after you go?
INTERROGATOR: Pardon me?
OMAR: And after you go?
INTERROGATOR: And after I go, then I'll listen to what, you know, then I'll come back down and talk to you again. Make sure everything is all right. Tell me what's changed from yesterday, today.
OMAR: I'm scared to tell you.
INTERROGATOR: Well, I'll tell you, there's not much we can do unless I know what you're talking about.
OMAR: Well, everything I said to the Americans was not right. I just said that, because they tortured me very badly in Bagram. So I had to say what I said.

MICHELLE SHEPHARD: The worst treatment that Omar received was after he was first captured, when he was in Bagram. And we still don't know a lot about Bagram.
OMAR DEGHAYES (Omar Khadr's cellmate): Bagram base was in Afghanistan, it's an American base, and we ... most of us who ended up in Guantánamo Bay first went through Bagram.

RICHARD BELMAR (Omar Khadr's cellmate): I was already imprisoned and, you know, they received some new detainees and he was one of them. Omar was injured really badly. He had like a broken foot or ankle, and he was blind in one eye. And I think he had another bone break somewhere else.

But he was in a real bad state. He couldn't walk, you know. They brought him in on a stretcher. And yeah, they put him in the same cage as me.

DAMIEN CORSETTI (former intelligence officer, US Army): The condition of Omar when I first met him was pretty bad off. Looking at him, you wouldn't think he was going to survive. He had a very large hole in his chest, large enough to fit a can of Copenhagen over top of it. He was covered in shrapnel from head to toe, which even months afterwards was still very prevalent through his skin. You could see the shrapnel in there."

MOAZZAM BEGG (Omar Khadr's cellmate): When I met Omar in Bagram, the way that they treated him, because the rumour was that he'd been responsible or involved in the killing of an American soldier, his treatment was worse than anybody else's. Despite the fact that he was a child, despite the fact that he was terribly wounded, they made him, I remember, drag him out of his cell chained up, make him stack up piles and piles of water, of water crate bottles, only to throw them down onto the floor and make him do it again.

DAMIEN CORSETTI: We were all so angry. Everyone was. You're talking less than a year after September 11th. The mindset of the average American soldier over there was hatred. We hated them.

DENNIS EDNEY (one of Omar Khadr's two Canadian lawyers): I recall the day when Nate and I were in Guantánamo and we realized that we needed an affidavit for the Supreme Court. And we sat down in his cell with him and here he is chained to the floor, sitting on a seat. And we're now approaching a very, very fragile subject – his torture.

FROM THE AFFIDAVIT OF OMAR KHADR, 22 FEBRUARY 2008: After about two weeks in the hospital I was immediately taken to an interrogation room at a military camp in Bagram.

During this first interrogation, the young blond man would often scream at me if I did not give him the answers he wanted. Several times, he forced me to sit up on my stretcher, which caused me great pain due to my injuries. He did this several times to get me to answer his questions and give him the answers he wanted. It was clear that he was making me sit up because he knew that it hurt. I cried several times during the interrogation as a result of this treatment and pain.

On some occasions, the interrogators brought barking dogs into the interrogation room while my head was covered with a bag. The bag was wrapped tightly around my neck, nearly choking me and making it hard to breathe. This terrified me. On other occasions, interrogators threw cold water on me.

Several times, the soldiers tied my hands above my head to the doorframe or chained them to the ceiling, and made me stand like that for hours at a time. Because of my injuries, particularly the bullet wounds in my chest and shoulders, my hands could not be raised all the way above my head, but they would pull them up as high as they thought they could go, and then tie them there.

DAMIEN CORSETTI: I knew his lead interrogator, Joshua Claus, consider him a friend, and I personally never saw him cross the line of what was acceptable at Bagram.

Unfortunately, though, what was acceptable at Bagram at that time was an outrage on human dignity. It was. I was not a nice person, and I did some very bad things. I became that monster that, that I was, that was written about me, I became that and I embodied it. And unfortunately I think that's going to come back to bite me in the ass, but you know, I have to own it, I have to say that I did these things, I have to admit that I took part in this ...

MOAZZAM BEGG: But Corsetti of all people treated Omar well, from what I understand. And the reason why is because although Corsetti may have been involved in some of those abuses, he recognized at least in this case, in Omar's case, that you don't treat a child like this.

DAMIEN CORSETTI: All I can say about his is that he was a kid, fifteen, that he was a typical fifteen year-old kid. Maybe, you know, raised a little differently than most of us, but that's ... the child was still there. That's what was prevalent in him, the child.

INTERROGATOR: So everything you told the Americans was because they tortured you?
OMAR: Yes.
INTERROGATOR: And you had to say what you said?
OMAR: Yes.
INTERROGATOR: OK. And what did you tell them that wasn't true?
OMAR: Everything is not true.
INTERROGATOR: Everything you told them is not true?
OMAR: Yes.
INTERROGATOR: What about what you told me yesterday, was that true?

OMAR: No.
INTERROGATOR: No? What parts weren't true? Be more specific. Tell me what you told me yesterday that wasn't true.
OMAR: That I saw OBL [Osama bin Laden]. That I've lived with him ... I don't know anything about him.
INTERROGATOR: You don't know anything about him?
OMAR: No.
INTERROGATOR: So none of that part is true?
OMAR: No. They tortured me very badly in Bagram.
INTERROGATOR: They tortured you very badly in Bagram?
OMAR: Yes.
INTERROGATOR: Now, who have you been talking to since yesterday about how you were going to be interviewed today?
OMAR: Nobody.
INTERROGATOR: Yes, you have. No Omar, let's be honest with each other. I won't sit here and lie to you and you don't sit there and lie to me. Who did you discuss this with last night?
OMAR: With nobody.
INTERROGATOR: With nobody?
OMAR: I knew you weren't gonna trust me.
INTERROGATOR: No, I'm not gonna trust you if you don't tell me the truth.

MAMDOU HABIB (Omar Khadr's cellmate): He tell me all the story, what happened. And I tell him, "Don't talk much with these people, because they are not going to let you go. Just quiet and let it go, leave it in the hand of Allah. Leave it in the hand of God, and that's it. Trust me, and be strong. Because if you lie, they want more lies. If you say the truth, they are not going to believe you. If you feel or you are showing weak, they are going to be stronger." And that's why they removed me and they were very upset, they dragged me and they take me away. Because they listened inside the cells.

OMAR: I knew you weren't gonna trust me.
INTERROGATOR: No, I'm not gonna trust you if you don't tell me the truth. No, Omar, the fact of the matter is –
OMAR (*lifting his shirt to expose his chest, then his shoulder*): I can't move my arms and all of these – is this healthy? I can't move my arm. I requested medical over a long time. They don't do anything about it.

INTERROGATOR: No, they look like they're healing well to me. I'm not a doctor but I think you're getting good medical care.
OMAR (*sobbing*): No, I'm not. You're not here.

DAMIEN CORSETTI: This is exactly why, as an interrogator, you wouldn't want cameras in the interrogation room. We fought that off both in Bagram and in Abu Ghraib. We didn't want cameras in there.

I'll say this. It looks, the treatment that he's getting is very harsh but if I were still in intelligence, that's probably how I would conduct my interrogations. It's not pretty, it is a very cold and callous manner that you have carry yourself in, in order to do this.

OMAR: I lost my eyes. I lost my feet, everything.
INTERROGATOR: No, you still have your eyes and your feet are still at the end of your legs, you know. Look, I want to take a few minutes, I want you to get yourself together, relax a bit, have a bite to eat, and we'll start again. I understand this is stressful, but by using this as a strategy to talk to us, it's not gonna be any more helpful.

OMAR DEGHAYES: Now, this reminds me, because once we were in the recreation yard together, one of the cages in the rec yard, and he showed me his eye, and he said to me that he lost sight in his eye. Because he could see that my eye was injured then, and he said to me, "Look, I can't see anything – you can see my eye from outside, but I can't see anything from my eye."

Now he mentioned it here to the Canadian interrogator, and the Canadian said "No, you're getting good medical care, your eye is all right." He doesn't know what happened to him.

INTERROGATOR: I mean we've got a limited amount of time and we've heard this story before.
OMAR: You don't care about me, that's why.
INTERROGATOR: Well, I do care about you, but I want to talk to the honest Omar that I was talking to yesterday. I don't want to talk to this Omar.
OMAR: It wasn't honest.
INTERROGATOR: Yes it was.
OMAR: You see, you're not going to believe me.

INTERROGATOR: Well, look me straight in the eyes and tell me that you're being honest.
OMAR: I am being honest.
INTERROGATOR: Omar, you can't even bear to look at me when you're saying that.
OMAR: I can't bear to look at you?
INTERROGATOR: Put your hand down.
OMAR: No, you don't care about me.

DR RAUL BERDICHEVSKY (psychiatrist): It gets to the point where the only thing you want is for the pain to stop, or for the mistreatment to stop, or the abuse. In this case it's psychological abuse, there is absolutely no question about it. He will potentially break down, it will lead to total regression.

INTERROGATOR: Look, let's take a few minutes, take a break, have a little bit to eat before your hamburger gets cold. Put your vest on. Relax a bit.
OMAR: Nobody cares about me.
INTERROGATOR: That's not true, people do care about you.
Second interrogator: Put the fan on so you're cool.
INTERROGATOR: We'll be back.

OMAR DEGHAYES: Now he is really crying, you can see the room is empty, nobody is in the room and he's really crying. And this is something I've never seen from him in prison, ever. So we've been locked up together maybe three years, two years in different camps, different cages, but you never see him cry like this.

GAR PARDY: These interviews basically were a continuation of the torture that he was being subjected to.

MOAZZAM BEGG: When I saw this interrogation that had been published, one sentence really picked up and that was "Nobody cares about me." And I remember when I met Omar last, which is in Bagram, that was the last time I saw Omar, and he said to me, "Nobody cares about me." And that remained with me, that will remain with me forever. The pity that I felt for him, I've never felt for anyone that I saw during all the time in Guantánamo and Bagram.

OMAR (*crying*): *Ya ummi* [O mother], *ya ummi, ya ummi* ...

DR STEPHEN XENAKIS (Omar's psychiatrist, Brigadier General, Ret., US Army): I think I know where this room was, and I know how bad he feels when he's in that room. I hate to see him so sad and I hate to see him feeling as hurt as he is. You know, I've spent a lot of time with this young man.

OMAR: *Ya ummi, ya ummi, ya ummi ...*

NATHAN WHITLING: You know, we've never seen that kind of emotion in Omar before. He has never displayed that to us before. And seeing it in a video was a pretty difficult thing to see, frankly.

OMAR: *Ya ummi, ya ummi, ya ummi ...*

ZAYNAB KHADR (Omar's sister): You go to your mother when you feel you need care, you need someone to take you out of danger and protect you. When things get so difficult you just go, anybody, an adult, a man, a woman, at the end of the time when you are in hardship, you know the only person in the world you can go to and will not ask you for any reason, will not expect anything in return, is but your mother.

MAHA ELSAMNAH (Omar's mother): That made me feel like, you know, I wished I can give him my life then. I just, I wish he would understand that I wanted to help, I wanted to answer. It's just I heard it so much later on in life, but ...

DR RAUL BERDICHEVSKY: I understand that he was actually watched and observed during this segment by the interrogators for approximately sixty minutes, and I believe that they were watching him to see if there was a chance for them to go back. See and use the opportunity, if he was going to be sort of vulnerable, to actually continue the interrogation.

OMAR (*tearing at his hair*): *Ya ummi ...*

DAY 3: BLACKMAIL

INTERROGATOR: Hi, Omar, how you doing? What kind of a day is it going to be today? Are we going to spend some time and have a good talk, or are we gonna ... What do you think?

DR RAUL BERDICHEVSKY: What changes here is immediately you see the difference in the layout of the room and the furnishing. He's on a couch that looks very much like anybody's living room. After the huge regression they produced in the previous one, they are sort of bringing him back, and this is all a demonstration of their power and control.

INTERROGATOR: Are you very hungry?
OMAR: I don't want to eat.
INTERROGATOR: Pardon me? You don't want to eat?
OMAR: I don't feel like eating.
INTERROGATOR: You don't feel like eating? Do you want a Coke?
SECOND INTERROGATOR: Maybe later.
INTERROGATOR: All right.

DR RAUL BERDICHEVSKY: The interrogators might be losing control of the situation because Omar is regaining his control. And he's regaining some of the elements of resistance that are still available to him, like saying no. If he's says no, that's the end of it. Nobody can actually make him say yes. Or they could, again in a situation of extreme torture, but what will be the value of that?

INTERROGATOR: Now look, I was very disappointed yesterday, but these things happen. We've only got a couple of days here, you and I, to speak. I think it's important that we try to get as much done as possible. I think we made a really, really good start, and I was very proud of you. I was very proud of the way you behaved. You behaved like a man. You were forthright and honest, and I think yesterday you got kind of upset, and you were kind of worried about things, and maybe you were talking to somebody.

But I mean you and I, we're both from the same area, we're both from Scarborough, and I want to be able to go home and tell the government that you've been cooperating. My organization has spoken to your father on a number of opportunities, he knows what we're about. We both know that we have a job to do. He knows what we're looking into. But your father, in our mind, is a lost cause. He's not going to come in and resume a normal life anywhere. He's committed to what he's doing, and that was a choice he made.
OMAR: He didn't do anything.
INTERROGATOR: Pardon me?

OMAR: He didn't do anything.

Omar's father, Ahmed Said Khadr, was killed during an attack led by the Pakistani security forces in South Waziristan, Pakistan. He died on 2 October 2003, eight months after this interrogation took place in Guantánamo.

INTERROGATOR: But what I do want to work on is, I'm worried about your mother. She's out there right now, she doesn't have any ability to come back to Canada, and her passport is expired. Nobody knows how to get in contact with her and I don't want, obviously, she's a Canadian, I don't want to see that for her. I particularly did not want to see that for your sisters or your little brother. Your situation is very different, and we both know why, but if I can go home and report to your service, pardon me, to my service, that you are being as cooperative as you can, then that will bode very favourably on the way our government deals with you. And I understand that you can't change the past, but what you can do is change the future. What do you think, Omar?
OMAR: I didn't do anything.
INTERROGATOR: Well, we're not talking about you right now. What I want you to do is, I want you to think, and help me to get in touch with your sisters and your brothers so that we can get them back to Canada. Who are your mother's friends in Pakistan who we might be able to go to, who can at least get a message to her, for us?"

ZAYNAB KHADR: He wasn't there, he doesn't know, it's a year later. Even if he knew where we were then, he wouldn't know a year later. He is telling them the truth.

MAHA ELSAMNAH: Omar probably did not know anything, if we are still alive, so how could he help them? How?

INTERROGATOR: We're not interested in getting anybody in any trouble. What we want to do is ... I don't even care if we can't see them. All I need is a phone number or an address that we can send a message to, and say... then give them instructions on how to come in to the Canadian mission and get a passport without getting arrested by the Pakistani authorities or getting shot by some trigger-happy dummy. That's what I'm interested in.

ZAYNAB KHADR: They are lying to him. I was almost always in touch with the embassy, and especially when they're talking about the passport, I went over and over and over again, I requested the passport many times over and they refused.

INTERROGATOR: If you want a pop now or something – I'm getting kind of parched. Take a second and just think – Pardon me? Are you hungry? Do you want a sandwich or something?
OMAR: I don't want to eat.
INTERROGATOR: We'll get you a pop. Let's get a pop. We'll be right back. But think about it, Omar. Is there anybody that you can think of, who would be, somebody who could sort of help us out.
(*Time passes.*)
OMAR: Can I pray?
SOLDIER: On the floor. We'll take your handcuffs off ... Which way are you praying? That way, right? Is it that way?
OMAR: To the east.

MOAZZIM BEGG: One of the most memorable sights of Omar for me was to watch him reading the Qu'ran. And we weren't allowed to raise our voices at all, in fact, we weren't allowed to talk, but with the Qu'ran sometimes you could get away with a little bit of melodic recitation. So I remember Omar's voice, particularly in a closed warehouse environment where the voice echoes. It was amazing – it was beautiful to the ears, his voice. It was one of the most uplifting things, because you knew when he was reading the Qu'ran, that he had some peace and tranquility in his heart. As long as he was doing that, it showed, and you could hear that in his voice.

OMAR DEGHAYES: I remember him when it's really late at night in the dark, I can hear his voice, he had a very beautiful voice and he used to sing. And his songs were so beautiful and at the same time very sad. I can hear him. He mentioned his father in his songs and he was calling as if he was speaking to his father. It was one of the moving things that I remember in Camp 5.

RUHAL AHMED (Omar Khadr's cellmate): We used to talk about religion sometimes, but the majority of times, we used to talk about films. Me and my two friends used to go every Sunday without fail, and we used to watch a movie. Because we were leaving, towards the end. We would come back and I would tell him about the film. So we watched a James Bond, *Tomorrow Never Dies,* and we watched *Harry Potter* in Guantánamo – we watched quite a few films in Guantánamo.

So every time I would come back, we would describe the whole film to him, which takes about two, three hours. You have to name every character – this person said this, this person said that – and we would stay awake until two in the morning, three in the morning, just talking about films.

INTERROGATOR: Here we go, are you done? Take a glass. All right. So, everybody's back and – Jesus, it's hot in here. Have you thought at all about what we discussed earlier? Tell me what you're thinking.
OMAR: I'm thinking of the day I'm gonna to get out of here.
INTERROGATOR: And what are you going to do on that day?
OMAR: Go back home.
INTERROGATOR: Where's home? To Canada?
OMAR: Yes.
INTERROGATOR: You want to go back to Canada? Well, there's not anything I can do about that. I want to stay in Cuba with you – can you help me with that?
OMAR: I don't think it's good to stay here.
INTERROGATOR: No? Weather's nice, there's no snow…
Audio erased by CSIS
INTERROGATOR: What other interesting things do you want to tell me about?
OMAR: I want to know when I'm going to go back home.
INTERROGATOR: Well, that's difficult to say. What I can tell you is, it certainly won't hurt you if you fully cooperate.
OMAR: I didn't do anything wrong to be here.
INTERROGATOR: Pardon me?
OMAR: I didn't do anything wrong to be here.
INTERROGATOR: Why don't you tell me what happened to you during the past three or four months of your time in Afghanistan? So we have that for our records.

MICHELLE SHEPHARD: In the months before Omar Khadr's capture, what we believe happened was that his father, Ahmed Said Khadr, lent his son to some militants in the area to act as a translator for them. And during the month before he was captured, he trained with them. And that's where the video comes of him allegedly making these unexploded devices. He was with these Taliban linked militants.

And at that time the US was working alongside the Northern Alliance, to try and combat the Taliban, and what the Pentagon has claimed was that Omar Khadr was training with some of these militants, to fight the US at that time.

INTERROGATOR: And when your dad left you or dropped you off with these people, what did he tell you you'd be doing with them?
OMAR: Just tell me to stay in this house-hotel until he's finished with my brother Kareem. Then he'd come back.
INTERROGATOR: Why couldn't you go with them?
OMAR: Maybe it was not safe or something.
INTERROGATOR: But it doesn't make any sense that he would just drop you off with these guys, and by happenstance you'd be sitting there taking apart mines for an attack on the Americans.
OMAR: It wasn't against the Americans.
INTERROGATOR: Who were you going to attack?
OMAR: The Northern Alliance.
INTERROGATOR: You were going to attack the Northern Alliance? But you can see that ... Is that something you always wanted to do?
OMAR: No.
INTERROGATOR: Then why would you go there?
OMAR: My father just told me to stay there.
INTERROGATOR: Because your father just told you. So you find yourself in this house, and they're getting ready to attack the Northern Alliance. And what kind of weapons?
OMAR: They had rifles.
INTERROGATOR: Rifles? Russian rifles or American?
OMAR: Russian.
INTERROGATOR: And did you have pistols as well?
OMAR: Yes.
INTERROGATOR: Hand grenades?
OMAR: Yes.
INTERROGATOR: So essentially, it was a fairly well-armed house. How did the Americans, or how did the Afghans and the Americans find you?
OMAR: I don't know.

MICHELLE SHEPHARD: On July 27th, 2002, the Americans got intelligence that there was a suspected al-Qaeda compound and they surrounded that compound. The militants inside the compound began firing, throwing grenades, and a massive battle ensued.

INTERROGATOR: So a firefight started. The Arabs shot at the Americans, the Americans shot back, and at the end of the day you were ... Did you guys make a decision that you were gonna fight until the end?
OMAR: They made the decision.
INTERROGATOR: They made the decision? What did they say, that there was nobody going to leave there or ...?
OMAR: Yes.
INTERROGATOR: And that you were all going to fight until you died? Did you want to do that, or did you believe in that when that happened?
OMAR: No.
INTERROGATOR: But you did it anyway even though you were the last person alive. What made you do that?
OMAR: I didn't do anything. I was in the house when the fighting started. Then I didn't have any choice.
INTERROGATOR: So the events overtook you.
OMAR: Yes.
INTERROGATOR: And you had to, in your mind, react to that.
OMAR: I didn't do anything, I had no choice.

MICHELLE SHEPHARD: The Americans eventually called in air support and decimated the compound. They believed that everyone inside was dead, and an elite unit that included Delta Force officer Christopher Speer went in to see if there was anyone alive. At that time a grenade was thrown.

LT-CMDR WILLIAM KUEBLER (Omar's former US Military lawyer, testifying before the Subcommittee on International Human Rights, Parliament of Canada): In a largely fictitious story first told by the Department of Defence in 2002, Omar was the lone survivor of a four-hour bombardment of an al-Qaeda compound near Khost, Afghanistan.

The story was that he waited in the rubble and then rose up wielding a pistol and hand grenade, taking a group of US soldiers by surprise and killing a medic before being shot in the chest.

No part of this story is true, however, and the Omar Khadr it describes does not exist.

FROM THE AFFIDAVIT OF OMAR KHADR, 22 FEBRUARY 2008: I was severely wounded in the battle where I was captured. I was shot at least twice in the back, at least once through my left shoulder exiting through my left breast, and once under my right shoulder, exiting out of my upper right side. I was also struck with shrapnel in my left eye, and was wounded in my left thigh, knee, ankle, and foot.

I believe I remained conscious after being wounded and captured. I remember being carried by my arms and legs to an area in the open where someone put some bandages on me. The soldiers were asking me questions about my identity. They then placed me on a wooden board and carried me into a helicopter. I lost consciousness during the trip in the helicopter.

After I regained consciousness after being unconscious for a week, the first soldier told me that I had killed an American with a hand grenade.

INTERROGATOR: Well, you have to own your own responsibility.
OMAR: What was my mistake, being in the house where they shot and killed the American?
INTERROGATOR: Exactly, being in the house was your first mistake.
OMAR: What's my mistake? My father put me in this house with all those people.
INTERROGATOR: Your father put you in this house. Well, all I know is that every day you get up in the morning, and there's a young American who every morning doesn't get up. How do you think his family feels?

MAMDOU HABIB: What's his problem? What's he done wrong to be in this position? He killed an American? How do they prove he killed an American? Who told them he killed an American? Maybe he defended himself. But no one knows. They have no evidence, they have no proof.

MICHELLE SHEPHARD: Sergeant 1st Class Christopher Speer was a member of the Delta Force unit. He was trained as a medic; however, he was there as a Delta Force soldier. And that's an important distinction to make, because a medic is a protected person of war. And under traditional laws of war, killing a medic is a war crime.

While Chris Speer was trained as a medic, he was there as part of this elite unit. The Delta Force unit is an elite counterterrorism unit that the US doesn't even acknowledge exists, and one former member recently was quoted in the *New York Times* as saying: "We don't issue search warrants. The Delta Force kills people that we want killed."

DENNIS EDNEY: One of the big issues that we've been facing is getting disclosure from the Americans. Something as simple as the fact when these planes flew over the compound Omar Khadr was in, they had cameras. Well, it just so happens those cameras have disappeared. And those cameras would have given us a bird's-eye view of what took place.

LT-CMDR WILLIAM KUEBLER: There are photographs that I have tried to get out publicly, but because of the secrecy rules of Guantánamo I have not been able to, that I think very clearly show that Omar Khadr could not have thrown the hand grenade that killed Christopher Speer.

INTERROGATOR: Your best course of action, this is all I can recommend to you, is you have to start realizing that complaining, whining, denying what happened, is counterproductive. It's never gonna help you from now on. I mean you've got to take ownership of what happened, take responsibility, and move on.
OMAR: You're saying that a sixteen-year-old can take responsibility?
INTERROGATOR: Pardon me?
OMAR: If you had a son, sixteen years old, could he take responsibility?
INTERROGATOR: Well, if I had a son, sixteen years old, and he went out and he got involved in a situation where he killed someone –
OMAR: I didn't kill anybody.
INTERROGATOR: I think I wouldn't take responsibility for him. His foot is in the grave.
OMAR: I'm not your son.
INTERROGATOR: Basically, you're old enough to do something, you're old enough to take responsibility for it.

DAMIEN CORSETTI: If he did it, which I think there is significant doubt if he did it, you can't hold a fifteen year old responsible for doing that, under those circumstances. I would have done it. I would have done it, if somebody came in and killed all my friends. I would have tossed a grenade at them. So it's very unfortunate what happened, but he's a fifteen-year-old child in a war zone.

CRAIG MOKHIBER (deputy director, United Nations High Commission for Human Rights): That means by definition that he is a child soldier. And child soldiers are the subject for the United Nations of protection, of rehabilitation, and not of the same kind of treatment that would apply to those who commit those kinds of offences when they are adults.

INTERROGATOR: You want to tell us anything that could help us? You know what we're concerned about. I'm sure you're aware that recently bin Laden has targeted Canada directly and said he's gonna strike out against them.
OMAR: Yeah.
INTERROGATOR: You told me the other night that you wanted to do something to help us, to help your country. Well now we've got this guy who's out trying to hurt us. Is there anybody you know who might be in Canada, or from Canada or on his way to Canada, who may be trying to hurt us?
OMAR: No.
INTERROGATOR: Because information like that, one piece of information like that, could go a long way to … to helping you if we could bring something like that in to the Canadian government. That would get you a lot of goodwill. Because there's nothing we value more than trying to save some lives. Do you understand what I'm saying?
OMAR: Yes.
INTERROGATOR: And I think you can do a lot to rehabilitate yourself if you can help us in that.
OMAR: Do you have any letters from my grandmother?
INTERROGATOR: Pardon me? Do I have any letters from your grandmother? No.
OMAR: I've sent lots of letters. I have no answers on my letters.
INTERROGATOR: Well, you'll get that through the … that'll have to be a Red Cross matter. I mean, now you have to put in your mind

who your real friends are. And your real friends aren't those guys behind that wire. Your real friends are the people in Canada who care about you.

STEPHEN HARPER, PRIME MINISTER OF CANADA: As you know, Mr Khadr is charged with extremely serious crimes. There is a legal process underway by American authorities and Canada, as I say, Canada sought assurances that Mr Khadr, under our government, will be treated humanely and we are monitoring those legal processes very carefully.

DENNIS EDNEY: Since we took over this case, which is approximately six and a half years ago, we have fought in every court there is – Supreme Court of United States, Supreme Court of Canada, federal court system here, federal court system in United States, and in military commissions in Guantánamo Bay – and along the way we've had absolutely no assistance from our government.

LT-CMDR WILLIAM KUEBLER: I will never have confidence in the military commissions. And that is not a function of some ideological issue or necessarily even distrust in the people that are responsible for the system. It goes back to the fundamental point that everyone is entitled to a fair trial. We know what fair trials are – we do them in the United States every day for terrorists in federal civilian courts. We know what fair trials in the military are – we do them in courts martial every day in the United States armed forces.

The only reason the military commissions exist is because the government has evidence in these cases that it can't use in regular courts. And so viewed from that perspective, this system will never in my mind will be fair. It will never be appropriate, because you are subjecting Omar, and you are subjecting these detainees, to a different level of justice, a sub-standard level of justice. In Omar's case the only reason he can be subjected to it is because he is not an American, he is from Canada.

DAMIEN CORSETTI: I think that the Canadian people need to look at themselves and figure out who they are. Because there's been elections since Omar was captured. So ultimately the blame now lies on the Canadian people – of how I, as a cold, callous son of a bitch, had more compassion for that boy than his own people.

MAXIME BERNIER (*speaking in Parliament, while he was Canadian minister of Foreign Affairs*): Mr Speaker, Omar Khadr is facing serious charges related to his capture in Afghanistan, charges such as murder in violation of the laws of war, attempted murder in violation of the laws of war, conspiracy, supporting terrorist activities, and spying. That being said …

DAMIEN CORSETTI: And if they want to allow one of their citizens to be treated like this, then think about the precedent that sets for the future, for you. Could be you. Who is America gonna say is our enemy next?

BILL GRAHAM (Canadian Minister of Foreign Affairs, 2001–03): I regret that we were not more aggressive in trying to get him back. But if I'd known then what I know now, we would have been far more aggressive. What we knew then was, here is a young man; he has been accused of killing an American soldier; we have been told "He's in American custody, he's being properly treated under American law, and he is being humanely treated in accordance with Red Cross rules." This by our best ally, a defender of freedom around the world with an impeccable reputation. And we accepted it.

And I said that in the House of Commons time and time over again, and I believed it when I said it. With historical hindsight I now know that things were different. So would I have acted differently then, if I knew it? Of course.

CRAIG MOKHIBER (deputy director, United Nations High Commission for Human Rights): All governments who are member states of the United Nations have an obligation to cooperate for the promotion and protection of internationally guaranteed human-rights standards. That means that if one state is engaged in violations of international human-rights protections, and another state, even though it doesn't have effective custody in that case, is in any way participating in or complicit in it, they share responsibility under international law.

GAR PARDY: The government of Canada, under law, has a duty to protect Canadians. No ambiguity whatsoever: all Canadians. But the government's position is that there is something called "Crown prerogative," which says in this area the government can pick and choose who it's going to help. And once you start picking and choosing, you are discriminating. Today you are discriminating against Muslims. A few years ago, we discriminated against the Sikhs. We discriminated against Jews coming out from Nazi Germany.

And you need absolute rules here, so that there is no ambiguity who you're going to help. A Canadian is a Canadian is a Canadian.

INTERROGATOR: So, we'll speak tomorrow, OK? Just relax here for a while, and we'll try to get by tomorrow if we have some time to see you. All right?
OMAR: Any books? Any books to read?
INTERROGATOR: I'll see what I can do.

DAY 4: FAILURE

INTERROGATOR: Hey Omar! How're you doing?
OMAR (*reading*): Good.
INTERROGATOR: It's good to see you. I brought you some McDonald's. I just have to throw it in the microwave – there's no delivery here. Why don't you have something to eat while it's still warm?
SECOND INTERROGATOR: Do you want me to turn this down?
INTERROGATOR: Yeah. It's nice and cool in here now.

I mean, let's just be honest with each other this one time. I wouldn't mind if you just said, "You know what, I'm not gonna tell you anything about that." But I don't like it when you say "I don't know" or you shrug your shoulders, because that leads me to believe that you do know, you're just not telling me. And if you don't know for certain, I'm pretty sure you're smart enough to have some very, very good theories as to what happened.
OMAR: What's theories?
INTERROGATOR: Theories are, it's an idea.
OMAR: Oh.
INTERROGATOR: You didn't just fall off the turnip truck. You're a very bright young guy and you see a lot and you've talked to a lot of people. And you've been in some very interesting places. And I think if you wanted to, you could probably tell us a lot of interesting things.
OMAR: I know, that's what I have.
INTERROGATOR: Pardon me?

OMAR: That's what I have. I told you already.
INTERROGATOR: Like when you told us that Sheikh Isa presided over Zaynab's wedding.
OMAR: Yeah, I think so.
INTERROGATOR: And OBL was there?
OMAR: No.
INTERROGATOR: No?
OMAR: There were lots of people.
INTERROGATOR: But not him?
OMAR: No.
INTERROGATOR: Why are you wavering on this today?
OMAR: I said that because I was scared.
INTERROGATOR: Of what?
OMAR: Of getting tortured again.
INTERROGATOR: Of torturing? Were we torturing you the other night?
OMAR: Not you, but –
INTERROGATOR: The sub was bad, but the –
OMAR: I didn't know who you were...
INTERROGATOR: No, I think ... I don't know why or what happened, that somehow you thought that you said too much and you decided to sort of change your ... So, were you lying to me then or you're lying to me now?
OMAR: Then.
INTERROGATOR: But ... How do I know? How do I know you're not lying to me now and you didn't lie to me then?
OMAR: How do you know that I was lying and now I'm not lying?
INTERROGATOR: Yeah, how would I know that?
OMAR: Because I admit that I was lying then.
INTERROGATOR: Yeah, but this could be just another lie. Right now, Omar, it doesn't get any worse. It's never gonna get any worse for you now, but –
OMAR: It may get worse.
INTERROGATOR: In what sense?
OMAR: More torturing. Get put in an isolated room with no stuff.
INTERROGATOR: Get put in an isolated room with no stuff? I wouldn't consider that to be torture.
OMAR: I don't think you could handle that for one night.
INTERROGATOR: No? Well, I mean, fortunately I'm not in a position where that has to be something I have to worry about. I'm not here

to change positions with you and I'm not here to tell you what your life is about right now because, quite honestly, that doesn't apply to me. It's a stupid game to get into anyway.

DR RAUL BERDICHEVSKY: I think it's one of the most cruel things that you can possibly say to anybody who's in that kind of a predicament. He's really saying, "You know what? You're the product of your circumstances and I don't have anything to do with it. So yes, we are both from Scarborough, you're a man, I'm a man, but you know what? When it comes to this, we're not equal."

And he's proud in saying "I'm not in trouble. You're in trouble. And what happens to people in trouble? They can be put into detention, they can even be tortured ... Fortunately, I don't have to worry about it."

INTERROGATOR: I'm in my position, you're in your position, but I can tell you –
OMAR: Why am I in my position?
INTERROGATOR: Pardon me?
OMAR: Why am I here?
INTERROGATOR: Yeah, but we don't want to go through that again, do we? I mean even yesterday you said that you were basically in there with a bunch of Afghanis and a few Arabs, and ended up in a firefight against the Americans. Well, that's why you're here.
OMAR: If I didn't fight anybody, why am I here?
INTERROGATOR: If you didn't fight anybody?
OMAR: Yeah. I'm saying, if you saw how I was sitting, just when an American came over and shot me with three bullets.
INTERROGATOR: And you were sitting?
OMAR: Yes.
INTERROGATOR: How did that American end up getting so dead then?
OMAR: I don't know, there's three people and the fight's on.
INTERROGATOR: So it was OK because it was a fight?
OMAR: It was not me, I don't even know who, maybe –
INTERROGATOR: Well, if three guys are sitting in a car and they go and they rob a convenience store, and one of them shoots somebody, everybody in the car is guilty of shooting that guy. That's the way the law works.

NATHAN WHITLING: What intelligence value is there in asking a question like that? I mean, is that a question that's going to elicit some information that's going to be of use to the Canadian government? No, it's trying to get him to admit that he's guilty. So it is an attempt to interrogate Omar and to get him to admit something that can be used against him in a prosecution. And so it belies this whole theory of theirs that they're not there to assist the Americans in prosecuting Omar.

DENNIS EDNEY: But not only that, the Canadian officials were aware when they were sharing information with the Americans from interrogating Omar Khadr, that the death penalty was still on the table.

INTERROGATOR: I have to go back and write a report on that. They're going to laugh at me because they're going to say, "This guy is not cooperating, this guy is jerking your chain, he's wasting your time. He's intent on lying to you."
OMAR: I'm not lying. If you were tortured like I was tortured, you'd probably say more than what I said. You're not in my position and that's why you're saying this.
INTERROGATOR: You're saying that like a robot. This is like a rehearsed speech. If I wanted a rehearsed speech or a recording, I'd get a tape recorder and I'd play it.

MOAZZAM BEGG (Omar Khadr's cellmate): I remember speaking to intelligence agents, and seeing clearly that they wanted to tick off boxes and go back and tell their superiors that we got this information now. It doesn't mean that the information is any good, that it's useful, it simply goes back and tells the people in charge that we're doing a good job. We can continue to receive the salaries that we're getting and continue to have this position that we have.

DENNIS EDNEY: When I look at that tape, I see the absolute callowness of the interrogators. But you also see the desperation. It's like the salesman whose job's on the line. He's gotta sell a car or he's fired, and he's pleading to a young kid, "Give us something, so we can take it back." And it's not something for Omar's benefit, it's for the justification of that interrogator's job.

INTERROGATOR: If you were bright, Omar, and I want you to think about this for a few minutes. If you're smart, tell me something that can help me – that can show my government that you're willing to help us against a group of people who are bent on doing bad things to us.
OMAR: You want me to lie?
INTERROGATOR: I don't want you to lie. I just want you to tell the truth.
OMAR: That's what I told you – the truth. You don't like the truth.
Audio erased by CSIS
INTERROGATOR: Well, we're leaving early tomorrow morning, and this is your last kick at the cat. So if you want to tell us something that you think we want, that we might be able to use and something that's going to be truthful, we want to hear it. But if not, well, thank you very much for your time, but we've got other things to do.
OMAR: You just want to hear whatever you want to hear.
INTERROGATOR: I just want to hear whatever I want to hear? No, I don't. I want to hear the truth. You think I want to sit here and listen to people talk about things? Not really, I'd rather be down on the beach. I'd rather go and get a boat and drive around, or I'd rather go do something fun, but we're here on a Sunday to hear what you're saying. Is there anything you want to tell me before we wrap this up? Omar?
OMAR: I told you everything. You can't believe me.
INTERROGATOR: I wish, you know, this was all a big mistake. But it's not. And I'm sure of what I know, as the sun comes up in the east in the morning and sets in the west at night. Anyway, Omar, thank you very much for your time.
OMAR: I want to call my grandparents.
INTERROGATOR: Pardon me?
OMAR: I want to call my grandparents.
INTERROGATOR: Well, I can't arrange that.
OMAR: You didn't do anything for me.
INTERROGATOR: Pardon me?
OMAR: You didn't do anything for me.
INTERROGATOR: We wouldn't do anything for you?
OMAR: You didn't do anything for me.
INTERROGATOR: I didn't do anything *to* you. We can't do anything for you, only you can help yourself. I'm telling you, if you ever get

the chance to speak with somebody like myself again, then I would think about your future. Not thinking about being loyal to somebody who was never loyal to you.

OMAR: It's gonna be after a month that I can call somebody.

INTERROGATOR: Pardon me?

OMAR: It's gonna be after a month that I can call somebody.

INTERROGATOR: All right, Omar, take care.

OMAR DEGHAYES: When I speak about those things, I see those conditions, I relive my own memories, and it's easier for me to keep quiet and live a quiet life. But when you ask about Omar Khadr, I feel there is a duty that I should speak about him, to make people know about his conditions and how he is living now in prison.

I'm a law graduate, I work as a human rights lawyer now. I was subjected to imprisonment – more than five years, about six years' imprisonment in Guantánamo Bay and Bagram. I was subjected to all kinds of torture. I lost the sight in my right eye by a guard pushing his fingers inside my eyes. I've broken ribs, my nose as you can see, and I can't breathe properly. My finger was broken in Guantánamo Bay. So I was subjected to physical mistreatment, and obviously the psychological mistreatment is even worse.

I was released in December 2007 without being charged of anything. After six years of imprisonment and torture, I was not charged of anything.

RUHAL AHMED: I was released from Guantánamo on the 9th of March 2004. I was going home and I knew that he's staying here, and it just didn't feel right, because, you know, he became like a brother to me. And it's like you leave your brother in the pit and you're gonna get released, it doesn't feel good. So it brought tears to my eyes, it brought tears to him but, you know, nothing we could do about it.

MOAZZAM BEGG: I will never forget his case, I will never forget the individual or what happened to him or how I saw him. For me, his case epitomizes everything that is wrong in Guantánamo and the "War on Terror." I'm director of the organization for human rights, Cageprisoners: I was held in Guantánamo Bay for two years and in Bagram for one year between 2002 and 2005. In January 2005, I was released without charge, without explanation, without compensation, and have been living and working in the United Kingdom since.

DAMIEN CORSETTI: I definitely feel a duty to do this. To your viewers I would say "Look at your own kids." And that's what he was: a child. He was not a hardened terrorist. He wasn't.

LT-CMDR WILLIAM KUEBLER: I'm a personally and philosophically conservative individual, but I have never found a contradiction or inconsistency between any of the things that I've had to do as a lawyer for Omar Khadr and my personal beliefs. I mean, conservatives believe in the rule of law, conservatives believe in limited government. Conservatives believe in things like fair trials. And those are the things that I have advocated for in my representation of Omar Khadr.

STEPHEN XENAKIS, (Brigadier General, retired): I am touched by him. And I think he has been treated unfairly. I think that good people and good citizens of Canada and the United States should know about him, and should speak up and advocate for him. And they should urge the governments to give him the opportunity to have the best possible life that he can.

On 29 January 2010, the Supreme Court of Canada ruled that Canadian agents had violated Omar Khadr's rights when they interrogated him at the Guantánamo Bay prison. The US government used the information obtained during these interrogations to build their prosecution against Omar Khadr.

On 25 October 2010, Omar Khadr pleaded guilty to all accusations of war crimes brought against him by the US government. His admission of guilt came after lengthy plea bargaining between his lawyers and American military prosecutors, who agreed to a maximum sentence of eight years in prison.

Omar Khadr, who had always maintained his innocence, thus avoided a forty-year prison sentence. He is the first child condemned for war crimes since the Nuremberg Tribunal defined the concept at the end of World War II.

The Canadian government never requested Omar Khadr's repatriation.

190

SECRET

DEPARTMENT OF DEFENSE
JOINT TASK FORCE GUANTANAMO
GUANTANAMO BAY, CUBA
APO AE 09360

REPLY TO
ATTENTION OF

JTF GTMO-CG

24 January 2004

MEMORANDUM FOR Commander, United States Southern Command, 3511 NW 9lst Avenue, Miami, FL 33172.

SUBJECT: (S) Recommendation to Retain under DoD Control for Guantanamo Detainee, Omar Ahmed Khader, ISN: US9CA-000766DP

1. (S) **Personal Information**: Omar Ahmed Khader is a Canadian national, born on 19 September 1986 (age 18) in Toronto, Canada (CA). He is in good health.

2. (S) **Detention Information**: Detainee claims that he lived in the Pakistan-Afghanistan region since 1996. In June 2002, detainee was encouraged by his father, a senior Al-Qaida leader in Canada and close associate of Usama Bin Laden, to travel to Khowst, AF, to translate for Al-Qaida personnel and to participate in Jihad against the United States. Detainee received training and instruction on how to build and plant Improvised Explosive Devices (IEDs) and how to plant land mines (it is not known where or when the detainee learned these skills). Detainee has also admitted to taking part in several mining and combat operations. In July 2002, detainee was present during a raid on a suspected Al-Qaida compound by US Special Forces, during which a gun battle ensued. During the raid, detainee threw a hand grenade and killed a US Special Forces soldier. Detainee was wounded and captured after killing the USSF soldier. Detainee was subsequently transported to Guantanamo Bay Naval Base, Cuba, on 27 October 2002 because of his part in the death of a US soldier and his affiliation with Al- Qaida.

3. (S) **Reasons for Continued Detention at GTMO**: Detainee's father is a senior Al-Qaida financier and reportedly the fourth in command underneath Usama Bin Laden in the Al-Qaida organization. The detainee and his brother were encouraged to travel to Afghanistan and fight against the US in support of Al-Qaida and the Taliban. Detainee, though only 16 years old at the time of his travel to Afghanistan, has been found to be intelligent and educated and understands the gravity of his actions and affiliations. Detainee excelled at his training in Afghanistan, which included small arms, explosives training, IEDs, mines, mine laying, and configuring IEDs for remote detonation using hand held devices. Detainee admits to having participated in several mining operations and harassing attacks against US Forces, in addition

CLASSIFIED BY: MG Geoffrey D. Miller, Commander, JTF Guantanamo
REASON: E.O. 12958 Section 1.5(C)
DECLASSIFY ON: 20290124

SECRET

191

SECRET

JTF GTMO-CG
SUBJECT: (S) Recommendation to Retain under DoD Control for Guantanamo Detainee, Omar Ahmed Khader ISN: US9CA-000766DP

to throwing the grenade that killed a US solider. Detainee has never expressed any genuine remorse for the killing of that soldier. He has direct family affiliations with senior Al-Qaida members, has received advanced specialized training in explosives, and has directly participated in hostile attacks against US Forces. Detainee claims that his entire family lived at one of Usama Bin Laden's compounds in Jalalabad, AF. Detainee continues to provide valuable information on his father's associates, and on non-governmental organizations that he worked with in supporting Al-Qaida, as well as other major facilitators of interest to the US. Detainee has also provided valuable information on the Derunta, Al-Farouq and Khalden training camps, indicating that the detainee has been to and likely trained at these locations; and he continues to provide valuable information on key Al-Qaida and Taliban members. Finally, detainee has been generally cooperative and forthcoming but has grown increasingly hostile towards his interrogators and the guard force and he remains committed to extremist Islamic values.

4. (S) **Assessment**: Based on information collected and available to Joint Task Force Guantanamo as of 20 January 2004, detainee ISN: US9CA-000766DP is assessed as being a member of Al-Qaida. Moreover, based on the detainee's folder, the knowledgeability brief, and subsequent interrogations by JTF Guantanamo, the detainee is of high intelligence value to the United States. Based on the above, detainee poses a high risk, as he is likely to pose a threat to the U.S., its interests or its allies.

5. (S) **EC Status**: Detainee's enemy combatant status was reassessed on 31 October 2003 and he remains an enemy combatant.

6. (S) **Recommendation**: Retain under DoD control.

7. (S) **Coordination**: JTF Guantanamo notified the Criminal Investigative Task Force of this recommendation on 22 December 2003. JTF GMTO and CITF agree on the threat assessment of this detainee as a high risk.

GEOFFREY D. MILLER
Major General, U.S. Army
Commanding

CF: CITF-GTMO

2

SECRET

192

Court File No. T-1228-08

FEDERAL COURT

BETWEEN :

OMAR AHMED KHADR

Applicant

- and -

THE PRIME MINISTER OF CANADA, THE MINISTER OF FOREIGN AFFAIRS, THE DIRECTOR OF THE CANADIAN SECURITY INTELLIGENCE SERVICE, and THE COMMISSIONER OF THE ROYAL CANADIAN MOUNTED POLICE

Respondents

AFFIDAVIT OF OMAR AHMED KHADR

I, OMAR AHMED KHADR, make oath and say as follows.

1. I am the Applicant in these proceedings and as such have personal knowledge of the matters hereinafter deposed to save and except where stated to be based upon information and belief.

2. I am a Canadian citizen. My date of birth is September 19, 1986.

3. I am a prisoner in Guantanamo Bay, Cuba. I was first taken prisoner by U.S. forces on July 27, 2002, when I was 15 years old. I was severely wounded in the battle where I was captured. I was shot at least twice in the back, at least once through my left shoulder exiting through my left breast, and once under my right shoulder, exiting out of my upper right side. I was also struck with shrapnel in my left eye, and was wounded in my left thigh, knee, ankle and foot.

4. I believe I remained conscious after being wounded and captured. I remember being carried by my arms and legs to an area in the open where someone put some bandages on me. The soldiers were asking me questions about my identity. They then placed me on a wooden board and carried me into a helicopter. I lost consciousness during the trip in the helicopter.

5. I was unconscious for about one week after being captured. When I began to regain consciousness I asked what the date was and knew that I had been unconscious for a week since being captured. I was awake, but I was not right and was out of my wits for about three days. I was in extreme pain and my pain

{E5501802.DOC;1}

was all I could focus on. I was in a tent hospital on a stretcher. There were two other detainees there with me, one had lost both his legs and often screamed for pain medication. The other detainee was an older man.

6. While at the tent hospital I was guarded day and night by pairs of soldiers. During the day, I was guarded by a young blond soldier who was about 25, and a Mexican or Puerto Rican soldier.

7. During the first three days I was conscious in the tent hospital, the first soldier would come and sit next to my stretcher and ask me questions. He had paper and took notes. During the first three days, they would shackle my feet and hands out to my sides with handcuffs when they did not like the answers I was giving to the questions. Due to my injuries, this caused me great pain. At least two of the interrogations during these first three days occurred when I was shackled by my hands and feet and in pain. I was unable to even stand at this time, so I was not a threat, and I could tell that this treatment was for punishment and to make me answer questions and give them the answers they wanted.

8. The Hispanic MP acted like he hated me, and would often shackle me and cause me pain. He would tell the nurses not to speak nicely or softly to me since he said that I had killed an American soldier. He would also insult me quite often.

9. There were no doctors or nurses present when I was interrogated. During the interrogations, the pain was taking my thoughts away. After I regained consciousness after being unconscious for a week, the first soldier told me that I had killed an American with a hand grenade. They would only give me pain medication at nighttime but the interrogations occurred during the daytime.

10. After about 2 weeks in the hospital I was immediately taken to an interrogation room at a military camp in Bagram. I was left in the room for about 1 hour by myself. Then someone came in and started interrogating me. This interrogation lasted for about 3 hours. It was a skinny white interrogator with glasses who seemed to be about 25 years old. He had a small tattoo on the top of his forearm. He wore desert camouflage pants but a different kind of shirt. They asked me all kinds of questions about everything and I don't remember all the questions today.

11. During this first interrogation, the young blonde man would often scream at me if I did not give him the answers he wanted. Several times, he forced me to sit up on my stretcher, which caused me great pain due to my injuries. He did this several times to get me to answer his questions and give him the answers he wanted. It was clear that he was making me sit up because he knew that it hurt and he wanted me to answer questions. I cried several times during the interrogation as a result of this treatment and pain.

12. During this interrogation, the more I answered the questions and the more I gave him the answers he wanted, the less pain was inflicted on me. I figured out right

away that I would simply tell them whatever I thought they wanted to hear in order to keep them from causing me such pain.

13. While detaineed in Bagram, I was held with other adult detainees in a building like an airplane hangar. I was still on a stretcher and still had holes in my body and stitching. I was kept with all the adult prisoners.

14. The soldiers at Bagram treated me roughly. I was interrogated many, many times by interrogators. For about the first two weeks to a month that I was there I could not get out of the stretcher and would be brought into the interrogation room on a stretcher.

15. During this time, my pain depended upon what I was doing. If I was just relaxing on the stretcher, the pain would be about a 4 or 5 on a scale of 1 to 10. If I was sitting up it was more severe. If I was treated roughly or if my wounds were touched, the pain would be a 10.

16. Everyday when I was at Bagram, five people in civilian clothes would come and change my bandages. They treated me very roughly and videotaped me while they did it.

17. On one occasion, interrogators grabbed and pulled me off the stretcher, and I fell and cut my left knee.

18. On some occasions, the interrogators brought barking dogs into the interrogation room while my head was covered with a bag. The bag was wrapped tighly around my neck, nearly choking me and making it hard to breathe. This terrified me. On other occasions, interrogators threw cold water on me.

19. Several times, the soldiers tied my hands above my head to the door frame or chained them to the ceiling and made me stand like that for hours at a time. Because of my injuries, particularly the bullet wounds in my chest and shoulders, my hands could not be raised all the way above my head, but they would pull them up as high as they thought they could go, and then tie them there.

20. They often made me sit up in the stretcher in order to create pain from my wounds. They knew it was painful for me because of my physical reaction and because I told them it was painful.

21. While my wounds were still healing, interrogators made me clean the floors on my hands and knees. They woke me up in the middle of the night after midnight and made me clean the floor with a brush and dry it with towels until dawn.

22. They forced me to carry heavy buckets of water, which hurt my left shoulder (where I had been shot). They were 5 gallon buckets. They also made me lift and stack crates of bottled water. This was very painful as my wounds were still healing.

4.

195

23. On several occasions at Bagram, interrogators threatened to have me raped, or sent to other countries like Egypt, Syria, Jordan or Israel to be raped.

24. When I was able to walk again, interrogators made me pick up trash, then emptied the trash bag and made me pick it up again. Many times, during the interrogations, I was not allowed to use the bathroom, and was forced to urinate on myself. They told me that I deserved it.

25. Sometimes they would shine extremely bright lights right up against my face, and my eyes would tear and tear and tear. These lights caused me great pain, particularly since both my eyes were badly injured and had shrapnel in them.

26. Sometimes when they were questioning me, they would tell me that they would let me go free if I told them something that enabled them to catch someone big.

27. One time, an interrogator gave me a pen and paper and told me to write out my story. While I was writing, the Hispanic MP from the tent hospital came up to me, turned around and farted in my face.

28. I think that I was interrogated 42 times in 90 days. I have a memory of 42 times, but I don't recall where I received that number.

29. In Bagram, I would always hear people screaming, both day and night. Sometimes it would be the interrogators screaming at prisoners to stand up or sit down or not to sleep, and sometimes it was the prisoners screaming from their treatment. I know a lot of other detainees who were tortured by the skinny blonde guy: Most people would not talk about what had been done to them. This made me afraid.

30. An old man who was captured with me was also brought to the Bagram camp. I saw bandages and injuries on his legs from where he had been tortured. Later, one of the interrogators told me that this man had died.

31. One time before I left, I had my hands chained above my head to the ceiling, and the skinny blond interrogator with the tattoo told me that I was lucky that I had been injured, he would know how to "treat me," meaning he would torture me.

32. After about three months, I was taken to Guantanamo. For the two nights and one day before putting us on the plane, we were not given any food so that we would not have to use the bathroom on the plane. They shaved our heads and beards, and put medical-type masks over our mouths and noses, and goggles and earphones on us so that we could not see or hear anything. One time, a soldier kicked me in the leg when I was on the plane and tried to stretch my legs.

33. On the plane, I was shackled to the floor for the whole trip. When I arrived at Guantanamo, I heard a military official say, "Welcome to Israel". They half-dragged half-carried us so quickly along the ground off the plane that everyone

had cuts on their ankles from the shackles. They would smack you with a stick if you made any wrong moves.

34. They left me in a waiting area for about one hour waiting for processing. They then took me into a room where I was stripped naked and subjected to a body cavity search.

35. I was feeling a lot of back and chest pain from my injuries, and I was also dizzy from the travel, pain and lack of sleep and food.

36. Two soldiers then took charge of me, one was black and one was white. These two soldiers then pushed me up against a wall. One pushed my back into the wall with his elbow, and the other pushed my face into the wall. Although the goggles and headphones had been removed, the mask was still over my mouth and nose and it was difficult to breathe. They held me like this, and I could not breathe, and passed out. When they felt me falling they would start to relax, but then when I began to wake up, they would do it again until I passed out and began to fall again. They did this to me about 3 or 4 times. There were other prisoners there who were not being treated like this.

37. During processing, they gave me a 2-minute shower, took blood, fingerprints and photographs, including photos of my wounds.

38. I was taken to the Fleet Hospital, where I stayed for two days. While in the hospital, two interrogators came and interrogated me for six hours each day. One interrogator was in civilian dress clothes and I think he told me he was with the FBI. The other was in military camouflage. They asked me questions about everything. I don't think there was anything new. They had papers with them and they took notes.

39. I did not want to expose myself to any more harm, so I always just told interrogators what I thought they wanted to hear. Having been asked the same questions so many times, I knew what answers made interrogators happy and would always tailor my answers based on what I thought would keep me from being harmed.

40. After those first interrogations, I was put into segregation. These are cells with walls, and only a small window that you can't look out of – the window just lets you know if its day or night. There is no human contact.

41. I would often be moved around depending on whether or not I had been co-operating with the interrogators.

42. I was not provided with any educational opportunities, no psychological or psychiatric attention, and was routinely interrogated.

43. While at Guantanamo, I have been visited on numerous occasions by individuals claiming to be from the Canadian government. These included four visits in the course of four days in a row, starting on March 27, 2003.

44. The first visit was by a group of three people: two men, one in his mid-30s and a second, older man, perhaps in his 70s, and a woman about 40-50 years old. The visitors introduced themselves as Canadians. They stated that they knew my mother and grandmother in Scarborough, Canada. We met in a special conference room, rather than the usual interrogation room, and this room was more comfortable. We met for approximately 2-3 hours. Rather than asking me how I was, the visitors had a lot of questions for me.

45. I was very hopeful that they would help me. I showed them my injuries and told them that what I had told the Americans was not right and not true. I said that I told the Americans whatever they wanted me to say because they would torture me. The Canadians called me a liar and I began to sob. They screamed at me and told me that they could not do anything for me. I tried to cooperate so that they would take me back to Canada. I told them that I was scared and that I had been tortured.

46. They came back three more days but I did not sob because they had no sympathy. They asked me about people, such as my father and Arar. They showed me pictures and asked who people were. I told them what I knew.

47. During this second visit, the visitors showed me approximately 20 pictures of various people, and asked me to identify them. The Canadian visitors never asked me how I was feeling or how I was doing, nor did they ever ask if I wanted to send a message to my family.

48. The next day, the two Canadian men who had visited me returned. I told them that if they were not going to help me then I wanted them to leave me alone.

49. On the third visit by the Canadians, I told the Canadian visitors that I wanted to return to my country, Canada, and that I would speak with them there.

50. After the Canadians left and I told the Americans that my previous statements were untrue, life got much worse for me. They took away all of my things except for a mattress. I had no Koran and no blanket. They would shackle me during interrogations and leave me in harsh and painful positions for hours at a time. One navy interrogator would pull my hair and spit in my face.

51. Approximately one month before Ramadan in 2003, two different men came to visit me. They told me that they were Canadian. One of the men was in his 20s and the other in his 30s. These two men yelled at me and accused me of not telling the truth. One of the Canadian men stated, "The U.S. and Canada are like

an elephant and an ant sleeping in the same bed," and that there was nothing the Canadian government could do against the power of the U.S.

52. One of the men returned alone approximately one month after the Eid al-Adha holiday. The visitor showed me his Canadian passport, the outside of which was red in color. The Canadian visitor stated, "I'm not here to help you. I'm not here to do anything for you. I'm just here to get information." The man then asked me questions about my brother, Abdullah.

53. Within a day of my last visit from the Canadians, my security level was changed from Level 1 to Level 4 minus, with isolation. Everything was taken away from me, and I spent a month in isolation. The room in which I was confined was kept very cold. It was "like a refrigerator".

54. Around the time of Ramadan in 2003, an Afghan man, claiming to be from the Afghan government, interrogated me at Guantanamo. A military interrogator was in the room at the time. The Afghan man said his name was "Izmarai" (Lion), and that he was from Wardeq. He spoke mostly in Farsi, and a little in Pashto and English. He had an American flag on his trousers. The Afghan man appeared displeased with the answers that I was giving him, and after some time both the Afghan and the military interrogator left the room. A military official then removed my chair and short-shackled me by my hands and feet to a bolt in the floor. Military officials then moved my hands behind my knees. They left me in the room in this condition for approximately five to six hours, causing me extreme pain. Occasionally, a military officer and the interrogators would come in and laugh at me.

55. During the course of his interrogation of me, the Afghan man told me that a new detention center was being built in Afghanistan for non-cooperative detainees at Guantanamo. The Afghan man told me that I would be sent to Afghanistan and raped. The Afghan man also told me that they like small boys in Afghanistan, a comment that I understood as a threat of sexual violence. Before leaving the room, the Afghan man took a piece of paper on which my picture appeared, and wrote on it in the Pashto language, "This detainee must be transferred to Bagram".

56. During one interrogation at Guantanamo in the spring of 2003, an interrogator spit in my face when he didn't like the answers I provided. He pulled my hair, and told me that I would be sent to Israel, Egypt, Jordan, or Syria – comments that I understood to be a threat of torture. The interrogator told me that the Egyptians would send in "Askri raqm tisa" – Soldier Number 9 – which was explained to me was a man who would be sent to rape me.

57. The interrogator told me, "Your life is in my hands". My hands and ankles were shackled, and the interrogator then removed my chair, forcing me to sit on the floor. The interrogator told me to stand up. Because of the way I was shackled, I

was not able to use my hands to do so, thus making the act difficult to do. As ordered by the interrogator, I stood up, at which time the interrogator told me to sit down again. When I did so, the interrogator ordered me to stand again. I could not do so, at which point the interrogator called two military police officers into the room, who grabbed me by the neck and arms, lifted me, up, and then dropped me to the floor. The military police officers lifted and dropped me in this manner approximately five times, each time at the instruction of the interrogator. The interrogator told me they would throw my case in a safe and that I would never get out of Guantanamo. This interrogation session lasted for approximately two to three hours.

58. On one occasion at Guantanamo, in the Spring of 2003, I was left alone in an interrogation room for approximately ten hours.

59. Around March of 2003, I was taken out of my cell at Camp Delta at approximately 12:00 – 1:00 a.m., and taken to an interrogation room. An interrogator told me that my brother was not at Guantanamo, and that I should "get ready for a miserable life". I stated that he would answer the interrogator's questions if they brought my brother to see me. The interrogator became extremely angry, then called in military police and told them to cuff me to the floor. First they cuffed me with my arms in front of my legs. After approximately half an hour they cuffed me with my arms behind my legs. After another half hour they forced me onto my knees, and cuffed my hands behind my legs. Later still, they forced me on my stomach, bent my knees, and cuffed my hands and feet together. At some point, I urinated on the floor and on myself. Military police poured pine oil on the floor and on me, and then, with me lying on my stomach and my hands and feet cuffed together behind me, the military police dragged me back and forth through the mixture of urine and pine oil on the floor. Later, I was put back in my cell, without being allowed a shower or change of clothes. I was not given a change of clothes for two days. They did this to me again a few weeks later.

60. When I was moved to Camp 5, I went on a hunger strike. I was very weak and could not stand. Guards would grab me by pressure points behind my ears, under my jaw and on my neck. On a scale of 1 to 10, I would say the pain was an 11. They would often knee me repeatedly in the thighs. Another time, when they took my weight, they pressed on my pressure points. I remember them videotaping me while they did this.

61. I continue to have nightmares. I dream about being shot and captured. I dream about trying to run away and not being able to get away. I dream about all that has happened. About feeling like there is nothing I can do. About feeling disabled. Besides my medical problems, the dreams are the worst right now. I continue to have back pain and pains in my joints.

62. I was first visited by lawyers in November of 2004. Before that, I had never been permitted to meet with lawyers.

63. In May 2005, they took all of my things including a calendar I had been keeping since sometime in 2004 regarding my treatment, events and other things. They never gave this back.

I solemnly affirm that all of the forgoing statements are true and complete to the best of my knowledge

Omar. A. Khadr

OMAR AHMED KHADR
30th July 2008

Reflections

Nail Biter: A One-Act Play

JUDITH THOMPSON

DAVID, *a* CSIS *agent in his mid-thirties, looks at a frozen video image of Omar Khadr in his orange jumpsuit. Quietly, he quotes him:*

"I have to follow my heart, because if I don't, it'll stop working."
I don't know what the hell he meant by that one –
It's bothering me, you know? Because it's like he was implying that we wanted him not to tell the truth; that we wanted to hear what we wanted to hear, and that is simply, totally NOT
The case.
Listen.
There are many things I don't like about myself –
FOR INSTANCE that my fingers are bitten right down to the quick; I'm a nail biter, okay a SERIOUS nail biter I can hardly pick up a pen without pain, it looks like hell, it's embarrassing as hell, but I can't seem to stop it, you know what I'm talking about? That urge comes on and I fight it and I fight it and I suck on a candy, I talk on the phone, I smoke a cigar but eventually, I get to the biting. I HATE THAT, ya know? About myself it reveals, it ADVERTISES a deep ... insecurity, not that I'M insecure NOW, in my late thirties, successful civil servant, fairly happy with myself now, quite a confident guy – life is good, you know? But I was, years ago, as a boy, like many of us, you know, AWKWARD, kind of funny looking, afraid not to be picked for the team, I know that's a cliché but its so TRUE, close to hysterical with fear about tests, about a girl's opinion of me, about my mom's cancer coming back, about my sister telling me I was a loser cause I was sometimes home on a Saturday night – so I bit, and

I gnawed, I bit like a dog with a bone, and I bit and I chewed and IT GAVE ME HUGE satisfaction,
Well …
Those are … very goddamned stressful years.
Going from a boy to … to the crazy hell of turning into a … man?

It's understandable that I would bite my nails. Isn't it?
But what I hate is
I STILL bite my nails.
Looks like fear, even though its NOT, it's just goddamned habit but it does LOOK
like it
And
I don't like that about myself.

Thing is, it actually allays anxiety, for a time, for a time, until the tips of your damn fingers start to KILL, and you are reminded, REMINDED that you are STILL a nervous wreck of a human being, a bit of a joke.
If nail biting was the only thing I hate about myself I'd be laughing.

I made a list, my shrink told me to write a list, and cross one thing off at a time, Because although they are all seemingly mundane, even trivial things they do add up … perhaps, to something bigger – something I need to … excavate … you know?
… After nail biting, comes LAZY I drive to the corner store two blocks away, I will lie in bed uncomfortable for hours rather than get up to go to the bathroom, I let the newspapers pile halfway to the ceiling, I don't clean the cat litter as much as I should sometimes go days without doin' my dishes have been known not to change my socks for two three four even five days in a ROW – with Karen not here to tell me my feet stink, why bother, you know? And what really BUGS me about it, what wakes me up at four in the morning with a headache RIGHT HERE is that it all … reveals an underlying, I don't know, character flaw, a lack of WILL, somehow, of of get-up-and-do-it-ness, that she did not like, that I do not like. Because I have always admired those guys that get up and do it, you know? I like, I admire men who take responsibility, who
Who are the first ones at the accident scene, who who have the vision to to change the way things are, who … who … don't …

I WANT that man to be me, so I am going to start, when this STORM has passed, and it will pass, by taking my personal life into my own hands, since my professional life is RIGHT out of control since the world is passing judgment on me, on my handling of the event since they seem to think I am responsible for for the boy since they seem to think that I am my government and that my government has abandoned a child.

We were given assurances. By the Americans. Our prime minister believed them, why shouldn't I believe them, I work for the prime minister I believe what he believes
And, I did believe. Those assurances.
They – those people they are very ... persuasive, have you ever met one?
An American intell officer, in full uniform? Can you say incandescent? ... It's like being the high school outcast and running smack into the star of the football team you can feel yourself visibly shrinking and blushing like a southern belle, you just want to say "yes sir, can I please shine your shoes or or get you a coffee?" You want to bask in that blinding light you will do anything to STAY in that light – well not anything, but let's just say it can be blinding.
I was stressed outta my head, I guess,
But what I did in the interrogation, that the whole world saw on YouTube? – is not one of the things I hate about myself. Oh no, THAT does NOT keep ME up at night.
We had credible intelligence that ... led us right to the boy's family, who are a first family of al-Qaeda AND running free in our country while putting DOWN our country and we needed to KNOW stuff about them that this kid could TELL US.

Do you know how many serious plots the secret services over the world have uncovered and dismantled?
Spain and London got past us, but if you KNEW what we have prevented!
I am SORRY that he is so young it is UNFAIR that he got caught up in his family's evil but we gotta do what we gotta do.

I mean he was havin' a good time at first, he was having a GREAT TIME, when we first came in.

When he saw us?
His face ...
Like a kid at Christmas!

He said "I'm so happy to see you guys."
He said "Oh! I have been asking for Canadians for so long." See? We were the GOOD GUYS
I said "we're happy to see you too, Omar." And I meant it.
His face. Was ...
Reminded me of myself actually, when I was his age? You know, kind of a goofball.
He was damn happy to see us
We gave him a Big Mac and a Coke, we gave him a Kit-Kat bar.
He ate it all up. I mean we all know food in Cuba is awful, even at the five-star resorts, right? So he ate HEARTY, and we had a great afternoon WHAT AM I SUPPOSED TO FEEL GUILTY FOR?
I never lied to the kid so next day when he said he wanted to go home I said, "I can't help you with that," I was not going to pretend I could help him with that.
So he was pissed at us, once he realized he wasn't goin' home? Of COURSE he says:
"You don't care about me."
Yah yah yah
"Yes we do, Omar, we do care about you." That's what I said, and I meant it.
I said, "We do care about you, Omar, but we want to see the Omar we saw yesterday."
See?
I am not
A cold heared bureaucratic bobblehead, I am NOT
But I'll be honest with ya, it was damn annoying, second day?
He wouldn't even take the Kit Kat.
He was SALIVATING over it but he turned his face away
Clearly he had been coached by the jihadi
He said, "I don't want your chocolate bar.
It's only temporal."
Temporal? Are you kidding me? A kid with a grade eight education using the word temporal?
"I want something real," he says, "something lasting," he says.

"I want to go home to Canada."
I told him "I can't help you with that," I was always honest. ALWAYS.
I joked around with him, I said, "I thought maybe you could help me stay in Cuba, BEAUTIFUL weather no snow … "
Okay, so he didn't find that funny … he was paranoid at that point, He asked us to protect him from the Americans, right in FRONT of the Americans!
The CIA guy looks at me, I don't know HOW the hell to arrange my face
He told me he said "I lost my eyes, I lost my feet. Everything." That's what he said
I said, "Well Omar, I'm not a doctor but I think you're getting good medical care." And I did, I mean he looked OKAY
He said – "You don't know, you're not here." And I thought, Omar, you are being a big baby, worse than my nephew
And then you heard him he's like "Kill me, Kill me Kill me."
Well. Okay, buddy.

I mean I felt sorry for the guy, I'm human, but I said to him, I said, "Omar, this strategy is not getting you anywhere and it's a waste of time. We got things to do, we can't sit here all day listening to you act OPERA for God's sake."
He was ACTING, don't you think?
He was acting his head off, he should get the bad acting award of the year. You know?

Listen, I was gathering intelligence, looking after the security of our country. And the security of our country is the security of America, Stephen Harper KNOWS this, he understands that their future is OUR future that that to defy them is to burn the hand that FEEDS us, he understands that America is our Big Brother and we gotta take the good with the bad because ultimately, your brother IS your brother, till death you do part, America and Canada, the PC's KNOW that the two are inextricably linked – the Liberals said no to Iraq causing a MAJOR problem and the NDP, Layton Layton'd be like the little Chihuahua with a mustache like biting the heels of his owner till his owner frickin' gives him away, he would have us stranded, man, alone on our ice floe, Harper? He gets it that WE NEED THEM, and this respect? that was the only way we even got in the door. The

Americans didn't have to let us near the kid. They WEREN'T going to let us near him until they realized that there were serious questions of national security because his family were residing IN Canada. An hour and a half from Buffalo.

He is their prisoner after all. I said to him I said "Omar, you are talking about an elephant and a mouse you think the mouse has any influence over the elephant?"
I mean come ON people ...

Listen. We are not stupid. We are not gullible
WE WERE GIVEN ASSURANCES.
And I did believe. Those assurances.
They – as I said, those people that are very ... persuasive, honestly, have you ever met one? Like I said before –
An American intell officer, in full uniform? You want to bask in his – charisma, you will do anything to STAY in the light including, maybe, compromising everything you believe in. I mean, of course I wouldn't do that, but I'm just SAYING.

I don't think ... he was tortured the way he said he was.
He looked FINE to me. I don't think things were quite as bad as everyone ...
I know that some people out there on the left think that we are patsies of the Americans but I want to ask you, where the hell would we be without them? If the terrorists attack Canada, who do you think is going to defend us? The Canadian army is superb but it just AIN'T big enough guys ...
Listen: the facts are the facts, are the – there he was, he may have been fifteen, yes, but he was in a compound, with a group of Taliban fighters, I don't know, translating or something and and when the Americans attacked the compound they did shoot back and and when Omar had four bullet holes in him, and everyone else was maybe dead, he ... it is said, it is conjectured that he threw a grenade that killed Christopher Speer, the American medic. Now it's true, nobody SAW this, and it IS true that one of the soldiers admitted they were "finishing off anyone who groaned," and that is against the law, technically, and it IS true that they were about to finish off Omar when one of them said "Let him bleed out" and the other said.

"No. We save this one. For interrogation" and I don't know what exactly what I think of that although we do need answers we DO need details but yes it is true that he was fifteen and could be deemed a child soldier but the Americans don't see it that way, they say he was a … terrorist, a spy, a … bomb maker, and … and the fact that he was fifteen doesn't …
The UN declaration on the rights of the Child does not apply because …
Well it's just like sometimes your Dad would change the rules and he would have a very good reason but he just couldn't tell you, I am sure there is a good reason I just can't seem to …

They didn't kill him, did they?
And they have promised us, that they. Will … abide by ... by ethical …
And we are their neighbours, we have to believe in them we …

But even we have always been in awe of America, haven't we? Behind all the famous America bashing most of us wish we were Americans. We think they're having more fun down there, you know, a better party. Because … Listen, because they are … we hadda show them WE KNOW HOW TO CONDUCT AN INTERROGATION and we will NOT be intimidated by a KID. A kid who pissed on the picture of his family. We gave him a photo of his family and you know what he does? He pisses on it.
Yes he did, I mean what kind of …
And the MP shackled him shorter so he wouldn't do it again
And then …
Undid his pants and he did it again
And then the MP cleaned it all up and shackled him shorter
And after an hour or so
He just lay his head down.
Beside the picture of his mother. And he kind of …
What do you make of that, I don't really know what the hell to make of that.
Was that some kind of … or …

Listen I tried to give him a pillow
They wouldn't let me because they apparently use the promise of a pillow as a reward. I tried to be nice to the kid, I'm a nice GUY …

listen when I was in Cambodia with Karen? You know how there's all those kids in the parking lots, selling their bracelets and books, one dollar, "one dollar mister," and … at first, you know, you buy, you buy five or six things, because the kids are so cute, but after a while you burn out. It's only natural so at the end of a long day in Angkor Wat we came out, my feet were killing me, I hadda go to the bathroom and this little girl came running up to me and said … "David! David you promised you would buy from me!" and I know this is a gambit, and I said I was sorry, but no. I didn't have anymore change, and I didn't want another bracelet, or guide book, I just wanted to go back to the hotel. "I'm sorry," I said, "I'm really sorry" and ya know what she said? She looked at me with her brown eyes and … suddenly no smile and she said "Sorry don't eat"
Well I could have died.
This … eight year old bitch. Coming up with something so … manipulative.

So call me stupid, I gave her twenty bucks. TWENTY BUCKS,
So I felt like a sucker, but.
it proves, that I DO have a conscience.
And that I respect … children.
I respected Omar Khadr. I CARED about Omar Khadr. I felt TERRIBLE when he started
Crying. And rocking. And saying that …
"Kill ME Kill ME Kill ME" … with the accent on the ME, you know?
That was … odd.
that was very … I mean some people said he was saying Ummi, which means Mommy in Arabic but I know he was saying KILL ME; he was being a Drama Queen, right? And he kept on saying it, and rocking and …
They gave us assurances. That …
even though they don't have to abide by the Geneva Convention? They were, basically abiding by the Geneva Convention … basically …
Okay. Ever since that final handshake with Omar, and I DID shake the kid's hand, I DID … my fingers … are … I have been biting again I have been biting in my sleep even, I hardly have friggin nails anymore.
"I have to follow my heart – because if I don't …"
that is very … you know I think he …

Maybe his dreams are good, you know? Maybe he's happy for eight hours every night, dreaming he's back home playing video games with his friends, goin' to movies, eating hot dogs

My fingers ache. They really fucking ache and … And so I bite them.

And for a minute?

Bliss.

But then? You know what happens then.

Hoping for Omar Khadr

MARINA NEMAT

I was arrested at home in Tehran at about nine o'clock at night on 15 January 1982, at the age of sixteen. I had attended protest rallies and written articles against the Iranian revolutionary government, which had come into power in 1979. My imprisonment lasted two years, two months, and twelve days. During that time, my mother and father suffered a great deal. They knew that political prisoners were tortured in Evin. They had heard about the rape of young girls and daily mass executions. Every day they waited for the phone call that would tell them to go to the prison gates to collect my belongings because I had been executed.

I was interrogated a few hours after my arrival in Evin. My interrogators, two men, were not satisfied with the answers I gave them, so they took me to a small room, tied me to a bare wooden bed, and lashed the soles of my feet.

Many of my friends did not survive the prison.

I have given many talks in high schools, and I sometimes speak to students about the Holocaust, a well-documented example of how countries can go completely mad. I sometimes read short passages from books about the Holocaust, including *Fatelessness* by Imre Kertesz. I love speaking to young people. They are open minded and inquisitive and ask unfiltered questions. At different schools, students have asked me exactly the same thing: "But, Miss, how is it possible that the police go to your neighbours' house, people you have been friends with forever, and take them away to kill them? How is it possible not to protest something like that and not do anything about it? How can it happen?"

I have told these young people that if I had not lived through the Iranian revolution, I would not have had an answer for them. "In history," I have explained, "horror doesn't usually happen overnight, but it unfolds little by little. We see danger signs popping up around us, but because we notice only one sign here and one there, we dismiss them as insignificant, and by the time we realize that something terrible has happened, it's too late. If we speak out at this point, we will be arrested, tortured, even killed. To give your life for your friend or neighbour is noble, but it's not easy, and even though a few people are willing to risk their lives for others, the majority of us usually remain silent."

After 9/11, I watched danger signs appear in Canada and the United States. The invasion of Iraq based on lies and deceit was the biggest of them, and of course there was the deportation of suspect Muslims, including Maher Arar, to countries like Syria and Egypt to be interrogated under torture. Arar would later protest and win a settlement from the Canadian government for this injustice. Paranoia and fear took over the world and caused people and governments to react to the situation instead of responding to it in a logical and lawful manner. The Guantánamo Bay detainment camp emblemizes that fear. And I find it terribly disturbing that, in many ways, Guantánamo is very much like Evin: a black hole into which people disappear, many without real evidence against them; a place where there is no access to due process, and prisoners can be terribly mistreated and humiliated and kept indefinitely for reasons that supposedly have to do with national security. The government of Iran imprisoned me because it believed I was a danger to Iran's national security. I was sixteen, but this didn't make any difference to Iranian officials.

As I write these lines, a young Canadian, Omar Khadr, languishes in the Guantánamo Bay prison camp. His trial, which unfortunately was not a real trial but a military tribunal, began after more than eight years of his imprisonment. He was shot and captured in Afghanistan at the age of fifteen. For three months he was held at the US prison in Bagram. Sedated and shackled, he was taken to his first interrogation hours after being discharged from a military hospital. International law tells us that because he was a child soldier, he should not be prosecuted but that every effort should be made to rehabilitate him. Omar needed help and compassion, not intimidation and punishment. He was in Afghanistan because his family had taken him there, where, it was alleged that he had killed an American medic, Sgt 1st Class Christopher Speer. In Guantánamo Bay prison camp, 25 October 2010, twenty-four-year-old Khadr, after eight years of denying he had killed anyone, pleaded guilty to five war crimes: attempted murder, spying, conspiracy, providing material support to terrorism, and murder for the fatal wounding of Sgt 1st Class Christopher Speer. Omar Khadr is the only person convicted of the murder of a US service member in Iraq or Afghanistan, even though about five thousand US service members have been killed in those counties. Also, Omar is the only Guantánamo detainee convicted of murder, and his case is the first war crimes prosecution of a juvenile since World War II.

Omar Khadr's confession allowed him to enter a plea bargain that would limit his sentence to another eight years in prison with the possibility of spending most of it in Canada after one more year in Guantánamo Bay. After torture and then spending a few months in Evin prison, I signed all the papers my interrogators told me to sign without even bothering to read them. I just wanted to go home. I can only imagine how Omar felt after eight years in Guantánamo with no hope of release, so I was not surprised at all to hear that he had confessed. Injustice is injustice, no matter if it is committed in the East or the West. The Canadian government refused to ask that Omar be returned to this country, even though he is a Canadian citizen. To me, this is a disgrace. Although he was a juvenile, Omar was subjected to unlawful interrogation techniques and was coerced into making confessions that could be used against him in court. Since 2000, both Canada and the United State have provided a great deal of aid for rehabilitating former child soldiers and have advocated for the elimination of the use of children in armed conflicts. Thousands of former child soldiers in Africa, many of whom have killed innocents, have benefited from these efforts and have never been put on trial – so why has Omar been treated the way he has?

In history, all horrors and massive disregards for human rights have occurred when societies have been divided into "us" and "them" and have been consumed by hatred. Democracy and human rights are for all, or they lose their meaning. The rule of law is supposed to protect all Canadians, and once it serves only specific groups, it begins to die. Our disregard for our own laws puts us on a slippery slope that can lead only to the destruction of our way of life and values.

In August 2010, Amnesty International's newly appointed secretary general, Salil Shetty, said that Canada was taking drastically different positions in areas such as torture and death penalty where it had traditionally been progressive. He mentioned that there was a big gap between what Canadians believed Canada did and what the reality was in term of government policy and action. He added that Ottawa's refusal to repatriate Omar Khadr was just one example of the shift in Ottawa's policy.[1]

During the military tribunal of Omar Khadr, members of the prosecution and a few witnesses stated that he was not a victim, when according to international law he is, and we have punished him for the crimes of the adults who put him in a terrible situation. Mahatma Gandhi has said, "Hate the sin, but love the sinner." Child soldiers have mutilated, tortured, and killed thousands of people around the world – and mutilation, torture, and murder are serious crimes. But does this mean that these children deserve our hatred and have to be punished? It seems as if the US and Canadian governments believe that child soldiers have to be dealt with and rehabilitated with sympathy and compassion – as long as they don't kill American citizens. We either imprison child soldiers, all of them regardless of whom they have hurt, and put them on trial, or we don't. It is our duty, not only as Canadians but also as human beings, to make sure that the rule of law is for all. Once we begin to make exceptions, we encourage revenge and reactionary measures instead of justice.

On 25 October 2010, the prosecution's forensic psychiatrist, Michael Welner, presented his argument against Omar Khadr, part of which relied on the research of the Danish psychologist Nicolai Sennels. Sennels has claimed that "massive inbreeding within the Muslim culture during the last 1,400 years may have done catastrophic damage to their gene pool."[2] Sennels has written a book titled *Among Criminal Muslims* and has called the Koran "a criminal book that forces people to do criminal things."[3] My question here is if a similar statement were made against Christians or Jewish people, wouldn't it have been considered hate literature and a racist statement, and wouldn't we have been outraged by it?

On 28 October 2010, Tabitha Speer, the widow of Sgt 1st Class Christopher Speer, testified for fifty-five minutes at Omar Khadr's hearing and brought many spectators to tears as she read letters by her children. Omar had confessed that when he was fifteen he had thrown a grenade that fatally wounded Sgt Speer in a firefight in

Afghanistan. During her testimony Ms Speer described her husband's smile and dedication to his children. Of course this is heartbreaking, and my heart goes out to her. But I can't help but to think of the victims of child soldiers in Africa. Didn't those victims have families? Didn't those victims smile? Didn't they love their children? In some cases, they were children themselves, so didn't they desperately call their parents' names as other children brutally ended their lives? If African child soldiers are not imprisoned, why should Omar Khadr face a military tribunal and spend years in prison? Why do we have such a double standard?

On 28 October 2010, in a courtroom in Guantánamo Bay, Omar took the stand for the first time since he was charged in 2005, and spoke for about five minutes. Since he had been in prison, he said, "I came to the conclusion that ... you're not going to gain anything with hate. Second thing, it's more destructive than it's constructive. Third: I came to the conclusion that love and forgiveness are more constructive and will bring people together."[4] He apologized to Ms Speer for causing her and her family pain. Then Ms Speer told him what she thought of him, that he would forever be a murderer in her eyes, and that it didn't matter what he said from that day on. She also said that she had heard over and over that Omar Khadr was the victim, that he was a child, but she couldn't see that. I wonder if she would have been able to see the child that Omar was if he had been tried within months of his arrest before spending eight years in Guantánamo.

Ms Speer has every right to be full of anger and hatred toward Omar. She is in pain. But I cannot help but see a terrible pattern here: tragedy leading to tragedy, hatred breeding hatred.

During Omar's military tribunal, many individuals gave their opinions about who the "real victim" in this case was, failing to see that this is not an either-or situation. Many of us tend to believe in absolute concepts: for example, that once you are a victim, you are absolutely and forever a victim, which is far from the truth. If a person is a victim today, that does not mean that he or she has never victimized others or never will. Killing is wrong, but so is treating a fifteen-year-old by the same standards we would use to treat adults. Omar deserves a second chance, mainly because he never had a first one, having been taken to Afghanistan at a very young age to be trained as a terrorist.

On Sunday, 31 October 2010, a military jury sentenced Omar to forty years in prison, unaware of the plea deal that had capped his term to one more year in Guantánamo before he could return to Canada. When I heard the news, I knew almost for sure that a civilian jury would have handed him a very different sentence. Let's imagine that a few members of the jury had been Iraqi-Americans or Iraqi-Canadian civilians who had lost family members in the Iraq war. How we see Omar and his case very much depends on our background and how well we understand the Middle East and its bloody conflicts that claim innocent lives on a daily basis, with no end in sight.

The Pentagon prosecutor, Jeffrey Groharing, said in his closing arguments of the Khadr tribunal that the world was watching the jury and their decision; they had to think about more than Omar Khadr's fate and that their verdict would send a message. So I have to ask if Omar was on trial in Guantánamo, or was the tribunal judging all those who have fought US troops in Afghanistan and Iraq? It is unjust to punish one individual to "send a message."

After the forty-year sentence was announced, Ms Speer cheered, pumped her fist in the air, and said that that day was the happiest of her life next to marrying her husband and having her children. I hope she finds peace, but the truth is that peace cannot be found in the midst of hatred and revenge, and I have no doubt that she will discover this sooner or later. There are many around the world who have lost loved ones but have decided to forgive, and, as a result, they have been able to make the world a better place and fight the vicious cycle of hatred that threatens us all.

The practical question now is whether Omar is a danger to society once he is released, probably in a few years. One thing I can say for sure: if, instead of being thrown into a notorious prison, he had received therapy, counselling, and education in a safe and controlled environment for the last eight years, he would now have been much closer to being a functional individual who is not dangerous to anyone. Is he now full of anger and hatred, or does he tell the truth when he says he believes in love and forgiveness? I guess we can't know for sure. I just know that what was done to him in Guantánamo was wrong, and we can't fix it now even if we want to. Many lives have been damaged and can never be the same, but eight years ago we had the opportunity to stop the damage from growing, we had a chance to show mercy to a fifteen-year-old, and we decided not to. Omar's family members who took him to Afghanistan and put him in terrorist camps should have been held accountable. This did not happen.

I hope for Omar Khadr. But hope and optimism are not the same concepts. Optimism ignores obstacles and assumes that all will be well, no matter what. Hope, on the other hand, is aware of the problems and encourages us to fight for what we believe in. Without hope, I would have died in Evin, and without hope, Omar would have died in Guantánamo.

NOTES

1 *Toronto Star*, Tuesday, 24 August 2010.

2 "Soldier Recounts How Khadr Altered His Life," *Toronto Star,* 28 October 2010, A6.

3 Ibid.

4 Michelle Shephard, "I'm Really, Really Sorry for the Pain," *Toronto Star*, 29 October 2010, A1.

Extreme Loneliness

KIM ECHLIN

> If we live long enough, we have to tell, or turn to stone inside. I try to release you from a pit in my heart but unburied and unblessed you imprison me.
>
> *The Disappeared*

We know.

We see. Electronic communications take us inside. We hear. We have photographs and videos from battlegrounds. We see shadowy figures, hear muffled voices from inside jail cells. We watch war on television. Missiles like fireworks in the sky. We watch what happens in interrogation rooms.

Where there are no pictures, we read written accounts. Truth commissions. Journalism. Fiction that tells the truth. We know what is happening in the world.

What do we do once we know?

> O you who believe! You have charge over your own souls.
>
> Koran 5:105

> The truth will set you free.
>
> John 8:32

Our oldest stories ask us to think about truth. Sophocles' *Oedipus Rex* tells the story of King Oedipus who discovers that the scourge in his kingdom can only be undone when a hidden truth is revealed. Oedipus pursues the truth and learns that he has unwittingly killed his father and married his mother. He discovers that *he* is the reason for his own kingdom's plight. When he uncovers this dread truth, he puts out his eyes and exiles himself.

We can admit the possibility that we sometimes do not know. Many people "did not know" about the concentration camps. Well-intentioned communists "did not know" about the Russian gulags. During the campaign of terror in Chile, people "did not know" what was happening to the disappeared. People "did not know" about the genocide inside the closed borders of Cambodia. How many places today don't we know about? When we finally figure things out – as Oedipus did – how can we stand the sight of what we have done?

Truth commissions and transcripts from international tribunals introduce us to investigators and witnesses who talk about "not knowing," to an international community that has "turned away." They often describe the events they record as *unspeakable* and *unbelievable*. But the very purpose of their work is to document and to accuse, to speak and to make believable.

To claim the past is to keep trust with those who will follow. As we work beyond borders and boundaries, we struggle with our capacity to do so. We try to articulate root principles that will allow us to sift through cultural difference and support each other. The best English phrase I can find is "shared humanity." Other languages do it better. In Cree, *witaskewin* means "how people, not necessarily coming out of the same nation, can live together." In Nguni, *ubuntu* describes human interconnectedness. Desmond Tutu, Anglican archbishop and chair of South Africa's Truth and Reconciliation Commission, explains *ubuntu* this way: "My humanity is caught up and inextricably bound up in yours ... [Those with *ubuntu*] know that they are diminished when others are humiliated, diminished when others are oppressed, diminished when others are treated as if they were less than who they are."

People who work in the aftermath of trauma invoke these concepts – shared humanity, *witaskewin, ubuntu*. Senator Roméo Dallaire wrote after witnessing the Rwanda genocide that we must "rise above race, creed, colour, religions and national self-interest and put the good of humanity above the good of our own tribe." Cleo Koff, a forensic anthropologist who has worked on massacre site exhumations, writes, "I was noticing that when I was talking about Kosovo, I was talking about Rwanda, and when I was talking about the dead, I was also talking about the living, and when I was talking about me, I was talking about the people in that room. The connections and similarities – and what was revealed by their differences – almost overwhelmed me."

I am not a religious leader or a soldier or a forensic anthropologist. I am a citizen who sees what anyone can see on television and computers, who reads the newspapers and sometimes suffers from the feeling that "humankind cannot bear too much reality." How am I to think about what I see? How am I not to turn away?

Omar Khadr is a Canadian citizen. He was fifteen when he was arrested after a battle in Afghanistan and transported to a "secret" prison in Guantánamo. During the battle he lost the vision in one eye, was shot twice in the back. He lived the remainder of his adolescence in a prison in Guantánamo with adult prisoners. He has been repeatedly interrogated. He has been tried and convicted, as an adult, for the murder of Christopher Speer in Afghanistan. The Rome Statue (entered in 2002) of the ICC states that *conscripting or enlisting a person under age 15 is a war crime.* Omar Khadr has lived since childhood with those who have practiced terrorism. No one has protected him. Christopher Speer's children have lost their father.

How can we stand the sight of what we've done?

People from many parts of the world live in my city. Most of the time, people do not tell their hard stories. They are trying to get on with their lives. Soldiers live among us, men and women who have served in Bosnia, Rwanda, Afghanistan. What do we know of their stories? What do we really know? A Cambodian woman runs a nail salon at the top of my street. She escaped in 1978 during the Pol Pot revolution. What do I know of her story? What do I really know? A former political prisoner from Asia runs a variety store a few streets away. He has no fingernails on his right hand. But what do I know of his story? What do I really know? I think of Virginia Woolf's novel, *Mrs Dalloway*, which describes a woman preparing a party while a shell-shocked soldier walks the streets of London among people who either do not see him or do not understand who they see.

No writer has taught me about my neighbours more eloquently than Jean Améry, who survived torture and incarceration during World War II. In *At the Mind's Limits,* he writes about the ongoing effects of trauma and torture. He reminds us that these ongoing effects belong to all of us.

He asks us first to understand that whoever has succumbed to torture can "no longer feel at home in the world." With the first blow, he writes, "trust in the world breaks down." The torture victim understands that no help is coming. And hope for help, writes Améry, is fundamental to humans, "as much a constitutional psychic element as is the struggle for existence."

Améry's view of his fellow man has been forever altered. He says that torture blocks a view of the world in which hope rules. Torture has taught him that a person can be transformed thoroughly into flesh – and that person's soul and autonomy, dignity and hope are destroyed.

Améry writes that the idea of "healing with time" is rooted in a metaphor drawn from the process of physical wounds. But it is not his psychological experience that the psychic wounds of trauma heal with time. He writes that he cannot forgive and forget. He calls social pressure to induce his forgiveness and forgetting "*anti*moral." He says he forgets nothing, and he names those who shared a last cigarette, who gave him bread, who listened to his fears, as well as those who tortured him. Time has been irreparably altered by torture, and "ordinary" chronological time is lost. Background and foreground merge, moments recur. His survivor's mind is marked by having lived "through death." He carries death inside forever: "Twenty-two years later, I am still dangling over the ground by dislocated arms."

Améry's writing is difficult to bear. It slashes its way toward truth.

It resists answers.

It resists forgetting.

It asks us to listen.

To act on international conventions meant to protect *all* of us asks us to imagine our own darkness. We must imagine being the one who throws the grenade. We must imagine being the perpetrator. We must imagine resistance to forgiveness. We must not forget and turn away. We must figure out ways to reason through insoluble problems. What do we do with a citizen who was raised in violence, who was convicted by a foreign military court for an action he committed as a child? Can we imagine a world in which we do not shave ourselves off from empathy? Can we imagine a world in which *every individual* matters?

Améry asks this: "We request of those whose peace is disturbed by our grudge that they be patient." He tells us that his experience of trauma separates him from us. He is lonely, and he also tells us that whatever we can say will not help. In concord with so many survivors of trauma, he speaks of his experience as "that of an extreme *loneliness*."

I sense this kind of loneliness in the story of Omar Khadr.

REFERENCES

Améry, Jean. *At the Mind's Limits: Contemplations by a Survivor on Auschwitz and Its Realities*. Trans. Sidney Rosenfeld and Stella P. Rosenfeld. Bloomington: Indiana University Press 1980.

Dallaire, Roméo. *Shake Hands with the Devil: The Failure of Humanity in Rwanda*. Toronto: Vintage Canada 2004.

Echlin, Kim. *The Disappeared*. Toronto: Hamish Hamilton, Canada 2009.

Eliot, T.S. *Four Quartets*. London: Faber & Faber 1959.

Koff, Clea. *The Bone Woman: A Forensic Anthropologist's Search for Truth in Rwanda, Bosnia, Croatia, and Kosovo*. Toronto: Vintage Canada 2005.

Tutu, Desmond. *No Future without Forgiveness*. New York: Doubleday 1999.

PART THREE

The Case of Omar Khadr

War Stories: A Reflection on Defending an Alleged Enemy Combatant Detained in Guantánamo Bay, Cuba

RICHARD J. WILSON

For nearly three years following July 2004, it was my privilege to represent one of the more than five hundred detainees then held at Guantánamo Bay, Cuba. I was one of several hundred volunteer lawyers who undertook to provide legal representation to detainees, named and unnamed, designated as "enemy combatants" and held in Cuba by the US military. The longest detentions then approached four years, and only four detainees currently faced formal criminal charges through suspect military commissions.

This essay presents my personal observations as of November 2005 on the general legal situation of the detainees, the situation of my client in particular, and my own perspectives more than a year into the litigation. My reflections are ongoing and incomplete because the litigation surrounding the detainees continues. (Some legal issues remain, even in 2012, as this article is reprinted.) Moreover, I now have a US government security clearance, necessitated when I undertook the representation, which permits me to see materials designated at the level of "secret" for national security purposes. Thus, the reflection also is necessarily incomplete because of the imposition of a protective order barring counsel for the detainees from disclosure of "secret" material provided to counsel by the government, or indeed, any aspect of their representation of a detainee that has not been reviewed and unclassified by a review team of government officials.

In addition to the plethora of literature on the legitimacy of actions by the US government in its detention policies in Guantánamo, many other lawyers involved in the litigation have written about the experience of litigating these cases as they are developing in the US courts. I approach this topic by addressing five questions. First, what is Guantánamo Bay, and what is its historic role in the implementation of US foreign policy through massive detentions? Second, who is our client, how did he end up at Guantánamo Bay, and what have been the major issues he has faced since his arrival there? Third, what law applies to the detainees, and why? Fourth, what are the legal issues presented before the US and other courts regarding the detainees in general, and our client specifically? Finally, what would be the ideal desired outcome of the litigation on behalf of the detainees in general, and Omar Khadr in particular? Let me now address each of those questions in succession.

WHAT IS GUANTÁNAMO BAY?

The United States Supreme Court, in *Rasul v. Bush*, one of a landmark trio of decisions holding that the US courts have jurisdiction to hear claims by individuals designated as enemy combatants, gives a good historical description of the military base at Guantánamo Bay:

> The United States occupies the Base, which comprises 45 square miles of land and water along the southeast coast of Cuba, pursuant to a 1903 Lease Agreement executed with the newly independent Republic of Cuba in the aftermath of the Spanish-American War. Under the Agreement, "the United States recognizes the continuance of the ultimate sovereignty of the Republic of Cuba over the [leased areas]," while "the Republic of Cuba consents that during the period of the occupation by the United States ... the United States shall exercise complete jurisdiction and control over and within said areas." In 1934, the parties entered into a treaty providing that, absent an agreement to modify or abrogate the lease, the lease would remain in effect "[s]o long as the United States of America shall not abandon the ... naval station of Guantánamo."[1]

The base was operated by a joint military command after the September 11 attacks, but is now back under the traditional control of the US Navy. Importantly, the court later said of the base, "By the express terms of its agreements with Cuba, the United States exercises 'complete jurisdiction and control' over the Guantánamo Bay Naval Base, and may continue to exercise such control permanently if it so chooses."[2] The extent of US control over the base was crucial to the court's later analysis about jurisdiction to hear petitions for habeas corpus filed by the detainees in the federal district court of Washington, DC. In effect, the court concluded that Guantánamo Bay is like any state in the United States for purposes of habeas jurisdiction.

During the early 1990s, the base also was used by the US government as an offshore detention facility for hundreds of Haitian "boat people" interdicted on the high seas by the US Coast Guard. The facility, seen to be beyond the reach of the US courts, guaranteed that the Haitians could not enter the US while it purported to protect them from return to Haiti. Litigation on their behalf went to the US Supreme Court, where the Haitians lost.[3] However, litigation and political activism on behalf of Haitian detainees with AIDS was eventually successful, the camp was closed, and the detainees were released.[4]

The new detention facility for enemy aliens began as Camp X-Ray when it was first opened in early 2002. The island of Cuba was picked after the military order of President Bush of November 2001 designated a process for the detention and trial of persons captured on the battlefield in Afghanistan. These new detainees could include anyone who "is or was a member of the organization known as al Qaeda" as well as anyone who "engaged in, aided or abetted, or conspired to commit, acts of international terrorism" or anyone who "knowingly harbored" such individuals.[5] The trials called for under the order were to be conducted by military commissions designed and implemented by the Department of Defense and without review in the civilian courts, with sentencing powers permitting the penalty of death. The camp at Guantánamo was later expanded and renamed Camp Delta. Since then, various facilities have developed in the area of the base known locally as "The Wire." They range from the minimum-security Camp 4, with open dorms for sleeping, to what the military calls a "state-of-the-art" maximum security prison at Camp 5.[6]

The military ultimately released the names or nationalities of detainees behind The Wire. At its peak, the camp held more than seven hundred persons.[7] As of the transfer out of Guantánamo in late August 2005, there were "approximately" 505 detainees, with

242 detainees reportedly having been transferred out of the facility.[8] In fact, in addition to detainees captured in Afghanistan, the facility holds prisoners seized in locations as diverse as Bosnia and Africa, with some forty nations represented among the detainee population. Numbers, names, and nationalities were released only after litigation under freedom of information laws.[9] In 2005, there were more than four hundred lawyers involved in the representation of detainees in federal habeas corpus, coordinated through the Center for Constitutional Rights in New York City. Still, a significant number of detainees have appeared in court under a general "John Doe" habeas petition on behalf of those whose identities were not known or who had not been formally contacted, nearly four years after the facility was first opened.[10] Although the government continues to deny or downplay accounts of severe mistreatment at Guantánamo, the evidence continues to mount. Nearly two dozen detainees have seriously attempted suicide at Guantánamo since it opened.[11]

Symbolically, the camp at Guantánamo is seen by many Americans as an offshore super-max prison that demonstrates the Bush administration's tough policy on dangerous terrorists. Others see it as a prisoner of war camp that keeps the detainees from returning to battle. Still others, in growing numbers, see the ongoing legal battle on the status and treatment of the detainees there as a series of jury-rigged justifications for exceptionalism that could have been avoided if the White House had simply followed the advice of military lawyers and used long-established procedures for the designation of combatant or civilian status, and for the interrogation and trial of detainee for serious war crimes under standard US military law. The facility can also be seen as a cynical distraction from the darker evils committed by the US military, which unquestionably has untold numbers of secret detentions at clandestine locations around the world or even at sea in moving prison ships.[12] For many outside of the United States, the facility is seen as an icon of American hubris, at the least an excellent recruiting tool for terrorists seeking to foment hatred of the United States, and at worst a justification for outlaw states to take similar action against captured US soldiers on some future occasion.

Whatever else it may be, the facility was designed and the policies there were implemented with three goals in mind. First, Camp Delta was set up to carry out the president's order to conduct war crimes trials before special military commissions. That goal has been frustrated to such an extent that only two military commission trials of detainees had begun in 2005, and those were suspended almost immediately, as is discussed below. Second, the facility was designed to provide a location for unmonitored interrogation of the detainees, purportedly to provide intelligence to fight the global war on terrorism.[13] However, aggressive interrogation of detainees such as that justified by White House and Justice Department lawyers clearly could not be conducted if they were entitled to prisoner of war status. So the administration's lawyers devised a third goal: the designation as "enemy combatant" of prisoners. As such, they would not be entitled to prisoner of war status and so could be endlessly interrogated. The detainees, so went the policy, would nonetheless be treated humanely, except when inconsistent with "military necessity." They could thus be kept from returning to battle or being freed, much as the law of armed conflict justifies the holding of prisoners of war, but only as the president saw fit, in his unilateral and exclusive discretion.[14] The last two policies have proved to be perversely tenacious, despite the best efforts of our large group of lawyers to seek the intervention of the courts on behalf of the detainees. [15]

WHO IS OUR CLIENT?

Our client's name is Omar Khadr. He is a Canadian citizen, the only person from that country known to be detained now at Guantánamo Bay. He was fifteen years old at the time of his capture near Khost, in Afghanistan, on 27 July 2002. In late October of that same year, after being held initially at Bagram Air Force Base outside of Kabul, he was transferred to Cuba. He has been there ever since, for nearly three years as of this writing. I've been to Guantánamo numerous times to visit with him.

Like virtually all of the other lawyers in the Guantánamo habeas corpus litigation, I am a volunteer, but I am not working alone. Within the law school at American University, another professor and I have been counsel for Omar from the moment the *Rasul* case was remanded by the Supreme Court to the local federal district court in Washington, DC, in July 2004. In addition, students enrolled in the law school's International Human Rights Law Clinic have worked on important aspects of the case from the beginning.

The clinic has, since 1990, provided legal services to clients seeking protection from human rights violations anywhere in the world. Our work has involved litigation in both domestic and international legal fora, as well as other projects for individual and group clients seeking human rights protection under international and domestic law.[16] In addition, we were joined by dozens of lawyers who also volunteered their time, coordinated through the efforts of the Center for Constitutional Rights in New York City.[17] That group of lawyers has grown to over four hundred, including private practitioners from small and large firms and a few academics like me. Some of our cases were consolidated for action, as will be discussed below, and our broader strategies have been discussed and coordinated through an email list and website devoted to our work. Finally, from the time that the Khadr family, now living in Toronto, discovered that Omar was in detention, they have retained the services of a law firm in Edmonton, Alberta. That firm has had signal success in protecting Omar's rights in the Canadian legal system. For example, in August 2005, a federal judge there ruled that Canadian authorities are prohibited, under the Canadian Charter of Rights and Freedoms, from conducting any interviews or questioning of Omar pending further consideration of the issue in Canada.[18]

Omar is distinguished by two crucial factors. First, his family is highly visible and controversial in Canada. They are not seen as sympathetic by the public and press,[19] and the presumptive prejudice against him and his family plays out strongly in the accusations against and custodial treatment of Omar. He and his family left Kabul, the capital of Afghanistan, shortly before the US invasion of that country in October 2001. On the road toward Pakistan, the family separated, and Omar was sent away alone. The Combat Status Review Board, discussed below, alleges that Omar later threw a grenade that killed an American soldier during the confrontation in which he was captured in July of 2002. He is also accused of being an "Al Qaeda fighter" alleged to have conducted certain activities on behalf of that group.[20] Omar was seriously wounded during his capture, shot three times in the back at close range, and lost the sight in his left eye from shrapnel fragments spread during a prolonged aerial assault. The press in Canada has published dozens of versions of the account of his capture – except for his own.

Second, Omar was a boy of fifteen, alone and isolated from his family at the time of his capture. When he arrived at Guantánamo, he had passed his sixteenth birthday, a factor that seems to have resulted in his treatment, along with other youngsters, as an adult. Omar is not the only detainee who was a juvenile at the time US authorities took custody of him. The information about other juvenile detainees at Guantánamo and throughout the war on terror is scant but deeply disturbing. In April 2003, after persistent press inquiries, the government admitted publicly that they were detaining children at Guantánamo. Those identified included children who were ten, twelve, and thirteen at the time of their capture. The military justified their detention by calling them "very, very dangerous people ... [T]hey may be juveniles but they're not on a little league team anywhere. They're on a major league team and it's a terrorism team." Dangerous as they may have been, these children were moved immediately into a separate facility, Camp Iguana, and treated much better than other detainees. All were released by January 2004.[21] A few juveniles between sixteen and seventeen years old at the time of their capture were never afforded treatment as children and were kept with adults without any formal legal justification. A letter sent by the government on 2 September 2004, during informal discussions with a judge hearing consolidated issues, indicates that as of that date, "no detainees known to be younger than age 16 are detained at Guantánamo Bay." It said that the government's policy was to provide special treatment of detainees under the age of sixteen at the time of their arrival, but the letter failed to note that detainees sixteen and up are treated as adults for purposes of status and treatment, particularly for interrogation.[22]

The government, through its actions, thus has recognized that children are entitled to treatment as specially protected persons when captured during armed conflict. Government actions in the transfer of some minors into Camp Iguana, where they were given special meals, education, and other benefits, and ultimately released to return to their families, were consistent with the requirements of international law.[23] Yet Omar, as well as a few other juveniles brought to the base after age sixteen, have been treated as adults at all times, without any formal justification of this legal step by the government.

WHAT LAW APPLIES TO THE DETAINEES IN GENERAL, AND TO OMAR IN PARTICULAR?

From the beginning, the goal of the Bush administration was to craft a policy with regard to captured enemy combatants that would allow the maximum flexibility to hold and interrogate them indefinitely. White House and Justice Department lawyers sought not only to prevent oversight or intervention by the US courts but to assure that no legal accountability would accrue to the actors controlling the detainees. As noted previously, for example, the initial order for capture and detention denied review of decisions by military commissions in the civilian legal system. The order also conspicuously failed to mention domestic or international protections accorded to prisoners of war, although the protections of the Geneva Conventions have generally been accepted and incorporated into procedures of domestic courts martial, the venue for military trials. Moreover, the presidential order explicitly stated that these detainees would not be treated as criminal accused entitled to constitutional protections in the United States, because it was "not practicable" to do so.[24]

The Defense Department obviously believed that by holding the captured detainees at Guantánamo Bay, it would avoid the application of US law through its interpretation of the doctrines of extraterritoriality and offshore detention. Moreover, memoranda written by Executive Branch lawyers during early 2002, and consistently endorsed for the president by then White House counsel Alberto Gonzalez, make clear that he and the highest ranking lawyers in the administration believed (accurately) that the detainees would not be susceptible to aggressive interrogation if protected by the Geneva Conventions as prisoners of war, but incorrectly concluded that such status could be denied them. Finally, and most outrageously, these same lawyers attempted to redefine torture in such a way as to permit the most heinous mistreatment of the detainees whenever military interrogators believed it to be necessary. The infamous "Bybee Memo" of 1 August 2002 attempted to redefine torture as "intense pain or suffering of the kind that is equivalent to the pain that would be associated with serious physical injury so severe that death, organ failure, or permanent damage resulting in a loss of significant body function will likely result."[25] A working group within the Department of the Air Force, set up in 2003 to review the legal issues involved in detainee interrogations, found in the most euphemistic of conclusions that extreme definitions of torture, if applied to interrogation techniques, "could have a negative impact on public perception of the U.S. military in general."[26]

Despite their later recasting of policy, then, the government's position was and is that it can hold enemy combatants outside of US territorial jurisdiction until the end of the "War on Terror" – that is, indefinitely – with limitless authority to interrogate them as necessary, just short of torture, because the detainees lack formal protection as prisoners of war and have no right to access to the courts of the United States for review of their status or the legality of their detention. Those of us challenging that policy have relied on an array of domestic and international norms. Our petition for habeas corpus review in Omar's case, for example, includes comprehensive domestic constitutional and statutory claims, including the Alien Tort Claims Act[27] as well as violations of customary international law. It refers to human rights treaties ratified by the United States including the following: the Geneva Conventions, the International Covenant on Civil and Political Rights, the Optional Protocol to the Convention on the Rights of the Child on the Involvement of Children in Armed Conflict ("Protocol on Child Soldiers"), and International Labour Organization Convention 182 concerning the Prohibition and Immediate Action for the Elimination of the Worst Forms of Child Labour ("ILO Convention 182").[28] However, the federal courts have been remarkably loath to apply treaties or international customary law as sources of individual rights in the absence of explicit implementing legislation from Congress. With the few exceptions noted below, the courts have relied almost exclusively on domestic sources as authority for protection of the rights of the detainees, in those limited circumstances in which they have elected to intervene.

We believe that the governments of both the United States and Canada have abdicated their responsibility to Omar Khadr as a child in military detention. Omar was detained at the age of fifteen and brutally mistreated immediately after his capture, as we note below. The government argues only that he has passed the age of majority while in detention, having celebrated his nineteenth birthday in September 2005, and that issues regarding his status as a juvenile have been rendered moot by that passage. While the government asserts, without any source to support its claim, that enemy detainees over sixteen years of age are treated as adults at Guantánamo, it has recognized that juvenile detainees have a right to be separated from the adult population, to be educated and otherwise protected and nurtured as children, and ultimately to be reunited with their families. The Canadian government, rather than protecting a juvenile citizen through the most minimal commitment to a consular visit permitted its citizens by international law, instead chose to send interrogators to Guantánamo to obtain its own intelligence, which was subsequently shared with American authorities. Whatever treatment may have been justified in the case of other child detainees, the treatment of Omar Khadr by his own government and by ours has been shameful.

The first body to review the legality of the actions of the US government in the treatment of detainees at Guantánamo Bay was not a US court but the Inter-American Commission on Human Rights, an organ of the Organization of American States. I was one of several lawyers who sought review by the commission in early 2002, in response to which it subsequently issued a request for precautionary measures to the United States asking the government to "take the urgent measures necessary to have the legal status of the detainees at Guantánamo Bay determined by a competent tribunal."[29] As has been its practice, the United States rejected both the jurisdiction of the commission over the US government and its ability to apply international humanitarian law.[30] Then in June 2004, as noted above, the US Supreme Court ultimately held, in *Rasul v. Bush*, that the federal courts of the United States have "jurisdiction to hear petitioners' habeas corpus challenges to the legality of their detention at the Guantánamo Bay Naval Base."[31] The cases regarding legality of detention were remanded to the federal district court in Washington, DC, where they continue to be litigated, one by one.

As for the conduct of criminal trials before military commissions, the purpose for which the detention facility was originally designed, the government provided the first non-exclusive list of offences setting out the commissions' jurisdiction a full year and a half after the first captives arrived at Guantánamo.[32] Then, in November 2004, a federal judge in Washington ordered a halt to one of the two military commission trials that had only recently begun at Guantánamo, finding violations of both the Geneva Conventions and domestic military law of the United States.[33] That decision was overturned in July 2005 by the US Court of Appeals for the District of Columbia, and a petition for review by the US Supreme Court was pending action at the time of this writing.[34] The Department of Defense announced its intention to resume military commission trials under newly amended instructions.[35]

WHAT IS THE PRESENT LEGAL SITUATION OF THE DETAINEES GENERALLY, AND OMAR KHADR SPECIFICALLY?

Remarkably, after more than a year of aggressive litigation on behalf of the detainees in domestic and international tribunals, little had changed on the ground in the treatment or release of detainees. While the government loudly touted the number of releases from Guantánamo – more than two hundred by 2005 – those releases occurred largely in cases where the detainee's name was unknown before release, and where he was not represented by counsel. Nonetheless, more than five hundred detainees remained in the camp, about half of whose identities were still unknown after more than three years of detention. In addition to the limitations on identity of detainees, counsel for detainees whose identities are known work under a series of national security limitations imposed by law and court order relating to access to and communication with clients. These limitations make active and open communication with clients nearly impossible.

The most immediate issue facing new counsel in the habeas litigation was the governmental and judicial concern with national security. Immediately upon entering an appearance as counsel, I was required to seek and obtain an FBI security clearance at the level of access to "secret" information. Access to classified information in the case is governed by federal law under Executive Order 12958, adopted in 1995. That order limits access to classified information to lawyers who are US citizens with appropriate security clearances. The government immediately sought consolidation of all of the cases then pending in the Washington, DC, court, which it obtained. Government lawyers then sought and obtained a protective order covering all cases.[36] That protective order imposed security processes that made communication and access to clients in Guantánamo incredibly burdensome.

First, all documents relating to the litigation are presumed to be classified, including all attorney-client communications. Documents that were not unclassified are kept in a secure facility on the outskirts of Washington, where lawyers have to travel if they wish to examine or review them. Second, incoming correspondence from detainee clients is considered classified, and all attorney-client correspondence is subject to screening for contraband. All such correspondence must pass through a court security office and is deposited in the secure facility after review. If the information is to be made public, review must be sought by an independent, government-named "privilege team" that makes decisions as to the level of public release. Mail between the secure facility and Guantánamo Bay takes an average of one month in each direction, and phone access has been granted in only the most extraordinary circumstances. All other incoming mail to the detainees, including family correspondence, Canadian attorney mail, and magazines, goes through a complex and time-consuming review process separate from that by which attorney-client correspondence is handled. Neither Omar's family nor any of his lawyers had communicated with him by phone by 2005; he had only three visits from us in a year following our appearance in the proceedings because of the costs of travel and difficulties of clearance to travel to the base. While base authorities are not to interfere with attorney-client mail clearly so marked except to review for contraband, some enclosures, including court papers, have not reached Omar.

Visits to clients at the base are also burdened with extraordinary precautions. Counsel must first obtain permission from the Pentagon to travel to the base and must receive theatre clearance orders in order to be able to board private planes flying to Guantánamo from Ft Lauderdale, Florida. Upon arrival, counsel are met by a military escort who accompanies them at all times. Counsel are housed on the leeward side of the island in a small hotel with few amenities and very limited access to telephones, Internet, or email. The trip to Camp Delta begins early with a bus ride to a ferry that transports counsel across the bay to the windward side where the detention camps are. All travel around the facilities must be in the company of the escort. Counsel have access to two public phones at a small shopping mall during lunch breaks or in the late afternoon. After extended screening and security clearances, interviews with clients are conducted inside a secure building at one of the camps, with only the client and counsel present, but with visual monitoring from a central command post. Clients are shackled to the floor and visiting times are limited. After each interview session, the escort takes the written notes produced by counsel during interviews and places them in a secure pouch. At the end of the visit, the notes are sealed and mailed from the base to the secure facility in Washington, again taking about a month on average to arrive. Counsel are not allowed to discuss particular aspects of client detention, such as their location, without prior clearance.

Even before the entry of a protective order in our collected cases, we decided to take immediate steps to protect the health and safety of our young client. We had received reliable reports that Omar had suffered physical and psychological injuries and trauma during his detention, first at Bagram in Afghanistan and later at Guantánamo. On 10 August 2004, we filed an emergency motion with our individual judge, seeking access to full medical records and to an outside physician to examine Omar to assure his competency to engage with us and the legal proceedings on which he was about to embark. We relied on the only available public information on the treatment of detainees, including reports by other detainees of Omar's mistreatment and expert affidavits noting the need for independent medical review. After full briefing of these emergency matters, the judge held the motion for two months without having heard oral argument on the issues, despite our requests to do so. The judge denied our request, holding that we had "failed to produce evidence that calls into question petitioner's mental competency such that the relief sought would be appropriate."[37]

The more central question presented in the consolidated cases was the government's bold assertion that despite the Supreme Court's ruling, the detainees were not entitled to constitutional protection in the US courts. Their arguments echoed much of what detainee counsel felt had been settled definitively in the *Rasul* litigation, but the judges seemed more than willing to indulge the government's arguments. After extensive informal discussion, followed by briefing and argument of the issues by all parties, two federal district court judges reached opposite conclusions as to detainee rights. First, Judge Richard Leon decided that procedures implemented by the government in the immediate wake of the *Rasul* decision were sufficient to provide the detainees with protection of their rights.[38] These mechanisms included a hastily created structure the Defense Department called Combat Status Review Tribunals (CSRTs), which were created just weeks after the *Rasul* decision. Despite their extremely curtailed processes, and the fact that all but a small number of the CSRT proceedings concluded that the detainees were enemy combatants,

Judge Leon held that there was no viable theory on which he could award relief through habeas corpus.

Two weeks later, Judge Joyce Hens Green, who handled a group of eleven consolidated cases in which Omar's was included, reached the opposite conclusion.[39] Judge Green condemned the overbroad definition of "enemy combatant" and found the CSRTs to deny due process. After a long discussion, largely of territorial jurisdiction, she concluded that the detainees had due process rights under the US Constitution and that the habeas claims could proceed. Her bold favourable decision was seen as the first significant vindication of the detainees' concerns, but there is a distressing downside to her decision. In a few short paragraphs, the judge dismissed most of the petitioners' international law claims,[40] as well as their allegations of violation of the Alien Tort Claims Act,[41] which permits a foreign national to bring suit in the US courts for torts committed in violation of the "law of nations." She did rule that most detainees were entitled to the protections of the Third Geneva Convention, save those "detained on the ground that they are members of [al-Qaeda, who] are not entitled to the protections of the treaties" because, she reasoned, a terrorist organization cannot be a state party to the Geneva Conventions. She also refused to dismiss the claims of Taliban prisoners who had not properly been determined to be prisoners of war by a competent tribunal, under Article 5 of the Third Geneva Convention. Finally, she found it unnecessary to address customary international law claims because she had already found protection for the detainees under domestic law.[42] Also of deep concern to petitioners' counsel was Judge Green's imposition of a stay, immediately following her favourable ruling, on all district court cases covered by her decision, pending appeal by the government. This meant that the detainees' ongoing concerns about conditions and access were presumptively barred until the appellate process ended, a prospect of long months of waiting for implementation of her favourable decision.[43]

The decisions by Judges Leon and Green were consolidated for review before the federal appellate court in Washington, the US Court of Appeals for the District of Columbia. Briefing and argument of the cases was completed in early September 2005, and the case was then under advisement before the court, with an opinion expected in a month or more. Depending on the decision, review would undoubtedly be sought before the United States Supreme

Court again, which could further delay consideration of the detainees' substantive claims in actual hearings.

One additional development in the Khadr litigation deserves mention. During the winter of 2004–05, because of revelations made to us during visits with Omar that were consistent with those made by other detainees and lawyers seeking open information on Guantánamo, we filed a petition seeking to enjoin further interrogation and torture or other cruel, inhuman, or degrading treatment of Omar while in control of US authorities. The mistreatment began immediately after his arrival at Bagram Air Force Base, when he was interrogated while in the hospital recovering from his near-fatal wounds. It continued aggressively through the first year of his detention at Guantánamo, including an incident during which he was "short-shackled" in painful positions and left for hours without questioning, during which he urinated on himself. Guards returned to the room on that occasion and, finding that he had soiled himself, spread a pine-smelling disinfectant on him and used him as a "human mop," swiping him back and forth through the mess. He was left to wear his soiled clothes for days.

Despite these serious allegations, the district judge denied injunctive relief on that claim and on a companion claim, arguing that there was a real risk that Omar could be transferred to another country and surrendered to authorities there who might subject him to the worst forms of torture or other mistreatment, a process called "irregular rendition" in US law.[44] The court framed the question of relief for physical mistreatment under interrogation on "whether this series of allegations – the most serious of which occurred more than eighteen months ago – warrants the exceptional remedy of a preliminary injunction respecting the conduct of [the government] in this setting." It concluded that "such relief is not warranted."[45] After reviewing the standards for the issuance of a preliminary injunction, the court further concluded: "Quite simply, even accepting petitioners' allegations of past misconduct as true, the record is barren of evidence of a "real and immediate threat" that petitioner will be subjected in the foreseeable future to mistreatment similar to that which he alleges occurred in 2003 ... Petitioners' mere speculation that this will happen is not a competent basis for the exercise of the Court's equitable powers."[46] The court's suggestion that the allegations of the risk of repetition were "mere speculation," in the face of a record in which the US government had actively promoted torturous treatment and was held to no discernable standards of conduct or limits on the length, frequency or intensity of interrogation, shows an impossibly high standard for challenge to governmental misconduct in a context in which full information as to the nature and extent of ongoing interrogation is almost impossible to provide.

WHAT WOULD BE THE IDEAL OUTCOME FOR THE GUANTÁNAMO DETAINEES?

At this writing, counsel for the detainees were awaiting the outcome of the consolidated appeal in the federal court of appeals. That decision would determine the extent to which appellate review would continue, and it might result in a decision that foreign detainees had a right to be heard on their claims of illegal detention through the writ of habeas corpus. If hearings were permitted to proceed, it would be months before they actually were held, and there were serious questions as to whether or not the government would bring the detainees to testify in court on their claims.

To my mind, the most favourable outcome for Omar would obviously be his release to return to Canada and his family in Toronto. There were, of course, obvious issues as to how a young man who had already lost more than three years of his life to custody in the most onerous of conditions would make the transition back into civil society, without appropriate schooling or health care, and certainly without the nurture of his family. Another option available to the authorities was simply to treat Omar as a legitimate prisoner of war, which would have unquestionably improved his quality of life and opportunities for self-improvement. It would also have ended his otherwise indefinite interrogation. The government argued, after three years of ongoing questioning, that there was still valuable intelligence to be gained from this young man and others like him. Finally, even the worst of options, charges of war crimes by a military commission, would be a more concrete status, in better conditions and with more clear access to counsel, than the endlessly ambiguous one accorded to a designated "enemy combatant" doomed to face detention until the end of the war on terror.

In September 2005 there was news that an increasingly aggressive hunger strike by the detainees was underway, the second in which they had engaged in recent months. It began spontaneously from within the detainee community. The newspapers reported that some two hundred detainees, nearly half of all detainees at Guantánamo Bay, were taking part in the strike. Nearly twenty of the detainees had been force fed, and their strike included a series of demands regarding their treatment, including the most fundamental claim that they were entitled to treatment "in accordance with the Geneva Accords."[47] The first strike had ended on 28 July 2005, with military officials agreeing to that demand, as well as to the creation of a six-member committee of detainees to act as spokespersons in talks with their military overseers. When the military broke the agreement after only a few days, the detainees returned to their strike. This time the detainees threatened to starve themselves to death.[48] The government asserted that they would not allow detainees to "starve themselves to the point of causing harm to themselves" and would provide "assisted feeding," with restraints, if necessary. One detainee recently told his attorney, "I'm dying a slow death in this place as it is. I don't have any hope of fair treatment, so what have I got to lose?" What, indeed?

POSTSCRIPT

After this article first went to press on 4 November 2005, the US government announced that five additional detainees would face trial by military commission for war crimes. Omar Khadr was charged with war crimes including murder by an unprivileged belligerent, attempted murder, conspiracy, and aiding the enemy. I continued representing him through the spring of 2006 and appeared in pre-trial proceedings of the first military commissions, the ones that were eventually struck down by the US Supreme Court in their decision in *Hamdan v. Rumsfeld*, 126 S.Ct. 2749 (2006) (the appeal mentioned at note 34). Our representation ended shortly after that, when Omar obtained the assistance of Canadian lawyers. The Supreme Court decided in the detainees' favour yet again in 2006, in *Boumediene v. Bush*, 553 U.S. 723 (2006), the appeal discussed after note 43.

At age twenty-three, after spending one-quarter of his young life in US custody pending trial, Omar eventually pled guilty to all charges before the newly reconstituted Military Commission at Guantánamo Bay on 13 October 2010. At no time did the US government, in or out of court, ever openly acknowledge his childhood or make any effort to treat him as a child under international or US law, both of which call for rehabilitation as the primary mission of juvenile justice.

The charges to which Omar Khadr pled guilty included the crimes of murder and attempted murder "in violation of the laws of war," conspiracy, material support for terrorism, and spying. In return for his plea of guilty, the Convening Authority for Military Commissions – the highest military authority overseeing commission operation – agreed not to approve a sentence of confinement of greater than eight years, with no credit for time served (as required under the new Military Commissions statute), and further, that after at least one more year at Guantánamo, Omar would be transferred to Canada to serve out the remainder of his sentence under Canadian law.

This complex plea agreement, however, did not settle the matter of sentencing. In what can best be described as a bizarre form of kabuki theatre, performed exclusively for the broad publicity, a full sentencing hearing in the Khadr case was held before a sentencing jury of military officers in Guantánamo just after he entered his plea of guilty. Although the jury imposed a sentence of forty years, trumpeted in the Defense Department's press release for the day, the eight-year sentence remained in place.

On reflection, an eight-year sentence for murder may be seen as the single manifestation of leniency required for minors in armed conflict, although strict compliance with international law would have called for no trial at all, with efforts to rehabilitate and reintegrate Omar into civil society based on his youth. Such is the Kafkaesque quality of Guantánamo "justice."

NOTES

This article was originally published in a slightly different form in November 2005. The notes below date from first publication.

1 *Rasul v. Bush*, 542 U.S. 466, 124 S.Ct. 2686, 2690-91 (2004) (footnotes omitted). The second of the trio of enemy combatant cases decided on the same day held that US citizens designated as enemy combatants also had the right to access to the US courts. *Hamdi v. Rumsfeld*, 542 U.S. 507, 124 S.Ct. 2633 (2004). The third case was *Rumsfeld v. Padilla*, 542 U.S. 426, 124 S.Ct. 2711 (2004), which was remanded for filing in the proper venue.

2 *Rasul, supra,* at 2696.

3 *Sale v. Haitian Centers Council Inc.*, 509 U.S. 155 (1993).
4 Michael Ratner, "How We Closed the Guantánamo HIV Camp: The Intersection of Politics and Litigation," *Harvard Human Rights Journal* 11 (1998): 187.
5 U.S.: Presidential Military Order – Detention, Treatment, and Trial of Certain Non-Citizens in the War against Terrorism, 66 Fed. Reg. 57, 833, 57, 833-34 (13 November 2001).
6 Kathleen T. Rhem, "Detainees Live in Varied Conditions at Guantánamo," Armed Forces Press Services, 16 February 2005, http://www.defenselink.mil/news/Feb2005/n02162005_2005021604.html (accessed 5 September 2005).
7 Diane Marie Amann, "Guantánamo," *Columbia Journal of Transnational Law* 42 (2004): 263.
8 "Detainee Transfer Announced," Armed Forces Press Services, 22 August 2005, http://www.defenselink.mil/ releases/2005/nr20050822-4501.html (accessed 5 September 2005).
9 The *Washington Post* compiled a list of some 367 detainees from unofficial sources. See "Names of the Detained in Guantánamo Bay, Cuba," *Washington Post*, http://www.washingtonpost.com/wp-srv/nation/ guantanamo_names.html (accessed 5 September 2005). Another website, Cageprisoners.com, claims to have the most comprehensive list of names, including the names of 480 detainees and the nationalities of another 174. At http://www.cageprisoners.com/page.php?id=10 (accessed 5 September 2005).
10 *John Does 1-570 v. Bush et al.*, Order Granting Petitioners' Motion to Proceed with a Petition for a Writ of Habeas Corpus Using Fictitious Names, D.D.C, 10 February 2005. The motion was granted.
11 Center for Constitutional Rights, "The Guantánamo Prisoner Hunger Strikes and Protests: February 2002–August 2005," 5 September 2005, www.ccr-ny.org.
12 An insightful report on global secret detentions comes from Human Rights First's "Behind the Wire: An Updating to Ending Secret Detentions" by Deborah Pearlstein and Priti Patel, March 2005, http://www.humanrightsfirst.org/wp-content/uploads/pdf/behind-the-wire-033005.pdf.
13 Kathleen T. Rhem, "Guantánamo Detainees Still Yielding Valuable Intelligence," American Forces Press Services, 4 March 2005, http://www.defenselink.mil/news/Mar2005/20050304_88.html (accessed 5 September 2005). Another document from the military offers what it alleges is evidence of that valuable intelligence. See "JTF-GTMO

Information on Detainees," http://www.defenselink.mil/news/Mar2005/d20050304info.pdf (accessed 5 September 2005).

14 Kathleen T. Rhem, "Government Attorney: Detainees Don't Deserve POW Privileges," American Forces Press Services, http://www.defenselink.mil/news/Mar2005/ 20050304_93.html (accessed 11 March 2005), asserts that detainees are held "for reasons of national security and military necessity, not because they're being punished."

15 There is no doubt that in time of armed conflict, "both international human rights law and international humanitarian law apply." See the Inter-American Commission on Human Rights, Organization of American States, *Report on Terrorism and Human Rights*, 2002, http://www.cidh.oas.org/Terrorism/Eng/toc.htm, para. 61. Moreover, as to the use of torture or other cruel, inhuman or degrading treatment, "in no other area is there greater convergence between international human rights law and international humanitarian law than in the standards of humane treatment and respect for human dignity" (id., at para. 147).

16 For a summary of the clinic's work, see the law school's website and the links on the clinic's homepage, at http://www.wcl.american.edu/clinical/inter.cfm.

17 The centre's website has two relevant locations summarizing our work. The first is the Guantánamo Action Center, which promotes civic activism, at http://www.ccr-ny.org/v2/gac/. The second is the legal docket of the center, collected under the general title of "September 11th," at http://www.ccr-ny.org/v2/legal/september_11th/ september_11th.asp.

18 *Khadr v. Her Majesty the Queen of Canada*, 2005 FC 1076, http://decisions.fct-cf.gc.ca/fct/2005/2005fc1076.shtml.

19 See, for example, the accounts in Isabel Vincent's "The Good Son," *National Post*, 28 December 2002, http://hvk.org/articles/1202/293.html; Doug Struck, "In Canada, An Outcast Family Finds Support," *Washington Post*, 9 June 2005, at A1.

20 *O.K. v. Bush*, Respondents' Factual Return to Petition for Writ of Habeas Corpus by Petitioner O.K., Sept. 15, 2004, D.D.C., No. 04-CV-1136, at Exhibit R-1, Combat Status Review Board (Unclassified).

21 Melissa A. Jamison, "Detention of Juvenile Enemy Combatants at Guantanamo Bay: The Special Concerns of the Children," *UC Davis Journal of Juvenile Law and Policy* 9 (2005): 136–7.

22 Letter from Thomas R. Lee, deputy assistant attorney general, US Department of Justice, Civil Division, to the Honorable Joyce Hens Green, 3 September 2004 (in the record of *O.K. v. Bush*).

23 See Jamison, "Detention of Juvenile Enemy Combatants," 146–55.

24 Presidential Military Order, at para. 1(f) (see note 5).

25 For a comprehensive description of the shaping of presidential views on the issues of prisoner of war status and the permissible range of interrogation techniques, see Jordan J. Paust, "Executive Plans and Authorizations to Violate International Law," *Columbia Journal of Transnational Law* 43 (2005): 811, 824–38. The Bybee memo was subsequently "superceded" by another Justice Department memo that more accurately defined torture but conspicuously failed to analyze the risk that abusive interrogations could also constitute violations of the prohibition against cruel, inhuman or degrading treatment under international law. See Memorandum from Daniel Levin, acting assistant attorney general, U.S. Department of Justice, Office of Legal Counsel, for James B. Comey, Deputy Attorney General, 30 December 2004. The memos and reports referred to in this section are available at http://www.humanrightsfirst.org/us_law/etn/gov_rep/ gov_memo_intlaw.htm.

26 Department of the Air Force, Office of the Judge Advocate General, "Final Report and Recommendations of the Working Group to Assess the Legal, Policy and Operational Issues Relating to Interrogation of Detainees Held by the U.S. Armed Forces in the War on Terrorism," 5 February 2003, http://dspace.wrlc.org/doc/bitstream/2041/70978/00601_030205_001display.pdf.

27 28 U.S.C. at 1350.

28 *Khadr et al. v. Bush et al.*, First Amended Petition for Habeas Corpus and Complaint for Declaratory and Injunctive Relief, No. 1:04CV01136, D.D.C., 17 August 2004.

29 Precautionary Measures in Guantánamo Bay, Cuba, Inter-Am. C.H.R., 13 March 2002, http://www1.umn.edu/humanrts/iachr/guantanamomeasures2002.html. The commission was interpreting, among other provisions, US obligations under Article 5 of the Third Geneva Convention.

30 Response of the United States to Request for Precautionary Measures – Detainees in Guantanamo Bay, Cuba, April 15, 2002, reprinted in 41 I.L.M. 1015 (2002).

31 124 S. Ct., at 2698.

32 Department of Defense Military Commission Instruction No. 2, "Crimes and Elements of Trials by Military Commissions," 30 April 2003, http://www.fas.org/irp/doddir/dod/milcominstno2.pdf.
33 *Hamdan v. Rumsfeld*, 344 F.Supp.2d 152 (D.D.C. 2004).
34 *Hamdan v. Rumsfeld*, 513 F.3d 33 (C.A.D.C. 2005).
35 Kathleen T. Rhem, "Military Trials for Two Guantánamo Detainees to Resume Soon," American Forces Press Services, 18 July 2005, http://www.defenselink.mil/news/ Jul2005/20050718_2108.html.
36 *In re Guantánamo Detainee Cases*, 344 F.Supp.2d 174 (2004).
37 *O.K. v. Bush*, 344 F.Supp.2d 44, 48 (D.D.C. 2004) (Omar's initials are used because such process is required for a juvenile appearing as a party in federal court.) We did not appeal the order.
38 *Khalid v. Bush*, 355 F.Supp.2d 311 (D.D.C. 2005).
39 In *re Guantánamo Detainee Cases*, 355 F.Supp.2d 433 (D.D.C. 2005).
40 Id. at 480–1.
41 28 U.S.C. at 1350.
42 *Guantánamo Detainee Cases*, *supra*, n. 39, at 480-1.
43 In *re Guantánamo Detainee Cases*, 355 F.Supp.2d 482 (D.D.C. 2005).
44 *O.K. v. Bush*, 377 F.Supp.2d 102 (D.D.C. 2005). No appeal was taken from the judgment.
45 Id. at 29 (citation to slip opinion only in Lexis-Nexis report).
46 Id. at 34–5.
47 Neil A. Lewis, "Guantánamo Prisoners Go on Hunger Strike," *New York Times*, 18 September 2005, http://www.nytimes.com/2005/09/18/politics/18gitmo.html?ei=5094&en=0e1376365dbc6773&hp=&ex=1127102400&partner=homepage&pagewanted=print.
48 The Center for Constitutional Rights has produced a comprehensive report on the strike as well as the medical and legal issues in similar life-threatening hunger strikes, in "The Guantanamo Prisoner Hunger Strikes and Protests: February 2002–August 2005," 5 September 2005, www.ccr-ny.org.

Khadr's Canadian Defence: Two Edmonton Lawyers, a Professor, and the Rule of Law

SHEILA PRATT

The jury of seven American military officers filed back into the courtroom in Guantánamo Bay at the end of eight long hours deliberating the fate of Omar Khadr. Sitting next to Khadr, watching tensely, were two Edmonton lawyers, Nate Whitling and Dennis Edney. For eight years the two Albertans had waged a determined battle for Khadr's legal rights. In Canada they had been to the Supreme Court twice, with much success, in their effort to bring the rule of law to bear on the case. They had travelled a dozen times since June 2007 to visit their client at this infamous US military prison and to help his American military lawyer, Lt-Col Jon Jackson, prepare the defence. This day, 31 October 2010, was a critical point in their journey: the fate of their client would finally be decided.

"Make no mistake, the world is watching," the military prosecutor told the jury. "Your sentence will send a message." Indeed. The military court had accepted Khadr's guilty plea (part of a plea bargain) the week before. Today it would recommend a sentence – and signal the kind of justice to be had from the new and contentious US military justice system.

Whitling and Edney knew the legal deck was stacked against their client at this hearing, given recently devised rules that violated fundamental principles of justice. For instance, in the military court, evidence obtained under torture was admissible – unthinkable in regular courts. The prosecution was not required to disclose its evidence, as required in regular courts. The Military Commissions system, set up by the Bush administration post-9/11 and modified by the Obama administration, was so stacked against the accused that the US government ruled its own citizens could not be sent to trial there. This was justice suitable for foreigners only.

But the US government was not the only one to ignore its own traditions concerning the rule of law when it came to Guantánamo. Unlike other Western countries, Canada under successive Liberal and Conservative governments had not publicly raised concerns about the lack of legal rights in Guantánamo nor taken steps to repatriate its citizen – as all other Western countries had done with their own Guantánamo detainees. Moreover, Canadian CSIS officials had actively participated in this flawed legal system by interrogating Khadr, and Edney and Whitling would eventually reveal the shocking circumstances through their battles in Canada's courts. In significant victories, the two lawyers managed to get Canadian courts to put an end to CSIS interrogations. They also had hopes of bringing Khadr back to Canada and avoiding his US military trial. While the Supreme Court of Canada eventually agreed Khadr's charter rights had been violated, the Harper government declined to bring the prisoner home as a remedy. For Edney, at that point, politics trumped the rule of law. A serious blow was dealt not just to Khadr's rights but also to legal protections that all Canadians rely on.

The defence of Omar Khadr, second youngest son of Canada's notorious al-Qaeda-linked Khadr family, was not a popular cause. The family's ties to terrorist Osama bin Laden were a shocking betrayal of national values and an affront to Canadians. For Whitling and Edney, however, a greater principle was at stake: the rule of law, so fundamental to democracy. Under the Charter of Rights and Freedoms, every Canadian citizen is entitled to the right to counsel, protection from torture, and a fair trial. Khadr had none of that in Guantánamo. Could the Canadian government simply abandon a citizen, albeit unpopular, to such a system?

The Edmonton lawyers are, as Edney likes to say, "as different as chalk and cheese." Whitling, mid-thirties, bookish, and reserved, is a brilliant legal mind. Raised in a middle-class Edmonton home, he went on to become the gold medallist in his University of Alberta law class. From there he studied at Harvard, clerked at the Supreme Court of Canada under Justice John Major, and then joined one of Edmonton's biggest downtown firms, Parlee McLaws.

Edney, twenty years older, a veteran criminal lawyer in a small Edmonton office, was a professional soccer player in Scotland before he went to law school. Behind his charming smile is a pugnacious, stubborn streak. He says it comes from his Scottish upbringing, which taught him to stand up for his rights or "be downtrodden." The notion of challenging the powers that be comes naturally to him. He also learned in his family a deep distaste for prejudice. His parents were a rare Catholic/Protestant marriage during the Second World War, much frowned upon by both sets of in-laws. To this day the Catholic side won't let his mother's ashes be buried with his father, says Edney, shaking his head.

In late 2002, Edney and Whitling joined forces to take on Khadr's case. The fifteen year old, captured in Afghanistan, was moved to Guantánamo where he was held for more than two years with no charges, no right to habeas corpus (to challenge his detention), and no access to lawyers. Whitling and Edney, who worked pro bono on this case, set out to see if Canadian law could force the federal government to intervene on Khadr's behalf or bring him home to face justice. The question: Under the Charter of Rights and Freedoms, what are Canada's obligations to one of its citizens detained in a foreign legal system that does not provide basic legal rights intrinsic to Canadian democracy?

In the post-9/11 era, the Khadr case tested the balance between the need for security in the West's "War on Terror" and the need to uphold Canada's long-standing civil liberties. The United States put Guantánamo deliberately offshore to exempt it from the US Constitution and the fundamental legal protections enshrined in it. So – could Canadian officials too turn a blind eye to the fact that Khadr was denied those basic legal rights and, as well, that he was a juvenile held in an adult system – contrary to Canadian domestic criminal law?

The case also tested Canada's commitment to its international obligations. Canada has signed both the UN protocol on child soldiers (which states that child soldiers should be rehabilitated, not sent to trial) and the UN convention against torture. But the federal government made no effort to protest when the United States put Khadr on trial in an adult court for crimes committed when he was fifteen years old. Human rights groups and many ordinary Canadians decried this as a sign that Canada was backing away from its commitments to international law. While all other Western countries got their citizens out of Guantánamo, mainly because they found its lack of legal protections repugnant, Liberal and Conservative governments in Canada left Khadr there to face whatever the US military had in store.

On a cold February morning in 2003, Whitling flipped through a newspaper and found the grounds for their first battle in Canadian courts. An article reported that Canadian Security Intelligence Service (CSIS) agents had gone to Guantánamo and interrogated Khadr about his role in the killing of US soldier Christopher Speer in a firefight in Afghanistan. At the time of those interrogations, Khadr was being detained with no charges, no right to a hearing, and no counsel. Whitling thought a pretty good argument could be made that Canadian officials could not go to another country and participate in detentions that would be illegal at home. The two lawyers wanted to stop the interrogations and force the government instead to start normal consular visits by Foreign Affairs officers to check on the welfare of the prisoner. They won on both counts.

In summer 2005, they went to the Federal Court of Canada (a separate court system which handles legal disputes with federal agencies, tribunals and the federal government) seeking an injunction against CSIS officials. On 10 August, the federal court upheld their case and handed down an injunction against further CSIS interrogations, citing Guantánamo's lack of legal protections. "Detention conditions, interrogation techniques used and rules of evidence employed at the US Combatant Status Review Tribunal do not comply with Charter standards," wrote Justice Konrad von Finckenstein.

"One of the best things we did was put an end to those interrogations," recalls Whitling. The reason why became clear in their next case which centred on the accused's legal right to disclosure of evidence. This case would go all the way to the Supreme Court of Canada, as federal officials fought to keep the CSIS evidence secret. The case would reveal the shocking treatment of Khadr before those interrogations. During the first trial, CSIS officials admitted to handing over the results of their 2003–04 interrogations to the US military as part of the evidence against Khadr. Canadian officials, in other words, were helping the US build the case against Khadr. Under the Canadian Charter, the accused has the right to see all the evidence against him. So Khadr's Edmonton lawyers decided to push for full disclosure of the CSIS interrogations – documents and videos – in accordance with the principles of fundamental justice.

They went back to Canada's Federal Court, and round one went against them. The Federal Court denied disclosure on national security grounds. But the Federal Court of Appeal upheld their case and ordered the documents released. The Canadian government then appealed the decision to the Supreme Court of Canada in an effort to keep the documents secret.

On 23 May 2008, the Supreme Court ruled in Khadr's favour. Canadian officials had violated international laws when they interrogated Khadr knowing he had been subject to cruel treatment that violated human rights. Some documents should be released, the court said. What those documents revealed stunned the country.

The documents revealed that Canadian intelligence officers had been told directly in 2004 that Khadr was subjected to severe sleep deprivation – moved every three hours for three weeks in what was known as the "frequent flyer program" – to soften him up for their interrogations. Canadian officials went ahead anyway, knowing Khadr had been subject to techniques deemed "cruel and degrading" under new US torture memos but simply called "torture" in many jurisdictions.

To this day Whitling is still shocked by that revelation, given that the Liberal government at the time was telling the public it was confident of US assurances of no ill treatment. "What we will do is what we have done so far, which is, at the end of the day, the US will proceed as they see fit," Edmonton MP Anne McLellan (minister of Public Safety in February 2005) told the *Edmonton Journal*. "We have sought assurances that he is not being ill-treated and those assurances have been given by the US." Yet officials in her department had clearly known otherwise.

Edney and Whitling moved on to the next step. If Canadian officials had violated Khadr's rights, there had to be a remedy and the two lawyers hoped to make it the repatriation of Khadr, by then the only Western citizen left in Guantánamo. This legal battle would prove to be far more complicated – and the outcome much more of a political proposition – than they'd imagined.

In *Khadr v. Canada (Prime Minister)* Edney and Whitling won the first two rounds in Canada's federal court. In April 2009, the Federal Court of Canada ruled that Khadr's Charter rights had been violated when Canadian officials participated in interrogations knowing about the torture and knowing no charges had been laid. To remedy the rights violation, the federal court ordered that the Canadian government must apply for repatriation. The federal government appealed and four months later, the federal appeal division upheld the lower court's decision. "While Canada may have preferred to stand by and let the proceedings against Mr. Khadr in the US run their course, the violation of his Charter rights by Canadian officials has removed that option," wrote the appeal court.

Prime Minister Stephen Harper's government soon announced it would appeal to the Supreme Court of Canada.

By 2008, citizen advocacy and legal groups began to pressure the Canadian government to bring Khadr home. Amnesty International, UNICEF, and the Canadian Bar Association called for action. But the Supreme Court in January 2010 wouldn't go that far. It agreed that Khadr's Charter rights to life, liberty and security of person were violated when "Canadian officials questioned [him] ... in circumstances where they knew that Mr. Khadr was being indefinitely detained, was a young person and was alone during the interrogations." While this represented another victory for Whitling and Edney, it also marked the end of their winning streak. The Supreme Court, rather than ordering the government to seek the repatriation of Omar Khadr as the lower courts had done, declared it would defer to the government to decide on a remedy "in light of its responsibility over foreign affairs."

The Harper government declined to repatriate Khadr and instead proposed a different remedy. It asked the US military not to use the information obtained in the interrogations by Canadian officials in its subsequent trial of Khadr. The US military declined the request. Under the rules of the Military Commissions Act, evidence obtained under duress would be just fine in court.

The Supreme Court decision in the Khadr case sparked a major controversy in Canadian legal circles. Human rights advocates said the judgment weakened the Canadian Charter of Rights and Freedoms. Declaring a rights violations with no remedy undermines the rule of law. Others said the court found the right balance in its decision, acceding to the federal government's exclusive jurisdiction in foreign affairs and wisely avoiding a showdown with the Canadian government – or the US government for that matter.

Edney points out that to this day there has been no remedy for the violation of Khadr's Charter rights. That is deeply troubling, he says. After the US government rejected Harper's request not to use the CSIS evidence, the federal government took no further action. By failing to come up with another remedy, the Harper government put itself above the law, Edney says. "By not taking that step, I feel it puts us all at risk. This government is saying it is above the law." (That legal battle is not over, he adds.)

Whitling says he is obviously disappointed that Canada's Supreme court did not order repatriation, but in the end the question of Khadr's repatriation came down to politics.

Having lost their bid to repatriate Khadr after eight years in Canadian courts, the two Edmonton lawyers knew their client would have to face the flawed Military Commissions the US had established. So they headed to Guantánamo in October 2010 for this final court hearing and sentencing. Their role here was limited to assisting American military defence lawyer Lt-Col Jon Jackson. In the end, Jackson called only two witnesses to speak on Omar Khadr's behalf at the sentencing hearing. One was a US military officer, Captain Patrick McCarthy, a senior legal adviser at Guantánamo between 2006 and 2008. During those years he saw Khadr regularly. He told the court he believed Khadr was not radicalized and could be rehabilitated. "Fifteen year olds should not be held to the same standard of accountability as adults," he told the jury.

The defence called only one other witness – and the only Canadian – an articulate English professor, Arlette Zinck, from a small Christian college in Edmonton. Her testimony contained a major surprise for the courtroom and many back in Canada. For two years Zinck had quietly corresponded with Khadr, their letters smuggled past military censors, often in the bottom of Dennis Edney's shoes. The letters were entered as evidence; some have been published by the *Edmonton Journal*. In this remarkable exchange, a unique friendship unfolds between the personable, engaging academic who takes seriously the Christian duty to comfort those in need, and the accused terrorist raised in Islam. Khadr's responses are a rare window to glimpse the young prisoner in the months before the Guantánamo trial

In her letters, Zinck took the role of academic advisor, sending lesson plans, lists of books to read, detailed instructions on how to write an essay. She urged Khadr to do a little work each day "to strike a balance between challenging yourself and putting undue pressure on yourself." She also wrote with warmth, her messages of encouragement and friendship urging him to "be strong." "God keeps you close," she wrote.

Khadr expressed his gratitude in handwritten responses: "I got your letter and picture, was very surprised by them. So thank you very much ... the true friend is not in the time of ease but in the time of hardship" (October 2008). A few months later, in January 2009, he wrote, "Your letters are like candles very bright in my hardship and darkness. About myself what can I say? We hold onto hope in our hearts and love from other to us and that keeps us going until we reach our happiness."

Zinck tried to keep his spirits up: "So Omar, don't feel discouraged about the time you are spending in Guantanamo ... Everything is an opportunity to learn, Omar. Some of the world's most important stories have been written by men in prison. Your circumstances will teach you things that other people will never know. Be a good student of the lessons of life."

Khadr also wrote about the books he'd read, a wide range from Nelson Mandela's biography to Dickens's *Great Expectations*, Ghandi, Barack Obama's *Dreams from My Father*, John Grisham novels and the Twilight series, which he described as "nonsense reading." "The problem is some things are so stressful you need some novels to get you out of this place," he wrote. In one of his last letters, in April 2010, he wrote down his thoughts in an essay on the book *A Long Way Gone: Memoirs of a Boy Soldier*, by Ishmael Beah, a boy forced at the age of thirteen into the Sierra Leone army. The Beah memoir, Khadr writes, "is the best example to what humans have reached from horrors they committed to the way they cured it and especially in the child field, a treatment that guaranteed succeeds and cureness – a way that leaves no traces of the horrors that have scard [scarred] the soul ... Children's hearts are like a sponge that will obserb [absorb] what is around it, like wet cement, until it is sculpted in a certain way."

Zinck told the courtroom that the young man she had come to know through their exchange of letters was polite, thoughtful, and intelligent. Though his formal education ended in Grade 8, he was making progress with his studies, she said. He was an eager student and a voracious reader. He expressed interest in coming to King's University College in Edmonton when he was released – an aspiration that Zinck encouraged.

Zinck had become involved in Khadr's case when Dennis Edney spoke at a college event on Khadr's plight in the legal blackhole of Guantánamo.[1] That was 2008. As Zinck was well aware, many

Canadians have another view of Khadr – a terrorist and murderer who sided with the enemy in the Afghanistan war where Canadian soldiers fought and died. But for Zinck, her appearance for the defence served to uphold the very values Canadian soldiers were fighting for – the rule of law, the right to a fair trial, and freedom from torture. All of these were violated in the handling of Khadr's case. Zinck was raised in a Canadian Air Force family, giving her a unique perspective. She had many lively discussions with her father, retired Master Warrant Officer D.C. Zinck. In the end, both agreed that upholding the rule of law – and participating in Khadr's defence – showed respect for Canadian soldiers in the field. "If we're sending our young men and women to die for those values, we should be willing to uphold those values at home," said Zinck.

In the Guantánamo courtroom that October day, Zinck had her first glimpse of Khadr. They exchanged smiles and later a few words before he was taken away to serve his sentence. It was a moment full of anguish. Tabitha Speer, widow of Christopher Speer, was also present and earlier had given powerful testimony about the impact of her husband's murder on herself and her young family. Asked by the defence if she considered Tabitha's plight, Zinck told the court she had also offered prayers for the widow in her time of loss. Zinck watched Khadr apologize to Tabitha Speer in his brief statement to the court.

Under the plea bargain, Khadr pleaded guilty to murdering Speer and to four other charges: spying, attempted murder, conspiracy, and providing material support for terrorism (planting roadside bombs). He agreed with an eight-page statement that called him, as an "alien unprivileged enemy belligerent," fully cognizant of his actions. In exchange for his guilty plea, he would be incarcerated for one year in solitary confinement at Guantánamo, then transferred to Canada for the remainder of his sentence.

The jury filed back into the courtroom, unaware that the plea bargain set a sentence of eight years. If the jury recommended a lower sentence, it would apply. A higher sentence would be largely symbolic. As Khadr's was the first trial held under the Military Commissions system – and as he was the only Western citizen remaining in Guantánamo – the world was paying close attention to see what kind of sentence, what kind of justice, would come from come from a jury of US soldiers passing judgment on an enemy combatant.

Whitling and Edney hoped the jury would recommend a lower sentence. The prosecution wanted the sentence increased to twenty-five years. The jury weighed two views of Khadr. Was he an unrepentant terrorist, radicalized, violent, and dangerous? Or was he, as the defence maintained, a teenager pushed into battle by his father and now a compliant prisoner committed to his studies and deserving of a second chance?

What came next was a jolt, says Whitling. The jury took their seats and announced their decision: a sentence of forty years. It is highly unusual, in regular courts, for a sentence to be so much longer than what the prosecution calls for. But then, this wasn't a regular court. "We were all shocked," said Whitling. "It just underscored the unfairness of the system."

As he looked over at Khadr in that dramatic moment, Edney recalled thinking, "Thank God we'd done the plea bargain deal. Otherwise Omar would be there for the rest of his life. Without that, I'd be picking him up at sixty-four years old."

Back in Edmonton, Edney sits in his favouite café pondering the lessons of his eight-year legal odyssey through Canadian courts and the final chapter in the Guantánamo courtoom. Canada's courts did an admirable job of upholding Khadr's legal rights and the rule of law, not hesitating to rule the government out of order when it violated those rights, says Edney. The courts forced an end to illegal interrogations by CSIS, forced disclosure of evidence obtained by CSIS, and ruled unanimously that Khadr's Charter rights had been violated. The trouble came from a federal government that refused in the end to uphold Khadr's rights and bring him home. "I may have lost faith in the government for failing to do the right thing, for acting on their own self-serving motives," he concludes. "But I haven't lost faith in the judicial system." What is disturbing, says Edney, is that a legal black hole like Guantánamo undermines respect for the rule of law in Canada too, not just in the United States. People begin to think the rule of law applies only to "good people. That's fatal for a justice system. Everyone deserves a fair trial."

Edney also suggests that the Canadian public demonstrated a disturbing complacency about the rule of law throughout the years of their legal battles for Khadr's rights. "I wish more people had stood up for this," he says. If a democracy does not protect the legal rights of its least desirable citizens, he notes, "no citizen can be sure they'll have those protections when they need them."

In early February 2011, Nate Whitling travelled back to Guantánamo to visit Khadr. The two spent half a day going over his schoolwork. But the main purpose of the visit was to prepare the application to transfer Khadr to a Canadian prison as the plea bargain stipulates.

"It's our job to be cautious," says Whitling. "But given that Canada's promise was made not only to Omar but also to the US government, we do not anticipate the government will go back on its word."

There was one more bump awaiting Whitling and Edney in this difficult case. In early August 2011, with just months to go before he was to return to Canada, Khadr suddenly fired his Edmonton counsel and hired two Toronto lawyers, John Norris and Brydie Bethell. Khadr's surprise move gave new resonance to a candid and affectionate letter he had written to Edney while awaiting his trial in Guantánamo, a trial they had both hoped to avoid. In May 2010, he wrote of his fears about the "unfairness" of the Military Commission and that his case would "show the world" what happens in Guantánamo. He also wrote of his love for Edney, a father figure for the last seven years. But, he warned, "The thought of firing everybody is on mind … Dennis, I'm sorry to cause you this pain, but consider it one of your son's hard decisions that you don't like but you have to deal with."

Khadr continues his long-distance lessons with Zinck in English and other subjects.

NOTE

1 See Dennis Edney's "The Politics of Fear" in this volume, which is based on the speech he delivered at this conference.

The Rule of Law, the Force of Law, and the Rule of Force

AUDREY MACKLIN

I became involved in Omar Khadr's case early in 2007. After I presented a scholarly paper about the Khadr family and citizenship at an academic conference in 2006, an American colleague who was representing Omar Khadr in a civil action asked me about the absence of political mobilization in Canada on Omar's behalf. After all, Omar was a Canadian citizen, and citizens of other US allies had successfully requested repatriation of their citizens and even, in some cases, permanent residents. The US rendition of Maher Arar to Syria, where he was tortured and detained for close to a year, incited the Canadian public to demand his return. It led to a public inquiry into Canada's role in Arar's ordeal and, ultimately, to a $10 million compensation package.[1] Omar was only fifteen when he was captured, and there was every reason to believe that US authorities did not spare him the brutality inflicted on older detainees.

In reply, I recounted the "Khadr effect" to my colleague: Prime Minister Chrétien had personally interceded in the mid-1990s to secure the release of Omar's father, Ahmed Said Khadr, from detention by Pakistani authorities on suspicion of complicity in the bombing of the Egyptian embassy in Islamabad. It emerged post-9/11 that Ahmed Said Khadr was an associate of Osama bin Laden. The Canadian government was stung by the allegation that it had been duped into rescuing a terrorist. The mistake would not be repeated. In 2004, Omar's mother and sister granted a television interview in which they made inflammatory statements to the media that further stoked public vilification. The travails of Omar's older brothers, Abdurahman and Abdullah, did nothing to improve the image of the Khadrs, by now dubbed Canada's "first family of terror." The litigation commenced on Omar's behalf by his Canadian lawyers in the Federal Court of Canada appeared to be stalled. When I contacted his Canadian lawyer by phone to ask for information about the legal case and to offer any assistance, the lawyer was very helpful but politely declined my offer.

My American colleague listened patiently to my explanation, and then said, "Yes, I know about the Khadr effect. But why isn't anyone in Canada doing anything to help Omar?" I had no answer.

Over the next three years, I assisted Omar's then US military defense counsel, Lt-Cmdr William Kuebler and Rebecca Snyder. My role consisted mainly in advocating for Omar's repatriation to Canada, and facilitating Lt-Cmdr Kuebler and Ms Snyder's efforts to engage the Canadian government and the Canadian public. I contributed to *amicus curiae* briefs submitted to the US Supreme Court and the Military Commission in Guantánamo Bay. I represented Human Rights Watch and the University of Toronto International Human Rights Program as co-counsel before the Supreme Court of Canada in both of Omar Khadr's appeals to that court. I twice attended the pre-trial hearings of Omar Khadr before the Military Commission in Guantánamo Bay as an observer for Human Rights, in October 2008 and again in May 2010.

The public advocacy efforts, in tandem with those of his dedicated Canadian lawyers, Nathan Whitling and Dennis Edney, yielded a measure of success in shifting public opinion and attracting the support of civil society and opposition politicians. However, they foundered before an implacable prime minister and a cautious Supreme Court of Canada.

I have approached Omar's case from many angles, yet I have never approached Omar himself. Lt-Cmdr Kuebler told Omar about me in the course of their meetings, and we acknowledged one another in an exchange of nods in the Military Commissions courtroom In Guantánamo Bay, one cannot simply speak with a detainee. Detainees do not move, eat, speak, go to the bathroom, read, write, sleep, or rise except by leave or command. This near-total annihilation of agency extends to life itself. Detainees who attempt to hunger strike are force fed, and those who commit suicide have their final act confiscated by the US military and recast as an act of aggression known as "asymmetrical warfare." Detainees are left with little more than a single autonomous act to perform in response to their circumstances: they can fire their lawyers. Which perhaps partly explains why Omar, like so many of his fellow detainees, has fired so many lawyers. Eventually, even that choice was withdrawn. Detainees could dismiss their particular civilian or military lawyers, but the Office of the Military Commissions would immediately detail another military lawyer to the case.

My experience with Omar's case educated me about how to speak to politicians, the media, and the public, and refined my ability to craft legal arguments for judicial audiences across jurisdictions. It also forced me to confront the fact that large swaths of the public seemed to regard the most basic human rights – the right to be free from torture, the right not to be detained indefinitely, the right to a fair trial – as privileges reserved for the popular. Canadian outrage over the rendition, detention, and torture of Maher Arar was underwritten to a significant degree by a contemporaneous and widespread public consensus that Maher was a morally innocent man. Omar Khadr, on the other hand, laboured under a presumption of guilt. If nothing else, he bore the stain of being the son of a terrorist. And if his innocence was not already immanent, he could claim no entitlement to a fair process to determine his guilt.

Working with Omar's defense lawyers taught me the invaluable lesson that the rule of law makes for strange bedfellows. Before meeting Lt-Cmdr Kuebler and Rebecca Snyder, I would have been unable to imagine what confluence of circumstances would lead me to make common cause with United States Judge Advocate General (JAG) attorneys. But thanks to that rare opportunity, I retain boundless and unqualified admiration for Ms Snyder and Lt-Cmdr Kuebler. I came to appreciate and respect their stance that fidelity to their constitutional duties as US soldiers and US lawyers not only permitted but required them to furnish the most vigorous defence of Omar Khadr.

I did not need to involve myself directly in Omar's case to know that the regime to which he was subject breached the most basic precepts of the rule of law. Viewed through a legal lens, the "black hole" of Guantánamo Bay would have been visible from outer space.[2] The invention of crimes, and their retroactive application to detainees, the routine use of torture, solitary confinement, and cruel, inhuman and degrading treatment, the lack of access to legal counsel, the indefinite detention without charge or trial, each and all extravagantly flouted international human rights law, international humanitarian law, the US Constitution, and US military law. Omar's particular circumstances as a minor and the indifference to his age and his status as a child soldier only exacerbated the brutality of the abuses.

As a legal academic, I could have remained seated at my desk and drafted legal arguments excoriating the conduct of the United States and Canada toward Omar Khadr. Indeed, demonstrating the illegality of the Guantánamo Bay regime was not difficult. What stymied me was that people knew it was illegal and did not care.

But when I travelled to Guantánamo Bay to observe proceedings, I learned what I could not have learned any other way. The almost instant labelling of Guantánamo Bay as a "state of exception" existing outside law had a certain resonance in the initial period after its conversion to a detention camp for alleged combatants/terrorists apprehended by the United States post-9/11. The work of Giorgio Agamben, in turn drawing on Carl Schmitt, Hannah Arendt, and Walter Benjamin, seemed to capture perfectly the character of Guantánamo Bay as a lawless zone and the detainees as outlaw bodies produced and contained by it. But the United States is probably the most legally saturated political formation in world history. Ironically, the "state of exception" both obscures and flattens the variegated legal and political topography of Guantánamo Bay in ways that do not do justice to the injustice.

The off-shoring of power to a US military base in Cuba could not fully deflect the pressure to paper over the regime with formal legal text. In *Rasul*, *Hamdan*, and then *Boumedienne*, the US Supreme Court ruled that the US government could not exempt Guantánamo Bay entirely from the reach of the US Constitution and judicial review. Congress enacted the Military Commissions Act and subordinate regulations to fill the apparent legal void. These legal instruments contained rules about liability, rules about procedure, rules about jurisdiction, rules about evidence, and rules about sentencing.

This proliferation of rules mainly had the effect of codifying the evisceration of the rule of law. In other words, it was a full-scale assault of laws against law. It is easy enough to grasp conceptually how a sovereign can, in a narrow positivist sense, deploy its legislative power to authorize that which contradicts foundation assumptions of a legitimate legal order – one need only think of the Nuremberg laws, or the laws of apartheid. But without witnessing the pre-trial proceedings in Guantánamo Bay, I could not have apprehended how the rule of law could decay and decompose at the granular level through the performance of ordinary courtroom rituals by legal actors schooled in the most intricate and rights-conscious legal system in the world. The team of mostly fresh-faced and eager military prosecutors seemed least conflicted by the demands of their role. Nevertheless, the Military Commissions Act's rigging of substantive rules of culpability and procedural rules of evidence virtually assured conviction.[3] The military judge deported himself like a grim and irritable technocrat; he swiftly mastered the text of the rules but determinedly refused to engage with any argument that went to the legality of the process or the basis of liability. Defense counsel oscillated between the internal gambit (play by the rules of the game) and the external strategy (expose the injustice of the rules themselves). And the better they performed, the worse they did: Omar's lawyers were caught by the paradox of legitimization writ large. The more zealously they denounced the injustice of the process, the more they proved that the system was just because it provided Omar with zealous defense counsel. Along with the media, we human rights observers performed a similar function: as long as our eyes were open in the courtroom, we proved that justice was seen to be done. What we said about what we saw mattered little.

The hearings in Omar's case were conducted in a small white courthouse encircled by spiralling bushels of barbed wire, in the heart of the Guantánamo Bay Naval Base (GTMO). The handful of observers from non-governmental organizations stayed in a nearby tent compound called Camp Justice. When I first read the sign, I wondered to myself whether there is a Department of Euphemisms deep inside the Pentagon responsible for the moniker "Camp Justice," along with the terms "asymmetrical warfare" (detainee suicide), "collateral damage" (killing of civilians), and "enhanced interrogation techniques" (torture).

First established in 1903, GTMO is a thriving community of over 6,000 US members of the military, non-military employees, and family members. It is a criminal offence (punishable by imprisonment) to harm or kill any of the iguanas that roam freely on the base. The US military cares about the welfare of iguanas.

Restaurants, bars, recreation facilities, and a lovely beach provide service personnel with relief from the tedium of military life. A couple of stores sell an impressive array of Guantánamo Bay souvenir towels, beer mugs, T-shirts, baseball caps, and snow-globes to take home as gifts for friends and family. There is even a school on the base, and the first time I went to GTMO, students were holding a fundraiser for their high school graduation. They set up a table advertising T-shirts printed with a slogan that went something like this: Beautiful beach: $100; Clear blue sea: $300; Year-round sunshine: $500; Detainees in orange jumpsuits in your backyard: Priceless.

I travelled to GTMO twice, first in October 2008 and again in May 2010. Each time I stayed for almost a week. One can fly directly from Toronto to Havana, and GTMO is a short trip from Havana in geographic space, yet the distance between Havana, Cuba, and Guantánamo Bay US Naval Base remains unbridgeable in political space. And so I flew from Toronto to Washington, DC, boarded a military flight from Andrews Air Force Base in Maryland, and flew directly to Guantánamo Bay without ever crossing into Cuban airspace.

The following vignettes do not present a comprehensive account of the pre-trial proceedings. They are, instead, despatches from the front row of the legal spectacle that was the Military Commission pre-trial hearing of Omar Khadr.

21–25 OCTOBER 2008

The charges against Khadr include "murder in violation of the laws of war" and providing material support to the enemy. The most serious allegation against him is that on 27 July 2002 in Afghanistan, he threw a grenade that killed US soldier Sergeant Christopher Speer. But the questions of what really happened on that day and what was done to Omar Khadr in the intervening years are nowhere on the agenda of these pre-trial hearings.

Instead, most of the time is consumed by arguments about scheduling of the actual trial. The prosecution accuses the defense of what, in hockey parlance, is called "ragging the puck": stalling until the clock runs out on the game. They cite defense counsel Lt-Cmdr William Kuebler's efforts to petition the Canadian government to seek the repatriation of its citizen (as every other industrialized country has done with respect to Guantánamo detainees) as evidence that the defense has no interest in proceeding to trial. Instead, the defense intends to delay the onset of the trial indefinitely in the hopes that a new US president may effect a political resolution to the running sore that is Guantánamo Bay – or at least do something about Omar's case. The defense counters that it is unable to prepare properly for trial because the prosecution has systematically refused to fulfill its obligations to disclose relevant and exculpatory evidence. The defense seeks discovery of evidence that the prosecution possesses or could obtain.

Arguments about delay are standard fare in ordinary litigation, and it is symptomatic of a military commission that is both like and unlike a normal trial. In a normal trial, it would not be unusual for the prosecution to accuse the defense of using discovery as a fishing expedition and to suggest that the defense has no reasonable basis for requesting the information. At Omar's hearing, the prosecution argued that the defense was engaging in just such a fishing expedition by seeking access to the military intelligence interrogators who interviewed Omar at Bagram Air Base in Afghanistan and at Guantánamo Bay.

Here is how the argument goes: the prosecution states that it intends to rely at trial solely on statements made by Omar to law enforcement interrogators, not to military intelligence interrogators. Therefore, defense does not need access to the intelligence interrogators, and their evidence is irrelevant.

The defense's main response is that, before and after Omar was interrogated by FBI and CIA law enforcement officials (who did not physically abuse him), he was tortured and subject to cruel, inhuman, and degrading treatment by military intelligence interrogators. The defense position is that, even if statements to the "clean team" law enforcement interrogators were not extracted contemporaneously with torture, they cannot be laundered of the stain left by past abuse and the fear of future abuse. Omar's past experience of abuse and legitimate fear of future abuse by military intelligence interrogators would have been present in his mind when he was interrogated by law enforcement officials. Statements made in an environment so saturated by brutality are contaminated and cannot be construed as voluntary.

Omar's military interrogators included the notorious Joshua Claus, who was subsequently implicated in torturing to death two other Afghan detainees around the same time. Discovery of these military intelligence interrogators is crucial to establishing a foundation for a motion to suppress statements Omar made to law enforcement interrogators in which he confessed, among other things, to throwing the grenade that killed Christopher Speer and wounded another US soldier, Layne Morris.

The prosecution's reply? That defense counsel's position regarding the use of coercive techniques by intelligence interrogators is mere speculation and assertion without factual support. So, the motion to obtain discovery of seven intelligence interrogators who interviewed Omar Khadr during three discrete periods (Bagram in July–August 2002; Guantánamo Bay in October 2002–February 2003, and late 2004) is an overly broad request built on unsubstantiated conjecture that US military intelligence personnel employed coercive interrogation techniques against detainees.

Only in a courtroom in Guantánamo Bay could a lawyer insist that assertions of detainee abuse at Bagram or Guantánamo Bay lack an air of reality, and do so without a trace of irony.

THIS IS NOT A NORMAL TRIAL

The other issue argued before the judge is more complex and exposes the incoherence produced by a legal order that stands outside criminal law and the laws of war, yet culls elements from both for normative support. The question is whether murder committed by an "alien unlawful enemy combatant" (later re-branded as "alien unprivileged enemy belligerent" under the post-Obama 2009 Military Commissions Act) is automatically a war crime, or whether something more is required to turn a killing into a violation of the laws of war.

A singular innovation of the laws of war is to bring within the domain of legal regulation that which is normally considered the ultimate criminal act – the wilful killing of another human being. Under the Geneva Conventions, members of a state's armed forces who kill enemy combatants on the battlefield cannot be prosecuted for murder under the domestic laws of the enemy state. That exemption is called "combatant privilege." Individuals who take up arms but who are not part of a state's armed forces, so-called unlawful (or, more properly, unprivileged) combatants, enjoy no such immunity from domestic criminal prosecution. This means that the Geneva Conventions authorized the US government to charge Omar Khadr with homicide under US criminal law and to try him in a US federal court. But the US government did not do that.

Instead Omar was charged under the Military Commissions Act with murder and attempted murder "in violation of the laws of war." While it is not a war crime to kill an enemy combatant on the battlefield, the prosecution insists that it becomes a war crime – a serious violation of the laws of armed conflict – if committed by an alien unlawful enemy combatant. Defense counsel Rebecca Snyder argues that according to international humanitarian law as articulated in the Geneva Conventions, a battlefield killing only becomes a war crime when a combatant – privileged or otherwise – targets a person with protected status or uses prohibited methods of killing. Protected persons include civilians, all persons in custody, incapacitated military personnel, or military medical or religious personnel. Prohibited methods include the use of human shields, poison gas, or intentional deception designed to induce the enemy into believing that one is a protected person (known as perfidy). Therefore, unless the prosecution can prove beyond a reasonable doubt that Sgt Speer was a protected person when killed (which he was not),[4] or that Omar used prohibited methods of killing (which he did not), his alleged actions can not constitute murder "in violation of the laws of war" even if he were a so-called alien unlawful enemy combatant at the time. Under international law, his unprivileged combatant status does not convert his acts into a war crime; at most, it can deny him the exemption from the purview of the ordinary criminal law of murder.

The prosecution's position is that international law does not matter. Congress can create a new war crime under US law – and has done so in the Military Commissions Act – even if it has never been considered a war crime under international law in this century or the last or at the time that Omar allegedly committed the act that was subsequently declared a crime. That virtually any iteration of the rule of law condemns retroactive ("ex poste facto") penal laws seems not to faze the prosecutors, or the judge.

Murder by an unlawful alien enemy combatant is only one of the war crimes invented by the Military Commission Act. Another is "providing material support" to the enemy. It turns out that the acts that constitute "providing material support" are meant to encompass anything that combatants might do, attempt to do, or assist others in doing, or fail to prevent others from doing in conflict situations. In effect, the offences created under the Military Commissions Act purport to criminalize the status of *being* an enemy.

While it may seem intuitively appealing to criminalize membership in al-Qaeda or the Taliban, the problem with calling it a war crime is that the laws of war are about regulating armed conflict between adversaries, not about making participation in armed conflict unlawful per se. Yet, once it labelled him an "alien unlawful enemy combatant," the Military Commissions Act made it a war crime for Omar Khadr to do anything other than surrender or die.

Arguing that any act of war by an alien unlawful combatant is, by definition, a war crime also points toward the "heads I win; tails you lose" quality of the Military Commissions process. Omar is a combatant when it comes to detaining him indefinitely but not when it comes to providing him the privileges and immunities of prisoners of war, such as "combatant privilege." He is a criminal defendant when it comes to charging him with murder but not when it comes to furnishing him with the most basic rights, protections, and defences available to persons charged with a crime. This includes the right not to have "confessions" obtained through coercion admitted as evidence.

There is a status that partly describes Omar but which is entirely absent from the text of the Military Commissions Act, the cages at Bagram Air Force Base, the cells of Camp Delta, or the courtroom of Guantánamo Bay. In none of these places was fifteen-year-old Omar Khadr a minor, much less a child soldier. The United States signed the Optional Protocol on Child Soldiers and committed itself internationally to the reintegration and rehabilitation of child soldiers. But as a political matter, the Optional Protocol is for child soldiers who kill foreigners in foreign countries. It does not apply to child soldiers who kill Americans in foreign countries. Omar Khadr, the adolescent boy whose youthful visage appeared so often on newspaper and television, never existed in the legal universe constructed by the Military Commissions Act. There is only the ageless, hypermasculine alien unlawful enemy combatant.

Omar sits ambiguously between being a criminal accused and a prisoner of war, bearing all the burdens and none of the protections of either status. His condition as a minor is invisible to the law. But he is indisputably an alien (non-citizen) to the United States. His designation as "enemy unlawful combatant" and subjection to the Military Commission process hinges on this status. Had he been a US citizen, he would not be here. He would be in the territorial United States, facing a trial under US law – including the US Constitution – in a US court, like Jose Padilla or John Walker Lindh. As it is, it doesn't actually matter if Omar is aquitted of the war crimes charges; the US position is that he can be detained indefinitely, or until the "War on Terror" is won, whichever comes first.

The Military Commissions regime is predicated on the fact that the US government cannot and will not inflict upon its citizens what it inflicts upon non-citizens.[5] This position may appear not to raise any problem – after all, except in civil war, enemies typically are citizens of foreign states anyway. But from another perspective, one might expect that the disloyalty – even treason – displayed by a US citizen who wages war against his country would exacerbate the wrongfulness of the acts. So the fabrication of a separate and unequal regime for enemy aliens cannot be rationalized by reference to the specific moral character of the impugned actions, or even by reference to the actor as enemy, for surely a traitor who kills a soldier is no better (and arguably worse) than a foreign enemy.

Instead, the Guantánamo Bay regime operates from a presumption of the lesser moral status of the actor as alien. The Military Commissions Act is predicated on the view that the alien is less human than the citizen, and so treatment, processes, and rules unfit for the citizen are suitable and available for the alien.

Of course, one state's foreigner is another state's citizen. Omar Khadr is a citizen of Canada. He was born on Canadian territory to Canadian citizen parents. In law, no amount of vilification based on his family, his absence from Canada, his religion, ethnicity, alleged beliefs, or conduct can compromise the tensile strength of his legal citizenship. That some regard him or his family as "bad" citizens does not alter the fact that Omar is a citizen in Canadian law.

Long before the advent of international human rights in the twentieth century, states understood that whatever treatment they felt free to inflict on foreigners in their midst could just as easily be reciprocated on their own citizens abroad. From the eighteenth century, states' rational self-interest led to the rise of consular assistance and diplomatic protection. States may intercede with other states through negotiation, advocacy, and even protest in order to protect their citizens from mistreatment. The formal legal rationale is that a violation of international law committed by state A against a citizen of state B constitutes a wrong against state B, thereby entitling state B to intervene through negotiation, consular assistance, representations, or litigation. This is how every industrialized state other than Canada secured the release and repatriation of its citizens (and even, in some cases, its permanent residents) from Guantánamo Bay. In fact, the Military Commission's former chief prosecutor, Morris Davis – a man who believes Omar to have killed Sgt Speer – put the matter bluntly: "I think the interesting question for the administration is that if this was a 15-year-old American being prosecuted in another country, would we condone the procedures that are in place in a military commission for an American citizen? And I hope the answer to that is no."[6]

Not only has Canada condoned US mistreatment of Omar through its inaction, it seized the opportunity of his detention in Guantánamo Bay to interrogate him repeatedly in 2003–04. In so doing, Canada effectively renounced its relationship to Omar as citizen. In functional terms, Canada exploited him as a Canadian in order to gain access to him in Guantánamo Bay, only to repudiate him as a citizen by availing itself of the opportunities presented by a regime that regarded him as an alien. The United States has perpetrated countless human rights violations upon Omar. It will not subject him to a criminal process in the continental United States that is governed by the rule of law because no such system could countenance or validate the abuses inflicted upon him. Although the "War on Terror" is invoked as justification for Guantánamo Bay, the specific normative distinction upon which the legal regime pivots is the alien/citizen distinction, and Omar Khadr has been consigned to the abyss reserved to aliens.

Canada has done something different to Omar: it has rendered him not merely an alien but a stateless man. Hannah Arendt famously described citizenship as the right to have rights, but that was at the dawning of the international human rights movement and well before theories of post-national citizenship encouraged the belief that human rights at the domestic level had gained lift-off from national citizenship. That was before 9/11. Today, Omar embodies a new and unheralded subject position: call it post-national statelessness.

The trial of Omar Khadr before the Military Commission is scheduled to commence on 26 January 2010, six days after the inauguration of the next US president.

3–6 MAY 2010 (PART 1)

Omar is currently represented by two US civilian trial attorneys. He fired his military counsel months earlier. The story of how and why he dismissed his military defense team is complicated, but it would be erroneous to infer that he lost personal confidence in Lt-Cmdr Kuebler. Civilian counsel took over after President Obama took office, and hopes were high that he would fulfil his pledge to close Guantánamo Bay. Had he followed through, Omar would have been repatriated to Canada or transferred to a civilian federal court in the territorial United States. Neither of these events transpired, and within a few months, Omar fired his civilian lawyers.

The pre-trial hearing I attended addressed a motion brought by the defense to suppress the admission at trial of evidence extracted by torture, by cruel, inhuman, or degrading treatment, or otherwise not given voluntarily. The 2006 Military Commissions Act did not prohibit the admission of evidence obtained up until 2005 through coercive methods deemed to fall short of torture, as long as the Military Commissions judge considered the evidence reliable and probative and concluded that the "interests of justice would best be served" by admission of the evidence.

The statements extracted from Omar were made prior to 2005. He was interrogated at Bagram in the summer and fall of 2002, less than a year after 9/11. Military intelligence interrogators at Bagram were under intense pressure from their superiors to generate usable battlefield intelligence and received no clear guidance on the limits of permissible interrogation techniques. This was also the political climate that generated the notorious "torture memos" in 2004, in which legal advisors to President Bush constricted the definition of torture to that which can precipitate organ failure or death. The goal was to ensure that techniques such as waterboarding did not constitute torture. If hypocrisy is the tribute vice pays to virtue, the torture memos were the tribute that raw power pays to legality. They indicated the lengths to which the Bush administration was willing to go to define torture out of legal existence in order to validate its use.

The amendments contained in the 2009 Military Commissions Act did exclude evidence obtained by torture or "cruel, inhuman or degrading treatment," whenever made. It also stipulated that statements made outside the battlefield or incident to capture had to meet a standard of voluntariness, determined according to the "totality of the circumstances." These included:

1 The details of the taking of the statement, accounting for the circumstances of the conduct of military and intelligence operations during hostilities.

2 The characteristics of the accused, such as military training, age, and education level.
3 The lapse of time, change of place, or change in identity of the questioners between the statement sought to be admitted and any prior questioning of the accused.[7]

As these provisions affirm, this regime does not lack for rules. The government has made up (and revised and amended) the regulations and the procedural manuals for the Military Commissions as they have gone along. The night before the suppression motion began, they delivered a 250-page procedural manual intended to govern the next day's proceedings. The rules of this game are always provisional and always proliferating and mutating. The absurdity would be comical were the stakes not so high. The government continuously adapts and revises the rules to better repel the claim that Guantánamo Bay is a lawless enterprise, even as it fails in the attempt – as it must inevitably do.

Omar has sworn an affidavit detailing allegations of torture, cruel, inhuman, and degrading treatment, and coercion. The prosecution counters that his statements were made voluntarily and that his allegations of abuse are fabricated.

As is typical in pre-trial motions, Omar does not testify. Over the course of the next few days, prosecution and defense lawyers ably perform their roles. They examine, cross-examine, leap to their feet with objections, and make prolix arguments about the proper interpretation of the relevant law. The Military Commissions judge, Patrick Parrish, listens with barely concealed impatience and doles out his dull sarcasm even-handedly to both sides.

Sitting in the courtroom, it is too easy to succumb to the enchantment of the spectacle and to mistake this facsimile of legality for the real thing. This should not surprise. After all, the United States arguably has the most elaborate and sophisticated legal apparatus in the world. One will not encounter here the vulgarity of a 1950s Soviet show trial, or the crudeness of a kangaroo court. The emperor in this legal chimera may have no clothes, but the clothes he is not wearing are impeccably tailored. And the daily media accounts simply report the progress of the parade.

Seven prosecutors, including two senior Military Commissions prosecutors, could see it: they resigned from their positions because their commitment to the rule of law would not allow them serve with integrity. But why? The most recent version of Military Commissions Act seems to comply with basic norms of legal process by requiring a judge to exclude evidence extracted by torture, or by cruel, inhuman, or degrading treatment, or otherwise obtained involuntarily. And here we are in a courtroom, watching and listening to witnesses testify before Judge Patrick Parrish about whether they tortured or abused Omar or saw or heard or learned of anyone torturing or abusing Omar. Every day the media dutifully recounts the day's events in court, just as they would in any other proceeding. And here we are, observers from human rights organizations, seeing that justice is done. Judge Patrick Parrish cares about the transparency of the process. I know this because he says so a lot. Judge Parrish is committed to ensuring that the United States and the world have a clear view of the first war crimes prosecution of a minor since World War II. Presumably, we NGO observers and the media serve as information conduits. So if the process is transparent and the process is odious, why is the rot not visible to the untrained eye?

What Judge Parrish seems to means by transparency is that we in the courtroom – media and NGO observers – can see and hear what he sees and hears. But transparency is not simply about seeing what is presented to a judge; it is also about what is withheld by the judge and from the judge.

Wherever national security is advanced, transparency retreats. When I first got involved in Omar's case, I was prepared to assume the veracity of the official story circulating in the public domain: that Omar Khadr threw a grenade in a battle that killed a US soldier and wounded another. Yet even if true, it could not amount to a war crime. Omar was a minor at the time. It could neither justify the violations committed against him or salvage the legality of a trial that amounted to both culmination and perpetuation of those violations. Only a year later, thanks to an inadvertent government leak, did we learn of evidence supporting the alternate hypothesis that another combatant might have thrown the grenade that killed Sgt Christopher Speer. Key elements of the prosecution narrative circulated freely in the media, while the cloak of national security confidentiality prohibited the release of any contradictory information that might raise doubts about Omar's guilt. It turned out that the battlefield report naming Omar as the grenade thrower initially identified another Afghan combatant as the perpetrator. That man (the only other survivor of the US air strike) was executed by US soldiers on the battlefield. Several months after submitting the battlefield report, the author altered the report to name Omar as the one who threw the grenade.[8]

The interior of the Military Commissions courtroom is certainly a reasonable facsimile of a real court, but in an ordinary court any interested member of the public can walk in off the street and attend. Not so in Guantánamo Bay. This is one of the most inaccessible, strictly controlled locations in the world. A limited number of observers from designated NGOs who obtained advance clearance attend the hearings at considerable inconvenience and expense. Parliamentarians from other states who wished to observe proceedings before the Military Commission were denied permission explicitly or else implicitly deflected through a tedious, bureaucratic process that never said no, but never said yes.

Ironically, the audience for Judge Parrish's assurances of transparency is steadily shrinking, since one US and three Canadian journalists have been banned by the Department of Defense from attending further proceedings in Omar's case. The Pentagon banished the journalists because they allegedly violated the Department of Defense "ground rules" by printing the name of Interrogator 1, Omar's lead interrogator. Interrogator 1's true identity – Joshua Claus – has long been in the public domain. Among other things, he gave an interview in 2008 to reporter Michelle Shephard (one of the four sanctioned journalists) of the *Toronto Star* and made no effort to conceal his identity or role. It is available to anyone with a passing acquaintance with Google, or who has seen the movie *Taxi to the Dark Side*. Claus faced a court martial for his role in the deaths by torture of two Afghan detainees at Bagram, though the charges were eventually bargained down to five months imprisonment for pleading guilty to relatively minor offences.

Not all intelligence officers who have testified so far have done so under condition of anonymity. Damien Corsetti had the same job as Claus, but unlike Claus, has expressed deep remorse and anguish about his actions. He testified under his real name, as did Greg Finlay and Tim Fehmer of the FBI's "clean team." At a press conference, Chief Prosecutor Murphy made it clear that he would not condescend to explain why Interrogator 1's identity could not be revealed. He avowed that military interrogators may require anonymity in case they deploy again, to avoid compromising ongoing operations, to safeguard former interrogators and their families, or to protect the interrogators' future employment prospects. Joshua Claus is no longer in the military, he is not connected to ongoing operations, and he will not be deploying again.

The only rationale for concealing Claus's name seems to be a desire to spare him whatever public opprobrium might ensue if he is exposed as an unrepentant torturer. We don't normally protect the identities of accused criminals from public disclosure and from possible conviction in the court of public opinion – as Omar knows all too well. Nor do we protect convicted criminals from vilification by those who learn of their wrongdoing. It is unclear why the Military Commission demands that we who are present in the courtroom protect the identity of an alleged torturer who happens to be an ex-soldier. But four journalists – the conduit through which the proceedings are supposedly rendered transparent – were expelled for publishing Claus's name.

The core of the suppression motion proceeds from a sworn statement by Omar that he was subject to abuse amounting to torture and/or cruel, inhuman, and degrading treatment over the course of three months in Bagram from July to August 2002 and subsequently during his detention in Guantánamo Bay. He was interrogated in Bagram hundreds of times, beginning twelve hours after he was transferred into the detention camp from the Bagram field hospital, where he was treated for two gaping bullet wounds in his chest and shrapnel in his eye. His affidavit enumerates long periods in painful stress positions, sleep deprivation, being denied pain medication, being subjected to barking dogs while hooded, urinating on himself and being used as a human mop, having bright lights deliberately shone in his shrapnel-wounded eyes, and more.

The prosecution seeks to discredit the affidavit by presenting the clean team interrogators whose evidence the prosecution intends to rely upon at trial. Meanwhile, the defense does not have access to the rest of the interrogators, except Joshua Claus. The defense does not even know how many people interrogated Omar. The defense brought motions to compel disclosure of the identities of all of Omar's interrogators and not only the clean team interrogators that the prosecution intended to rely upon. But the defense never got the names.

Over the next few days, the prosecution leads a troop of clean team interrogators from Bagram and Guantánamo. Each witness testifies that he or she did not abuse Omar. No witness saw, heard, or learned of any abuse of Omar in the interrogations that happened before or after their own. Their evidence is intended to demonstrate that Omar is lying when he says he was tortured and subject to cruel, inhuman, or degrading treatment. According to the prosecution witnesses, the teenage Omar freely admitted to throwing the grenade that killed Sgt Speer. Indeed, not only did he confess to throwing a grenade after he had been shot twice in the chest and took shrapnel in his eye, he conveniently managed to glance at his watch before throwing the grenade so that he could provide the interrogators with the precise time that the grenade was thrown (3 PM). At least, that's what the interrogators' reports tell us. The witnesses confirmed that Omar was relaxed, cooperative, and unafraid as he volunteered his statements to them.

These clean team witnesses are professional interrogators; many were also professional witnesses. Each testifies directly, cogently, and confidently. One FBI witness does concede that Omar told him that he had been tortured by other interrogators. When asked how he responded to the disclosure, the witness replies that Omar did not give him enough specific information to merit pursuit of the issue, and so he neither reported the torture complaint to anyone else nor inquire further himself. A fellow observer and I find this interesting. The FBI is a law enforcement agency. A law enforcement officer is trained to investigate crime. Torture is a crime. When a teenage kid reports being tortured, one might have thought that a highly trained law enforcement officer might know how to follow up with appropriate inquiries to ascertain the basis of the complaint.

Insofar as the prosecution has set out to discredit Omar by leading witnesses who did, saw, or heard nothing amiss, the prosecution performs ably. The only slip-up occurrs when a medic assigned to check on Omar's post-operative condition testifies about attending him in the days following his transfer from the hospital to the detention camp. The medic came upon Omar in a cage known as a "sally port" with his arms shackled above his head to the top of the cage. Omar was hooded. At this time, he was sixteen years old and recovering from the bullet wounds that nearly killed him. When the medic removed the hood, Omar was weeping. Guards had chained him up like that for hours to punish him. For what? That was never made clear.

Omar's allegations of abuse are consistent with the widespread documentation of systematic torture and abuse that occurred at

Bagram and at Guantánamo. This documentation has been reported, recorded, and disseminated by the media, by human rights organizations, by documentary filmmakers, detainees, and former interrogators. In a real judicial proceeding, demonstrating a pattern of abuse similar to what Omar alleges would be relevant and admissible for purposes of establishing the plausibility of his account of what was done to him.

Inside this courtroom, however, that evidence does not exist. In this pre-trial hearing, a crucial task performed by the Military Commissions judge is the creation of the legal and factual universe within which he will assess the credibility of Omar's allegation of abuse and torture. In this hermetically sealed space of his own making, Judge Parrish deems that any torture, abuse, or cruel and inhuman treatment that occurred in Bagram to anyone other than Omar is neither visible nor audible to him. Judge Parrish declares that he will not admit any testimony about any treatment or interrogation methods applied to anyone other than Omar. If any such evidence slips in inadvertently, the judge announces, he will give it the weight he deems appropriate: none. The hooding and chaining of Omar is not eligible as torture because it was not perpetrated by an interrogator for purposes of extracting information. In a real criminal court or court martial, these rulings would be regarded as absurd. In the Military Commissions court, the cliché "justice is blind" takes on a whole new meaning. So all that is left is Omar's word against a phalanx of US military, FBI, and CIA interrogators who did nothing, saw nothing, and heard nothing except the spontaneous, voluntary confessions of a fifteen-year-old.

3–6 MAY 2010 (PART 2): ON TORTURE-INDUCED MEMORY LOSS

I have long known that torture can impair the memory of survivors. What I learn from observing the Military Commissions proceedings of Omar Khadr is that it can impair the memory of perpetrators too.

Consider the testimony of Joshua Claus. The convening authority of the Military Commissions prohibit public disclosure of his name. In court, he is addressed as Interrogator 1. We observe him testify by videoconference from an undisclosed location in the United States. He was Omar's lead military intelligence interrogator at Bagram airbase in Afghanistan, where Omar was detained for around three months after his capture on the battlefield on 27 July 2002.

Claus is a defense witness. This may seem odd, since he extracted most of the statements that the clean teams subsequently "confirmed" in their interrogation of Omar. Claus is a hostile witness called by the defense and compelled to testify against his wishes. Why didn't the prosecution call him as their star witness? After all, Claus extracted the original statements that the clean team later confirmed with Omar in their interrogations.

As noted earlier, Claus was also one of several interrogators and guards implicated in the death of two Afghans detained at Bagram around the same time as Omar was detained there. Along with the other American soldiers (none of whom were convicted), Claus was offered and accepted a plea bargain in late 2005 wherein he admitted to three incidents of detainee abuse in exchange for a sentence of five and half months. At the time, Omar's prosecutors requested clemency on Claus's behalf because of the valuable contribution he could make to securing Omar's conviction. Claus also received immunity from prosecution for torture or detainee abuse in exchange for speaking to the Khadr prosecutors, in order that he could testify against Omar free of any risk that he would himself face sanction for his conduct.

What changed between Claus's court martial and the suppression motion that might have led the prosecution to decide not to rely on his testimony? First, the public backlash that accompanied the publication of the "torture memos," along with the revelations of widespread abuse in Bagram, Abu Ghraib, and Guantánamo, made it more challenging to characterize the conduct of men like Claus as honorable. Secondly, the Military Commissions Act of 2009 also made evidence obtained by cruel, inhuman, or degrading treatment inadmissible. Even if the interrogation methods employed at Bagram did not meet the threshold for torture, it would be difficult to evade their depiction as "cruel, inhuman, or degrading." Suddenly, Claus was no longer so attractive a witness to the prosecution.

He was, however, perhaps the only, and certainly the most important, military interrogator whose identity was known to the defense. Claus began interrogating Omar less than twelve hours after Omar's discharge from hospital where, according to the nurse and doctors who testified, he received first class medical treatment for the two gaping bullet wounds in his chest and the shrapnel in his eye. Fifteen-year-old Omar was served up to Claus on a stretcher.

Omar's affidavit identifies his chief interrogator as a "skinny blond man" with a tattoo on his forearm. Claus is no longer skinny, but he is still blond and tattooed. When questioned by Omar's defense lawyers, Claus cannot recall the promise of immunity or the clemency plea written on his behalf by the Khadr prosecutors. As for the interrogations themselves, Claus's memory fails him again and again. As he explains, it all happened a long time ago, and it is hard to remember details. One thing he can remember is the story that he and his fellow interrogators concocted about the gang rape of a fictitious young Afghan kid by "four big black guys" in a US prison that ended with the death of the victim. Since another military witness admitted that he heard that Omar was threatened with rape, Claus cannot not easily disavow any recollection of it. Indeed, he does not merely confirm the rape story, he re-enacts his recitation of it for us. He throws in the nuances, small asides, fake pauses, and colourful detail that a practised storyteller uses to make his delivery seem natural and spontaneous. Today his audience is in the courtroom, but it was originally performed before a fifteen-year-old lying on a stretcher with bullet holes in his body and shrapnel in his eyes, whom Interrogator 1 believed had thrown the grenade that killed a US soldier. Interrogator 1 tells the story with impressive flair, and he knows it.

As for the rest – well, he can't recall if he ever shone a bright light into Omar's shrapnel-injured eyes. He cannot recall shackling Omar to a cage for hours at a time with hands bound at head level, eye level, head hooded. He does remember prisoners shackled in cages – he likens this practice to a "time out" that a parent might impose on a misbehaving child. But he isn't sure about whether it ever happened to Omar. He can't remember forcing Omar to sit up on his stretcher after arriving from the hospital tent in order to cause him excruciating pain. He can't recall setting barking dogs on Omar while he had a hood over his head. He does not recall making Omar stand for hours to inflict both physical pain and sleep deprivation – though he does acknowledge that sleep deprivation was a technique used at Bagram; in his court martial Claus swore that it was "the practice" to do it to new detainees. He explains his understanding that the Geneva Conventions only required prisoners to receive four hours of sleep over a twenty-four-hour period (the Geneva Conventions say nothing of the sort). He does not recall tightening the hood around Omar's neck – something he admitted doing to one of the detainees whose death precipitated the court martial. He cannot recall grabbing Omar and throwing him off his stretcher. He does not actually deny using this or any other "non-traditional interrogation techniques" (the prosecution's euphemism) – he just cannot recall one way or the other.

These interrogations of Omar happened eight years prior to the Military Commission hearing at which Claus testified, and Claus was a busy man at Bagram. It might well have been difficult to retrieve specific knowledge about what was done or not done in the course of his self-described "six hour a day, seven day a week" interrogations of Omar.

In fairness to Claus, if someone asked me whether, between August and October 2002, I sat on the subway next to a skinny blond man with a tattoo on his forearm, I would almost certainly declare that I don't recall. I definitely rode the subway in August to October 2002, but it was so long ago, and riding the subway is so routine for me and I have sat next to so many people that I just can't remember if I sat next to a skinny blond man with a tattooed forearm. On the other hand, if someone asked me if I jumped off a bridge between August and October 2002, I would say no without hesitation. I may not recollect what I was doing every minute of every day of those three months, but I do know that I did not jump off a bridge because I have never jumped off a bridge in my life.

So why is it that Joshua Claus can't recall whether he tortured Omar Khadr?

I am listening to a torturer testify. But that's not the worst part. The worst part is that he is not the one on trial.

AUGUST 2010

Judge Parrish renders his written decision in the suppression motion. In it, he recounts the evidence led by the prosecution, recites the relevant law, and concludes that there is no evidence before him to support Omar's allegations that confessions made by him to the clean team interrogators were extracted involuntarily. In any case, the inculpatory video showing his participation in the construction of real evidence was obtained independently of any statements he made.

Parrish's decision is largely devoid of judicial reasoning, and so the logical chain that leads him to his conclusions remains opaque. But the judgment is freely available to anyone who wishes to download it. Yet more transparency.

The opportunity to observe proceedings before the Military Commission in Guantánamo Bay has taught me an important lesson in transparency. I have had a clear and unobstructed view of a brick wall.

POSTSCRIPT

On 13 October 2010, Omar Khadr accepted an offer of a pre-trial agreement. In fulfillment of that agreement, he pled guilty to all offences brought against him and entered into a Stipulation of Fact in which it was "stipulated and agreed, by the Prosecution and Defense, with the express consent of the accused" that the facts contained in the document were true. The stipulation of fact contained a detailed confession that comprehensively rehearsed the version of events asserted by the prosecution.

In exchange for pleading guilty, agreeing to the stipulation of fact, and surrendering or waiving various other rights or entitlements Omar would otherwise have, the Convening Authority undertook to approve a sentence of confinement of eight years in addition to the time already spent in the custody of the United States. The Convening Authority further undertook to support his transfer to Canadian custody after he served one more year of confinement at Guantánamo Bay. By an exchange of diplomatic notes dated 24 October 2010, the Canadian government conveyed that, "as requested by the United States, the Government of Canada is inclined to favourably consider Mr. Khadr's application to be transferred to Canada to serve the remainder of his sentence, or such portion of the remainder of his sentence as the National Parole Board determines."

As part of the plea agreement, Omar was required to undergo a sentencing hearing before a jury of US military officers empanelled under the Military Commissions Act, even though any sentence they imposed beyond eight years would be disregarded. The plea agreement restricted the defense's discretion to call witnesses on Omar's behalf; the prosecution was unrestricted. Their star witness was Michael Welner, a forensic psychiatrist and media pundit. After interviewing/interrogating Omar on a single occasion, Welner testified at length and depicted Omar as an incorrigible, unrepentant, and depraved terrorist. The defense was not able to use the legal mechanisms available in ordinary US courts to discredit

Welner as an expert witness. His testimony remains on the record as expert evidence.

The plea agreement and the events around it are unlikely to change anybody's view about Omar. For those already committed to viewing him as a monster, his stipulation of fact and the sentencing hearing merely confirm what they have known all along. Others will doubt the probity of the guilty plea and view Omar's confession as the unfree choice of a boy-man facing the hideous alternative of a rigged trial, followed by certain conviction and decades more imprisonment.

As for me, I am no longer seeking an answer to the question of whether fifteen-year-old Omar Khadr threw a grenade on a battlefield in the course of a firefight in Afghanistan on 27 July 2002. I have so many other questions about guilt and responsibility, but they are not addressed to Omar.

NOTES

1 A non-public inquiry into Canadian involvement in the detention and torture of three other Canadians also made findings of Canadian complicity. As of late 2011, the government has refused to compensate any of the three men, and litigation is ongoing.

2 I invoke Guantánamo Bay as a metonym for the regime of capture, detention, interrogation, and torture applied by the United States and its partners in various locations outside the territorial United States, ostensibly to evade the reach of the US Constitution and legal constraint more generally.

3 Notably, seven Guantánamo prosecutors did resign, including chief prosecutor Morris Davis, who initially prosecuted Omar Khadr.

4 The media circulated the story that Sgt Speer was a medic and therefore a protected person. He was apparently training to become a medic, but he was not a medic or performing in that role at the time of his death.

5 In the case of Yaser Hamdi, a dual US-Saudi citizen captured on the battlefield, the US government ultimately coerced Hamdi into surrendering his US citizenship and accepting permanent exile from the US in exchange for release from potentially indefinite detention. In this way the United States avoided having to confront further litigation before

US courts in which its violations of Hamdi's constitutional rights would be repeatedly exposed before a civilian court.

6 "Khadr Plea a 'Lose-Lose' Situation: Former Prosecutor," CTV website, 25 October 2010, http://www.ctv.ca/CTVNews/Canada/20101025/khadr-prosecutor-101025/ (accessed 7 October 2011).

7 Military Commissions Act 2009, 10 U.S.C., at 948r(d).

8 In testimony, the author of the report explained the revision by stating that he meant to identify Omar as "the one who threw the grenade."

291

UNITED STATES OF AMERICA

v.

OMAR AHMED KHADR
a/k/a "Akhbar Farhad"
a/k/a "Akhbar Farnad"
a/k/a "Ahmed Muhammed Khali"

Offer for Pre-trial Agreement

13 MGS CK
~~12~~ October 2010

1. I, OMAR AHMED KHADR, ISN 0766, am presently the accused under military commission charges, dated 24 April 2007. I read the charges and specifications alleged against me, and they have been explained to me by my defense counsel, Lieutenant Colonel Jon Jackson, and Major Matthew Schwartz, and Mr. Nate Whitling, a Canadian foreign consultant (hereinafter collectively referred to as "defense counsel"). I understand the charges and specifications, and I am aware I have a legal and moral right to plead not guilty and to leave the prosecution with the burden of proving my guilt beyond a reasonable doubt by legal and competent evidence.

2. Understanding the above and under the conditions set forth below, and in consideration of this agreement by the Convening Authority to approve a sentence in accord with the limitations set forth in this agreement, I offer and agree to:

a. Plead Guilty to all charges and specifications.

b. Admit I knowingly and intentionally committed each of the acts set forth in each charge and specification referred on 24 April 2007. I understand, as explained to me by my defense counsel, that my admission of committing these acts constitutes a sufficient basis, under United States law, for me to be found guilty beyond a reasonable doubt to the aforementioned charges and specifications.

c. Enter into the Stipulation of Fact that is Attachment A, dated ~~8~~ 13 [MGS CK] October, 2010, a nine (9) [MGS CK] page document (hereinafter Attachment A). I understand that I have an absolute right to refuse to enter into Attachment A but I knowingly and voluntarily agree to enter into Attachment A with the United States Government. I understand a stipulation of fact ordinarily cannot be contradicted. If Attachment A should be contradicted during or after my guilty plea, I understand the United States Government may withdraw from this pretrial agreement. I further understand and agree that Attachment A will be used to determine my guilt and to determine an appropriate sentence. I have discussed this decision with my defense counsel and believe it is in my best interest to enter into Attachment A with the United States Government for the herein stated purposes.

d. Knowingly and voluntarily waive and relinquish any request for any forensic or scientific testing of any physical evidence in the United States Government's possession, including, but not limited to, DNA testing. I fully understand that as a result of this waiver I will

APPELLATE EXHIBIT 341
PAGE _____ OF _____

not have another opportunity to have any physical evidence in this case submitted for any testing or to employ the results of any testing to support any claim of innocence regarding the offenses to which I am pleading guilty. In addition, I understand the United States Government may dispose of such physical evidence upon sentencing by a Military Commission in this case.

e. Waive any claim to confinement credit for any period of time I have been detained prior to the sentence being announced. Notwithstanding my waiver to any claim to confinement credit prior to the sentence being announced, this waiver in no way shall be construed as to limit the Convening Authority's ability to reduce the sentence imposed pursuant to paragraph 6 *infra*.

f. Sign and execute the document found at Attachment B, a two (2) page document that is Military Commission Form 2330, Waiver/Withdrawal of Appellate Rights, within the specified timeframe found within Attachment B and R.M.C. 1110. In doing so I understand I will, at the time of execution of Attachment B, waive my rights to appeal this conviction, sentence, and/or detention to the extent permitted by law, or to collaterally attack my conviction, sentence, and/or detention in any judicial forum (found in the United States or otherwise) or proceeding, on any grounds, except that I may bring a post-conviction claim if any sentence is imposed in excess of the statutory maximum sentence or in violation of the sentencing limitation provisions contained in this agreement. I have been informed by my counsel orally and in writing of my post-trial and appellate rights.

g. Not initiate or support any litigation or challenge, in any forum in any Nation, against the United States or any official in their personal or official capacity with regard to my capture, detention, prosecution to include discovery practice, post conviction confinement and/or detainee combatant status. I further agree to move to dismiss with prejudice any presently pending direct or collateral attack challenging my capture, detention, prosecution and/or detainee combatant status; to implement this aspect of this agreement, following announcement of the sentence in this case, I direct my counsel to submit a motion to dismiss the petition for habeas corpus in my case currently pending in the United States District Court for the District of Columbia as well as all claims currently pending in the United States Court of Appeals for the District of Columbia Circuit.

h. Not to engage in or materially support, directly or indirectly, hostilities against the United States or its coalition partners as defined in 10 U.S.C. § 948(a), or any other organization that I know engages in hostilities against the United States or its coalition partners.

i. While in the continued custody of the United States, submit to interviews whenever and wherever requested by United States law enforcement officials, intelligence authorities, and prosecutors. I understand the requesting parties will notify my legal counsel of the interviews. However, I waive any right I may have to my attorneys being present for the interviews. I understand I must be completely truthful during these interviews. I also agree, while in U.S. custody, to appear, cooperate, and testify truly, before any grand jury, any court, military court or hearing, military commission or any other proceeding requested by the United States Government.

293

j. I agree and understand that if I am not truthful in any testimony I may provide, I may be prosecuted for perjury, false statement or other similar offense before any court or Military Commission having jurisdiction over me.

k. In further exchange for consideration of the benefit I am receiving, I also agree, after I am transferred to Canadian custody, to never enter into the United States of America or any of her territories or military installations. If I enter into said area(s), the remaining portion of any approved sentence, if any, shall be carried out in United States custody, explicitly revoking the provisions of paragraph 6 of this agreement. I understand and agree that I will also waive any legal actions that may or may not be brought at that time, in any forum, whether in the United States or otherwise, as a result of my violation of this agreement by entering the United States of America or any of her territories or military installations. This includes United States airspace.

l. I hereby assign to the Government of Canada any profits or proceeds which I may be entitled to receive in connection with any publication or dissemination of information relating to the illegal conduct alleged on the charge sheet. This assignment shall include any profits and proceeds for my benefit, regardless of whether such profits and proceeds are payable to me or to others, directly or indirectly, for my benefit or for the benefit of my associates or a current or future member of my family. I hereby represent that I have not previously assigned, and I agree that I will not circumvent this assignment to the Government of Canada by assigning, the rights to my story to an associate or to a current or future member of my family, or to another person or entity that would provide some financial benefit to me, to my associates, or to a current or future member of my family. Moreover, I will not circumvent this assignment by assisting or facilitating his or her profiting from a public dissemination, whether or not such an associate or other family member is personally or directly involved in such dissemination. I agree that this assignment is enforceable through any applicable provision of law that would further the purpose of this paragraph's prohibition of personal enrichment for myself, my family, or my heirs and assigns, through any publication nor dissemination of qualifying information, and I acknowledge that my representations herein are material terms of this agreement.

3. Subject to the Rules for Military Commissions (R.M.C.), the Military Commissions Rules of Evidence (M.C.R.E.) and the limitations described below, I understand the prosecution and defense may call witnesses and present evidence, subject to any rulings by the Military Judge, regarding matters in aggravation and extenuation and mitigation for sentencing consideration. I further agree to the following:

a. I will not seek to offer any testimony, in any form, from any detainee presently held at Naval Station Guantanamo Bay;

b. I will not seek to obtain any depositions to be offered at the presentencing hearing, nor will I offer any depositions at the presentencing hearing;

3

c. I will not seek to offer the testimony, either in court or via VTC of any witness, other than: (1) Dr. Katherine Porterfield: (2) Dr. Steven Xenakis. (3) Captain McCarthy; and (4) Dr. Arlette Zinck, all of whom the Government has agreed to produce at U.S. Naval Station, Guantanamo Bay. Cuba for sentencing. I understand that sentencing proceedings will not be delayed to if these witnesses are unavailable.

d. I will not seek to offer the expert testimony, in any form, of any expert other than Dr. Katherine Porterfield and Dr. Stephen Xenakis. I recognize that it is the responsibility of my defense counsel to ensure that fees for these experts have been properly requested and approved and that sentencing proceedings will not be delayed if the Defense fails to submit proper requests sufficiently in advance of the sentencing hearing to allow the Convening Authority to review and approve appropriate hours to accommodate these witnesses' testimony.

4. I understand that this offer. when accepted by the Convening Authority, constitutes a binding agreement. I assert that I am, in fact, guilty of the offenses to which I am offering to plead guilty, and that I have been apprised of the evidence against me and agree that the evidence could and would prove me guilty beyond a reasonable doubt of the offenses to which I am pleading guilty. I understand that this agreement permits the Military Commission to find me guilty for all offenses to which I plead guilty without the need for the government to present evidence that would prove my guilt beyond a reasonable doubt. I offer to plead guilty because it will be in my best interest that the Convening Authority grants me the relief set forth in this agreement. I understand that I waive my right to a trial of the facts and to be confronted by the witnesses against me, and my right to avoid self-incrimination insofar as a plea of guilty will incriminate me.

5. In making this offer, I further state that:

a. I am satisfied with Lieutenant Colonel Jon Jackson and Major Matthew Schwartz my detailed defense counsel who advised me with respect to this offer and consider them competent to represent me in this Military Commission.

b. No person or persons made any attempt to force or coerce me into making this offer or to plead guilty. I enter into this agreement voluntarily of my own free will.

c. My counsel fully advised me of the nature of the charges against me, the possibility of my defending against them, any defense that might apply (including other defense motions that have not yet been filed), and the effect of the guilty plea that I am offering to make, and I fully understand their advice and the meaning. effect. and consequences of this plea.

d. I understand that I may withdraw my plea of guilty at any time before the sentence is announced but not after the sentence is announced and that, if I do so, this agreement is canceled and of no effect. This agreement will also be canceled and of no effect. if any of the following occurs:

(1) The Military Commission refuses to accept my plea of guilty to any charge and specification, as set forth above, or modification of the plea by anyone during the trial to "not guilty," or to lesser charges;

(2) Either party withdraws from the agreement before the trial; or

(3) I fail to enter into Attachment A and Attachment B as described in paragraph 2(g) and (j) *supra.*

e. I understand the Convening Authority's obligation to approve a sentence no greater than that provided in this agreement may be canceled if, between the announcement of sentence and the Convening Authority's approval of any sentence, I commit any offense chargeable under the Military Commissions Act of 2009 or fail to otherwise fulfill the terms of this agreement.

f. I understand that in the event this plea agreement is not approved by the Convening Authority or is not accepted by the Military Commission, or if I withdraw from this agreement prior to the Military Commission announcing my sentence, this offer cannot be used against me in any proceeding in this case to establish my guilt to these offenses.

g. This document includes all of the terms of this pretrial agreement and, to the extent consistent with the authority granted to the Convening Authority by section 948(h) of the Military Commissions Act of 2009, this prosecution and agreement disposes of all acts of commission or omission which have been referred to this military commission. I have taken into account that other U.S. federal government agencies have indicated their willingness to positively endorse my prisoner transfer application after I have completed one additional year in U.S. custody after my sentence is approved; however, I recognize the decision to approve my transfer is ultimately made by the Canadian Government, and this agreement cannot bind Canadian Officials to accept my prisoner transfer application. No other inducements have been made by the Convening Authority, or any other person, which affect my offer to plead guilty.

h. It is a condition precedent to this agreement that duly authorized officials of the United States and Canada exchange diplomatic notes reflecting United States and Canadian Government support for my transfer to Canada to serve the remainder of my approved sentence after completing no less than one additional year in United States custody after the date of approval of my sentence, and that the United States provide copies of these diplomatic notes to my detailed defense counsel. I understand that my transfer to Canada is contingent upon the consent of the Government of Canada, and that this plea agreement cannot bind the Government of Canada to consent to my prisoner transfer application. I further understand that the Government of Canada cannot accept my application until it is submitted and that any acceptance of a prisoner transfer agreement is a separate agreement from the pre-trial agreement I am entering into with the Convening Authority. I understand that if the Government of Canada ultimately does not accept my application for transfer, it will have no impact on this agreement. No other inducements have been made by the Convening Authority, or any other person, which affect my offer to plead guilty.

6. As consideration for my offer to plead guilty set forth above:

a. The Convening Authority will not approve a sentence of confinement of greater than eight (8) years.

b. The Convening Authority agrees to take all appropriate actions, to the extent of his authority, including the execution of all necessary documents, to support transfer of the accused from the custody of the United States to the custody of Canada after the accused has served one year of confinement in the custody of the United States after the announcement of sentence, provided the accused otherwise complies with the terms of this agreement. The remainder of the approved sentence will be served in Canada, consistent with Canadian Law.

c. The parties acknowledge that the authority of the Convening Authority is limited by the Military Commissions Act of 2009, the Rules for Military Commissions, and the Regulation for Trial by Military Commission, which limit the authority of the Convening Authority to action related to the prosecution of cases by military commission, such as the approval of the terms of pretrial agreements, the approval of the findings and the sentence of military commissions, and taking action on clemency requests, if any. The parties acknowledge the Convening Authority does not have the authority to:

(1) Control the location of confinement, the conditions of confinement, or whether such confinement is served in military or federal institutions;

(2) Release the accused from military or federal confinement after taking formal action on the findings and sentence of the military commission;

(3) Bind the government of the United States to release the accused from law of war detention;

(4) Bind the government of Canada to allow the accused to enter the country, or to direct, control or otherwise influence the accused's confinement, transfer, parole, or release while in the custody of the government of Canada.

7. The accused and defense counsel understand and agree that this agreement consists of seven (7) numbered paragraphs and seven (7) pages. This document represents the accused's entire agreement with the United States Government. The parties further understand and agree that there are no other agreements, letters, verbal promises or notations that will affect this agreement. The accused and defense counsel further agree that no other inducements have been made by the United States Government which affect the accused's offer to plead guilty.

13 OCT 2010
Date

Omar A Khadr
Omar Ahmed Khadr

297

I certify I gave the accused the advice referred to above. I explained to him the elements of the offenses and I witnesses his voluntary signature to this offer for a pretrial agreement.

13 OCT 2010
Date

JON S. JACKSON,
Lieutenant Colonel, USAR
Defense Counsel

13 Oct 2010
Date

MATTHEW G. SCHWARTZ,
Major, USAF
Defense Counsel

I recommend (acceptance) (rejection) of this offer.

OCT 1 3 2010
Date

Michael C. Chapman
Michael C. Chapman
Legal Advisor to the Convening Authority

The foregoing instrument, dated OCT 1 3 2010 is (approved and accepted) (disapproved).

OCT 1 3 2010
Date

Convening Authority

7

Torture as Foreign Policy: The Omar Khadr Decision

GAIL DAVIDSON

The decision of the Supreme Court of Canada in the Omar Khadr[1] case implies that remedies to prevent torture and punish perpetrators are a privilege to be granted or withheld at the pleasure of the prime minister. This is wrong.

In the Khadr decision, the Supreme Court of Canada declared "that through the conduct of Canadian officials in the course of interrogations [of Khadr] in 2003–2004, as established on the evidence before us, Canada actively participated in a process contrary to Canada's international human rights obligations and contributed to Mr. Khadr's ongoing detention so as to deprive him of his right to liberty and security of the person guaranteed by s. 7 of the Charter, contrary to the principles of fundamental justice."[2] The court was referring to the fact that officials from Canada's Department of Foreign Affairs and International Trade (DFAIT) interrogated Omar Khadr at Guantánamo Bay prison and gave their interrogation records to his American captors. They did this after being told that US officials had tortured him by prolonged and severe sleep deprivation[3] for the three weeks prior to "make him more amenable and willing to talk" to the Canadians. They also knew that he would be placed in isolation after their interrogation.

Ignoring the imperative international duties triggered by these appalling facts, the Supreme Court of Canada went on to rule it appropriate to leave it "to the government to decide how best to respond."[4] The court set aside the 23 April 2009 order of the Federal Court of Canada,[5] confirmed by the Federal Court of Appeal on 14 August 2009,[6] compelling the prime minister, the minister of Foreign Affairs, the commissioner of the RCMP, and the director of CSIS (the

Canadian Security and Intelligence Service) to "request that the United States return Mr. Khadr to Canada as soon as practicable."

The Federal Court order was in keeping with the will of Parliament expressed by majority votes in both the Senate and the House of Commons. In June 2008 the committee struck to study the Omar Khadr case recommended to Parliament "that the Government of Canada demand Omar Khadr's release from U.S. custody at Guantánamo Bay to the custody of Canadian law enforcement officials as soon as practical."[7] On 23 March 2009, Parliament voted to accept that recommendation, thereby directing the prime minister to request Khadr's release and repatriation. The Senate had voted approval of the committee's recommendation in June 2008.

To set aside the Federal Court order and override the will of Parliament, the Supreme Court of Canada relied on a text published in 1915: long before the prohibition of torture became a peremptory norm of international law from which no derogation is permitted; long before the "use of torture ... by state authorities ... had come to be regarded as an attack upon the international order";[8] long before the individual's right to freedom from torture took precedence over the right of states to conduct their affairs free from interference by other states; and long before Canada's Constitution[9] and the rule of law became the supreme law in Canada.[10]

Under current international law, the duties of states to enact and enforce effective remedies to prevent and punish torture are not subservient to any other domestic or international purpose or circumstance including "comity" between states. Under current domestic law, governments, including the executive branch, are bound by the Constitution. As acknowledged by the Supreme Court of Canada in an earlier case, government officials "may not transgress its provisions: indeed, their sole claim to exercise lawful authority rests in the powers allocated to them under the Constitution, and can come from no other source."[11]

The prohibition against torture creates obligations to the international community as a whole, with the consequence that each person has a "legal interest" in its observance and a legal entitlement to demand respect for the prohibition.[12] Enforcement of the torture prohibition through effective measures to prevent, punish, and remedy torture relies on domestic legal systems and on maintenance of the rule of law within those legal systems. The refusal of the prime minister, the minister of Foreign Affairs, the commissioner of the

RCMP, and the director of CSIS to take proper actions to prevent and punish the torture of Omar Khadr and to ensure his removal from the control of his torturers is a frightening example of power politics trumping the law and the rule of law. By such refusal, both the executive and heads of Canada's national law enforcement agencies gave the United States carte blanche to continue to violate Khadr's internationally protected rights.

In taking the extraordinary step of failing to enforce the only available remedy, based on the existence of an arbitrary power not supported by law, the Supreme Court of Canada was simply wrong. It was wrong for the court to conclude that characterizing a remedy for torture as a foreign affairs policy matter displaces the imperative legal duties arising from the Convention against Torture and other instruments binding on Canada to take effective action. Neither the prime minister nor the executive can clothe themselves with the power to do what is prohibited by international and Canadian law. By law, torture against a Canadian citizen must be remedied through investigation and prosecution of suspects. Obviously the victim – in this case, Omar Khadr – must be removed from the control of the perpetrators of crimes against him. Neither the prime minister nor "government" has any "residual" right to override Parliament or to "speak freely with a foreign state"[13] on the suspension or relaxation of the absolute prohibition against torture.[14] Torture can never be considered a legitimate act of state. Neither can suspending or refusing remedies be legitimated as foreign policy.

Ignored by the Supreme Court decision are over fifty years of law reform. Both internationally and within Canada, the imperatives of human rights enforcement and rule of law maintenance have displaced the arbitrary prerogatives enjoyed by states in the past. As observed by the House of Lords in the Pinochet decision, the terms of the Convention against Torture "demonstrate that the states that have become parties have clearly and unambiguously agreed that official torture should now be dealt with in a way which would otherwise amount to interference in their sovereignty."[15] In earlier decisions, the Supreme Court of Canada has recognized that the rule of law now "excludes the idea of any exemption of officials or others from the duty of obedience to the law which governs other citizens or from the jurisdiction of the ordinary courts,"[16] guarantees executive accountability to legal authority, and provides a shield from arbitrary state action.[17]

The language used by the court to describe key facts and principles creates the erroneous impression that US accusations against Omar Khadr are more serious than, and therefore take precedence over, the crimes the United States is known to have been committed against him.

Here are examples of the misleading language used by the court in the Khadr judgment:

- "Frequent flyer program" is used to refer to the torture of Khadr by subjecting him to prolonged and severe sleep deprivation to enhance extraction of information by Canadian officials.
- "Trial" is used to refer to the Military Commissions process found by the US Supreme Court to illegally violate the right to a fair trial by a "regularly constituted court affording all the judicial guarantees which are recognized as indispensable by civilized peoples."[18]
- "War crimes" is used to describe charges against Khadr that have been challenged as illegitimate as being unknown to the laws of war; created after they are alleged to have been committed, for which reason prosecution is absolutely barred;[19] and inapplicable to Khadr because of his status as a child.
- "The trial *is proceeding*" refers to a delay[20] of almost eight years – a delay that violates the right to be tried within a reasonable time under Canadian and US law.[21] Were Khadr before a regularly constituted court, the prosecution would indubitably be stayed on the basis of that delay.
- "Government" is used to refer to Stephen Harper, the commissioner of the RCMP, the minister of Foreign Affairs, and the director of CSIS rather than to Parliament.[22]
- "Mr. Khadr's rights under s. 7 of the *Canadian Charter of Rights and Freedoms* were violated" camouflages the most grave violations of his rights to liberty:[23] due process,[24] freedom from torture and other cruel, inhuman and degrading treatment or punishment,[25] freedom from arbitrary imprisonment,[26] freedom from prosecution for *ex post facto* crimes, a fair trial, timely and confidential legal representation, determination of criminal charges by an impartial and independent tribunal, habeas corpus, equality before the law and equal access to the protection of the law,[27] and rights arising from the Convention on the Rights of the Child including rights to rehabilitation, education, and reintegration into free society.

Finally, the Supreme Court of Canada decision in the Khadr case ignored the legal reality that without remedies there are no rights.[28] The chief justice of the Supreme Court of Canada has observed that, had freedom from torture and other basic rights been enforced, the Holocaust could not have occurred.[29]

Allowing the executive to decide what action to take to remedy or prevent ongoing violations of the internationally protected rights of a Canadian citizen laid the foundation for more inaction. In response to the SCC decision, Canada essentially did nothing. On 3 February 2010, Harper and the minister of Foreign Affairs, Lawrence Cannon, released a statement indicating that their position had not changed and they would not seek Khadr's repatriation. Then on 16 February the Canadian embassy requested, by diplomatic note, assurances that the United States would not use any information turned over by Canadian officials as a result of their interrogations of Khadr. The United States refused to give the assurances, stating that the use of evidence and statements provided by Canadian officials would be governed by the Military Commissions Act.

When Khadr's Canadian lawyers applied for a judicial review of this inaction, the Federal Court of Canada ruled (5 July 2010)[30] that repatriation would be an effective remedy and that doing nothing was not a legal option. Mr Justice Zinn found that the executive's response to the Supreme Court decision (sending a diplomatic note) violated Khadr's right to procedural fairness and that the Canadian government was bound, first, to try to provide an effective remedy for violations of his rights to life until all potentially curative remedies were exhausted and then, to attempt ameliorative remedies. The court ordered the respondents (Harper et al.) to provide to Khadr within seven days and before the recommencement of the Military Commission proceedings a list of remedies that the executive would seek, with the proviso for Khadr to respond to the government's proposals within seven days of receiving them.

In response, the prime minister et al. filed an appeal and an application to stay the Federal Court order pending hearing of the appeal. The chief justice of the Federal Court of Appeal granted the stay (16 July 2010), stating that allowing a judicial review of the exercise of the Crown prerogative "could be seen ... as an affront to the division of powers that would cause irreparable harm ... and would result in improper interference by the Court in the conduct of foreign relations."[31] There was no evidence of harm.

Following the collapse of these attempts to access a determination of Khadr's rights and remedies through an independent court willing and capable of applying the law, the US military proceedings recommenced. US Army Col. Parrish, presiding over the Military Commission proceedings, ruled on 17 August 2010 that all of Khadr's statements, including those made as a result of torture and other cruel, inhuman, and degrading treatment or punishment, would be admitted.

Subsequently Khadr accepted the US offer to place an eight-year cap on any additional sentence and to allow him to apply to serve the balance of his sentence in Canada after "at least" one year, in exchange for a guilty plea on all counts. He was required to sign a fifty-paragraph "Stipulation of Fact" recording his agreement that he is not and was not covered by the Geneva Conventions. Securing this agreement was perhaps seen as necessary, because the Geneva Conventions specifically prohibit sentencing by the Military Commission. Article 3 common to all four Geneva Conventions and Protocol I prohibits – at any time and in any place – the passing of sentence when charges have not been determined "by a regularly constituted court, affording all the judicial guarantees which are recognized as indispensable by civilized people."[32] Denial of a fair trial, such as occurred in the Khadr case, violates the Geneva Conventions, the Rome Statute of the International Criminal Court, and Canada's Geneva Convention Act and Crimes against Humanity and War Crimes Act.

In addition, Khadr was absurdly required to sign the "Stipulation of Fact" and confirm as true statements about which he cannot have known anything: for example, events reputed to have taken place between 1989 and 1998 when he would have been between two and twelve years old; al-Qaeda activities in Afghanistan, the United States, Kenya, Tanzania, Pakistan, and "other countries," and a declaration that al-Qaeda was responsible for the 11 September 2001 collapse of the Trade Towers in New York

Minister of Foreign Affairs Lawrence Cannon subsequently told Parliament, "The government of the United States has accepted that Omar Khadr return to Canada and we will carry out the agreement between Mr. Khadr and the U.S. government."

By allowing the prime minister to refuse to take the remedial action approved by Parliament, ordered by the Federal Court and confirmed by the Federal Court of Appeal, on the basis that the remedy involved interacting with another state, the Supreme Court of Canada compromised the rule of law. State duties to guarantee internationally protected rights such as freedom from torture do not stop at the border. As observed by the European Court of Human Rights, "States must endeavour with all legal and diplomatic means available *vis à vis* foreign states to continue to guarantee the enjoyment of rights and freedoms."[33]

The prevention and punishment of torture and other international crimes will almost always be a matter of foreign affairs: a matter of one state holding another state accountable for the commission of international crimes that were perhaps committed in a third state. These crimes of torture, genocide, war crimes, and crimes against humanity, considered by the world community as the gravest threat, after the crime of aggression, to world peace and order, are almost always committed by state actors. Prevention and punishment will rarely be conducted by the state whose officials are accused as perpetrators.

The capacity of human rights and humanitarian law to ensure global peace and universal rights is threatened throughout the world by both a lack of political willingness to enforce restrictions or accept accountability and executive control of the divisions of the legal systems mandated with enforcement of these laws. In the Khadr case, legal and diplomatic remedies were prevented by executive control and refusal to act. Diplomatic means were used by Australia, Belgium, Demark, France, Russia, Spain, Germany, Sweden, and the United Kingdom to secure the release and repatriation of their nationals imprisoned at Guantánamo Bay.

Enforcement of the prohibition against torture and other international crimes involving state actors depends on laws being in place and in force. Canada has the laws in place. Laws in force depend on the maintenance of the rule of law, which includes access to courts that are independent and impartial and willing to properly balance the public interest in enforcing the law and maintaining the rule of law with the political interest of a few in retaining arbitrary powers. The decision of the Supreme Court of Canada in the Omar Khadr case failed to achieve this balance and put the rights of all at risk.

NOTES

1 *Prime Minister of Canada, Minister of Foreign Affairs, Director of the Canadian Security Intelligence Service and Commissioner of the Royal*

Canadian Mounted Police v. Omar Ahmed Khadr, Supreme Court of Canada, 29 January 2010, http://scc.lexum.umontreal.ca/en/2010/2010scc3/2010scc3.html.

2 *Infra,* para. 48.

3 Sleep deprivation used to extract information from a prisoner is torture according to a variety of authorities. UN experts, reviewing international law, confirmed in a 2006 report on Guantánamo Bay that sleep deprivation, even for several consecutive days, is torture. The US Army Field Manual on Interrogation in force in 2004 listed sleep deprivation as a form of torture. The Canadian government publication *Torture and Abuse Awareness* lists the United States as one of the ten countries worldwide known to engage in torture and lists sleep deprivation as a form of torture.

4 *Supra* note 1 at para. 39: "in view of the constitutional responsibility of the executive to make decisions on matters of foreign affairs and the inconclusive state of the record. The appropriate remedy in this case is to declare that K's *Charter* rights were violated, leaving it to the government to decide how best to respond in light of current information, its responsibility over foreign affairs, and the *Charter*."

5 *Khadr v. Canada*, 2009 FC 405, [2010] 1 F.C.R. 34.

6 *Canada (Prime Minister) v. Khadr*, 2009 FCA 246, [2010] 1 F.C.R. 73.

7 OMAR KHADR Report of the Standing Committee on Foreign Affairs and International Development: Subcommittee on International Human Rights, June 2008, para. 3, p. 6, http://www.jlc.org/files/briefs/khadr/Parliament%20Report%2017%20Jun%2008.pdf.

8 *R v. Bartle and the Commissioner of Police for the Metropolis and Others, Ex Parte Pinochet; R v. Evans and Another and the Commissioner of Police for the Metropolis and Others, Ex Parte Pinochet*, [1999] UKHL 17, Lord Millett.

9 Constitution Act, 1982, being Schedule B to the Canada Act 1982 (U.K.), 1982, c. 11 s. 52 (1), provides that the "Constitution of Canada is the supreme law of Canada, and any law that is inconsistent with the provisions of the Constitution is, to the extent of the inconsistency, of no force or effect."

10 The Canadian Charter of Rights and Freedoms, preamble: "Whereas Canada is founded upon principles that recognize the supremacy of … the rule of law …"

11 *Reference re Secession of Quebec*, [1998] 2 S.C.R. 217, 1998 CanLII 793 (S.C.C.), (1998), 161 D.L.R. (4th) 385, *1998-08-20*, from the unanimous judgment of the court composed of Lamer CJ and

L'Heureux-Dubé, Gonthier, Cory, McLachlin, Iacobucci, Major, Bastarache, and Binnie JJ.

12 *Prosecutor v. Kupresic* (ICTY) 14 January 2001, para. 518-520.

13 *Supra*, note 1, at para. 33.

14 Instruments that impose a mandatory duty to provide effective remedies against torture include the Geneva Conventions of 1949; Rome Statute of the International Court; International Covenant on Civil and Criminal Rights; Convention against Torture and Other Cruel, Inhuman or Degrading Punishment or Treatment; Basic Principles and Guidelines on the Right to Remedy and Reparations for Victims of Violations of International Human Rights and Serious Violations of International Humanitarian Law; the Vienna Declaration and Programme of Action, articles 56 and 60; Body of Principles for the Protection of All Persons under Any Form of Detention or Imprisonment.

15 *Supra*, note 8, at para. 170.

16 *R. v. Campbell*, [1999] 1 S.C.R. 565, 1999 CanLII 676 (S.C.C.), 1999-04-22, para. 18.

17 *Supra*, note 11.

18 *Geneva Conventions*, common Article 3, adopted 12 August 1949; entry into force 21 October 1950. Ratified by 194 countries. Protocol Additional to the Geneva Conventions of 12 August 1949, and relating to the Protection of Victims of International Armed Conflicts (Protocol I), 8 June 1977, article 75.

19 Freedom from *ex post facto* prosecutions is absolute and cannot be displaced by any authority under any circumstances.

20 Factors contributing to the delay include rulings by the US Supreme Court that the military commissions are illegal; dismissal of the charges; non-disclosure by the prosecution; leaked documents indicating falsification of evidence by the US military; the Pentagon sacking of the military "presiding officer" in charge of the Khadr case; investigation of professional misconduct complaints against Khadr's lead military attorney; a 120-day adjournment imposed by President Obama in January 2009 for a review the process; a four-month suspension imposed by the president in May 2009 to alter the military commissions.

21 The US Constitution, art. VI, cl. 2, guarantees a trial within a reasonable time, as does the Speedy Trial Act. In Canada this right is guaranteed by the Charter of Rights and Freedoms s. 11 (b). The Supreme Court of Canada recently ruled that a two-year delay violated Charter

rights and that the appropriate remedy was to stay the prosecution (*R. v. Godin*, 2009 SCC 26).

22 *Supra*, note 4, at para. 3, p. 6.

23 The right to liberty and not to be deprived thereof except in accordance with the principles of fundamental justice is guaranteed by the Charter of Rights and Freedoms, the International Covenant on Civil and Political Rights, and the Universal Declaration of Human Rights.

24 Due process rights, including rights to a lawyer, notice of charges and evidence, a fair trial before a competent and independent tribunal, habeas corpus, an appeal, and the presumption of innocence are guaranteed by a number of Canadian statutes and international instruments binding on Canada, e.g., the Canadian Charter of Rights and Freedoms, the International Covenant on Civil and Political Rights, Third Geneva Convention, Crimes against Humanity and War Crimes Act, Convention on the Rights of the Child, Hague Conventions, Annex, art. 23(h).

25 Freedom from torture is a non-derogable right of all humankind that cannot be displaced by any circumstances, guaranteed by the Convention against Torture and Other Cruel and Inhuman Treatment or Punishment, the Criminal Code, the Crimes against Humanity and War Crimes Act, the Rome Statute of the International Court, the Geneva Conventions, the Convention on the Rights of the Child, and other laws binding on Canada and the United States.

26 Freedom from arbitrary imprisonment is guaranteed by the Charter of Rights and Freedoms, the International Covenant on Civil and Political Rights, the Convention on the Rights of the Child, the Third Geneva Convention, the Universal Declaration of Human Rights, and the Magna Carta.

27 Rights to equality before the law and equal access to protection by law and to legal remedies for the prevention and punishment of violations are guaranteed by the Charter of Rights and Freedoms, the International Covenant on Civil and Political Rights, and the Convention on the Rights of the Child.

28 "Our High Commissioner has reminded us that 'Rights which are violated or ignored are rights in name only.' It is in this spirit that we must abolish the culture of impunity. States that fail to prosecute human rights abusers are failing in their 'responsibility to protect.'" Canada's International Human Rights Policy website, http://www.dfait-maeci.gc.ca/foreign_policy/human-rights/statement_hr_item9-en.asp (accessed 2 August 2005).

29 "The most basic human rights are those guaranteed by the criminal law – the right to life; to liberty; to freedom from arbitrary detention, abuse and torture ... Rights, that had they been in place and in force, would have made impossible the atrocities of the holocaust." The Right Honourable Beverley McLachlin P.C., chief justice of Canada, *The Changing Face of International Criminal Law*, 14.

30 *Khadr v. Canada*, 2010 FC 715 CanLII.

31 *Supra,* note 6, at paras. 19 and 20.

32 *Supra,* note 18.

33 *Ilascu and Others v. Moldova and Russia*, 48787/99, Council of Europe: European Court of Human Rights, 8 July 2004, http://www.unhcr.org/refworld/docid/414d9df64.html (accessed 22 January 2011).

Reflections

Omar Khadr: America's Injustice, Canada's Shame

MAHER ARAR

Forty years in prison: this was the sentence in October of 2010 that was pronounced by the jury panel for a child soldier. While shocking, it was no surprise to those who closely followed the Omar Khadr saga at Guantánamo Bay. How fair could this jury be, given that it included a Navy captain, a Marine colonel who was wounded in a firefight in Iraq, an Army lieutenant-colonel who served more than a year at an unnamed detention centre, a Navy commander, an Army lieutenant-colonel who once served as a military policeman, a Navy lieutenant-commander who is a submarine officer, and an Army major in military intelligence.

This is how the American Military Commission at Guantánamo Bay decided to put an end to one of the most embarrassing human rights cases and all that goes along with it in terms of abuse, neglect, and vendetta. The United States, with the tacit approval of Canada, supposedly two democratic countries and champions of human rights, not only decided to set up a military tribunal to judge a child soldier who was only fifteen years old at the time of his capture but also kept him in a military camp for over eight years, during which he was harshly interrogated and abused.

After claiming his innocence for eight years, Omar Khadr saw no hope of being cleared by this sham process and decided to plead guilty to the charges of murder, terrorism, and spying in exchange for an additional eight-year prison term. He has to spend one of these years at a maximum-security facility at Guantánamo before he can seek repatriation to Canada to serve the remainder of his sentence.

"Everything about Omar Khadr's ordeal at Guantánamo Bay over the past eight years has been a fiasco," said Alex Neve, secretary general of Amnesty General Canada. How did all of this could have happened in the civilized Western world?

To start with, the creation of Guantánamo camp was wrong. The transfer of prisoners who were captured in Afghanistan shouldn't have taken place. Since its inception in 2002, 770 prisoners have been detained at this notorious camp. As of today, 192 prisoners still remain locked up. Nearly 580 have been released over the past few years. More than 530 of those were released during the rule of the previous administration. In 2008, during his presidential campaign, President Obama described Guantánamo as a "sad chapter in American history." He promised that if he became the next president of the United States, he would immediately close down this camp. Here we are, almost two years after he took office: the camp remains open, and it is unclear whether it will ever close.

Recently, a high-ranking US colonel stated in an affidavit that top US officials had known for a long time that the majority of the detainees initially shipped off to Guantánamo were in fact innocent. In other words, the detainees had been kept there for reasons of political expedience.

Australian David Hicks, who recently published a memoir entitled *Guantanamo: My Journey*, spent over six years in Guantánamo before he decided to plead guilty. As a result, he was allowed to return home to serve the remainder of his sentence. Hicks's legal team attributed his acceptance of the plea bargain to his "desperation for release from Guantanamo." It looks like history is repeating itself with a twist: Mr Hicks was an adult when he was captured, while Khadr was only fifteen years of age and international law governing child soldiers' treatment should have applied to him.

In Canada, the past and present governments refused to help repatriate Omar Khadr back to Canada. It seems that it was too dangerous, for electoral reasons, to show any interest in the case. Without his consent, Omar Khadr became a pawn in a game where political parties could score points.

But the ostrich policy that so far has been adopted by successive Canadian governments is no longer feasible. This case is now coming to haunt the current government and to tarnish its legacy forever.

Navy Captain John Murphy, the military prosecutor presiding over Khadr's trial, said immediately after sentencing, "I hope it sends a message to terrorists." I am afraid this sham trial has already sent the wrong type of message, that of injustice, arrogance, and double standards.

NOTE

This article was first published online at the *Huffington Post*, 2 November 2010.

The Politics of Fear

DENNIS EDNEY

My topic here is the culture of fear and Islamophobia. I speak not as an academic, or as someone who has studied the subject matter of fear: I come from the perspective of a lawyer who has witnessed how fear is used as a manipulating tool to control public opinion. And I can bear witness to how fear is being used as a manipulating tool to control public opinion in the "War on Terror."

I want to share with you my perspectives and, more importantly, the story of my client, Omar Khadr. Justice has been denied to him, this young Canadian who was born in Scarborough and has been detained in Guantánamo Bay for almost nine years, since the age of fifteen.

Let's talk about Islamophobia. There is no better present-day example of Islamophobia than the raging debate taking place south of the border. At issue is the extent to which the Muslim faith and Muslim citizens should be allowed to freely express their religious views within American society.

Many will be aware of the recent activities of "Pastor" Jones,[1] the head of a small Florida church, who planned to commemorate the 9/11 tragedy by burning three hundred Korans and encouraging others in the United States and throughout the world to follow his example. When asked how he would feel if Muslims burned the Bible, he admitted he wouldn't like it, but emphasized that it was his "right" to burn the Islamic text, "because we live in America" and the Koran is an "evil book."

Jones's threat to burn ancient texts is, of course, nothing new. He is simply following a long history of people burning books because those books embody ideas that we cannot tolerate. Those books contradict our own extreme beliefs or are in competition with them. What is significant about this previously unknown pastor's book-burning stunt is that he was able to gain worldwide attention and put the entire planet's political-military-media complex on a high alert, with the White House, the Pentagon, the State Department, and leaders across the Muslim world pleading with him to call it off. President Obama expressed concern that such an act would simply be a recruitment tool for al-Qaeda. He expressed fears it would lead to the "recruitment of individuals who would be willing to blow themselves up in American or European cities."

Robert Gates, the US secretary of Defense, personally phoned the formerly unknown "pastor" to express his grave concerns about the security of American troops in Afghanistan and Iraq.

Even the former vice-presidential candidate Sarah Palin inserted herself into the debate by requesting that Jones give up his book-burning intentions – but only after General Petraeus, a hero to Republicans, had also phoned the good pastor to cease and desist. In attempting to deflect criticism of "Pastor" Jones, Palin informed the media, "There is a Muslim cleric who is running for parliament in Afghanistan who is calling for the murder of American children in response to burning Korans. Which is worse?"

Meanwhile, the media fed the frenzy of fear with rumours of impending riots in Afghanistan, Pakistan, and elsewhere.

"Pastor" Jones's threat to burn a sacred text came weeks into a hostile argument about Islam's place in America, a debate fuelled by the proposed construction of an Islamic mosque near the former site of the World Trade Center. The president of the United States was equivocal at best on that subject, stating that if "someone wants to build a mosque, they cannot be legally stopped."

Around the same time, an Internet evangelist named Bill Keller held a meeting in a makeshift church not far from what used to be the World Trade Center. He called upon the gathered faithful to help him build a Christian church as a counterweight to the proposed Islamic mosque. He also went on to say that anyone who attended the proposed Islamic mosque would be guilty of murder by association: "After all, it was their Muslim brothers who flew planes into the Twin Towers and killed three thousand people." He told the *New York Times*, "Muslims can go to their mosques and preach the lies of Islam and I'll come here to preach the truth of the gospel."

In another time, no one would have paid attention to these "pastors." They would have been seen as pathetic, attention-seeking bigots. Jones's ungodly behaviour would have disqualified him from any form of Christian leadership. But in today's world, the paradigm is different. We seem to live in an age where fear trumps common sense.

Think about how the media reported what the president of the United States said: Obama was quoted as worried about the "recruitment of individuals who would be willing to blow themselves up in American or European cities." We didn't hear that he stood up and condemned Jones as a hateful publicity seeker, intent on reducing American society to anti-Islamic sectarianism. Unfortunately, instead of deflating the anti-Muslim sentiment, Obama sent the same message of fear prevalent since 9/11, that Muslims and terrorists are linked.

Think about that: Muslims and terrorists are linked. These comments fan the flames of intolerance. That may well please the bigots of Palin's far-right Tea Party, but do others accept these statements? What has become of the principle that racial equality and religious tolerance are among the most important hallmarks of a developed and mature society? In a globalized world where we are all interconnected, every single incident of intolerance and fear bears the potential of escalation.

It is my belief that we cannot tackle intolerance in all of its various forms until we understand the role that fear plays in our everyday life. We cannot fight intolerance until we understand how that fear influences our thoughts and our actions. So let us look at the few examples of fear statements that I have mentioned. Very quickly we see the common message that Islam and people of Islamic faith are to be feared. Islamophobia, the message of fear of Islam, has become repetitious in our everyday society and is sitting far too comfortably in the psyches of our people.

Consider the stereotypically linked words such as "threat," "evil," "Islam," and "terrorists." They resonate in our everyday psyches to such an extent that they create a moral panic within us. And with that panic comes the implication that action must be taken to defeat this enemy.

Quite easily, we are led to understand that drastic measures must be taken in the interest of our security. Our security is such a priority that it means the suspension of civil liberties, a limitation on ethics, and infringement on the rule of law – for the greater good of our society.

That same manipulation of fear has allowed military escapades into countries beyond those who bombed the Twin Towers. That same message that has been exploited by governments to reduce civil liberties and infringe upon human rights by allowing places such as Guantánamo Bay to exist.

We are witnessing sanity slipping out of our grasp as our apathy has allowed anti-Muslim whispers to become part of the mainstream conversation. Anti-Muslim sentiment is not limited solely to the United States but is also alive and well in Canada.

Joseph Goebels, the Nazi minister of propoganda, once stated that you can make society do anything – all you need to do is give people a target and create fear. And Goebels would know, for he perfected the fear game. It was he who stated, "If you tell a lie big enough and keep repeating it, people will eventually come to believe it." Hence, the present-day strategy of connecting all Muslims with terrorism.

Guantánamo Bay, Cuba, where Omar Khadr is detained, exemplifies what I am talking about. For those of you who may not be familiar with him, let me take a few minutes to tell you a bit about Omar. He was fifteen years of age when his father dropped him off in a house in Afghanistan with the instructions to remain there until his return. The house was in a compound controlled by the Taliban. After several weeks, the compound was attacked by US forces who killed everyone except Omar. He suffered extensive, life-threatening injuries. On regaining consciousness in a military hospital on a US naval base in Bagram, Afghanistan, little did he realize that his suffering was only starting. He experienced extensive abuse and torture on that naval base and was later transferred to Guantánamo Bay, where the torture and abuse continues.

Guantánamo Bay is a necessary propaganda tool for the "War on Terror." It is a place, we are told, where terrorists are held, where the worst of the worst are detained – including Omar Khadr. We are led to believe that as a result we are now safer, that we can now all sleep better. That governments know what they are doing and should be left to get on with the job.

However, Amnesty International and other human rights organizations have stated that many of the detainees are simply innocent taxi drivers and farmers sold to the Americans for money by the

Northern Alliance. We will never know the truth, as many of these detainees have now been quietly released after years of detention, without being charged with any offence, or given any explanation, and returned to their homeland or other countries.

There are now approximately 145 detainees remaining in Guantánamo Bay, including my client Omar Khadr. It is left up to our imagination to consider what kind of horrible people these remaining terrorists in Guantánamo Bay are, as we never get to see or hear them.

Yet we do not question why the detainees in Guantánamo Bay are not allowed to be seen or heard, why they are not permitted access to the media, or visits from human rights organizations, or consular visits, or visits by family and friends. Or why they are not allowed to communicate with the outside world. These detainees are hidden behind a curtain of silence.

And do we ever consider why no American charged with a terrorism offence has been sent to Guantánamo Bay? Or why all Western nations except Canada refused to allow their detainees to remain in Guantánamo Bay, and demanded their release from Guantánamo, which was granted?

These other Western nations had no concern over releasing these so-called "terrorists" into the public on their return home. But Guantánamo is a place good enough for a young Canadian Muslim who has been there since the age of fifteen.

Nor do we question why all these detainees have been kept in indefinite detention without being charged or brought to trial for the past nine years. This is despite the fact that in May 2002 a UN panel said that holding prisoners indefinitely at Guantánamo Bay violated the world's ban on torture and that the United States should close the prison.

Is it that we have become apathetic and unsympathetic to human suffering simply because the detainees are branded as Muslim terrorists?

Last year I attended a press conference arranged by the Pentagon, which invited a select group of family members of those who had died in the 9/11 attack. The purpose of the press conference was to have these people publicly state to the world press that Guantánamo must never be closed and that the detainees there do not deserve justice.

We have been told that these detainees are being treated well, despite reports by the Red Cross and numerous other witnesses that many of them have simply been locked away for years without trial, without scrutiny, and abused and tortured in the process. At least four suicides and hundreds of attempted suicides are public knowledge. The Pentagon has reclassified suicides as "manipulative self injurious behaviours" because camp physicians alleged that detainees do not genuinely wish to end their lives.

The inhumanity of the place is clear in a video released in 2008 of an interrogation of Omar Khadr between the Canadian Security Intelligence Service (CSIS) and the CIA in Guantánamo Bay in which Omar repeatedly cries "help me" and cries out for his mother. He was sixteen at the time.[2] And now, having experienced all that I have described, he faces a military trial in Guantánamo – a legal process condemned internationally, including by former US military prosecutors.

The story of Omar and Guantánamo Bay reflects the failure of civil society, its institutions, and its people to speak out in ensuring our shared values of a just society are carried out. When we cave in to fear and apathy, when we fear to speak out in opposition, there are no longer boundaries between state action and impermissible behaviour.

And, if we walk away from our duty, who will speak for us when our time comes?

EDITOR'S NOTES

This text is edited from a speech originally delivered on 15 September 2010 during the Interdisciplinary Studies Conference at King's University College, University of Alberta, in Edmonton. Students attend this biannual for credit. The topic in 2010 was "Know Fear." Listen to the original talk at http://www.kingsu.ca/IS-conference/2010/index.html.

1 "Pastor" Jones, a high-school contemporary of Rush Limbaugh, does not have a theological degree. The unaccredited college that earlier gave Jones an honorary degree has sought to distance itself from him. In 2008, Jones left a church he led in Cologne, Germany, after being charged with fraud, according to a Florida newspaper.

2 This interrogation tape became the key material for the documentary film *You Don't Like the Truth: 4 Days inside Guantánamo* by Luc Côté and Patricio Henriquez. Excerpts from this screenplay appear in this volume. Omar Khadr's cries of "Oh Mother" are traditional Arabic cries of lament.

PART FOUR

Omar Khadr, Child Soldier

How to Unmake a Child Soldier

ROMÉO DALLAIRE

What I know for certain from studying child soldiers for the better part of a decade is this: picking up the pieces of broken children after a conflict is hugely difficult, the necessary and ongoing effort is hard to sustain, and success is unpredictable to gauge. In this chapter I will sketch some of the features of this troubling terrain, which the UN, peacekeeping, and humanitarian communities have labelled DDR, for disarmament, demobilization, and reintegration. That final *R* stretches to cover many other *r* words – reinsertion, rehabilitation, reconciliation, reconstruction, repatriation – all of them so difficult to achieve. I will say it again: it's better to stop the recruitment and use of children within belligerent forces before it happens than to deal with the complexities of reintegrating children into their home communities – if they even exist – after the conflict is over. Former child soldier and rapper Emmanuel Jal eloquently captured the nature of the damage and the struggle of healing in the lyrics to his song "Baakiwara": "I'm in another war / This time / It's my soul that I'm fighting for."

... The fact also stands that no matter the good intentions and agreed-to protocols, dealing with war-affected children and child soldiers is rarely a top priority among the international and domestic players as they attempt to put together the pieces of a viable nation state after a conflict has ended. This shouldn't be a surprise. What political entity in developed and stable countries actually pays more than lip service to putting the needs of children first or to "remembering" how important it is to our future to protect a child's sense of wonder and imagination, his or her capacity to dream and grow?

...We are still dropping the ball far too often when it comes to dealing with some of the most vulnerable populations in conflict and post-conflict settings. The UN has taken a significant leadership role, supported by its own agencies, such as UNICEF, and within some of its missions by the special representatives of the secretary general, and by dedicated work done by several field focused NGOs, such as Save the Children, War Child, Search for Common Ground, World Vision, and a number of others.

But nonetheless, we responsible and reasonable adults still seem far off the mark when dealing with rehabilitating war affected children and child soldiers. I would contend that most of the "r" problems stem from weak performance from the same agencies I've just mentioned, who enter the field with great ambition and resolve, and talk a great battle, but seldom manage to muster the capacity to sustain the fight to achieve their own declared objectives. They also risk being mired in dogma, which can hamper new initiatives.

... The age criterion is one of the most challenging aspects in DDRR [demobilization, disarmament, rehabilitation, and reintegration programming]. How does one determine the age of a child who arrives at a disarming post with no identification, a child for whom chronological age probably was never really that important? Chronological age figures in all international standards. The UN Convention on the Rights of the Child establishes the legal age of majority, but how is the concept of majority measured in reality? These children have often endured experiences that many adults in the developed world would fail to cope with, and as a result it is rare that the signpost of chronological age adequately captures their level of maturity. Age is not a universal construct delineating youth and childhood from adulthood. Though agencies are trying to recognize this issue, we still face considerable interpretive problems when we start drawing the age line among groups with respect to who is or isn't entitled to participate in DDRR programs.

There are too many examples where children have fallen through cracks and as a result have not been able to benefit from education, skills training or adoption opportunities, mostly because they have been denied any recognition as having been a child soldier due to lack of proof and witnesses who would speak on their behalf. During the course of a conflict, the child soldiers who do escape from their armed groups do not always have a designated safe place to go. If they attempt to surrender to whatever recognizable authority exists, they are not necessarily turned over to a benevolent NGO programme for demobilized children. Instead ... they can face summary execution or lengthy imprisonment for war crimes. Many child soldiers who desert have to flee in order to avoid both or all sides in the conflict and cannot return home ... Many leaders force children to commit atrocities on friends, neighbours, and even their own families expressly so they can't go home again.

... Child soldiering is a serious threat to regional stability even in the post-conflict nation-building phase. Investments in effective, long-term reintegration programs are investments in the security and stability of the nation and even the region. Successful reintegration plans must cover all the phases of the conflict, from the beginning of a crisis right through to the conclusion of a peace agreement and well beyond. And they must commit, with depth and sophistication, to the deliberate rehabilitation of conflict affected children away from evil toward good, from abuse toward restraint, from survival toward living with hope that they can have a better future.

... Canada made the argument that small arms were the primary tool used by children and youths in conflicts around the world, putting a face to the subject as well as recommending registering the transit and ownership of these guns, and the destruction of them on the spot if they were found in unauthorized or illegal hands. In 2008 the secretary general's report finally widened the discussion to include issues of production, marking, and tracing. But it is as if the whole exercise has really stood still, as millions of small arms continue to be produced and distributed with near impunity.

If we can revive the campaign against small arms, especially if we stress the link to child soldiers, we can end the overproduction of these weapons and munitions and start eating away at their distribution.

... One of the alternatives we can present children with is education. Education is a critical need of the former child soldier, but also a critical element for the prevention of the use of child soldiers. Careful thought must be given to the type of programs offered. During the Child Soldiers Initiatives' Ghana simulation exercise in Accra in 2007, several former child soldier participants spoke of their desire to pursue the education they missed because of the time they spent as combatants. The international community and local authorities must carefully consider the type of education to be offered. How many times have I heard youths say that the vocational courses that were offered to them in post-conflict settings were inadequate? How many cobblers, bakers, and seamstresses does one community need? Are we actually paying attention to the needs of the children and the community or rather training children in short-term programs that we deem cost-effective? Whose needs are we really trying to fulfill? In his book, *A Long Way Gone*, Ishmael Beah mentions the large number of boys who were trained as mechanics in Sierra Leone after the war – how many mechanics does Sierra Leone need for a population that can barely afford cars?

... If we truly want to make a dent in the number of children who are re-recruited into gangs or other armed groups in post-conflict settings, then we must make sure that the training we are providing is actually filling a need that either already exists or serves to improve the world in which these children live. We must be serious about moulding children and youth into productive individuals who can give back to their communities. In Sierra Leone some programs have begun to train former child combatants for professions that are desperately needed. Water sanitation experts, agricultural specialists – these are professions that will make their graduates indispensable to their communities.

And it is not only the child *soldiers* we need to think about when it comes to DDRR. The Paris Principles noted the harm caused by focusing reintegration support exclusively on child combatants; other youths and children in need feel envious and abandoned. This tension between focused support for former child soldiers and wider support for all war-affected children, many of whom are discernibly worse off than those who fought, is of concern for those working on this issue. Moreover, attempts solely focused on the individual are doomed to fail since the child is not to blame for what's happened. It is not as simple as "fixing the children" and putting them into a community. The community also needs "fixing."

... If we condone the prosecution of children, we may have an even more difficult time persuading ex-child soldiers to come in from the cold. And at this point I can't help but comment on the stance the government of Canada has taken on a young man and Canadian citizen, who by every definition must be considered a child soldier. Canada – one of the drafters and first signatories of the Optional Protocol to the Convention on the Rights of the Child, an instrument to protect such children from prosecution and a guarantee that they would be put through a formal process of DDRR – has kept Omar Khadr in the illegal jail at Guantánamo for more than seven years without lifting a finger to repatriate him. And as this book goes to press Khadr is standing trial before a military tribunal at Guantánamo.[1] The Canadian government insists it has confidence in the U.S. justice system and clings to the fact that though Canada has ratified the convention, we have not yet implemented it by legislation. (I will be introducing legislation to the Senate just after this book goes to press to rectify this loophole.) The Khadr case is a black mark on my own country's international reputation and standing in the fight for child rights and human rights as a whole.

... But what of the child soldiers who paid the ultimate price? What can we say about those whose bones are spun across the landscape of these nation states at war or in civil conflict? We know so little of them. We don't even have decent statistics on where and when they fell to bullets, machetes, land mines, and grenades in multitudes of ambushes, attacks, patrols, and undercover insertions, or in the mining of gold and diamonds for the sustainment of their adult leaders' cause.

Who cries for them? Who accounts for their loss to humanity? In the scheme of important things to resolve when stopping conflict, who has stopped to weep over their unmarked places of death, the blood-soaked ground where they were abandoned by their "warrior" ethic, failed by their fighting machine, lost their drug-induced fearsome-killer mantra and died – lonely, heartbroken children sacrificed to the evil ends of adults? Who actually sings their songs of sadness and promises, "We shall never forget?"

Probably no one.

EDITOR'S NOTE

This chapter is excerpted from Roméo Dallaire's book, *They Fight Like Soldiers, They Die Like Children: The Global Quest to Eradicate the Use of Child Soldiers* (Toronto: Random House Canada, 2010).

1 After the October 2010 US Military Commission trial ended in Guantánamo with a plea bargain, this *Toronto Star* headline appeared: "Omar Khadr Trial a Travesty of Justice, Says Dallaire." Olivia Ward writes:

The Guantánamo Bay trial of Omar Khadr was a perversion of justice that delivered a major blow to children's rights, says Gen. Roméo Dallaire, an outspoken advocate for child soldiers.

And, worse, he says, Canada was a silent partner in the proceedings.

"The jury that delivered that 40-year sentence went overboard," he said. "They seemed to be living in a bubble that had lost contact with the whole context of human rights."

Dallaire ... said that Canada had also "acquiesced" in the military trial – which denies normal rights of due process – "in response to the panic that 9/11 created."

And he said, the trial has also damaged an optional protocol to the UN Convention on the Rights of the Child, which forbids the recruitment of children under 18.

"It's affected the credibility of any Canadian or American who is arguing for the application (of the protocol), and I would extend that to anybody in the developed world who is trying to stop child soldiers from being treated in a less than fair way" ... He said that the Khadr trial could undermine progress, including the International Criminal Court's ability to prosecute war criminals for recruiting child soldiers, some 250,000 of them now fighting worldwide, many forced into brutal militias where they are drugged, tortured, and beaten into killing to order. (*Toronto Star*, 1 November 2010; http://www.thestar.com/specialsections/omarkhadr/article/884272--omar-khadr-trial-a-travesty-of-justice-says-dallaire [accessed 30 November 2011])

International Law and the Recruitment of a Child Soldier: Omar Khadr and Family Ties

W. ANDY KNIGHT AND JOHN MCCOY

In October 2010 a United States military panel of seven officers sentenced Omar Ahmed Khadr to forty years in prison for war crimes committed in Afghanistan in July 2002. He was convicted of a total of five so-called war crimes, including the most publicized crime of killing US Sergeant 1st Class Christopher Speer. Among the additional charges to which Khadr pleaded guilty on 25 October 2010 were spying, attempted murder, provision of material support for terrorists, and conspiracy.

The plea bargain and sentence represented what can best be described as a mostly symbolic and highly unorthodox legal proceeding against Omar Khadr (who at the time of his arrest in Afghanistan was a fifteen-year-old minor), which was shaped by the extraordinary legal environment that has followed the attacks of 11 September 2001. The sentencing was largely symbolic because, as widely reported, the American and Canadian governments entered into a diplomatic agreement that would see him repatriated back to Canada after serving one additional year in custody at the Guantánamo military prison. Upon his repatriation his fate will be an open question – Omar's case has become a highly contentious and embarrassing one for the Canadian government, which has largely tried to distance itself from the Canadian citizen since his incarceration in 2002.

It is difficult to overstate the unorthodox nature of the legal proceedings against Omar Khadr. As his Canadian lawyer Dennis Edney commented after the sentencing, "The fact that the trial of a child soldier, Omar Khadr, has ended with a guilty plea in exchange for his eventual release to Canada does not change the fact that fundamental principles of law and due process were long since abandoned in Omar's case."[1] Not only did his conviction represent the first prosecution of a child soldier since the Nuremberg trials that followed World War II, but it was also the first case of an individual being charged, put on trial, and convicted of a battlefield murder in Afghanistan, despite the fact that more than 1,200 US troops were killed in that country since the US invaded in 2001. As noted by Jennifer Hyndman, Khadr's murder-related charges in Afghanistan are "not technically possible" in war under international humanitarian law.[2] His detention, charges, trial, and prosecution violate a myriad of international customary and criminal laws regarding child soldiery and the protection of the rights of a minor. Most specifically, and arguably most importantly in terms of universal legal standards, his detention and prosecution violate the UN Convention on the Rights of the Child (CRC) and its Optional Protocol on the Involvement of Children in Armed Conflict, both of which Canada has signed and ratified. (Note that the United States has signed but still has not ratified the CRC.) In addition, there are other international treaties that address the legality of child soldiery.[3]

A 1996 United Nations study on the impact of armed conflict on children highlighted the complexity of the issue of child soldiers: "The dilemma of dealing with children who are accused of committing acts of genocide illustrates the complexity of balancing culpability, a community's sense of justice and the best interest of the child. The severity of the crime involved, however, provides no justification for suspending or abridging the fundamental rights and legal safeguards accorded to children under the Convention on the Rights of the Child."[4]

No fewer than three sets of laws apply to Omar Khadr – international law and the domestic laws of the United States and Canada. To date, a number of advocacy groups have been highly active in lobbying on Khadr's behalf, among them the Canadian Bar Association, Amnesty International, and Human Rights Watch.[5] Much of the legal and humanitarian scrutiny in this case has focused on the violation of the CRC and the prosecution of a minor. However, this focus tends to obscure another central part of international criminal law that applies to child soldiers – the prosecution of those who recruit children into armed militia groups. The criminal act of child soldiery involves both recruiting child soldiers and encouraging these children to fight and engage in illegal activities on the battlefield. Attempts to prosecute the recruiters of child soldiers reflect the general understanding that many more children are coerced and pressed into military service than those who participate voluntarily.[6]

Arguably, Omar Khadr's misfortune largely stems from his association with extremist members of his family. His deceased father, Ahmed Khadr, was a highly contentious and shadowy figure, both in Canada and internationally, who was accused of having close ties to al-Qaeda and its leader, Osama bin Laden. Omar, along with his older brothers, is said to have been indoctrinated in the violent ideology of al-Qaeda and put into training camps runs by that extremist group. These accusations, if accurate, would shift culpability from Omar to his family, specifically to his father, who played an active role in embedding Omar and his siblings into al-Qaeda's irregular armed group in Afghanistan. Inexplicably, relatively little attention has been paid to this aspect of the case. We approach this subject by first examining the legal concept of recruitment of child soldiers – a crime that has recently been recognized to have moved from the realm of customary international law to international criminal law.[7] Second, we examine the charges against Omar Khadr and argue that the CRC, together with other domestic and international laws and treaties, was violated in his detention, prosecution, and sentencing. We further argue that the CRC, together with the 2000 Optional Protocol, firmly establishes the legal protections which Omar Khadr should have been afforded upon his arrest – that is, protection as a minor who was associated with a non-state militant organization.

OMAR KHADR AND INTERNATIONAL LAW REGARDING THE RECRUITMENT OF CHILD SOLDIERS

Child soldiering is not as uncommon a phenomenon as some may think. Around the world, some government armies, rebel groups, paramilitaries, warlords, and various militia groups use children in various roles on the battlefield – today, an estimated 250,000 to 300,000 children.[8] The exact number is difficult to ascertain, primarily because as some conflicts involving children come to an end, others are heating up. But the problem of child recruitment into armed conflict is so serious that states, intergovernmental organizations, and NGOs have been actively establishing a body of international law to arrest the problem. A review of international and state legal statutes dealing with child soldiers reveals the influence of political and cultural/normative precepts on this often contentious area. A contemporary epicentre of this debate is the ongoing war against international terrorism. As Judith Butler has stated, the former Bush administration did not simply wage a "war of law" but rather waged a war *through* law, as that administration showed little regard for international legal standards.[9] Omar Khadr found himself caught within this "war through law" which consistently denied him his legal rights as a child and as a citizen of Canada. The Canadian government was complicit in this.

After his 2002 incarceration, Khadr was held for over three years at Guantánamo Bay before being formerly charged in 2006 under the first set of military commissions established by the Bush administration. These cases were dismissed when the US Supreme Court declared the commissions unlawful after the 2006 *Hamdan v. Rumsfeld*. The charges against Khadr were, however, reinstated under reformed commissions authorized by the US Congress.[10] Despite having extraterritorial jurisdiction to prosecute Khadr in domestic courts, the Canadian government purposely allowed him to stay in Guantánamo,[11] where he was reportedly tortured. According to Amnesty International, he was subjected to sleep deprivation and disruption under a technique known as the "frequent flyer program."[12] Other reports indicate that he was subjected to ritualized humiliation and degradation such as being short-shackled for up to six hours (during which time he would soil himself), having cleaning fluid poured on him, not being allowed to wash for days, and being ridiculed by the guards.[13]

Labelling Omar Khadr as an "enemy combatant" rather than a child soldier is just another example of the US claim of "exceptionalism." It provided the United States with a way of getting around the legal protections that should have been afforded to a sixteen-year-old child. One legal argument that has been neglected in this case is that Omar Khadr ought to have been viewed not as a perpetrator of war crimes but rather as a victim of a controlling and extremist father who indoctrinated him and recruited him as a child soldier. There are several international treaties and agreements that explicitly refer to the issue of the recruitment of child soldiers. Article 77 of the Additional Protocol to the Geneva Conventions (1977) states, "The Parties to the conflict shall take all feasible measures in order that children who have not attained the age of 15 years do not take a direct part in hostilities and, in particular, they shall refrain from recruiting them into their armed forces."[14] The 1977 protocol represents an early attempt at addressing the legal vacuum that existed with regards to child recruitment into armed conflict. But these legal provisions do not apply to irregular militia such as al-Qaeda.[15] Both the CRC and the 1977 additional protocol to the Geneva Convention primarily refer to the issue of the recruitment of child soldiers within the context of state conflict and state sovereignty, leaving children involved in non-state conflict and with irregular armed groups in a legal grey area. Moreover, they establish the age of fifteen as the threshold that separates a child from an adult. However, in 2000, Article 4 of the Optional Protocol to the Convention on the Rights of the Child on the involvement of children in armed conflict expressly banned "Armed groups that are distinct from the armed forces of a State" from recruiting or using persons under the age of eighteen in hostilities.[16] David Rosen notes that the push for the recognition of what has become known as the "straight-18" position finds its origins in the universal definition of childhood found in the UN Convention on the Rights of the Child, which defines childhood as beginning at birth and ending when an individual turns eighteen.[17] The 1989 CRC and 1977 additional protocol to the Geneva Convention were later codified through Article 8 of the Rome Statute, making the conscription or enlistment of children under the age of fifteen in armed forces or using them to participate in hostilities a war crime. This protocol gives the International Criminal Court (ICC) the authority to indict, try, and sentence recruiters of child soldiers.[18] In addition to these international agreements are UN Security Council resolutions and regional legal documents, such as the African Charter on the Rights and Welfare of the Child, which contribute to sources of customary international law governing this issue area.

It has been alleged that Omar Khadr and his older brothers were sent by their parents to attend al-Qaeda training camps where they were taught to use a variety of weapons and indoctrinated in the extremist ideology of al-Qaeda. As with other reports surrounding the Khadr family, many of these claims are disputed. However, in several instances, the Khadrs themselves admit that the sons participated in al-Qaeda training camps and in combat missions in Afghanistan. Much of the available information regarding Omar

Khadr's activities in Afghanistan remains subject to debate, but what does emerge from the history of the Khadr family is a portrait of a family that encouraged its children to participate in extremist militant activities.

Ahmed Khadr, an Egyptian by birth, immigrated with his family to Ontario in the mid-1970s. He studied computers at the University of Ottawa and worked for Bell Northern Research.[19] However, this early career path was short lived. After the 1979 invasion of Afghanistan by the Soviet Union, he became increasingly focused on the Afghan conflict and its consequences.[20] It was during this period that he began operating what he described as refugee camps along the Pakistan/Afghanistan border. He set up a registered charity called Human Concern International (HCI) and listed himself as its regional director. Ahmed carried out significant fundraising drives in Canada and even received funds from the Canadian International Development Agency (CIDA) for his organization. However, by the early 1990s, suspicion had been cast on the verity of his charitable activities. According to freelance journalist Tim Deagle, who in 1988 visited one of the camps Ahmed was said to have been running, within the camp there were heavily armed young men and very little in the way of humanitarian activity.[21]

The controversy surrounding Ahmed Khadr grew intensely during the mid to late 1990s. In 1992, he sustained a serious injury in Afghanistan, purportedly from a land mine. It was then that he returned with his family to Canada in order to receive medical treatment. The incident marked one of the several times when he and his family moved between Pakistan/Afghanistan and Ontario. In 1995, he was accused of financing a bomb plot that targeted the Egyptian embassy in Islamabad, killing seventeen people. Pressure from the Egyptian government led to his arrest in Pakistan. There was significant lobbying by those associated with his charitable activities in Canada to have him released from prison. In 1996, Prime Minister Chrétien asked the then Pakistani president Benezir Bhutto to ensure a fair trial for Khadr. He was released without charges in the spring of that year.[22] In 1996, a *Toronto Star* reporter quoted Chrétien as saying, "I wanted to be sure due process is followed, and she [Bhutto] gave me all the guarantees I could wish (for)."[23] However, members of the Khadr family drew the ire of Canadian officials after it was learned that Ahmed had links to al-Qaeda. In a 2008 address to the Moynihan Institute of Global Affairs, University of Toronto law professor Audrey Macklin, in explaining why the Canadian government did nothing to get Omar Khadr out of Guantánamo, chalked it up to the "Khadr effect" – the public and government distaste for the Khadr family based on the historical dealings between the family and the government.[24] This "effect" was reflected in Canadian public opinion polls in which two-thirds of Canadians believed Omar Khadr would not receive a fair trial at Guantánamo, and yet only 43 percent of them wanted him repatriated to Canada for his legal proceedings.[25] But the real issue here should be the extent to which the Khadr family was guilty of an international crime – that is, recruiting a child into conflict situations.

Like most of Ahmed Khadr's life story, his ties to al-Qaeda remain somewhat obscured. The primary accusation is that he had been a "founding member of al-Qaeda," that he was known as "al Kanadi" (the Canadian) in militant circles, and worked as a financier for the organization while using his charitable work as cover.[26] His daughter has admitted that he "knew Osama bin Laden"; she said in a *National Post* interview, "If you want to say they were friends, well, they were friends 20 years ago. During the Afghanistan war, Osama bin Laden and my father were taking money into Afghanistan."[27]

In 2001 when the invasion of Afghanistan commenced, Ahmed disappeared into that country. Only later was it discovered that he had been killed in a firefight, described as a shootout between the Pakistani military and al-Qaeda members in a Pakistan-Afghanistan border town.[28] According to an al-Qaeda document posted online, he had become an al-Qaeda commander in Logar Province following the invasion of Afghanistan by coalition forces in 2001.[29] At the time of his death, he was accompanied by his fourteen-year-old son, Abdul Karim Khadr, who was shot in the spine and paralyzed during the fighting. While the events surrounding Ahmed's death remain the object of speculation and debate (there are a variety of conflicting accounts regarding the firefight in which he died), the fact that he was accompanied by his fourteen-year-old son while in the company of known militants indicates the extent to which he was willing to expose his children to war.

As confirmed by various sources, and indeed by his own family, then, Ahmed Khadr was to some extent involved in various Afghan skirmishes. There is also evidence that he indoctrinated his children to embrace al-Qaeda's extremist ideology and recruited them as child soldiers. Again, as with much of the reports on Ahmed and his family's activity in Pakistan/Afghanistan, there are many unanswered questions in this regard. According to some, such as an anonymous "senior RCMP investigator," Ahmed Khadr "created his own 'terrorist cell' and indoctrinated his children from an early age in the values and beliefs of criminal extremists, specifically al-Qaeda."[30] A recently released al-Qaeda biography praised him for "tossing his little child in the furnace of the battle" and described Omar as an "injured lion cub" following his shooting in Afghanistan.[31]

While many details about the lives of the Khadr children remain unknown, one certainty is that they lived a dual existence – split between the very different environments of the Pakistan/Afghanistan border and Ontario. It is believed that Omar went to school in Scarborough before leaving Canada when he was about ten years old.[32] In Pakistan, according to Stewart Bell, Ahmed Khadr sent a majority of his eldest male children to train in "al Qaeda training camps." One of these was Abdurahman, who was said to have trained in al-Qaeda's Khaldun camp for three months around the age of fifteen. Ahmed said of his sons' training, "It's a normal thing in Afghanistan." On the same subject Omar's mother, Maha Elsamnah, stated, "We wanted to get him something just to be disciplined."[33] Zaynab, Omar's sister, confirmed these reports in an interview stating that her brothers "did go to training camps and the past 20 years many people have been going." She described their undergoing of weapons training and stated quite frankly, "From a religious point of view, a Muslim had to know how to defend himself."[34] Zaynab has been a controversial figure in Canada and has claimed that Osama bin Laden attended her wedding in 1999. She has been known to make inflammatory public remarks,[35] such as her comments in a CBC documentary that she would "love to die like" a martyr and that "if carrying my father's beliefs – and I believe that my father had great beliefs and he did not do anything wrong – is supposed to be poison, then maybe all of us need to have poisoned heads."[36]

In a series of interviews given by the family to the PBS television program *Frontline*, the Khadrs confirmed that Ahmed Khadr's sons attended training camps in Afghanistan. When asked by the interviewer if her children went to "the bin Laden training camps" the mother, Maha Elsamnah, replied, "The big boys did," referring to her eldest male children.[37] When asked by the same reporter how a mother could send her children to these camps for this kind of military training, she replied, "Would you like me to raise my child in Canada and by the time he's 12 or 13 he'll be on drugs or having some homosexual relation or this and that? Is it better? For me, no. I would rather have my son as a strong man who knows right and wrong."[38] In the same set of interviews, Abdullah Khadr, the eldest son, admitted that he attended Khalden camp, at that time run by Ibn al-Ahaykh al-Libi, one of Osama bin Laden's confidants, who was eventually captured in 2001 by Pakistani security forces. Abdullah would have been fourteen years old when he attended the camp.[39] When asked whether he was "ever sympathetic to Al Qaeda," he stated, "To what they do? Building a homeland for Muslims, yes."[40] Abdullah described the normalcy with which he viewed this form of militant training: "Anyone who wants to get trained can get trained in Afghanistan. If you want to fire a Kalashnikov it is like in Canada going and learning hockey. Anybody can do it. A ten-year-old boy can fire a Kalashnikov in Afghanistan. So it's not a big deal."[41]

Based on remarks made by the Khadrs, it is clear that participation in military training in Afghanistan was considered normal and that the parents actively encouraged this activity for their teenage sons. However, while there have been reports that Omar received military training, it is unclear whether this was actually the case. His sister Zaynab described him as a "very sweet, simple and easy going person" and has denied that he attended these camps. On the other hand, Stewart Bell contends that Omar fell "into the grip of Al Qaeda, training in weapons and explosives near Khost, in eastern Afghanistan. For the Khadrs, it seems holy war was a family affair."[42] How Omar ended up in Afghanistan where he was eventually captured is also somewhat mysterious. In a PBS interview, his mother was asked, "Why was Omar not with the others? Why was he in a different place [at the time of the capture]?" She replied, "I remember his father told me that he was just going with some group of people to translate for them or to do some work because he is much better in English, even in Pashto, Farsi. And that's all I know. Actually I was shocked when I heard that Omar was injured, or captured or killed or whatever at the beginning."[43] Other reports also indicate that Omar may have been sent by his father to act as a translator for Abu Laith al-Libi. When Maha Elsmnah was asked if she was "proud" of her son for killing an American soldier, she stated, "Of course. He defended himself."[44]

There is little direct testimony or evidence of the actual process through which the sons of Ahmed and Maha were indoctrinated by, and trained to be part of, the al-Qaeda militant group. However, as seen in comments made by family members, including those of Maha Elsmnah, at least some of the Khadr sons were as young as fourteen when they attended al-Qaeda training camps. It seems quite certain that Ahmed Khadr, as a senior member and financier for al-Qaeda, brought his children into the world of militancy and fed them an ideology of hate. He recruited his children to take part in the Afghan conflict. In his words, and in the words of his wife, a portrait emerges of a family for which armed conflict was a normal activity. Ahmed Khadr repeatedly put his family in harm's way – including his youngest son, who was paralyzed in the firefight in which Ahmed lost his life. Considering the established customary and criminal international law in this area, one is left to wonder why Omar's case has not been viewed as a case of illegal recruitment of a child into a non-state and irregular military organization.

It should be noted that the legality surrounding the recruitment of child soldiers has been the subject of some debate. For instance, scholars Rachel Brett and Irma Specht have challenged the contention that a majority of child soldiers are pressed into service. In their comprehensive study they found that a majority of children "choose" to become soldiers.[45] However, this choice can only be understood by examining the specific constraints and the various structural factors such as poverty, ideological influences, culture, family environment, peer group factors, and normalization of war that lead children to make that decision.[46] Yet, for legal observers like Pilar Villanueva Sainz-Pardo, "The existing legislation criminalising child recruitment as a war crime and the precedents set by the international courts have led to the conclusion that there is sufficient state practice, which is virtually uniform, extensive and representative, to establish the rule of prohibiting child recruitment as a norm of customary international law, whether committed in the context of a conflict of an international character, or not of an international character."[47]

In the case of Omar Kadr's becoming a child soldier, the role of ideology and the family environment seems clear. While this legal aspect of the case has received little attention, human rights groups such as Human Rights Watch (HRW) held his recruiters culpable. In a 2007 document HRW noted, "According to the US' own policies,

Khadr's recruiters should be held responsible for exploiting Khadr as a child combatant, and ongoing efforts should be made to educate and rehabilitate him."[48] As noted by multiple observers, there are sufficient precedents in international customary and criminal law, together with ad hoc proceedings such as what took place in Sierra Leone, to arrive at that conclusion. Roméo Dallaire in his book *They Fight Like Soldiers, They Die Like Children* has also decried the despicable practice of extremist adults who recruit children into armed groups, turning children into "killing machines."[49]

THE QUESTION OF AGE AND NON-STATE COMBATANTS IN INTERNATIONAL LAW ON CHILD SOLDIERS

We now turn to aspects of the law that have received much legal and media attention: Omar's age at the time of his capture and his status as a non-state combatant. At the centre of the legal controversy, and arguably at the centre of the case, rest two central questions: whether Omar's age at the time of his detention allowed him legal protections under international law as a minor, and whether non-state child combatants should be afforded the same protections as state combatants. The fact that Omar was fifteen when he was captured placed him within the accepted limits at the time (in terms of enforced international law) of an adult soldier. However, increasingly there have been calls for international law in this area to change this age standard to reflect the now generally recognized definition of a minor (in terms of many states' domestic laws) as anyone under eighteen years old. This position, the "straight-18" standard, has been promoted by several international bodies – including the UN under the CRC and its Optional Protocol.[50]

The recognition of the legal standing of children involved in non-state conflict is also controversial. Omar Khadr has been labelled under the moniker of the "war on terror" as an "enemy combatant" or "terrorist" – terms that Jennifer Hyndman contends are based more on current geopolitical considerations than anything else.[51] As David Rosen points out, lawful combatants are privileged in theatres of war: "Under the laws of war, they are legally entitled to kill other combatants; in addition, if they are captured, they are entitled to protection as prisoners of war and may not be treated as criminals. With certain exceptions, rebel groups, insurgents, or other dissident forces in an internal conflict within a state are not considered to be lawful combatants."[52] Yet within the CRC and its Optional Protocol we find the inclusion of children under the legal protection of child soldiers within international law.[53]

While the Geneva Convention of 1949 did not address the issue of child soldiers, additional Protocols I and II delineated two categories of conflict within the convention: conflict between states (Protocol I) and intra-state conflict between state and non-state actors or between non-state actors (Protocol II). These protocols applied to both younger children (below fifteen years) and older children (fifteen to eighteen) depending on the type of conflict.[54] The age issue was addressed more definitively under the UN Convention of the Rights of the Child (CRC), which was adopted in 1989, and its 2000 Optional Protocol. Article 38 of that convention specifies that fifteen is the minimum legal age for state recruitment; therefore, children between the ages of fifteen and eighteen can voluntarily take part in combat.[55]

A number of NGOs (together with some state governments), recognizing the lack of protection of those children over the age of fourteen, agitated for raising the legal age of protection for children from recruitment into armed conflict to eighteen years of age.[56] As of July 2007 the CRC was ratified by 192 states – all UN member states with the exception of the United States and Somalia.[57] According to Pilar Villanueva Sainz-Pardo, "It can be said that the Convention has received a nearly universal ratification, which implies that the age limit of 18 can be regarded as the general legal rule for defining childhood, and, more importantly, that this universal ratification could amount to custom."[58] However, as numerous observers of law in this area have noted, the phrase "feasible measures," which appears in a number of CRC documents, represents weak international legal language. The wording reflects a compromise, based on political considerations, that was made in order to encourage many states to sign the treaty.

Additionally, the protocol states in Article 4 (1) that non-state groups "should not, under any circumstances, recruit or use in hostilities persons under the age of 18 years."[59] Other international agreements that can be said to reinforce the CRC and the Optional Protocol include the International Labor Convention No. 182, which addresses forms of child labour, prohibits the recruitment of children in armed conflict, and encourages states to hold to the straight-18 position.[60] In addition, the Paris Principles of 2007, signed by sixty states, affirms that child soldiers should not be criminalized but rather viewed as victims; it also promotes protection of children in conflict.[61]

Among some states and scholars, the straight-18 position remains controversial. According to Augustine Park, "While in negotiating the CRC some states and NGOs proposed to raise the minimum age for participation to 18 years, the US delegate 'categorically refused' to exclude 15 to 17 year olds from direct participation in hostilities."[62] Based on these trends, Sainz-Pardo concludes that "it is therefore commonly accepted that 15 is the age limit under which the prohibition of child recruitment has crystallised today as part of customary international law."[63] Some observers, such as Park, have questioned the usefulness of a universalized age limit on child soldiery by arguing that "there is a wealth of sociological and anthropological literature that aims to denaturalise the idea of childhood and posits that there are a multitude of childhoods across cultures, throughout history and across geographical spaces. Thus, the age at which childhood is thought to end, the presumed character and competencies of children, and the beliefs, customs and norms about what is appropriate for children to do are highly contingent rather than universal."[64]

Yet, in the context of the Bush administration's war through law and the extra-legal space of Guantánamo, the United States has, according to Joseph Pugliese, imprisoned children as young as twelve.[65] In 2008, US representatives appeared in front of the UN Committee on the Rights of the Child as that treaty body examined US compliance with the Optional Protocol to the Convention on the Rights of the Child on the Involvement of Children in Armed Conflict (ratified by the United States in 2002). At that time the committee called on the United States to "conduct investigations of accusations against detained children in a prompt and impartial manner, in accordance with minimum fair trial standards. The conduct of criminal proceedings against children within the military justice system should be avoided"[66] – a call that was obviously not heeded. Human rights organizations like Human Rights Watch have pointed out that the United States' international position with respect to child soldiers runs counter not only to its commitments under international law but also to its own domestic law. They note, for example: "In Eddings v Oklahoma, the Court noted youth is more than a chronological fact. It is a time and condition of life when a person may be most susceptible to influence and to psychological damage. Our history is replete with laws and judicial recognition that minors, especially in their earlier years, generally are less mature and responsible than adults. Particularly during the formative years of childhood and adolescence, minors often lack the experience, perspective and judgment expected of adults."[67]

The US position on the age of combatants is shaped in part by its foreign policy, especially within the context of the "war on terror." According to Rosen, "The most important development in proscribing the use of child soldiers is the 1998 Rome Statute establishing an ICC in The Hague in the Netherlands";[68] The ICC represents the only permanent international court that can prosecute individuals related to child soldiery. Rosen notes, "The Rome Statute came closest to establishing a universal legal standard, but only by addressing the recruitment of younger children (below age 15) and by avoiding the issue of the criminal culpability of children."[69] The ongoing debate continues between the so-called straight-18 position supported by many NGOs and the United Nations (as found in the universally accepted definition of childhood in the UN Convention on the Rights of the Child), and the position of many states that hold fifteen as the age limit.[70] The ICC and some state courts generally hold to the fifteen age limit, while a vast majority of states and NGOs have advocated for eighteen. While these debates rage, the UN secretary general released a report on children and armed conflict in 2009 that detailed some progress in establishing monitoring and reporting aimed at eliminating the recruitment and use of child soldiers in conflicts; however, the report also noted a lack of accompanying enforcement mechanisms.[71]

CONCLUSION

Inevitably, with the glaringly evident breeches of international and domestic law in the Omar Khadr case, it is expected that his repatriation will be accompanied by discussions of compensation and rehabilitation. Some analysts have suggested that, to avoid further embarrassment, the Canadian government may follow the lead of other Western governments, such as the United Kingdom and Australia, which have compensated citizens who were said to have been tortured while in custody at Guantánamo. With the revelation of many of the details surrounding the complicity of the Canadian government and its security organizations in Khadr's illegal detention, it is very likely that there will be some form of settlement.[72] At least seven of the British detainees released from Guantánamo have received financial compensation – with some claims surpassing the $1 million mark. Considering Khadr's status as a minor in Canadian domestic and international law (under the CRC optional protocol), it is likely that his compensation could be higher than the amounts paid out to adult detainees with British citizenship. At the very least, he should be given the chance to be rehabilitated.

Should it take place for Khadr, rehabilitation would arguably represent his first exposure to the normative and legal rights normally ascribed to other child soldiers. For instance, under the Paris Principles, a child involved in armed conflict should be enabled to "play an active role as a civilian member of society, integrated into the community and, where possible, reconciled with her/his family."[73] But, ultimately, many questions will persist in the Khadr case; for instance, to what extent can his treatment and his ability to be rehabilitated and reintegrated into Canadian society be successful if he is reunited with his toxic family members? In our opinion, any rehabilitation program for him would have to include a clean break from a family that continues to espouse unrepentantly extremist views.

In effect, then, the case of Omar Khadr must be considered within the overall context of the development of international law in regards to child soldiery and with regard to his being a victim of the extra-legal environment of exceptionalism that has existed in the US since 11 September 2001. He falls into the grey area between the two dominant positions in the age debate: that of the UN, a majority of states and NGOs who advocate for a straight-18 categorization of child soldiers, and the position of the United States and the ICC (under the Rome Statute), which places the age limit as under fifteen. The debate is tied to the other primary area of debate in this aspect of international law – the role of the recruiter. No doubt children may volunteer to participate in conflict under the influence of a variety of structural and non-structural push and pull factors. But there are other cases in which children are pressed into service for armed groups through the most coercive of measures. In Khadr's case, the role of his family, especially that of his father, and of an ideology shaped by hate, was central in radicalizing Omar Khadr and turning him into an extremist child soldier. Yet again the issue of age enters this debate, as no currently existing court holds to the straight-18 position despite the virtually universal ratification of the CRC and its Optional Protocol. For Canadians, this breaks with our normative precepts and domestic laws, which would have viewed Omar as a child. Yet as suggested by Augustine Park, despite these recognitions, the current legal debates over child soldiery in international law may in fact miss the root problem within this phenomenon: "Thinking about child soldiery requires a paradigmatic shift from conceptualising it as a legal problem aimed at recruiters to conceptualising it as social, political and economic problem aimed at why children join up in the first place. This is not to suggest there should be no legal standards; and, certainly, international agreements and efforts at prosecution hold enormous symbolic and moral value. But unequal social, political and economic structures may well undermine any success that might be attained through legal strategies."[74]

NOTES

1 *CBC News Online,* "Omar Khadr Sentenced to Symbolic 40 Years," http://www.cbc.ca/world/story/2010/10/31/guantanamo-khadr-sentencing.html (accessed 30 November 2010).

2 Jennifer Hyndman, "The Question of 'the Political' in Critical Geopolitics: Querying the 'Child Soldier' in the 'War on Terror,'" *Political Geography* 29, no. 5 (2010): 253.

3 Among these treaties are the 1977 Additional Protocols (I and II) to the Geneva Conventions; the 1998 Rome Statute; and the 1999 International Labour Organisation Convention No. 182. See Augustine Park, "Child Soldiers and Distributive Justice: Addressing the Limits of Law," *Crime, Law and Social Change* 53, no. 4 (2010): 331.

4 Pilar Villanueva Sainz-Pardo, "Is Child Recruitment as a War Crime Part of Customary International Law?," *International Journal of Human Rights* 12, no. 4 (2008): 556.

5 Hyndman, "The Question of 'the Political,'" 247–55.

6 Recent ad hoc legal proceedings, for instance, in Sierra Leone, have focused on prosecuting those who recruited children as soldiers during the civil war in that country. In 2007, the Special Court in Sierra Leone prosecuted three members of the Armed Forces Revolutionary Council for "conscripting or enlisting children under the age of 15" (Sainz-Pardo, "Child Recruitment as a War Crime").

7 Ibid., 555–612.

8 See Park, "Child Soldiers and Distributive Justice," 330; Michael Wessells, *Child Soldiers: From Violence to Protection* (Cambridge: Harvard University Press 2006), 2

9 As Butler contends, "law is a site of political struggle not only in its suspension but also in its formulation, interpretation, and application" (quoted in Hyndman, "The Question of 'the Political,'" 251).

10 Human Rights Watch, "The Omar Khadr Case: A Teenager Imprisoned at Guantanamo," 2007, http://hrw.org/backgrounder/usa/us0607/us0607web.pdf (accessed 12 November 2010).

11 Unlike other OECD countries, including Australia and Britain, which made the decision to repatriate their citizens (Hyndman, "The Question of 'the Political,'" 252).

12 Amnesty International, "Military Commission Proceedings against Omar Khadr Resume, as USA Disregards Its International Human Rights Obligations," http://www.amnesty.org/en/library/asset/AMR51/029/2010/en/7b1d3e2c-9824-4c80-9657-4392d18dfff3/amr510292010en.pdf (accessed 11 November 2010).

13 Joseph Pugliese, "Apostrophe of Empire: Guantanamo Bay, Disneyland," *Borderlands E-Journal: New Spaces in the Humanities* 8, no. 3 (2009): 13.

14 ICRC, "Protocol Additional to the Geneva Conventions of 12 August 1949, and Relating to the Protection of Victims of International Armed Conflicts (Protocol I), 8 June 1977," http://www.icrc.org/ihl.nsf/7c4d08d9b287a42141256739003e636b/f6c8b9fee14a77fdc125641e0052b079 (accessed 29 November 2010).

15 In 1989 the CRC also referred to specific provisions in regards to the issue of recruitment of child soldiers. Article 38 of the CRC states, "States Parties shall refrain from recruiting any person who has not attained the age of 15 years into their armed forces. In recruiting among those persons who have attained the age of 15 years but who have not attained the age of 18 years, States Parties shall endeavour to give priority to those who are oldest."

16 OHCHR, "Optional Protocol to the Convention on the Rights of the Child on the Involvement of Children in Armed Conflict," 2000, http://www2.ohchr.org/english/law/crc-conflict.htm (accessed 29 November 2010).

17 David Rosen, "Child Soldiers, International Humanitarian Law, and the Globalization of Childhood," *American Anthropologist* 109, no. 2 (2007): 296.

18 Further, the Paris Principles of 2007 defined child soldiers in a broader way to include children under 18 years old who are "associated with an armed force or armed group" who have been recruited or used by an armed force or armed group in any capacity – not just in hostilities.
19 Stewart Bell, *Cold Terror: How Canada Nurtures and Exports Terrorism around the World* (Etobicoke: Wiley 2004).
20 According to Bell, Ahmed was drawn to the conflict zone "to participate in jihad" and eventually became so involved in the region he decided to move his family to neighbouring Peshawar Pakistan (ibid., 158).
21 Bell, *Cold Terror.*
22 Ibid.
23 Rosemary Speirs, "Canadian Faces Charges of Terrorism," *Toronto Star*, 16 January 1996, A9.
24 Quoted in Hyndman, "The Question of 'the Political,'" 252.
25 Ibid., 253.
26 *CBC News Online,* "Omar Khadr Sentenced."
27 Stewart Bell, "Khadrs Reveal bin Laden Ties," *National Post*, 24 January 2004, A1.
28 Michelle Shephard, "Hurt Teen Hopes for Swift Return to Canada; Pakistan Holding Son of Ahmed Khadr Paralyzed in Attack That Killed His Father," *Toronto Star*, 24 January 2004, A22.
29 *CBC News Online,* "Khadr Patriarch Disliked Canada, Says al-Qaeda Biography," http://www.cbc.ca/world/story/2008/02/07/khadr-bio.html (accessed 24 November 2010).
30 Michael Friscolanti, "The House of Khadr," 2006, http://www.macleans.ca/article.jsp?content=20060807_131499_131499&source=srch (accessed 29 November 2010).
31 *CBC News Online,* "Khadr Patriarch."
32 Colin Freeze and Christine Boyd, "U.S. Holds Canadian Teen as al-Qaeda Assassin," *Globe and Mail*, 6 September 2002, A1.
33 Bell, *Cold Terror,* 169.
34 Bell, "Khadrs Reveal."
35 *PBS Online,* "Son of al Qaeda," 2004, http://www.pbs.org/wgbh/pages/frontline/shows/khadr/interviews/abdullah.html (accessed 30 November 2010).
36 Friscolanti, "House of Khadr."
37 *PBS Online,* "Son of al Qaeda."
38 Ibid.
39 At the camp training would have included instruction on using light weapons, handguns, small machine guns, rocket-propelled grenade

launchers (RPGs), explosives (including TNT, C4 plastic explosives, and black plastic explosives), poisons (including cyanide), and poison gas. They were also trained in the art of sabotage, target selection, urban warfare, tactics (including assassinations), and security (NEFA 2010).

40 *PBS Online,* "Son of al Qaeda."

41 Ibid.

42 Bell, *Cold Terror.*

43 *PBS Online,* "Son of al Qaeda."

44 Ibid.

45 Rachel Brett and Irma Specht, *Young Soldiers: Why They Choose to Fight* (Boulder: Lynne Rienner 2004).

46 Park, "Child Soldiers and Distributive Justice," 338.

47 Sainz-Pardo, "Child Recruitment as a War Crime," 592.

48 Human Rights Watch, "The Omar Khadr Case."

49 Roméo Dallaire, *They Fight like Soldier, They Die like Children: The Global Quest to Eradicate the Use of Child Soldiers* (Toronto: Random House 2010); W. Andy Knight, "Children as 'Weapon Systems': A General Dedicates His Life to Ending the Use of Child Soldiers Worldwide," *Literary Review of Canada* 28, no. 3 (2011): 28–9.

50 Sainz-Pardo has advocated for this position: "It is therefore commonly accepted that 15 is the age limit under which the prohibition of child recruitment has crystallised today as part of customary international law. Despite this huge step forward in the development of international criminal law, a last effort is needed in the fight against impunity for the most serious crimes, among which is that of the conscription, enlistment, or use of children during armed conflict. This is a call on states to include, through an increasing state practice that will lead to the required opinio juris, children between 15 and 18 years in the customary definition of child recruitment, all in respect of the universal definition of 'child' provided by the Convention on the Rights of the Child" ("Child Recruitment as a War Crime," 592).

51 Hyndman, "The Question of 'the Political,'" 252.

52 Rosen, "Child Soldiers, International Humanitarian Law," 300.

53 In terms of international law relating to child soldiers, the following represents the relevant international treaties: the 1977 Additional Protocols (I and II) to the Geneva Conventions; the 1989 Convention on the Rights of the Child; the 1990 African Charter on the Rights and Welfare of the Child; the 1998 Rome Statute; the 1999 International Labour Organisation Convention No. 182; and the 2000 Optional Protocol to the CRC (Park 2010, 331); and the 2007 Paris Principles.

54 Rosen, "Child Soldiers, International Humanitarian Law," 300.
55 Hyndman, "Question of 'the Political,'" 251.
56 Park, "Child Soldiers and Distributive Justice."
57 The 2000 Optional Protocol to the Convention on the Rights of the Child attempted to raise the minimum age of recruitment to eighteen, stating that state parties "shall take all feasible measures to ensure that persons below the age of 18 do not take a direct part in hostilities and that they are not compulsorily recruited into their armed forces" (Hyndman, "Question of 'the Political,'" 251).
58 Sainz-Pardo, "Child Recruitment as a War Crime."
59 Quoted in Park, "Child Soldiers and Distributive Justice," 332.
60 Human Rights Watch, "The Omar Khadr Case."
61 Hyndman, "Question of 'the Political.'"
62 Park, "Child Soldiers and Distributive Justice," 331–2.
63 Sainz-Pardo, "Child Recruitment as a War Crime," 592.
64 Park, "Child Soldiers and Distributive Justice," 332.
65 Pugliese, "Apostrophe of Empire," 12.
66 Amnesty, "Military Commission Proceedings."
67 Human Rights Watch, "The Omar Khadr Case," 3–4.
68 Rosen, "Child Soldiers, International Humanitarian Law," 301.
69 Ibid.
70 Ibid., 296.
71 Park, "Child Soldiers and Distributive Justice," 334. There have been recent examples of indictments and charges being successfully brought by the ICC against individuals who recruit child soldiers; for instance, against Thomas Dylio, president of the Union des Patriotes Congolais in the DRC and against five leaders of the Uganda's Lord's Resistance Army (LRA). In all of these recent examples, the individuals were charged with recruitment of children into armed groups.
72 Paul Koring, "Omar Khadr Pleads Guilty to All Terrorism Charges," *Globe and Mail*, 25 October 2010, http://www.theglobeandmail.com/news/world/americas/omar-khadr-pleads-guilty-to-all-terrorism-charges/article1771325/ (accessed 29 November 2010).
73 Human Rights Watch, "The Omar Khadr Case," 6.
74 Park, "Child Soldiers and Distributive Justice," 342.

Omar Khadr: Canadian Child Soldier

DEBORAH GORHAM

On my computer screen the boy in the orange shirt is being interrogated by a man with a cold, bland voice. The interrogator never displays emotion, but the boy is upset, and finally he is sobbing.

"I want you to tell me the truth," says the interrogator.

"You don't like the truth," says the boy.

The boy takes off his orange shirt, to show the damage to his body.

"They tortured me very badly at Bagram," he says. (Bagram is an American air base in Afghanistan. There is a "black prison" on the base.)

To which the interrogator replies, "I think you're getting good medical care."

"No, I'm not," says the boy, his voice cracking as he begins to cry. "You're not here."

This footage was filmed in February 2003 at the American maximum-security prison at Guantánamo Bay, Cuba.[1] The boy is Omar Khadr, barely sixteen when this interrogation took place. The interrogators are Canadians. Although Omar was at first happy that "finally" he could talk to Canadians, the footage reveals that these people did not come to Guantánamo as his friends. They were agents of the Canadian Security Intelligence Service, and they were cooperating with the US government.

Like other contributors to this book, I find many things appalling about the Omar Khadr case. When Omar was detained, he was a child under Canadian, American, and international law. He was born in Toronto on 18 September 1986. He was captured on 27 July 2002 by American forces after a firefight in a village in Afghanistan between a group of Muslim militants, of whom he was one, and American soldiers. He was so severely wounded that when the US medic at the scene of the firefight was treating him, he said to him – in English – "Shoot me."[2]

Omar was first sent to Baghram. In October 2002 he was transferred to the detention camp run by the United States at Guantánamo where he remains as I write this. He was accused, among other things, of throwing a grenade that killed US Sgt Christopher Speer and was deemed by his American captors to have committed "murder in violation of the law of war."

As W. Andy Knight and John McCoy point out in their essay in this volume, "International Law and the Recruitment of a Child Soldier Omar Khadr and Family Ties," there is convincing evidence that American personnel tortured Omar as a prisoner at Bagram and at Guantánamo Bay and that Canadian officials knew about this. American officials decided that Omar was to be tried not in a regular US court of law but by a Guantánamo Military Commission tribunal.

We know that while Omar was reluctant to do so, he and his lawyers and officials at the highest level in Canada and in the United States did negotiate a plea bargain in October 2010. The negotiators agreed that Omar would be returned to Canada after he spent an additional year at Guantánamo, to serve a sentence that could not be longer than eight years. In return, he pleaded guilty to five charges, including throwing the grenade that is alleged to have killed Christopher Speer.

How should we interpret these facts? How do I interpret them, as a citizen of Canada and of the United States (my country of birth), as a grandparent, and as a historian who has written about women, gender, and childhood?

The Guantánamo Bay Naval Base has been, de facto, US property since the 1903 Cuban-American treaty. When Fidel Castro came to power, his government repudiated the agreement, and Cuba has refused to take the "rent" the US government pays for its "perpetual lease." The occupation of the base is a deplorable example of American imperialism. The establishment of the "detention center" or prison after 11 September 2001 as part of President George W. Bush's "war on terror" is even more reprehensible than the existence of this US military base on the soil of a country that objects to its presence.

The Bush administration selected Guantánamo precisely because it was territory under American control but outside the boundaries of the United States. American law and principles of justice and human rights could, the administration believed, therefore be violated.[3] To justify its behaviour to prisoners at Guantánamo, the administration created the concept of "unlawful enemy combatant." As one American military lawyer has said, this concept, which violates international law, amounts to saying "anyone in Afghanistan who resisted the U.S. invasion was guilty of a war crime."[4]

Illegal methods of interrogation have been used at Guantánamo, including torture. The use of torture by American personnel violates the Eighth Amendment of the Constitution of the United States, which George W. Bush, as president, swore to uphold. President Obama, to his great credit, immediately after his inauguration in January 2009 stated that he intended to close down Guantánamo. Sadly, his administration has not succeeded in doing so.

And Canada? For years the government of Prime Minister Stephen Harper chose not to seek the repatriation of Omar Khadr. Harper and other representatives of the Canadian government repeatedly stated that they believed Omar would be treated fairly by the United States – despite representations from Amnesty International, the Canadian Bar Association, and UNICEF, among other organizations, that the Canadian government demand his repatriation, and despite a Canadian Supreme Court ruling in January 2010 that his rights under Canada's Charter of Rights and Freedoms have been violated.

The brave and outspoken General Roméo Dallaire has written that the "Khadr case is a black mark on my own country's international reputation and standing."[5] For me, the Khadr case is a black mark on both my countries: the United States and Canada.

Omar Khadr is now an adult, and it is as an adult that he was forced into making the plea bargain in October 2010. It is as an adult that he will spend another year at Guantánamo. As an adult he is one of hundreds of thousands of victims – in Iraq, in Afghanistan, and in the United States itself – of the tragic decisions made by the Bush administration after the events of 11 September 2001. President Obama unfortunately has not succeeded in stopping the wars in Afghanistan or even in Iraq, nor in bringing to an end the travesties of justice at Guantánamo, although matters have improved during his administration.

Is the violation of Omar Khadr's status as a minor in July 2002 the most egregious of the injustices he has endured? He certainly was engaged in violent conflict on 27 June 2002, the day of his capture, but as Knight and McCoy point out at length, human rights activists insist that he should never have been imprisoned or tried at all, because he was a child soldier.

I agree with this interpretation, but I also think that we need to be fully cognizant of what we are advocating when we defend Omar Khadr's rights as a child and when we deplore the use of children as soldiers. First, we need to understand that the use of children as soldiers is not new: it is the condemnation of this practice by humanitarian organizations and individuals that is new. Consider ancient Sparta where boys were trained from childhood to be warriors. Consider the Janissaries, Christians forcibly converted to Islam by the Turks during the Ottoman Empire. These boys could be as young as ten, and they wore uniforms and fought and died in battle. Consider the drummer boys of the American Civil War. There were over 100,000 of them, some as young as nine. Consider the use of boys as young as thirteen as midshipmen (officer cadets) in the British navy, a practice that continued well into the nineteenth century. These are a few of many examples.

It is true, however, that the use of child soldiers appears to be expanding, even as the condemnation of their use also expands. As Knight and McCoy note, there are at least an estimated 250,000 children under the age of eighteen all over the world who are child soldiers. Some are as young as seven.

In *They Fight Like Soldiers, They Die Like Children,* Roméo Dallaire focuses on African countries, arguing that the use of children, mostly boys but also girls, is growing because the insurgent groups and governments that recruit them consider them to be dispensable: there are so many poor, abandoned, orphaned children available. As Dallaire says, "Children are faceless, and they are considered expendable."[6] The recruiters' methods are brutal: often the children's family members are killed before their eyes. Sometimes the children are coerced into killing family members themselves under threat that unless they do so, they themselves will be killed. They are often drugged to make it easier to force them to fight. The girls who are coerced into being soldiers are usually abused sexually as well and often become pregnant. These little soldiers are frequently forced into battle in the front lines, ahead of adult soldiers, or forced to cross areas where there may be land mines. After all, there are more expendable children where they came from.

Dallaire and others point out that technology has contributed to this sorry situation. Small arms that are easy to use and light enough for a child to carry (most notably the AK-47 rifle) are now readily available to governments and to groups opposing government forces, and this has facilitated the use of children in combat. In short, Dallaire declares, "Man has created the ultimate cheap, expendable, yet sophisticated human weapon, at the expense of humanity's own future: its children."[7]

The use of child soldiers rends the heart. It is, after all, happening today when a humanitarian point of view opposing it has been fully articulated. There is a wider history of behaviour that humanitarians would now consider child abuse. Take the question of culpability under the law. In England, for example, right up to the middle of the nineteenth century, a child age seven or more could be held criminally responsible and hanged for capital offences. And even in the nineteenth century, some children were executed.[8] In this same era, boys and girls as young as four worked in coal mines underground. The pittance they earned was paid to their fathers.

In our European and North American past, then, children were not seen as individuals with inherent human rights. Legal and cultural structures were patriarchal, and children were subject to the will of their fathers.[9] The status of children, like that of adults, depended as well on race and social class, but in all situations children were regarded, if not as possessions, then as individuals subject to the will and decisions of others.

But what exists today, with respect to child soldiers – and other forms of child abuse as well – is a confusing situation. On the one hand, there is a well-articulated humanitarian position opposing such practices and defending the rights of children under eighteen as individuals with inherent human rights, and with special needs as children. This approach is fully articulated in the Knight and McCoy essay.

But in spite of this law and this rhetoric, children are still recruited as child soldiers. Children, girls for the most part, are still forced to participate in the international sex trade, and in India and Bolivia, for example, children still work in mines. How can these abuses continue in the face of organized international condemnation?

The American human rights lawyer David Kennedy, in his book *The Dark Sides of Virtue: Reassessing International Humanitarianism*,[10] suggests some reasons for these woeful failures. Kennedy believes, first of all, that we need to recognize that human rights is a Western concept, a product of enlightenment liberal thinking, and that it may not be understood or easily assimilated in non-Western situations.[11] Moreover, Kennedy believes that human rights advocates have created a bureaucracy of human rights advocacy. Activists hold conferences, pass laws, and make high-sounding pronouncements. We attempt to intervene in situations where human rights are violated, yet the violations continue. Too often, Kennedy says, we mistake rhetoric for change: "As human rights advocates, we have too often treated our norms as true – rather than as reminders of what might be made true."[12] "People inside the movement can mistake reform of their world for reform of the world."[13]

But in the case of Omar Khadr, I believe it is not only right but may be useful, perhaps even to Omar himself, to see him as a child victim. We must speak out as Canadians in defence of this Canadian imprisoned and tortured when he was a teenager.

Omar became a "child soldier" because of the influence of his family, most especially his father. He was not the kind of child soldier – orphaned by war or by HIV/AIDS or abandoned – whom we encounter in Roméo Dallaire's account. Omar was, it appears, the favourite son in a close family. But his father and his mother believed it was their right and their duty to impose ideas on him and their other children, and these ideas included encouraging their sons to become Islamist soldiers, prepared to fight and die for what the parents clearly saw as a just cause.[14]

Omar's father, Ahmed Said Khadr, born in Egypt in 1948, came to Canada in 1975 to study. An observant Muslim when he first came to Canada, he was also secular in his beliefs and practices. But at the University of Ottawa, he joined the Muslim Student Association and became committed to an Islamist view of the world.

From 1982, Ahmed Khadr and his family moved around a lot, within Canada and then to Bahrain, Pakistan, and Afghanistan, where he was involved in charitable work but also with Islamic militancy. He was killed in Pakistan on 2 October 2003.

What were these circumstances like for Omar, the fifth child in the family? As a child, he had multiple identities. He loved the

Tintin stories and his favourite food was Jell-O, but he also learned to speak Pashto. He was a Canadian boy but also at home in the Islamist world of Pakistan and Afghanistan. "Omar, like all the Khadr children, was comfortable in both worlds," says journalist Michelle Shephard.

That Omar as a child experienced many shifts in scene does not make his parents bad parents or the children victims in need of protection from the law, although it is clear that Ahmed Said Khadr put his support of Islamism ahead of the needs of his family. He did become convinced that he and his sons should fight and die for Islam. He wanted his sons to become martyrs, even suicide bombers. It was Ahmed Khadr who allowed and even encouraged Omar to train with Abu Laith al Libi. This led directly to Omar's participation in the firefight that day in July 2002 and to his wounding and capture by the Americans.

In my view, Ahmed Khadr's encouragement of Omar's participation in violent conflict when he was in his early teens was child abuse. (Knight and McCoy agree.) Omar's family may have been close, but Omar was a victim of his family's political beliefs. No one should encourage a boy of fifteen to engage in armed conflict. Because this particular boy is a Canadian, as Canadians we have a right and a duty to speak out against this violation of his rights as a Canadian child.

Omar has also been a victim of anti-Muslim sentiment within Canada, although these sentiments are usually presented as simply anti-terrorist and accompanied by statements about "good" Muslims. When Maha Elsamnah, Omar's mother, returned to Canada in 2004 after her husband was killed, here's what Don Martin, of the *National Post* had to say: "Clearly, the words of this matriarch and her outspoken daughter, the actions of her deceased husband and terrorist-suspect sons, and the notoriety of their infamous ringleader friends render the entire clan unworthy of citizenship or its benefits."[15] Shockingly, Stockwell Day, then foreign affairs critic for the Stephen Harper Conservatives, struck the same note: "Canadian citizenship is diminished when we allow it to be extended to people like the Khadrs."[16]

True, Omar's mother and his older sister, Zaynab, have openly expressed their support for Islamic militancy. But both are naturalized citizens of this country, and Omar was, of course, born here.

Moreover, he is not responsible for anything that his mother, sisters, or brothers say or do, or for the words or actions of his dead father. Under Canadian law and as a Canadian, he is a separate individual, not just part of the "Khadr clan." It is appalling that Stockwell Day, a member of Parliament and spokesperson for the Conservative Party, should make statements about removing the citizenship of all of the Khadrs.

"I like my son to be brave ... I would like my son to be trained to protect himself, to protect his home, to protect his neighbour."[17] So said Omar's mother when she was interviewed in 2004.

Omar Khadr was fourteen going on fifteen on 11 September 2001. The Khadr family was in Kabul at the time. They moved because it was dangerous in Kabul after the Americans started bombarding the city. By January 2002, Omar was living with his mother, and his younger sister Maryam, moving from place to place in South Waziristan. He chafed at being responsible for the two women. On one occasion he had to wear a burqa so that he could travel without being noticed, and this reportedly infuriated him.[18] He wanted to be a soldier: he wanted to be with the men. Finally, his father agreed that Omar should go to join the jihadist forces of Abu Laith al Libi. "Khadr allowed his son to go and Omar was delighted to finally be away from the women."[19]

It matters that Omar Khadr is male. Yes, there are girl soldiers, and women now serve in the armed forces of many countries, but war remains a male activity, and the vexed questions connected with gender and war and gender and violence are of great importance to a general analysis of these issues, as well as to Omar's particular case.

Throughout history and across cultures, wars have been fought by men, and not just by men but by young men, although their commanding officers are usually older men. Yes, we have much rhetoric about how dreadful it is to coerce children into becoming soldiers – and it is – but even Roméo Dallaire thinks it is all right to welcome eighteen-year-olds into the Canadian armed forces. Eighteen is very young. Armies like young soldiers: they are more easily indoctrinated than older recruits, and they fight more fiercely. They are not included in the category "child soldier," but the distinction between a sixteen-year-old and an eighteen-year-old is in fact arbitrary. I would suggest that both are victims, just as both may also be perpetrators: people who harm others.[20]

The association of war with masculinity encourages misogyny. The Marine Corps book camp refrain comes to mind:

This is my rifle
This is my gun [penis]
One is for fighting
One is for fun.[21]

Again, through history and across cultures, warfare sanctions rape, and rape has been and continues as I write this to be used as an act of war. Nicolas Kristof and Sheryl WuDunn cite one sixteen-year-old soldier in Congo who told them, "If we see girls, it's our right ... we can violate them."[22]

Everyone suffers in war, but women and girls suffer disproportionally: women and girls experience an increase in sexual violence; they also suffer more severely than men or boys as displaced persons in refugee camps. And children suffer not only as child soldiers but also from hunger, disease, and loss in war-torn parts of the world. As the great human rights activist Graca Michel has said, "Protecting children from the impact of armed conflict is everyone's responsibility – governments, international organizations and every element of civil society. Therefore my challenge to each of you ... is that you ask yourself what you can do to make a difference. And then take that action, no matter how large or how small. For our children have a right to peace."[23]

No one knows what the future holds for Omar Khadr. One person who knows more about him than most people is the Scottish-Canadian lawyer Denis Edney from Edmonton who was Omar's lawyer for many years. Edney, who has vowed to help Omar upon his release, made a powerful speech at the Festival de Nouveau Cinema in Montreal on 14 October 2010, following the launch of the documentary *You Don't Like the Truth*.

In this speech Edney talked about his meetings with Omar at Guantánamo. "Is he lost?" Edney asked. He had suffered so much. But Edney has hope: "Along the way [Omar's] dignity has shown through." Edney asks each of us to confront and challenge governmental power, as individuals committed to "human compassion": "You'll be surprised at the power that you have."[24]

Edney's tireless work on Omar Khadr's behalf is truly an inspiration. We must strive to prove him right.

NOTES

1 Excerpts from the film *You Don't Like the Truth: 4 Days inside Guantánamo*, made by filmmakers Luc Côté and Patricio Henriquez, are included in this volume and available at http://www.youtube.com/watch?v=dZrERVO19Dg.

2 See Michelle Shephard, *Guantanamo's Child: The Untold Story of Omar Khadr* (Toronto: Wiley, 2008), 16. Shephard is a journalist with the *Toronto Star*. Her book is an important contribution to our knowledge about Omar and the Khadr family, along with the actions of the US and Canadian governments and those lawyers and human rights activists who sought Omar's freedom in Canada and in the United States.

3 Many Americans and the American courts do not agree. See, for example, the timeline at http://projects.washingtonpost.com/guantanamo/timeline/.

4 This is William Kuebler. The quotation is from his address to the Canadian Bar Association delivered 11 August 2007. In that speech Kuebler urged the association to pressure the Canadian government to ask for Omar Khadr's repatriation. See Shephard, *Guantanamo's Child*, 216.

5 Roméo Dallaire, with Jessica Dee Humphreys, *They Fight Like Soldiers, They Die Like Children: The Global Quest to Eradicate the Use of Child Soldiers* (Toronto: Random House Canada, 2010), 181. An excerpt from the book is included in this collection.

6 Ibid., 3.

7 Ibid.

8 It was still the case that theft for anything worth more than five shillings could be punishable by death. However, by the eighteenth century the death penalty was used less often than it had been: punishment as reform was emerging as an idea, along with the idea of juvenile status. But the transformation was gradual.

9 In English law, if they were "legitimate," that is. If they were born out of wedlock, the law saw them as "nobody's child." Girls and women were also subjected to patriarchal law.

10 David Kennedy, *The Dark Sides of Virtue: Reassessing International Humanitarianism* (Princeton: Princeton University Press, 2004).

11 "Although there are lots of interesting analogies to human rights ideas in various cultural traditions, the particular form these ideas are given in the human rights movement is the product of a

particular moment and place: post-Enlightenment, rationalist, secular, Western, modern and capitalist" (ibid., 18).

12 Ibid., 352.

13 Ibid., 24.

14 Dennis Edney, Omar's Canadian lawyer, points out that we don't know for sure that A.S. Khadr supported al-Quaeda, but the evidence that he did is strong. He was killed in a shootout in 2003. Khadr's mother, who now lives in Toronto, said in 2004, "[Omar] would have been so proud to die as a *shahid*, a martyr, as a soldier of Islam, as his father now is" (Shephard, *Guantanamo's Child*, 152).

15 See http://vladtepesblog.com/?p=4862. Martin's was an op-ed byline on 15 April 2004.

16 Day, speaking to reporters and quoted in the *National Post*, 10 April 2004, cited in Shephard, *Guantanamo's Child*, 149.

17 Omar Khadr's mother, Maha Elsamnah, in 2004, quoted in Shephard, *Guantanamo's Child,* 146.

18 Shephard, ibid., 81.

19 Ibid., 82.

20 This victimization of very young soldiers is a theme in two novels I have recently read. David Bergen's *The Matter with Morris* (2010) is a Canadian novel that features the death of the protagonist's young son in Afghanistan. Bergen's intention here is to say that teenaged Martin Shutt volunteers impulsively. He's really just a confused boy. In American novelist Lorrie Moore's *A Gate at the Stairs* (first published in 2009), the protagonist's brother Robert volunteers right after high school and is also killed in Afghanistan. The protagonist, Tassie, who unlike Robert did well in high school and is going to university, suffers from "survivor guilt." She dreams about her dead brother, and in one dream he appears "holding a sign that read YES I AM A MAN" (Toronto: Anchor Canada edition, 2010, 309).

21 For a depiction of this Marine Corps chant, see http://www.youtube.com/watch?v=4kUoXCVey_Uhttp://www.youtube.com/watch?v=4kUoXCVey_U. For an analysis, see Richard Allen Burns: "The link between firing of weapons and sex becomes more forceful when considering the words of a Vietnam veteran who compared carrying a gun to having a permanent erection: 'It was a sexual trip every time you got to pull the trigger'" (Grossman quoted by Goldstein 2001, 349). By extension, maleness becomes a weapon of destruction; a man's penis (gun) becomes an instrument of power (ibid., 350)." See Richard Allen Burns, "'This Is My Rifle, This Is My Gun ... ':

Gunlore in the Military," http://www.temple.edu/english/isllc/newfolk/military/rifle.html

22 Nicholas D. Kristof and Sheryl WuDunn, *Half the Sky: Turning Oppression into Opportunity for Women Worldwide* (New York: Vintage Books, 2010, first published in 2009), 86.

23 Michel was the main force behind the 1996 report "Promotion and Protection of the Rights of Children: Impact of Armed Conflict on Children," a study sponsored by UNICEF, http://www.un.org/rights/introduc.htm.

24 See http://www.wikio.co.uk/video/omar-khadr-lawyer-dennis-edney-fnc-4424658.

How the Supreme Court of Canada Undermined the Convention on the Rights of the Child in the Case of Omar Khadr

GRACE LI XIU WOO

What makes the Omar Khadr case so troubling in terms of hard-won juridical values? Omar was a child when he was detained. He was only fifteen years old. Yet, at twenty-three he was the only citizen of a Western country who had not been repatriated from illegal detention by the United States at its Guantánamo Bay naval base. When the Supreme Court of Canada reversed a Federal Court order requiring the prime minister to request Omar's repatriation, it violated the Convention on the Rights of the Child and *jus cogens*, which prohibits torture. Although the court provided consolation to some by condemning the involvement of Canadian officials in Omar's mistreatment, it ignored the gravity of this situation, not only for Omar but for us all. The court failed to take account of the way that international law has been incorporated in Canadian law. It also misstated Anglo-Canadian constitutional tradition by claiming that it lacked jurisdiction over the executive prerogative on matters touching on foreign policy. As a product of the British Empire, prerogative powers under Canada's constitution have always been legally limited by the will of the nation, which is now expressed by the legislature and in international human rights instruments. The failure of Canada's highest court to uphold this principle has undermined the Rights of the Child. In doing so it also undermined the concept of the rule of law, a fundamental tenet of both parliamentary democracy and modern international relations. The court's disturbing acquiescence to the illegal detention of a child by the party responsible for torturing him also impugns the Canadian constitution, putting us all at risk.

Omar Khadr's experience demonstrates the extreme vulnerability of children and of the fundamental human rights that many of us take for granted. Every now and then, we are shocked to discover that some seemingly normal individual has abducted a child to sequester in a secret bunker. The inevitable media blitz feeds our horror. Reporters scramble to find out how the crime was discovered and how it remained hidden for so many years. But once the act is known, we depend on the law to put things rights. Glimpses of the shackled perpetrator being led into court play before our eyes as we listen to the plans made to rehabilitate the unfortunate victim. There is no question of putting such children on trial. Some cases come to light when the abducted child escapes. He or she may have grown to adulthood and waited years for the opportunity but, once free, has headed straight for the police, confident that protection will be offered and the world will defend the right to common decency.

For Omar Khadr, that trust in the law has been extinguished. His sequestration was publicly known. The United Nations and some of the most respected courts in the world have confirmed that he was the victim of torture. Canada's House of Commons and Senate both recommended his repatriation. Yet in January 2010 the Supreme Court of Canada reversed the order of two lower courts, requiring Canada to ask the United States for his return from detention at Guantánamo.[1] The judgment left him under the control of his abusers while the violation of his fundamental human rights continued. This failure of due process is of concern to everyone who hopes to establish a culture of peace and leave behind the injustices and bad habits entrenched during the age of colonial aggression and imperial domination.

The breakdown in the web of protection that should be inviolable, especially for children, happened despite the fact that Omar is a citizen of Canada, which is a founding member of both the League of Nations and the United Nations. Canada is widely considered a leader in the field of human rights, as the chief justice of the Supreme Court herself has claimed.[2] Moreover, the state that tortured Omar and that continued to hold him under conditions that ignore his rights is the United States of America, whose constitution inspired the opening words of the Charter of the United Nations.[3] As stated in the Universal Declaration of Human Rights, this organization is dedicated to "the inherent dignity and the equal and inalienable rights of all members of the human family." Why did this breakdown occur? Why is the Convention on the Rights of the Child (CRC) so difficult to uphold in Canada when it has been ratified by every state except Somalia and the United States, making it the most successful and widely accepted human rights treaty in the world?[4]

WHAT HAPPENED TO OMAR

When a child has been abducted by a twisted individual, no one waits for a court to establish evidence concerning the abuse. The child is removed immediately to safety. In Omar's case, however, he has remained the captive of a state that tortured him and violated his human rights, even though its institutions are expected to provide public protection. That state justified its actions by claiming that the confinement of those transported to its naval base at Guantánamo Bay was necessary to prevent enemy combatants from taking up arms against the United States.[5] The failure of both Canada and the United States to uphold international norms has obscured many facts, preventing an orderly judicial examination of what happened and denying Omar any opportunity to tell his story.

FACTS ABOUT OMAR KHADR THAT HAVE GONE MISSING IN ACTION

Photos purporting to show Omar Khadr's bloody, twisted body being dug out of the rubble after the battle in which he is alleged to have thrown a grenade have been published on the Internet. Shot twice in the back, permanently blinded in one eye by shrapnel, he might not have survived were it not for onsite American medical attention.

Internet postings are not subjected to the same rigorous scrutiny as evidence submitted in court. However, undisputed evidence referred to in the factum presented by Omar's lawyers to the Supreme Court of Canada indicates that he was later severely tortured. After being hospitalized at Bagram, this seriously injured fifteen year old was pulled off his stretcher onto the floor; his head was covered with a bag while dogs barked in his face. Cold water was thrown on him; he was forced to stand for hours with his hands tied above his head and to carry heavy buckets of water to aggravate his wounds. He was threatened with rape; bright lights were shone in his injured eyes. One of his interrogators at Bagram has confirmed that prisoners were tortured there.

After being transferred to Guantánamo, Omar was pressed against a wall until he passed out. He was shackled in painful positions for hours, exposed to extreme temperatures, threatened with rendition and sexual violence, forced to urinate on himself and used as a human mop to clean up the mess. He was then denied clean clothes for two days as well as being subjected to a sleep deprivation technique known as the "frequent flyer program." This technique was recognized as torture and prohibited by the 1992 US Army Field Manual.[6] The horror of his treatment should not have slipped the attention of the Supreme Court of Canada, because the factum took the unusual step of beginning with an extract from the 14 February 2003 CSIS interrogation of Omar in which he expressed his fear of the Americans and asked repeatedly for protection, reporting that his admissions had been made under torture.

Despite the rigours of court procedure, controversial cases are often accompanied by advocacy in the media. In 2007 a video found in the wreckage of the village where the battle in which Sgt Speers was killed was leaked to the press. It showed Omar laying land mines and playing with detonating cord. Yet the bluster surrounding US justification for Guantánamo and its treatment of Omar has obscured the negative example that the United States has set for young people. This state has shown little commitment to stopping the use of weapons that injure innocent parties, including children. Unlike 80 percent of the states in the world, the United States has yet to become a party to the 1997 Mine Ban Treaty. Nor has it signed the Convention on Cluster Munitions. Ignoring the threat they pose to civilian populations, it continues to manufacture lethal weapons.[7] UNICEF has expressed concern over the insidious danger such weaponry presents to children.[8] Yet the focus in the Khadr case has been on the culpability of a child caught in a battle zone rather than on the adult responsibility of the state that violated his rights. The ongoing need for disarmament and better communications skills has likewise been ignored. Moreover, in 2008, military reports accidentally released to the press indicated that US operatives were less than honest. Soldiers at the scene initially reported that the grenade that killed an American soldier was thrown by the Mujahadeen, not Omar, but the report was later changed to implicate the captured child.

Media accounts based on US military documents concerning events leading up to the battle in which the contested grenade was thrown raise other concerns. The incident began when American troops approached a mud-brick village. They saw children playing outside and an elderly man asleep under a tree. Some men were sitting around a fire in the main house where AK-47s were visible, as might be expected in a war-torn region. Everything was quiet until the old man awoke and started screaming in Pashto. The children acted as interpreters for the Americans and said the man was "just angry." Things were calm enough for someone to take photographs of the children. Then the Americans sent an Afghan militiaman to demand the surrender of the men with the weapons. He retreated when someone fired a gun. The US soldiers insisted on a search even after they had been informed the men were Pashtuns. Things degenerated quickly, and a battle broke out with no apparent consideration for the safety of civilians. When the US soldiers requested medical aid, helicopters strafed the village with cannon and rocket fire, and reinforcements threw grenades at the houses. In other words, this was not a planned aggression. It erupted because people on both sides mistrusted each other and both responded inappropriately.

We will probably never hear the villagers' side of this story or find out whether any other children were killed or injured. Arguments concerning what happened have focused almost exclusively on how to interpret US military reports and policy statements, ignoring the confusion concerning the actual relationship between the United States and the various warring factions in the Afghan region. After the attacks of 9/11, Osama bin Laden and other members of al-Qaeda reportedly fled for the Pakistan-Afghanistan border. Omar's father, Ahmed Said Khadr, is believed to have followed them and was officially placed on the United States list of terrorists at that time.[9] However, former US President George W. Bush is also alleged to have been heavily involved with the bin Ladens for several years prior to 9/11.[10]

The sharp contrast in the treatment accorded to the associations of the Bush and Khadr families with the bin Ladens may be attributable to the differentiation of the "other" used to justify western domination as identified by Edward Said.[11] North Americans are so conditioned to see Muslims and Middle Eastern people as desert nomads engaged in terrorist activities that those with overactive imaginations fail to perceive points of commonality. Omar's Egyptian-born father,

Ahmed Said Khadr, was a computer engineer who had graduated from the University of Ottawa,[12] so the family had access to ordinary Canadian middle-class life. Ahmed worked for charitable nongovernmental organizations helping Afghan refugees and setting up agricultural projects, orphanages, a hospital, and several medical clinics. He is said to have been skilled at brokering peace between warlords. After Western intelligence agencies accused him of using his humanitarian aid activities to funnel funds to terrorists, he was arrested for complicity in bombing the Egyptian embassy in Islamabad but was eventually released for lack of evidence. In 2003, not long after Omar's capture, he was killed in or shortly after a battle in which one of Omar's brothers was shot in the spine and paralyzed from the waist down.

We may never know the truth about Omar's father. Was he subverted into supporting terrorism? Or was he just a humanitarian who got caught in the cross-fire? Omar's perception of the family conflicts with that of his brother Abdurahman who was released from Guantánamo and returned to Canada after being recruited by the United States as a double agent.[13] Moreover, the reports of intelligence agencies have been tainted by their implication with evidence obtained under torture. In 2006 Justice O'Connor's Commission of Inquiry into the Actions of Canadian Officials in Relation to Maher Arar investigated US rendition of a Syrian-born Canadian telecommunications engineer to Syria, where he was tortured. O'Connor found that despite exhaustive efforts to find incriminatory information, there was no indication that Arar was ever involved in any illegal or terrorist activity, concluding that the United States had sent Arar to Syria on the basis of false information provided by the Royal Canadian Mounted Police. As a result, an apology was issued and compensation paid.[14] An FBI agent later testified to a US military commission that Omar Khadr had reported seeing Arar in al-Qaeda safe houses and training camps. Arar was elsewhere and Omar's report has been discounted as the product of torture.[15]

The convoluted circumstances surrounding Omar Khadr's detention contrast sharply with the treatment accorded by the United States to Patty Hearst, the wealthy heiress who, at nineteen, was an adult when she was kidnapped by the Symbionese Liberation Army. Bank security cameras recorded her active participation in an armed robbery. Even after her rescue, she continued to defend the "urban guerilla" movement, but despite undisputable evidence of her criminal activity, her thirty-five year sentence was commuted to seven years, and she was released after serving only twenty-two months. She was later given a presidential pardon in accord with public recognition that she had been a victim of Stockholm syndrome, a psychological condition that induces hostages to sympathize with their captors. The evidence in Omar Khadr's case is much more ambiguous than that against Patty Hearst. He was only eleven years old when he was taken into a war zone. If he did throw a grenade, he was only fifteen at the time, and the act took place in the heat of an impromptu battle in a remote area where he had been left by his father. Subsequently, he was tortured repeatedly and spent over seven years in confinement with not so much as a trial. What was left of his family was not able to pay for top-flight legal defence. Nor did he have the benefit of the rule of law as defined by Canada, the United States, and international human rights instruments that these states are parties to. Indeed, by 2008 he had been permitted no visits and only two telephone calls from any family member.[16]

THE FORGOTTEN LEGAL FRAMEWORK FOR CHILD PROTECTION

The Convention on the Rights of the Child, so flagrantly violated in Omar Khadr's case, is part of a radical legal reordering that emerged during the twentieth century and is not yet complete. In 1832 the English jurist John Austin defined "laws" as "commands,"[17] and this model prevailed in European domestic and international relations during the age of colonial conquest and aggrandizement. The principles of human equality and consent as defined in international organizations like the United Nations and implemented through multilateral treaties like the International Covenant on Civil and Political Rights and the Convention on the Rights of the Child have been changing generally accepted concepts of legality. During the imperial age, treaties may have been the product of a monarch's prerogative, but with the rising importance of democratic norms, international procedure now allows states to ensure that international agreements represent the consensus of their people. Texts presented for signature are agreed upon through comprehensive discussion processes. States may register reservations to provisions that they do not support and, prior to ratification, may present a treaty or convention for approval according to their varying domestic legislative processes.

A convention comes into force when the required number of ratifications has been received from other states. However, once a treaty has been signed, a state is obligated to refrain from acts that would defeat its object and purpose (Vienna Convention on the Law of Treaties, Art. 18). Some international law is considered *jus cogens* or non-derogable. It is binding even on states that have not agreed to its terms. As the Supreme Court of Canada has acknowledged, the prohibition against torture is one such pre-emptory norm.[18] Since all members of the United Nations except Somalia and the United States have completed ratification of the Convention on the Rights of the Child, it has arguably reached non-derogable status. Despite the reservations that have been registered by some states, it certainly represents universally accepted norms.

The Convention on the Rights of the Child replicates some of the provisions that can be found in other international treaties and conventions as well as in the domestic law of most states. As set out in Justice O'Reilly's trial judgment when Omar Khadr's case was heard in Canada's Federal Court, it stipulates that "no child shall be subjected to torture or other cruel, inhuman or degrading treatment or punishment"; "no child shall be deprived of his or her liberty unlawfully or arbitrarily"; and that the "arrest, detention or imprisonment of a child shall be in conformity with the law." It further provides that every child in custody "shall have the right to prompt access to legal and other appropriate assistance, as well as the right to challenge the legality of the deprivation of his or her liberty before a court or other competent, independent and impartial authority, and to a prompt decision in any action" (Article 39).[19] All of these provisions were obviously violated in Omar Khadr's case. The Convention on the Rights of the Child also includes special provisions for children. Article 1 defines a child as a person under the age of eighteen. Article 39 specifies that "arrest, detention or imprisonment ... shall be used only as a measure of last resort and for the shortest appropriate period of time." Article 37(c) requires children deprived of their liberty to be separated from adults and declares a right to maintain contact with family through correspondence and visits except in exceptional circumstances. Article 39 requires states to "take all appropriate measures to promote physical and psychological recovery and social reintegration" of a child victim of torture, cruel or degrading treatment or armed conflict. Article 19.1 specifies that states have a duty to "take all appropriate legislative, administrative, social and educational measures" to protect children from maltreatment by parents, legal guardians, or any other person.

There is broadly based popular support for international human rights in Canada, and many pieces of legislation have been passed that implement the human rights conventions that Canada has agreed to uphold. The Canadian Charter of Rights and Freedoms, which is included in the Constitution Act, 1982, replicates several provisions found in both the International Covenant on Civil and Political Rights and the Convention on the Rights of the Child. The Geneva Conventions Act prohibits torture, and the Crimes against Humanity and War Crimes Act implemented the Statute of Rome establishing the International Criminal Court to prosecute the perpetrators of genocide, war crimes, and torture. As well as ratifying the Convention on the Rights of the Child on 13 December 1991, Canada became the first state to ratify the Optional Protocol to the Convention on the Rights of the Child on the Involvement of Children in Armed Conflict on 7 July 2000. The National Defence Act was amended to comply with its terms.[20] Through this kind of process, international law has become part of Canadian law.

In its 2008 *Khadr* decision, the Supreme Court of Canada confirmed that Canada's commitment to international human rights norms is reflected in the laws that it enacts. Its earlier reasoning in *Suresh* found that "both domestic and international jurisprudence suggest that torture is so abhorrent that it will almost always be disproportionate to interests on the other side of the balance, even security interests."[21] The 2008 Canadian Parliamentary Report to the Standing Committee on Foreign Affairs and International Development recommending Omar Khadr's repatriation was tabled in Parliament, although the Conservative Party dissented, focusing on the serious crimes Omar was accused of committing.[22] The Senate likewise adopted Senator Roméo Dallaire's motion urging Omar's repatriation.[23] Both houses of Parliament expressed particular concern with maintaining Canada's leadership role in support of children's rights. In summary, there was little to prepare us for the Supreme Court's 2010 *Khadr* decision, which contradicted the object and purpose of both the Convention on the Rights of the Child and the Optional Protocol by prolonging Omar's detention and leaving him in the hands of the state that had tortured him.

US RESPONSIBILITY UNDER INTERNATIONAL LAW

Primary responsibility for Omar's mistreatment must fall on the United States. In 2006 the United Nations Economic and Social Council issued a report on the "Situation of Detainees at Guantánamo Bay."[24] Although the United States denied access to some members of the investigating panel and refused to allow private interviews of any of the detainees, the information the council was able to compile was disturbing. Although the United States has not ratified the Convention on the Rights of the Child (CRC), it is a party to the International Covenant on Civil and Political Rights (ICCPR), and it has violated many of the covenant's provisions without registering any official derogation from this or any other human rights treaty to which it is party. The UN investigation concluded that the "War on Terror" did not constitute an armed conflict for the purposes of international humanitarian law. It expressed particular concern over systematic violations of the Convention against Torture and of the right not to be subjected to cruel and degrading treatment under s. 7 of the ICCPR. It also found that practices at Guantánamo had led, in some instances, to serious mental illness. There were 350 acts of self-harm in 2003 alone, individual and mass suicide attempts, and widespread and prolonged hunger strikes.[25] Noting that Omar Khadr's detention contravened the CRC,[26] it pointed out that even though the United States had not ratified this convention, it was a signatory and so had an obligation to refrain from acts that would defeat its object and purpose.[27]

Many citizens of the United States have been just as concerned as the United Nations over the Guantánamo regime. The slow struggle to defend both international human rights and domestic legal rights in US federal courts includes the ruling in *Rasul v. Bush,* which found that President George W. Bush acted illegally when he issued orders considering Guantánamo detainees to be unlawful combatants with no standing to seek remedies in any court, no protection under the Geneva Conventions and no right to habeas corpus. *In re Guantánamo Detainee Cases* found that due process had been denied by the same Combatant Status Review Tribunal that had classified Omar Khadr as an enemy combatant. In *Hamdan v. Rumsfeld*, the US Supreme Court found that the Guantánamo regime violated the Geneva Conventions by denying detainees access to regular courts. However, before Omar's lawyers challenged Prime Minister Stephen Harper's decision not to request his repatriation, the US Congress had passed the Military Commissions Act of 2006 removing the jurisdiction of US federal courts to receive habeas corpus applications from Guantánamo detainees.[28]

Immediately after taking office in January 2009, US President Obama signed an order closing the Guantánamo prison. However, in May, the House of Representatives and Senate voted to prevent the transfer of the detainees to the United States, and Omar Khadr remained the last westerner held at Guantánamo.[29] The United States had transferred about 435 detainees from Guantánamo including Omar's brother, and repatriated both citizens and permanent residents to Australia, Denmark, France, Germany, Belgium, Russia, Spain, Sweden and the United Kingdom.

With international and domestic concern mounting over Omar Khadr's treatment, the new US administration was strongly motivated to find a face-saving resolution. His case finally moved to trial but ended in October 2010 when he agreed to plead guilty to the charges against him. According to the settlement reached, he was sentenced to eight years imprisonment with the first year to be served in the United States and no credit for time served. He was also required to agree not to participate in any lawsuit against the United States or profit from publication of his story.[30] Omar apologized to the widow of Christopher Speer, the man killed by the grenade, but does this mean he did it? Lest we forget, the whole plea agreement was reached under the duress of prolonged illegal detention that included torture. Like victims of Stockholm Syndrome, Omar has learned to act as if the truth is whatever those who imprisoned him say it is. Given the types of decisions being made by courts in the United States, the terms he agreed to appear to have been designed to preclude his ability to initiate proceedings that could reveal the culpability of American personnel. If the American courts could find the president guilty of violating the law, who else could they convict? This anomaly only underscores that represented by the failure of Canada's Supreme Court to support the order to request Omar Khadr's repatriation and defend Canada's obligations under the CRC and the ICCPR.

OBSTACLES TO CANADIAN JUDICIAL PROTECTION

Although Omar Khadr was born in Toronto and is a Canadian citizen, the fact that he was being held by the United States presented several obstacles to the efforts that have been made to secure Canadian protection for his rights. To begin with, the Federal Court of Canada has jurisdiction only to grant relief against the Crown for the better administration of the laws of Canada.[31] There must be an identifiable decision that can be challenged,[32] and even though anyone incarcerated in Canada has access to legal aid, this is provided under provincial jurisdiction. Since Omar is outside the country, no funding was available. The appeals made on his behalf in Canadian courts were an entirely volunteer effort, initiated by Dennis Edney, a lawyer with sons of Omar's age. Edney seems to have brought the case to Federal Court at his own expense and, since Omar could not participate, proceedings were initiated by his grandmother acting as his best friend.

THE FACTS AND LAW AS SEEN BY THE FEDERAL COURT OF CANADA

Several decisions of the Federal Court of Canada concerning Omar Khadr demonstrate this institution's capacity to provide the legal infrastructure required to uphold international conventions including the Convention on the Rights of the Child. Following Omar's interrogation by agents from CSIS and the Department of Foreign Affairs and International Trade (DFAIT), Justice von Finckenstein granted an injunction against further interrogations.[33] An application was also made to review a decision of the minister of Foreign Affairs not to seek further consular access to Omar.[34] When the Federal Court rejected an application for disclosure of documents,[35] the decision was reversed by the Federal Court of Appeal,[36] and the minister's subsequent appeal was dismissed by the Supreme Court of Canada.[37] Canadian courts have accordingly proven capable of upholding both domestic and international law to prevent improper conduct by Canadian officials and obtain some disclosure.

Because he was being held abroad, Omar was not available to testify in any of these proceedings. Justice O'Reilly's trial judgment in *Khadr v. Canada (Prime Minister)*, 2009 F.C., which addressed the decision not to seek repatriation, began with a brief overview of the factual background establishing that Omar was born in Canada in 1986 and moved to Pakistan with his family in 1990. In 1995, when his father, Ahmed Khadr, was charged with complicity in bombing the Egyptian embassy in Islamabad, the rest of the family went back to Canada but returned to Pakistan in 1996 when Ahmad was released. In 2001 they again returned to Canada for a few months so Ahmed could recover from an injury caused by a land mine. They moved to Afghanistan in July 2001 and, following the events of 11 September 2001, Omar and his older brothers attended training camps associated with al-Qaeda. In July 2002, Omar was present at the fateful gun battle near Khost, Afghanistan, where a United States soldier was killed by a grenade. Omar was charged with throwing the grenade but maintained his innocence. He was seriously injured by bullets and shrapnel, held in custody at Bagram Airbase for several weeks, then transferred to Guantánamo Bay on 28 October 2002. Beginning in 2005, Canadian consular officials checked on him regularly.[38]

This skeletal focus on what was required to resolve the issues before the court did little to dislodge the suspicions of those who are susceptible to negative stereotypes about Islamic culture. The judgment did not even refer to Omar's partial blindness or describe the more horrible aspects of the torture he was subjected to. Sticking strictly to his limited jurisdiction over Canadian government action, Justice O'Reilly founded his reasoning on three significant facts that were agreed upon by both parties:

First, on detention, Omar Khadr was "given no special status as a minor" even though he was only fifteen when he was arrested and sixteen at the time he was transferred to Guantánamo Bay.

Second, he had virtually no communication with anyone outside of Guantánamo Bay until November 2004, when he met with legal counsel for the first time.

Third, at Guantánamo Bay he was subjected to the so-called frequent flyer program, which involved depriving him of rest and sleep and moving him every three hours over a period of weeks. Canadian officials became aware of this treatment in the spring of 2004 when Omar was seventeen, and proceeded to interrogate him (*Khadr v. Canada [Prime Minister]*, 2009 FC 405, 8–11).

O'Reilly found that Canadian consular inquiries concerning Omar began in November 2003 and were initially concerned with his welfare; however, he concluded that the interviews in 2003 by CSIS and

DFAIT were conducted for intelligence purposes. By the spring of 2004, Canadian officials were knowingly implicated in subjecting Omar to sleep deprivation techniques at a time when he was a seventeen-year-old minor, detained without legal representation, with no access to family and no Canadian consular assistance (ibid., 17). After referring briefly to judgments in the United States concerning the illegality of the Guantánamo regime, he noted that Omar faced five charges under the US Military Commissions Act: (1) murder in violation of the laws of war; (2) attempted murder in violation of the law of war; (3) conspiracy; (4) providing material support for terrorism; and (5) spying (ibid., 22). He found that the issues in this case had not been previously decided and that Prime Minister Stephen Harper's declaration to a journalist that Omar's repatriation would not be requested was evidence of a decision that could be judicially reviewed. He also found that there was an ongoing policy against requesting repatriation reflected in the dissent registered by Harper's government to the Parliamentary committee's recommendation of repatriation (ibid., 36–7).

After reviewing several judgments concerning adult Guantánamo detainees, Justice O'Reilly found that there was no clear duty to protect citizens under international law or the common law, but following the approach taken by the Constitutional Court of South Africa in *Kaunda v. President of South Africa*, he concluded that the government's decision was reviewable under the Charter although its determination concerning how to deal with the matter was entitled to "particular weight" (49). Within this context, he found that "When a person's life, liberty or security is at stake, s.7 of the *Charter* requires Canadian officials to respect the principles of fundamental justice" (53). In 2002 the Supreme Court of Canada had established in *Suresh v. Canada (Minister of Citizenship and Immigration)* that the principles of fundamental justice are informed by Canada's international obligations. Invoking the Supreme Court of Israel's finding that severe sleep deprivation for the purpose of breaking a suspect violates the Convention against Torture and Other Cruel, Inhuman or Degrading Treatment or Punishment, O'Reilly concluded that Canada had an obligation to prevent torture, prosecute offenders, and ensure that statements made as a result of torture were not used in any proceeding.

He then outlined Canada's duties under the Convention on the Rights of the Child, finding that Canada was required to protect

Omar Khadr from "physical and mental violence, injury, abuse or maltreatment" and that it had implicitly condoned the use of sleep deprivation techniques by conducting interviews with knowledge that Omar had been subjected to them (63). Although he found that the Optional Protocol on the Involvement of Children in Armed Conflict raised no specific legal obligation on Canada in respect to Omar, he found the principles set out in its preamble recognized the special needs of children "who are particularly vulnerable to recruitment or use in hostilities." He also identified the need to strengthen international cooperation to implement the Protocol "as well as the physical and psychosocial rehabilitation and social reintegration of children who are victims of armed conflict" (66–8). On this basis he determined that Canada's constitutional duty to uphold the principles of fundamental justice under s.7 of the Charter included a duty to protect Omar by ensuring that he was treated in accord with international human rights norms. He also found that a request for repatriation "as soon as practicable" was minimally intrusive on the Crown's prerogative over foreign affairs (89, 91).

In short, Justice O'Reilly's reasoning, which was upheld by the Federal Court of Appeal, was a model demonstrating how a state can use domestic legal infrastructure to uphold its international human rights commitments. Omar's circumstances are unprecedented in Canada, and it can only be hoped that they will never be replicated. Had the Supreme Court of Canada refused leave to appeal, all would have been well.

HOW CANADA'S SUPREME COURT SUBVERTED CHILDREN'S RIGHTS

Given the facts of Omar Khadr's situation, Canada's legislative support for human rights, and the Supreme Court's previous reasoning, its reversal of the order to request repatriation is both shocking and mysterious, particularly since the court failed to address children's rights and the issue of torture that figured so prominently in the Federal Court reasoning. The Supreme Court did confirm that the interrogations conducted by Canadian officials with knowledge that Omar had been subjected to sleep deprivation techniques signified Canada's active participation in a process that violated international human rights and deprived Omar of his right to liberty and security of the person guaranteed by s. 7 of the Charter. It even found that the order to request Omar's repatriation was an appropriate remedy. It is the reversal of this order on the grounds that it touched on the Crown prerogative over foreign affairs that is troubling. What does it mean to grant government officials such broad discretion to suspend the laws of Canada with regard to a particular individual, especially when that person's rights were violated as a child? Its rationale for doing this was poorly explained, revealing some rather ominous cracks in what people have generally assumed to be an enviable legal regime.

THE PRIME MINISTER'S SUBMISSIONS TO THE SUPREME COURT OF CANADA

The appeal to the Supreme Court of Canada was prepared by Canada's Department of Justice on behalf of the prime minister, the minister of Foreign Affairs, and the director of the RCMP. In other words, arguments against the recommendation for repatriation tabled by both houses of Parliament were prepared at the expense of Canadian citizens on behalf of government agencies that had already been implicated in serious violations of Canadian law in relation to Omar Khadr. This raises many questions. Do these agencies have something to hide? Should the Department of Justice be formulating arguments on behalf of administrative departments against the express will of Parliament? Who represents Canada? And, given Omar Khadr's lack of resources, can justice be assured in the face of such a David and Goliath imbalance in access to legal representation? Given the serious nature of both the prohibition against torture and the rights of children, it also leads us to wonder whether the governmental veil should not be lifted in some circumstances to consider the personal responsibility of individuals purporting to act on Canada's behalf.

The partisan nature of the application for leave to appeal can be seen in the fact that it made not one mention of the Convention on the Rights of the Child or of the prohibition against torture, even though these were the foundation of the trial judgment. It referred only to an international obligation to fight terrorism, protesting against any governmental duty to protect citizens abroad and what it claimed was an emerging trend to issue specific orders impinging on foreign relations. It even went so far as to accuse the court of using the Charter to reverse foreign policy,[39] when the problem might more properly be seen in terms of an increased tendency of government agents to violate both Canadian and international law. Unfortunately, the Supreme Court crumbled under this allegation and granted leave.

The extreme rarity of Omar Khadr's circumstances limited the scope of the protection represented by a request for his repatriation. However, the Crown's factum raised the spectre of an unmanageably expanded duty to protect Canadian citizens abroad. It paid little attention to the Convention on the Rights of the Child except to make an incorrect and unsubstantiated suggestion that it had not been incorporated in Canadian law and to claim that Canada's obligations under this instrument were territorially limited.[40] Most of its assertions were not relevant to Omar's particular situation. For example, the remedy of requesting repatriation did not require any extraterritorial action. Similarly, although the Crown pointed out at paragraph 99 that a citizen who leaves for another state must expect to be answerable to the justice system of that state, it failed to acknowledge that Omar was only eleven years old when he left Canadian territory and was taken to Pakistan and Afghanistan. He did not in any sense choose to enter the jurisdiction of the United States. There were so many split ends in the Crown's tangled argument that it would have been impossible for the court to address them all. The dishonest quality of the submissions certainly leaves us to wonder whether a state can be considered to be respecting its international obligations when its agencies exhibit such wilful blindness to its commitments.

Overall, the Crown's submissions were so biased and so lacking in understanding of the aspirational and mutually supportive character of international human rights law that it would have required at least a term at law school to correct some of its misperceptions. Its assertion of territorially defined sovereignty contradicts the colonial processes through which Canada became incorporated in the British Empire, and its ardent denial of any duty to protect deviates from the exchange of loyalty for protection that is central to the English concept of constitutional monarchy to which Canada is heir.[41] There have been a great number of changes in the political structure of both Canadian and international relations during the past century, yet s. 9 of Canada's Constitution Act, 1867, still vests "Executive Government and Authority" in the Queen, and the Queen is still subject to the coronation oath that she swore upon taking office confirming the monarch's traditional obligation to protect, as seen specifically in the duty to uphold the laws of the land. Indeed, the Constitution Act, 1982, begins by stating that Canada is founded on the rule of law. In short, the Crown's submissions seem to have been based on a fundamental misunderstanding of both Canadian constitutional history and international law.

THE REASONING OF AN ILL-INFORMED COURT

Fortunately Omar Khadr's situation is highly unusual. There is no Canadian precedent for such extraordinary mistreatment of a child by an allied state. Yet, if the Supreme Court had decided to uphold O'Reilly's order, all it needed to do was to reiterate the reasoning in some of its previous judgments. Justice Binnie's supplementary reasons in *R. v. Hape,* 2007 SCC [184] included a well-articulated explanation of the wisdom of the common law case-by-case approach in areas that have yet to be fully defined, such as that governing the relationship between Canadian and international law. This approach could have been used to counter the Crown's fears concerning an expanded duty to protect Canadians abroad. The main body of *Hape* also includes a careful analysis of the effect of changes in international law on the interpretation of domestic legislation. The court concluded that Canada follows the English tradition and, by the doctrine of adoption, "rules of international law are incorporated automatically, as they evolve, unless they conflict with legislation."[42] *Suresh*, 2002, is chock full of statements confirming that torture outrages Canadian standards of decency as well as "Canada's constitutional commitment to liberty and fair process."[43] It also supports the incorporation of international law in Canadian law, saying, "When Canada adopted the *Charter* in 1982, it affirmed the opposition of the Canadian people to government-sanctioned torture by proscribing cruel and unusual treatment or punishment in s. 12."[44]

Suresh touches on foreign policy in that it is concerned with deportation. The Supreme Court had no problem limiting executive discretion in that case, stating, "The Minister is obliged to exercise the discretion conferred upon her by the Immigration Act in accordance with the Constitution ... [and] the principles of fundamental justice under s.7 of the Charter."[45]

In other words, the *Khadr* case contradicted seemingly established legal principles. In keeping with its previous reasoning, the court did confirm that the conduct of Canadian officials had violated s.7 of the Charter, and that the request for repatriation was an appropriate and fair remedy. But this is of little consequence. The reversal of O'Reilly's order left Omar Khadr in the hands of his torturers. Equally sinister and foreboding, the court's meek acceptance of the Crown's boldly asserted prerogative over foreign affairs ignored the ancient and fundamental principle that the law applies to everyone, including prime ministers and monarchs. The astonishing conclusion is that the Supreme Court of Canada has abdicated from its traditional role as guardian of the rule of law.

In taking the tack it did, the court failed to acknowledge the most serious concerns raised both by Justice O'Reilly in his trial reasoning and by the factum presented by Omar Khadr's lawyers. The court did not even mention the barbarity of Omar's treatment at Bagram and Guantánamo. The word "torture" only occurs once in its judgment, at paragraph 20, with reference to a US case. Instead of identifying what had happened to Omar by using the appropriate word that invoked the appropriate Canadian and international law, the court adopted the euphemisms of his abusers, referring to the specific mistreatment in which Canada was implicated as "sleep deprivation" or the "frequent flyer program." It also turned its back on children's rights, presenting no discussion whatsoever on this topic in relation to the Crown's concerns despite the primordial role of the Convention on the Rights of the Child in Justice O'Reilly's reasoning and in the submissions made in both Omar Khadr's factum and in those of some of the interveners, most notably that of the Canadian Coalition on the Rights of the Child.[46] Even if Omar is guilty of having thrown the grenade, it can hardly be considered that, as a child, he was a leading al-Qaeda operative responsible for plotting war crimes. He had already been incarcerated far longer than Patty Hearst, although there is no doubt that Hearst used a machine gun to hold up a bank. Former child soldiers who killed more people in less ambiguous circumstances walk Canadian streets and tell their stories.[47] So how can the Supreme Court's refusal to uphold O'Reilly's order be reconciled with the concept of equality before the law or Canada's obligation to "take all appropriate measures to promote physical and psychological recovery and social reintegration" of children caught in war?

The justification the court offered for its extraordinary denial of its supervisory duties was extremely sketchy, barely two pages in length. Ignoring the democratic processes required to establish modern legality and the substantial changes that took place during the twentieth century as Canadian independence from the British Empire emerged, it cited the *Reference as to the Effect of the Exercise of the Royal Prerogative of Mercy upon Deportation Proceedings*, a 1933 case that defined "prerogative power" as the "residue of discretionary or arbitrary authority, which at any given time is legally left in the hands of the Crown."[48] This is a direct quote from A.V. Dicey, whose 1885 review of British constitutional history paints a very different picture from the autocratic deference condoned by our modern court. Dicey stipulated that constitutional conventions such as prerogative power "must be carried on in accordance with the will of the House of Commons, and ultimately with the will of the nation as expressed through that House."[49] According to him, "the supremacy of the law of the land means in the last resort the right of judges to control the executive government" (ch. 15).

Although treaties in Dicey's day could be made by the Crown or by Cabinet without the sanction of Parliament (ch. 15), he noted the "danger lest the use of the prerogative should supercede the supremacy of law" (ch. 12), concluding that "treaty-making power ought not to be exercised in opposition to the will of Parliament" (ch. 14). For Dicey, the issue was not just whether a prerogative power existed but whether it was exercised within the proper limits, which, as he saw it, were set by the will of the nation as expressed by an elected legislature. Dicey was writing well before democratic norms found expression in international law such as the International Covenant on Civil and Political Rights. Yet, if the court had considered Dicey's theory of the Constitution in its entirety instead of relying on a snippet taken out of context from a case decided before Canada was fully independent, it would not have granted the executive prerogative such extraordinary deference. It might even have been led to consider how to weigh domestic laws, the international conventions that Canada has ratified, and the recommendations for repatriation tabled by both houses of Parliament against the personal preferences of the prime minister and his minority government.

In the *Khadr* decision, the court correctly claimed that its role is to establish the legal framework within which executive decisions may be made.[50] It also acknowledged its ability to give specific directions to the executive branch in matters of foreign policy, citing *United States v. Burns*, 2001 SCC, in which it had rejected extradition for two Canadian youths charged with bludgeoning to death the family of one of the youths in the State of Washington. However, it distinguished *Burns* on the grounds that Omar Khadr is not in the control of the Canadian government, paying no heed to the fact that O'Reilly's order concerned only the actions of Canadian officials operating within Canadian territory. Despite the repatriation of so many other Guantánamo detainees at the request of so many other governments, even when many were not citizens and the rights of the child were not in issue, the Supreme Court then claimed that the effectiveness of requesting repatriation was "unclear." It did not explain why we should assume that Canada would be treated differently from other nations by the United States.

The court went on to misrepresent *Kaunda v. President of the Republic of South Africa,* 2004 S.A. Const. Ct, claiming that it could not uphold O'Reilly's order because courts should not interfere with the timing or language of diplomatic representations.[51] O'Reilly's order was not that restrictive: it only directed a request for repatriation "as soon as practicable." Moreover, *Kaunda* is not authority for the abdication of judicial supervision over foreign affairs. Chief Justice Chaskalson and all of the judges who wrote complementary reasons made strong assertions upholding South Africa's obligation to act in accord with its constitution and with international law. For example, Judge Sachs stated, "In my opinion, the government has a clear and unambiguous duty to do whatever is reasonably within its power to prevent South Africans abroad, however grave their alleged offences, from being subjected to torture, grossly unfair trials and capital punishment."[52]

In short, the Supreme Court did not offer a well-founded explanation either for its refusal to uphold O'Reilly's order or for its abdication of its duty to uphold Canada's international commitments and the will of Parliament. It is an alarming development because the court granted executive prerogative an unprecedented level of deference, contradicting the very idea of democracy and the rule of law.

ACTION NEEDED AND LESSONS TO BE LEARNED

Omar Khadr's story presents the obscene spectacle of child abuse and torture committed before the eyes of the world. The fact that the Convention on the Rights of the Child can be so easily ignored, especially in circumstances that demonstrate violation of the prohibition against torture, is a matter of serious concern for all members of the international community. This is especially so in this case, where the violations were perpetrated and effectively condoned by Canada and the United States, both of which claim to be leaders as far as democratic rights and the rule of law are concerned. Despite the fact that the United States is responsible for the atrocities, Canada's complicity is particularly troubling because Canada has ratified the conventions that its prime minister and Supreme Court now choose to ignore.

The case has revealed serious institutional problems in Canada, and it does not bode well for the future. The partisan stance adopted by Canada's prime minister and Department of Justice with regard to an individual who was a child at the time of the alleged offence is troubling to say the least. If the arguments submitted to support government officials who have violated both international law and the will of the Canadian people as represented by Parliament do not represent a lack of good faith, they certainly demonstrate ignorance concerning both international law and Anglo-Canadian constitutional history. The unwillingness of the Supreme Court of Canada to exercise its traditional supervisory role is even more disconcerting, especially since the decision was unanimous, and not one of the judges who have reasoned so impeccably in previous cases bothered to write dissenting reasons. It is obvious that a great deal of advocacy and educational work remains to be done. The *Khadr* case is a stark reminder that mere ratification is not sufficient to ensure respect for international norms, even when they are as widely accepted as the prohibition against torture and the Convention on the Rights of the Child.

NOTES

1 *Canada (Prime Minister) v. Khadr,* 2010 SCC.
2 McLachlin, 2004.
3 Goodrich, Hambro, and Simmons, *Charter*, 2.
4 United Nations Treaty Collection 2009 Ch. IV; Schabas, "Reservations to the Convention."
5 UN Economic and Social Council, 2006, para. 19.
6 University of Toronto, Khadr Factum, para 15–20.
7 http://www.icbl.org.

8 http://www.unicef.org/graca/mines.htm.
9 University of Ottawa, "Repatriation of Omar Khadr," 7–8.
10 CBC, "Conspiracy Theories."
11 Said, *Orientalism; Culture and Imperialism.*
12 University of Ottawa, "Repatriation of Omar Khadr."
13 *CBC News,* "Time Line, Guantánamo Bay."
14 Arar, "Right to the Truth"; City News, "Maher Arar Accepts."
15 *CBC News,* "Guantánamo Bay History."
16 University of Ottawa, Repatriation of Omar Khadr," 44.
17 Austin, *Province of Jurisprudence Determined.*
18 *Suresh,* 2002 SCC [61-65, 72].
19 *Khadr*, 2009 FC, [21].
20 University of Toronto, "Canadian Coalition on the Rights of Children," 11.
21 *Suresh,* 2002 SCC [76].
22 House of Commons, 40th parl. 2nd sess.
23 Canada, Senate, "Senator Roméo Dallaire's Motion."
24 UN E/CN.4/2006/120.
25 Ibid., para. 71. These included "the capture and transfer of detainees to an undisclosed overseas location, sensory deprivation, and other abusive treatment during transfer, detention in cages without proper sanitation, and exposure to extreme temperatures, minimal exercise and hygiene, systematic use of coersive interrogation techniques, long periods of solitary confinement, cultural and religious harassment; denial or severely delayed communication with family; and the uncertainty generated by the indeterminate nature of confinement and denial of access to independent tribunals."
26 Ibid., n. 93.
27 Ibid., para. 66 citing the *Vienna Convention on the Law of Treaties*, art.18.
28 *Khadr*, 2009 FC, [21].
29 *CBC News,* "Guantánamo Bay History."
30 Schwartz, "Omar Khadr's Return."
31 *Constitution Act, 1867,* s. 101; *Federal Court Act*, s.17.
32 *Khadr*, 2009 [36-38]
33 *Khadr* 2005 FC.
34 *Khadr,* 2004 FC.
35 *Khadr*, 2006 FC.
36 *Khadr,* 2007 FCA.
37 *Khadr*, 2008 SCC.

38 *Khadr* 2009, FC, 12–18.
39 University of Toronto, Crown Application, [38-39].
40 University of Toronto, Factum of Crown, [53-55].
41 *Halsbury's Laws of England* (4th), 1996, vol. 8(2) 26; *Calvin's Case*, 1608; *Coronation Oath Act, 1688*; Starkey, *Monarchy*; Woo, *Ghost Dancing with Colonialism*, ch. 3.
42 *R. v. Hape*, 2007 SCC [65]. *Suresh v. Canada (Minister of Citizenship and Immigration).*
43 *Suresh*, 2002 SCC [58].
44 Ibid. [51].
45 Ibid. [77].
46 University of Toronto, Canadian Coalition on the Rights of Children.
47 See, for example, Moran, "L. Gen. Romeo Dallaire."
48 *Khadr*, 2010 SCC [34].
49 Dicey, *Law of the Constitution*, ch. 15.
50 *Reference re Secession of Quebec.*
51 *Khadr*, 2010 [44].
52 *Kaunda*, 2004 S.A. Const. Ct. [275].

BIBLIOGRAPHY

Laws, Treaties, and Conventions

Act of Settlement. 12 & 13 Will.3; 6 Statutes 496, 1700 (UK).

British Nationality Act. c. 61, 1981.

British North America Act, 1867, 30-31 Vict. c. 3.

Canadian Citizenship Act S.C. 1946 c.15.

Charter of Rights and Freedoms, included in the Constitution Act, 1982, enacted by the Canada Act, 1982 (UK), 1982 c.11, Sched. B. (Can.).

Charter of the United Nations, 26 June 1945. R.T. Can. 7 (UN-Can.).

Constitution Act, 1982, enacted by the Canada Act, 1982, c.11, Sched. B (UK).

Constitution Act, 1867 (UK), R.S.C. 1970 Appendix II, No. 5 (formerly the British North America Act).

Convention on the Rights of the Child, 20 November 1989, in force 2 September 1990, in force for Canada, 12 January 1992, GA Res. 44/25; CTS 1992/3 (UN-Can.).

Coronation Oath Act, 1688 (1 Will. and Mar. c. 6) (UK).

Crimes against Humanity and War Crimes Act, 2000, S.C. c-24. (Can.).

Department of Foreign Affairs and International Trade Act, 1985, R.S.C. c-E-22 (Can.).
Federal Court Act, R.S.C.1985, c-F7 (Can.).
Geneva Conventions Act, 1985, R.S.C. c G-3 (Can.).
International Covenant on Civil and Political Rights (19 December 1966, in force 23 December 1976, in force for Canada 19 May 1976), 999 U.N.T.S. 171, Can. T.S. 1976 No. 47. (UN-Can.).
National Defence Act, R.S.C. 1985, N-5 (Can.).
Optional Protocol to the Convention on the Rights of the Child on the Involvement of Children in Armed Conflict, 25 May 2000, in force for Canada, 12 February 2002, GA Res. A/RES/54/263; CTS 2002/5 (UN-Can.).
Quebec Act, 1774, R.S.C. 1970, Appendix II, No. 2 (UK).
Rome Statute of the International Criminal Court, 17 July 1998, in force for Canada, 1 July 2002. A/CONF.183/9; CTS 2002/13 (UN-Can.).
Vienna Convention on the Law of Treaties, 23 May 1969, in force 27 January 1980, consent to by bound in Canada 14 October 1970. U.N.T.S., vol. 1155, p. 331, CTS 1980/37 (UN-Can.).

Legal Cases

(Canadian cases are available through the Canadian Legal Information Institute at http://canlii.org)
Abbasi v. Secretary of State, EWJ No. 4947, [2002] EWCA Civ. 1598, [106] (UK Court of Appeal (2002).
Baker v. Canada (Minister of Citizenship and Immigration). CanLII 699 (SCC) (Can. 1999).
Black v. Canada (Prime Minister). 199 D.L.R. (4th) 228 (Ont. C.A.) (Can. 2001).
Calvin's Case. 7 Co. 1a at 10b, 77 E.R. 377 (K.B. and Exch. Ch.) (UK 1608).
Campbell v. Hall. 1 Cowp. 204; Loft. 635 ; 98 E.R. 1045 (UK 1774).
Canada (Attorney General) v. Canada (Commission of Inquiry into the Actions of Canadian Officials in Relation to Maher Arar. FC 766 (CanLII) (Can. 2007).
Copello v. Canada (Prime Minister). FCA 295 (CanLII). (Can. (2003).
Hamdan v. Rumsfeld. 126 S. Ct. 2749 (US 2006).
Kaunda v. President of the Republic of South Africa. ZACC 5, 136 I.L.R. 452 (Constitutional Court of South Africa 2004). South African Legal Information Institute at http://www.saflii.org/za/cases/ZACC/2004/5html.

Khadr: Canadian Legal Information Institute at http://canlii.org.
Prime Minister of Canada, Minister of Foreign Affairs, Director of the Canadian Security Intelligence Service and Commissioner of the Royal Canadian Mounted Police v. Omar Ahmed Khadr, 2010 SCC 3.
Canada (Prime Minister) v. Khadr 2009 FCA 246 *at* 70.
Khadr v. Canada (Prime Minister), 2009 FC 405 *(CanLII); 188 C.R.R. (2d) 342 at 8–11.*
Canada (Justice) v. Khadr. SCC 28, *[2008] 2 S.C.R. 125 (2008).*
Khadr v. Canada. FC 1076, *[2006] F.C.R. 505, at 46 (2005).*
Khadr v. the Attorney General of Canada and the Minister of Foreign Affairs, FC 1076 *(CanLII) (2005).*
Khadr v. The Minister of Foreign Affairs. FC 1145 *(CanLII) (2004).*
Operation Dismantle v. The Queen. 1 S.C.R. 441. (Can) (1985).
In re Guantánamo Detainee Cases. 355 F. Supp. 2d. 443. (US 2005)
Public Committee against Torture in Israel v. Israel, 38 L.M. 1471 (Israel).
Rasul v. Bush. 142 U.S. 466 (US 2004).
Reference as to the Effect of the Exercise of Royal Prerogative of Mercy upon Deportation Proceedings. S.C.R. 269 at 272 (S.C.C.) (Can. 1933).
Reference re Secession of Quebec. 2 S.C.R. 217. (Can. 1998).
R. v. Hape. SCC 26, [2007] 2 S.C.R. 292. (Can. 2007).
Suresh v. Canada (Minister of Citizenship and Immigration). SCC 1, [2002]1 S.C.R. 3. (Can. 2002).
Trendtext Trading Corp. v. Central Bank of Nigeria. 1 Q.B. 529 (C.A.) (UK 1977).
United States v. Burns. SCC 7, [2001] 1 S.C.R. 283. (Can. 2001).

Books, Articles, and Websites

Arar, Maher. "We All Have a Right to the Truth." 2010. http://www.maherarar.ca.
Austin, John. *The Province of Jurisprudence Determined.* 1832. Reprint London: Weidenfeld & Nicolson 1955.
Barnet, Laura. "Canada's Approach to the Treaty-Making Process." Library of Parliament, 24 November 2008. http://www2.parl.gs.ca/Content/LOP/ResearchPublications/prb0845-e.htm.
Brode, Patrick. *Sir John Beverley Robinson: Bone and Sinue of the Compact.* Toronto: Osgoode Society 1984.
Canada. Foreign Affairs and International Trade Canada. "Canada and the Court: Canada's ICC Leadership at Home." 12 February 2010. http://www.international.gc.ca/court-cour/icc-Canada-cpi?lang=eng.

– Implementing the Statute of Rome. 12 February 2010. http://www.dfait-maeci.gc.ca/rights-droits/policy-politique.aspx.
– "Canada's International Human Rights Policy." 12 February 2010. http://www.dfait-maeci.gc.ca/rights-droits/policy-politique.aspx.
Canada. House of Commons. "Omar Khadr: Report to the Standing Committee on Foreign Affairs and International Development," by Kevin Sorenson and Scott Reid. June 2008, 39th Parl., 2nd Sess. http://wwwe.parl.gc.ca/HousePublications/Publication.aspx?DocId=3572352& Language=E&Mode=I & Parl=39&Ses=2&File=30.
– Senate. "Senate Adopts Senator Roméo Dallaire's Motion Urging the Repatriation of Omar Khadr." 9 June 2008. http://sen.parl.gc.ca/SenWeb/news/details.asp?langen&sen=47&newsID=167.
– Treaty Information. "Policy on Tabling of Treaties in Parliament." 12 February 2010. http://www.treaty-accord.gc.ca/section.asp.
Canadian Coalition for the Rights of Children. "The Rights of Children in Armed Conflict and the Omar Khadr Case." 12 September 2009. http://rights of.children.ca/media-release-for-khadr-hearing-on-november-13.
CBC. "Conspiracy Theories: The Saudi Connection, Conspiracy or Coincidence." *Fifth Estate*, 29 October 2003. http://www.cbc.ca/fifth/conspiracytheories/Saudi.html.
– "The U.S. v. Omar Khadr." 16 October 2008. http://www.cbc.ca/documentaries/doczone/2008/omarkadr/.
– "Guantánamo Bay History." 21 May 2009. At http://www.cbc.ca/world/story/2009/05/21/f-gitmo.html.
– "Time Line, Guantánamo Bay, The Omar Khadr Case." 12 November 2009. http://www.cbc.ca/Canada/story/2009/11/12/f-omar-khadr-time-line.html.
City News. "Maher Arar Accepts Ottawa's Apology – and $10.5 Million Compensation." 26 January 2007. http://www.citytv.com/toronto/citynews/news/local/article/25897.
Dicey, A.V. *Introduction to the Study of the Law of the Constitution.* 8th ed. Oxford: All Souls College 1914. http://constitution.org/cmt/avd/law_con.htm.
Goodrich, Leland M., Edvard Hambro, and Anne Patricia Simons. *Charter of the United Nations, Commentary and Documents*. 3d rev. ed. New York: Columbia University Press 1969.
Halsbury's Laws of England. 3rd ed. London: Butterworths 1968.
Hailsham of St Marylebone, Lord. *Halsbury's Laws of England*. 4th ed. London: Butterworths 1996.

International Campaign to Ban Land Mines. February 2010. http://www.icbl.org.

McLachlin, Beverley. "Globalization, Identity and Citizenship." Ottawa, October 2004. http://www.scc-csc.gc.ca.

Moran, Andrew. "L. Gen. Romeo Dallaire, Ex-Sudanese Child Soldier Talk Zero Force." *Digital Journal*, 10 December 2010. www.digitaljopurnal.com/article/301295.

Riddell, Walter A. *Documents on Canadian Foreign Policy, 1917–1939*. Toronto: Oxford University Press 1962.

Said, Edward W. *Orientalism*. London: Routledge 1978.

– "Orientalism Reconsidered." *Cultural Critique* 1 (1985): 89.

– *Culture and Imperialism*. New York: Vintage Books 1994.

Schabas, William. "Reservations to the Convention on the Rights of the Child." *Human Rights Quarterly* 18, no. 2 (May): 472.

Schwartz, Daniel. "Omar Khadr's Return to Canada." CBC, 19 November 2010. www.cbc.ca/Canada/story/2010/11/10/f-omarkhadr-returns-faq.html.

Starkey, David. *Monarchy*. Channel 4 (UK), 2004–06. http://www.chanel4.com/programmes/monarchy/.

UNICEF. "Land-Mines: A Deadly Inheritance." February 2010. http://www.unicef.org/graca/mines.htm.

United Nations Economic and Social Council, Commission on Human Rights. "Situation of Detainees at Guantánamo Bay." E/CN.4/2006/120. 15 February 2006. http://www.law.utoronto.ca/faculty_content.asp?itemPath1/3/4/0/0&contentId=1617.

University of Ottawa Faculty of Law, Common Law Section. "Repatriation of Omar Khadr to Be Tried under Canadian Law: An Overview of the Case against Omar Khadr and the Prospect of Canadian Criminal Jurisdiction." Brief Submitted to the Senate Standing Committee on Human Rights, January 2008. http://www.law.utoronto.ca/faculty_content.asp?itemPath1/3/4/0/0&contentId=1617.

University of Toronto Faculty of Law. "The Omar Khadr Case." http://www.law.utoronto.ca/faculty_content.asp?itemPath1/3/4/0/0&contentId=1617.

– Crown Application for Leave to Appeal, Supreme Court of Canada. 24 August 2009.

– Factum of Crown, Supreme Court of Canada. 21 September 2009.

– Factum of Omar Khadr, Supreme Court of Canada. 9 October 2009.

– Canadian Coalition on the Rights of Children Intervener Factum. 2009.

Woo, Grace Li Xiu. *Ghost Dancing with Colonialism: Decolonization and Indigenous Rights at the Supreme Court of Canada*. Vancouver, UBC Press 2011.

Reflections

From Congo to Guantanamo: Omar Khadr, the Invisible Child Soldier

MONIA MAZIGH

Last week my teenage daughter came back from school and proudly showed me her newly bought T-shirt. The shirt had an intriguing slogan: "THE INVISIBLE CHILDREN."

After I asked her a few questions, she told me, "An organization from the United States came to our school and spoke to us about child soldiers in Congo and other African countries. This organization is on a school tour in North America. It sells crafts and other items to help raise money for cholarships for these kids ... Isn't that great?"

She was very enthusiastic. Of course this is great!

But what about other child soldiers, like Omar Khadr? Can't he be rehabilitated and sent to school as well? Or is the child soldier status only reserved for those war-ravaged countries where Americans have interests in keeping things safe and stable?

Unfortunately, according to the US and Canadian governments, the answer to my question seems to be an outrageous "No." Indeed, the following sad fact has now been recorded by history: Omar Khadr is the first convicted child soldier since World War II. His conviction came at an end of a shameful military trial where not a single basic principle of transparency and justice was followed and where the torture and abuse he endured was simply brushed away.

This trial concluded eight long years, during which both Liberal and Conservative Canadian governments refused vehemently to repatriate him. The acts and words that have been posed and uttered by other members of Khadr's family seem to have overtaken the ability to discern between justice and guilt by association.

Omar Khadr became a hot potato that no one was ready to keep, with the exception of very few human rights groups. Unfortunately, these groups, despite their best efforts, were unsuccessful in their attempt to make this issue a mainstream one.

Even the Canadian legal system didn't dare go to the end of the tunnel: while acknowledging that Omar's Charter rights were violated, the federal court stopped short of forcing the federal government to ask the United States to return him to Canada.

Moreover, the light hope of the closure of Guantánamo Bay faded away after two years of the presidency of Barack Obama.

All these facts forced Omar and his legal team to accept a guilty plea for the charges of murder, terrorism, and spying. In exchange, he received an additional eight-year prison term.

In the midst of the plea "bargain," another sad decision was announced by President Obama. It slipped from of the radar of many mainstream media and it had to do with child soldiers. The US president decided that "it is in the national interest of the United States to waive the application of section 404(a) [Child Service Prevention Act] to Chad, to the Democratic Republic of the Congo, to Sudan, and to Yemen." This means that the United States will continue to work with and potentially provide aid to these four countries known for their use of underage soldiers.

"What the president has done is basically given everybody a pass for using child soldiers," said Jo Becker, the children's rights director at Human Rights Watch.

Many observers interpreted this move as a setback for the rights of child soldiers.

I don't want my scepticism to overshadow my daughter's enthusiasm for the rights of child soldiers. But, inside of me, the conviction of a child soldier, in the person of Omar Khadr, changed a lot of meanings.

Delta Force

LOLA LEMIRE TOSTEVIN

> What have children got to do with it? I can understand the solidarity
> Of men in sin, but not the solidarity of children in the sins of men.
>
> Ivan Karamazov

1
I know little of Omar Khadr.
Except that he was fifteen years old when
he was incarcerated at Guantánamo Bay.

I don't know whether he was aware of his father's
terrorist activities; whether he helped put together
hand grenades; whether he visited Osama bin Laden's compound
and played with bin Laden's children; whether he threw
the grenade that killed Sergeant Speer, the trained American
soldier from the Delta Force Unit.

All of which makes it difficult to write a poem
on the incarceration of Omar Khadr. A poem
should capture a moment that generates new reality.
It should generate an understanding of that reality.
Yet there is an absolute obscenity in trying to understand
the incarceration of a fifteen year old.

2
I have read that Omar Khadr sometimes quoted from
The Adventures of Tintin. As any child would.
That he slept with an English version of a Mickey Mouse book.
As any child would. There is a photograph of him standing
alongside a Batmobile. As any child would.

He may have played the computer game
Delta Force, whose mission is to ambush, eliminate,
intercept, capture, and kill. A game invented by men for children.

Omar Khadr may be the perfect model of infantile terror
where the hunter becomes the hunted and the hunted
becomes the hunter as in a computer game.

He may be the perfect model of infantile vengeance where
the deaths of thousands requires the deaths of millions.

It's all so easy.
Take a child full of life and sew him up inside
the tenets of old men where the command
to obey is stitched under furrowed skin. That is how
the worth of some men is measured. By the number
of children who are brainwashed, ambushed, eliminated,
intercepted, captured, tortured, and killed.

3
There is little doubt that Omar Khadr was tortured
at Guantánamo Bay. There is no doubt that vengeance
visited on a child is never a legitimate substitute for justice.
Except perhaps in infantile cultures where people obey
in the hope of rewards. As any child would.

In cultures where infantile terror reigns and
children follow in the footsteps of adult games.

Children fashioned by men who stand
by their Batmobiles, quote Tintin,
and sleep with Mickey Mouse comic books.

"Child Soldier"

RACHEL ZOLF

A child has an imposition from which he can redeem himself with
six points

Planets move so that soldiers sketch with chalk over the singe

Women feel burning and pricking of heat inside

Tracing their hands or pictures of ships where paws and bellies hung

But sand has a terrible secret

I think plain, clear language could make it stronger

"Very good, only *they breathe*"

In the background is a piece of classical architecture

He holds a small camouflaged pillow in his left hand

I forgive your ancestor's beautiful thoughts

Statues representing dancing figures

What the Boardroom shoves through the porthole to sea

With this little soldier doomed grow monster

Tribunal earrings shown full face and aligned in depth

While writing this, I am bloody as well as greasy

Hot about the mouth of the womb

If the vest of childhood the thread of peace

Sometimes the colour of humid ashes

Outside the veins and in the hollowness

Small black bodies mingled with milk

If unable to deliver antibiotic borders

Inside and aching, pricking and hardness

And if such humours turn into cold wind

And they fly up to the heart and lungs

NOTE

This poem was composed through the process of searching for the words "child" and "soldier" in the Tolerance Project Archive. Eighty-six writers, artists, and thinkers donated their poetic DNA to the Tolerance Project (thetoleranceproject.blogspot.com). Each piece of donated poetic DNA was assigned a barcode and Zolf wrote a series of poems composed solely from the donated material.

PART FIVE

Omar Khadr, Oh Canada

Reading Khadr: Making Sense of Canada's Reluctance to Do the Right Thing

ROBERT DIAB AND ALNOOR GOVA

Omar Khadr's case was initially part of a larger story about Guantánamo and other black sites, as a state of exception, a "pure *de facto* rule" of sovereign power over bare life.[1] But toward the end of the decade, the focus of the story shifted. The number of detainees left in Guantánamo had dwindled, while Omar remained the only Western national whose government had strongly resisted calls for his repatriation. Many Canadians wondered why.

The question links Omar Khadr's case to a series of other recent cases that implicate the Canadian government in human rights violations of its own citizens on foreign soil. Muslim men and women have been arrested, detained without charge, and sometimes tortured, on information provided by Canadian officials, or acting at their behest. In each of these cases the government has resisted accountability, often vigorously. Remarkably, in the same period, Canada was quick to assist some of its non-Muslim citizens in trouble abroad. Many Canadians wondered what, if any, message was being sent to them about being Canadian.

Consider the record.

The facts in Khadr's case are well known, but those relating to Canada's involvement are worth noting. Well after a host of Western governments had intervened on behalf of their citizen detainees at Guantánamo, Canada stood silent, forsaking its obligations as a signatory to the UN Convention on the Rights of the Child and the Geneva Conventions. Both the Federal and Supreme Court of Canada found unequivocally that Canada's dealings with Omar

Khadr and the circumstances of his detention had violated the most essential of his constitutional and human rights.[2] The courts had repeatedly urged the government to intercede. Adamantly opposing these decisions, the Harper government forced Khadr to submit to a detention process and military tribunal regime universally denounced as unfair. Evidence against him was tainted by allegations of torture, in a trial in which a conviction and life sentence were foregone conclusions. Canada would only agree to accept his plea deal and transfer back home at the obvious direction of a US State Department eager to move the case out of the media spotlight.

Equally distressing in its own way is the lesser-known case of Canadian citizen Abousfian Abdelrazik. A Muslim living in Montreal in the 1990s, Abdelrazik had, by chance, formed acquaintances that made him a person of interest in the climate of heightened fear and suspicion following 9/11. He came to know Ahmad Ressam, the would-be bomber of the Los Angeles airport, but would testify for the prosecution at Ressam's trial. Another acquaintance was that of Adil Charkaoui, a Canadian resident detained on a "security certificate" for suspected links to terror but eventually released. Later investigation by both CSIS and the RCMP would clear Abdelrazik of any involvement in criminal activity.

However, in 2003, when he visited his ailing mother in Sudan, CSIS took the opportunity to investigate Abdelrazik on foreign soil. It gave the Sudanese secret police information leading to his arrest, interrogation, and imprisonment. CSIS agents then travelled to the prison in Sudan to interrogate him directly. His ordeal lasted eleven months, during which time he describes being frequently "beaten with a rubber hose, made to stand at attention for hours at a time, subjected to confinement in a freezing cold cell, and also [having] his asthma medicine and eyeglasses taken away."[3]

Upon Abdelrazik's release, Canadian consular officials attempted to assist him to return home. But on the eve of his departure in July 2004, his name appeared on an airline no-fly list. Further arrangements that were attempted fell through, yet Canada would not provide him with a new passport or arrange a flight home. The following summer, still stuck in Khartoum, Abdelrazik received a letter from the Sudanese Ministry of Justice clearing him of any involvement with al-Qaeda. Three months later he received a summons to meet with Sudanese authorities. Before doing so, he sought counsel from Canadian consular officials. They encouraged him to meet with the

Sudanese, assuring him they would "follow up" if issues arose.[4] Abdelrazik met with Sudanese authorities and was detained for a further nine months. He was once again beaten and tortured repeatedly.[5] Canadian officials attempted unsuccessfully to make contact with him.[6] Upon his release in July 2006, he was designated a terrorist by the US State Department, which claimed he maintained links with "high level" members of al-Qaeda. Soon after, the UN Security Council's 1267 Committee also listed him as a terrorist.[7] As a consequence, he became subject to a "global asset freeze" and "global travel ban."[8]

Abdelrazik's lawyer in Canada petitioned the minister of Foreign Affairs to have Canada seek his removal from the UN list. The minister made inquiries and was told by both CSIS and the RCMP that they had no information linking him to terror (the RCMP's letter stated, more broadly, that it was "unable to locate any current and substantive information that indicates Mr. Abdelrazik is involved in criminal activity"[9]). The minister sent the UN a formal request for his delisting. Notably, it stated that "the Consular Branch fully supports [Abdelrazik's] eventual return to Canada" and that "Abdelrazik retains the right to return to his own country of nationality. International law expressly provides for a right of return, and prevents a state from denying return to own state of nationality."[10] The delisting request was denied without explanation.[11] On the basis of its submissions to the UN, however, one would expect the Canadian government to have responded by arranging for Abdelrazik's return directly. It was in a position to do so and should have done so.

Not only did Canada choose not to assist Abdelrazik in this way but it denied his further requests for a passport. At this point, fearing for his safety, he sought shelter in the foyer of the Canadian embassy in Khartoum. He stayed there for almost eighteen months, when the Federal Court finally ordered Canada to arrange for his immediate return.[12] After returning, he remained on the UN Security Council's 1267 list, and as a consequence was prevented from working and was virtually destitute.[13] In November 2011, the UN finally acceded to Abdelrazik's request to be delisted, despite the fact that the Harper government refused to support his request. Along with various civil liberties groups, Abdelrazik has launched a constitutional challenge to Canada's implementation of the UN 1267 regime.[14] He has also brought a tort action against the Government of Canada for its complicity in his torture and cruel treatment in Sudan.

The experiences that formed the basis of the Iacobucci inquiry tell a similar tale of Canada's complicity in torture abroad, followed by a reluctance to make amends. Canadian citizens Abdullah Almalki, Ahmad El Maati, and Muyyed Nureddin were travelling independently through Syria in 2002 when they were arrested, detained, and tortured. Frank Iacobucci, a former Supreme Court justice, found that while information that CSIS gave to Syria did not directly result in the three men's imprisonment and torture, in two of the cases it clearly contributed to it. Consular officials and intelligence agents in all three cases acted in ways that Justice Iacobucci found seriously "deficient." In one of the cases, as was done with Maher Arar and later Abdelrazik, questions prepared by CSIS were put to a Canadian citizen in foreign custody. Canada has resisted offering any of the men an apology or compensation. Much of the evidence in the inquiry was censored, and no one has been held personally responsible.

The cases of Maher Arar and Suaad Haji Mohamud are only partial exceptions to this pattern. In 2003, acting on erroneous information provided by CSIS and the RCMP, US customs officials detained Arar on a stopover in New York on return from vacation. They rendered him to Syria for an ordeal that involved interrogation, torture, and imprisonment lasting over a year. Months after news of the case had surfaced, Arar continued to languish in a damp, windowless, underground cell, which he described as a grave. Due in large part to the heroic efforts of his wife, Monia Mazigh, the Canadian government eventually intervened, and an inquiry was held that cleared Arar of wrongdoing. It also confirmed that he had been tortured, and pointed to CSIS and the RCMP as a primary cause of the entire episode. Arar was generously compensated and received an apology in the House of Commons.

These were important gestures of accountability, but they were still marred by a large degree of resistance and state secrecy. Virtually all of the RCMP and CSIS testimony at the Arar inquiry was censored, as were significant portions of the final report. No one was held personally accountable, nor have any of Justice O'Connor's many recommendations been adopted. One wonders what might have happened to Arar if his wife hadn't been so tenacious, or if his case for compensation hadn't been so strong. Canadian Muslims, in particular, are left wondering how easily this could happen again.

Suaad Haji Mohamud's experience in a Nairobi detention centre in 2009 was shorter and there was no allegation of physical torture, yet it reflects a similar pattern of reluctance to aid a citizen in serious trouble, a lack of accountability, and the spectre of religio-racial discrimination. At the conclusion of a visit to her birth country, Kenya, Mohamud attempted to board a plane home to Canada. Kenyan officials doubted her identity and arrested her. She was charged with identity fraud and jailed for eight days. A Canadian consular official interviewed her in Kenya and wasn't satisfied of her identity, despite her having presented other evidence including her Ontario driver's licence, receipts from her dry-cleaner in Toronto, and Shoppers' Drug Mart card.[15] Canada asked Kenya to prosecute. Only after her lawyer arranged for a DNA test did Canada reluctantly concede its error and allow her to come home. This was after Mohamud had spent close to three months on bail in Kenya, waiting for the matter to be sorted out with Ottawa. Although the Harper government indicated on her return that it would seek a "full accounting" in the matter, no significant steps have been taken.[16] No compensation or apology has been offered.

To juxtapose these cases with the recent experiences of white non-Muslim Canadians in trouble abroad is illuminating. Brenda Martin is a Canadian who was jailed in Mexico from 2006 to 2008 for her involvement in a Ponzi scheme run by a former Canadian resident for whom she had worked illegally in Mexico. In April 2008, a Mexican court convicted her of money laundering and sentenced her to five years in prison. While in jail, she was visited by former Prime Minister Paul Martin (no relation), MP Jason Kenney (minister for Multiculturalism and Canadian Identity at the time), and several other consular officials. A month before she was convicted, Prime Minister Stephen Harper had called Mexican President Felipe Calderon on her behalf. Our then Foreign Affairs minister, Maxime Bernier, also met with his Mexican counterpart to discuss Martin's case. Nine days after her conviction, she was released to Canadian officials, flown in a chartered plane to a prison in Waterloo, Ontario, and parolled nine days later.

In December 2008, Nigerian militants kidnapped Robert Fowler, Canadian UN special envoy to Niger, and his assistant, Louis Guay, on their return from a visit to the Canadian-owned Samira Hill Gold Mine. The two men were held for four months in the Sahara Desert. The Canadian government worked quietly behind the scenes to negotiate their release. They were freed, along with a German and a Swiss woman, after a prisoner exchange. "Ultimately," Stephen Harper said at the time, "a great deal of effort went into a large number of activities by Canadian government officials from all departments and agencies over the past few months to help secure the release of these hostages."[17] Fen Hampson, director of the School of International Affairs at Carleton University and a friend of Robert Fowler said, "Foreign Affairs operated a special Fowler rescue team that quietly worked 24/7 to free him."[18]

What are Canadians to make of their government's inconsistency in these cases? Is it irrational, or pure folly, to suggest that Canada's reluctance to take accountability for rights violations points to a deeper set of motivations? Is it reasonable to suggest that these cases provide empirical evidence of a religio-racial bias in the treatment of citizens regardless of the political affiliations of the executive? Is it fair to look at these cases and question whether Canadian Muslims enjoy the full benefits of citizenship?

Or are we open to the charge of skewing the facts? Did we not spend millions to help thousands of Lebanese Canadians return home during the 2006 war between Israel and Hezbollah? Did we not intervene in the recent case of Mohammed Kohail, a twenty-four-year-old Canadian sentenced to death in Saudi Arabia following a schoolyard fight? Have we not also been active in cases of Muslims suffering human rights abuses abroad, regardless of their citizenship – including people like Hossein Derkhshan, a Canadian resident and Iranian blogger sentenced to twenty years, or Nazia Quazi, a Canadian whose father would not let her return from Saudi Arabia to marry her non-Muslim boyfriend, or Sakineh Ashtiani, an Iranian woman who faced death by stoning?

We suggest that there are at least three ways of reading Canada's actions in these cases. The first is what might be called the "good faith reading." On this view, there may appear to be a pattern in some of these cases, but in truth each turns on its own facts. Omar Khadr allegedly lobbed a grenade that killed an American medic. He is not being held without a reason. That reason distinguishes his case from the many others in which Western governments intervened on behalf of their citizens. Canada simply chose to defer to America's choice of legal regime. Our deference in that respect is in keeping with other current policies, including that of refusing to assist with any transfers of Canadians serving jail sentences in the United States.

Similarly, in every other case involving our complicity in the arrest and detention of our citizens abroad, there were suspicions based on certain associations. Abelrazik, Arar, and others, for example, had associated with persons of interest to CSIS in the early part of the decade. The associations were benign, but in the aftermath of 9/11 there was some argument for casting a wide net. We made mistakes, but we made them out of an abundance of caution, not to oppress citizens out of bias.

Finally, among other possible arguments in defence of Canada's record, we have to concede that it did, after all, comply with various court orders that offered a remedy for rights violations. The Supreme Court of Canada requested, and the government did seek, assurances that the United States would not use the evidence obtained by CSIS at Guantánamo. At the Federal Court's behest, the government helped to arrange Abdelrazik's flight home from Khartoum. In other cases, the issue was addressed without a court order. Suaad Haji Mohamud got her passport, Almalki, El Maati, and Nureddin got an inquiry, and of course, Arar got an apology and $10 million.

A second interpretation of Canada's conduct in these cases can be called the "national security reading." On this view, the reluctance to take accountability, to offer compensation, to adopt inquiry recommendations, and to expose CSIS or the RCMP to greater transparency reflects a desire to maintain the widest possible leeway for national security investigations. Why would we want to concede responsibility for any of these violations if we intend to maintain the authority and freedom to do more of the same in the future? Why, in short, would we seek to hamper our defences if an act of nuclear or mass terror on Canadian soil may be only a few years or even months away? We may quibble over the applicable law and processes to use Canadian, Geneva Conventions, or a US Military tribunal regime; *but if you only knew what we know ... you would know we're not being paranoid.*

A third interpretation, the "reading from exile," is sceptical of the "good faith reading" and attempts to make sense of the deeper political motivations of the "national security reading." It has its roots in the response of Canadians to the experiences of the citizens noted above.[19] It begins with the assumption that although the government may have responded to court orders, held inquiries, agreed on a repatriation deal for Khadr, and offered Arar generous compensation, in a larger sense it has done no more than what was absolutely necessary. It complied with court orders in letter but not in spirit. It ignored the various concerns raised about Canada's role in extraordinary rendition, torture, and arbitrary detention in commissions, court hearings, and the press. It made amends in Arar's case, where its culpability was clear, but failed to answer for any of the serious lingering damage caused in the others. On the contrary, in some cases – Khadr, Abdelrazik, Almalki, El Maati, and Nureddin – the government vigorously opposes efforts to be held accountable. And to be clear: in each of the cases at issue, the person had not been convicted of an offence or had not received due process. Nobody had been held personally responsible for any of the torture, imprisonment, or trauma that these individuals have suffered. No changes to law or policy had been made. The government's conduct would therefore seem to imply that the core human rights of these citizens are non-existent.

The "reading from exile" also suggests that "the national security reading" may explain the government's conduct in part but that there's much more to it.[20] The cases have unfolded in a religio-political context of a "clash of civilizations" that shapes their meaning. The government's use of the rhetoric of "national security" and "terrorism" to justify extraordinary detention, exile, torture, surveillance, and no-fly lists exhibits clear links between narrowing parameters of legitimate democratic dissent, declining civil liberties, and related forms of discrimination. The Harper and previous Canadian governments have thus either ignored or exploited the undeniably racial or ethnic dimension here, a fact that necessarily follows from its continual resistance to make amends.

In this light, Canada's complicity takes on a different meaning for Muslim Canadians in particular. Immediately after 9/11, a certain historically familiar tendency to scapegoat was inevitable. But "Islamophobia" has been on the rise over the past decade. Muslims have faced greater discrimination, fear, and harassment than any other "ethnic" group in Canada. Many report experiences of racial profiling, aggressive surveillance, and security visitations by CSIS and the RCMP in their homes, at work, in mosques, and in Islamic centres. Many feel a general sense of mistrust by the majority (and other) cultures and by official state institutions. Attitudes south of the border are distinct in some respects but indicative of a wider cultural shift of which Canadians are very much a part. Thus, a 2004 poll conducted by Cornell University's Media and Society Research Group found that 44 per cent of American respondents suggested the need to curtail the civil liberties of Muslim Americans, while 29 per cent agreed with undercover infiltration of Muslim civic and volunteer organizations. A further 26 per cent said mosques should be monitored, 27 per cent agreed that all Muslim Americans should be required to register with the federal government, and 22 per cent said Muslims and those of Middle Eastern origin should be profiled due to the potential threat they pose. Here in Canada, according to an EKOS poll in 2002, 48 per cent agreed with the statement "Given current circumstances, I think that it is acceptable that airline, police and customs officials give special attention to individuals of Arabic origin." A 2006 Environics poll for the Trudeau Foundation found that 51 per cent of respondents reported a negative impression of Islam and Muslims. A 2010 poll by Leger Marketing in Canada and Caravan in the United States reported a majority belief, 55 per cent of Canadians and 50.3 per cent of Americans, stating that Muslims do not share common values. A 2010 Environics poll for the CBC asked Canadians of all backgrounds whether they believed that people of certain races in Canada were the "targets of discrimination." Thirty-four percent of respondents said that Muslims are targeted, surpassing the 33 per cent of Canadians who believe that Aboriginals suffer a bias and only 13 per cent who perceive Jews to be so targeted.

For Muslim Canadians, these facts can't be disconnected from perceptions of the government's indifference to its complicity in torture and other violations. It seems only fair to suggest that the government's indifference reflects a lower regard for the dignity and equality of these citizens, or of their very claim to citizenship itself. It also suggests a certain political licence – that given the widespread discrimination against or negative impressions of Muslim or Middle Eastern Canadians, a differential treatment may be politically acceptable. Whereas Canadians would likely expect consular assistance in the case of a white non-Muslim Canadian languishing in a Mexican prison, *despite her having committed a crime*, more of them are likely to seem indifferent to the neglect of a black Canadian Muslim in Kenya or the torture of a black or Arab Canadian (in Sudan, Syria, or Egypt), *who happens to be innocent*.

Our point is not that only one interpretation of Canada's conduct in these cases is the right one, or that the three we describe are mutually exclusive. We argue instead that the lingering ambiguity – the uncertainty as to why Canada has committed and then neglected to address a series of similar human rights violations involving Muslims – does violence to our very idea of citizenship, multiculturalism, and liberal democracy. An ambiguity as to the value Canada places on the rights of Muslim citizens contributes to a kind of psychological internment and social death of these communities, a perception of criminality, exclusion, and disentitlement to citizenship and human rights.

These cases also represent a failed opportunity on the part of our government to demonstrate leadership in the never-ending fight against bigotry and intolerance. The very idea that forms the bedrock of modern Canadian citizenship – what has made Canada an example for the world – is its insistence that all people are equal under the rule of law and that people of all ethnic backgrounds are equally welcome, have something important to contribute, and are worthy of equal dignity and respect. At a time when multiculturalism and the fabric of liberal, tolerant societies are under strain everywhere, Canada should have set a better example.

We take comfort in the thought that the government's reluctance to aid Omar Khadr, or take accountability for abuses in other cases, does not reflect the wisdom of an otherwise quite tolerant and harmonious society. We suspect that whatever reading history favours of our government's reluctance to do the right thing in these cases, its conduct will be a mark of lasting shame.

NOTES

The authors would like to thank Asifa Akbar for her comments on an earlier draft.

1 Giorgio Agamben, *State of Exception*, trans. Kevin Attell (Chicago: University of Chicago Press, 2005), and *Homo Sacer: Sovereign Power and Bare Life*, trans. Daniel Heller-Roazen (Stanford: Stanford University Press, 1988).
2 *Canada (Prime Minister) v. Khadr* 2009 FCA 246; *Canada (Prime Minister) v. Khadr* 2010 SCC 3.
3 *Abdelrazik v. Canada*, 2009 FC 580, para. 16.
4 Ibid., para. 20.
5 Ibid., para. 21.
6 *Abdelrazik v. Canada*, 2009 FC 580.
7 Justice Zinn states: "It is not known which government asked that Mr. Abdelrazik be listed. There has been speculation that his listing was at the request of the United States of America. That suggestion is reasonable in light of the evidence before this Court" (ibid., para. 24).

8 Ibid., para. 26.
9 Ibid., cited at para. 27.
10 Ibid., cited at para. 28.
11 Justice Zinn notes, "There is nothing in the listing or de-listing procedure that recognizes the principles of natural justice or that provides for basic procedural fairness ... It can hardly be said that the 1267 Committee process meets the requirement of independence and impartiality when, as appears may be the case involving Mr. Abdelrazik, the nation requesting the listing is one of the members of the body that decides whether to list or, equally as important, to de-list a person. The accuser is also the judge" (ibid., para. 51).
12 *Abdelrazik v. Canada*, 2009 FC 580.
13 The 1267 regime continued to subject Abdelrazik indefinitely to severe sanctions in Canada – including an asset freeze and domestic and international travel bans. Further, it made it a crime to provide him with financial assistance such as a loan, gift, salary, or social assistance. As well, his children were refused child assistance benefits by the Régie des rentes du Québec.
14 The case of Canadian citizen Liban Hussein offers a precedent for Canada's resistance to the implementation of the 1267 regime where an innocent person has been listed. Hussein was added to the UN list in November 2001, in response to allegations of involvement in the financing of terrorism. An RCMP investigation eventually cleared him of wrongdoing. In response, the Chrétien government successfully petitioned the 1267 Committee for Hussein's delisting in 2002.
15 Christopher Hume, "Is Citizenship Now Defined by the Colour of Your Skin?," *Toronto Star*, 12 August 2009; Margaret Wente, "The Strange Case of Suaad Mohamud," *Globe and Mail*, 9 October 2009.
16 *CBC News* notes that although the consular official who interviewed Mohamud has since been reassigned to another posting, the Department of Foreign Affairs has indicated that the move was not made in response to this case. In the fall of 2009, Mohamud's lawyer told the CBC that "consular documents show that little was done after the initial assessment [of the case] in late May" ("Suaad Hagi Mohamud's Detention in Kenya," *CBC News*, 5 October 2009.
17 Mike Blanchfield and Steven Edwards, "Canada Paid No Ransom, PM Says," *National Post*, 24 April 2009.
18 Blanchfield and Edwards, "Canadian Diplomats Free after Four Months in Captivity," *National Post*, 22 April 2009.

19 The "reading from exile" also incorporates a response to the ordeal of what have become known as the "Secret Trial Five." Over the course of the past decade, five Muslim men have been imprisoned in Canada for between two and nine years, on secret evidence and without being charged with an offence. This situation has been made possible by the "security certificate" regime under Canada's Immigration and Refugee Protection Act, which allows for arrest and indefinite detention of non-citizens on secret evidence where are there "reasonable grounds to believe" that a detainee poses a danger to Canada.

20 See, for example, Sherene Razack, *Casting Out: The Eviction of Muslims from Western Law and Politics* (Toronto: University of Toronto Press, 2008); Sunera Thobani, *Exalted Subjects: Studies in the Making of Race and Nation in Canada* (Toronto: University of Toronto Press, 2007); and Himani Bannerji, *The Dark Side of the Nation: Essays on Multiculturalism, Nationalism, and Gender* (Canadian Scholars' Press, 2000).

Pray or Pay: The Rights of Canadians Abroad

NATHALIE DES ROSIERS

The Omar Khadr tragedy may be told through many angles. One could see it as a test of Canada's commitment to the International Convention on the Rights of the Child: a failure. One could see it as a test of the dedication of our intelligence forces to the eradication of torture around the world: a failure. Or, it could be narrated as the story of a child's trial by the media that portrayed the Khadr parents as committed to terrorism and hence led the Canadian public to condemn and judge the child through the views of the parents. And the politicians followed.

I want here to analyze a different aspect of the Omar Khadr story: the fragile and amorphous legal context for the duty of Canada toward its citizens when they are incarcerated in other countries. I analyze first how the current understanding of the rights of Canadians abroad and the corresponding duties of the government is flawed and potentially dangerous. I then suggest some alternatives to structure and limit the discretion of a government to decide whether or not it wishes to help a Canadian imprisoned outside of Canada.

THE INADEQUACIES OF THE CURRENT MODEL

There is very little law on the subject of what to expect from one's government when one is accused, arrested, detained, tried, or incarcerated in a foreign country.[1] Section 10 of the Department of Foreign Affairs and International Trade Act (DFAIT Act)[2] provides that the minister of Foreign Affairs has discretion to "determine whether and when to request the repatriation of a Canadian citizen detained in a foreign country." The Vienna Convention on Consular

Relations[3] prescribes the corresponding obligations of the foreign countries in response to the exercise of consular and diplomatic services by the Canadian government. The International Transfer of Offenders Act[4] does prescribe the criteria to be weighed when a prisoner asks for the transfer of his or her sentence to Canada from a foreign jurisdiction. This only applies when the person has been sentenced by a foreign court, and not when one is being detained prior to sentencing, and only when the detaining jurisdiction has agreed that a transfer is appropriate. Therefore, the International Transfer of Offenders Act will be applicable to Omar Khadr in the course of his sentence now imposed by the American courts and has already been the subject of an agreement between the two governments.

The limits to the exercise of the discretion provided by section 10 of the DFAIT Act raise issues. Canadians travel, and the Canadian government has actively pursued a policy to lessen the impediments to the exchange of people and services through the North American Free Trade Agreement, among other international agreements fostering free trade. People travel for work, study, business, family reunification, leisure, and culture. In addition, many Canadians live in other countries. Many have dual or multiple citizenships. In a romanticized vision of their relationship to Canada, Canadians expect to be rescued if and when they are in danger in a foreign country. DFAIT is quick to demystify this belief: it will not seek preferential treatment for Canadians; it will not provide legal advice; it will not post bail; it will not rescue.[5] Canadians travelling should essentially look after themselves.

Nevertheless, there are examples of rescue efforts that lead the average Canadian to expect that the "privilege" of rescue ought not to be restricted and must be provided in a fair and equal manner. This is where the lack of transparency, lack of clarity, and apparent arbitrariness of the decision-making process hurts our perceptions of fairness. Nobody debates that Brenda Martin or Robert Fowler should be rescued, but they ask why it took a Federal Court decision to provide a passport to Mr Abdelrazik, or why Ms Suaad Hagi Mohamud also had to seek judicial intervention to obtain her passport.

More transparency with respect to the scope and availability of consular services is asked for, but as in the Omar Khadr case, more is also asked with respect to the range of diplomatic actions, which is traditionally the realm of absolute discretionary policy-making. Indeed, the Omar Khadr case represents the limits of the current legal regime where the Supreme Court resigns itself to a role of declaring unconstitutionality but not mandating a specific remedy in light of the traditional Crown prerogative in the context of international relations.

However, the case for greater accountability, transparency, and limits on discretionary powers does not seem to be proceeding in the right direction. Indeed, in the context of the International Transfer of Prisoners Act, the government is moving in the opposite direction. The Omnibus Bill enacted in late 2011 amends the International Transfer of Offenders Act by changing the words "the Minister shall" to "the Minister may." It also adds new factors that the minister "may" take into account. It does transform a rule-bound framework into a discretionary ministerial remedy. The purpose of International Transfer of Offenders legislation is to allow for the transfer of convicted offenders to serve their sentence in the country of their citizenship pursuant to international treaties and bilateral arrangements. In other words, it allows Canadians convicted in another country to request a transfer to serve the remainder of their sentence in Canada and provides similar transfers for foreign nationals incarcerated in Canada. All transfers must have the consent of the foreign country and of the offender.

Canada has been party to transfer of prisoners agreements since 1978, and the current legislation was enacted in 2004. Most countries have similar legislation. The rationale behind offender transfers is that both for the rehabilitation of offenders and the interest of their family, a sentence in a prison of the country of citizenship is often preferable. Language barriers, isolation, difficulties in contacting families and friends, and, in some countries, prison conditions may make the sentence particularly harsh or undermine any rehabilitation for offenders. For families, the difficulty and costs of maintaining contact with the offender may be significant. Since citizens can return to their country after their sentence is completed, there is an interest in ensuring that they have access to rehabilitation programs while in prison. It is for these reasons that most countries enter into multi-state conventions of bilateral arrangements to provide for such transfers. It is indeed viewed as enhancing public security and not diminishing it to ensure proper rehabilitation to offenders who are likely to come back in the country.

The amendments suggest additional criteria such as whether, in the opinion of the minister, the offenders have sufficiently accepted responsibility for the offence for which they have been convicted or whether they have cooperated with the police, as well as "any other factor that the minister considers relevant." These criteria are problematic: cooperation with the authorities in certain countries would be problematic if it involved exposing other people to torture. Requiring that the offender admits his or her guilt and accept responsibility may also force people innocently accused to plead guilty in order to avoid remaining in a foreign jail. The increased discretion is what should concern us all. Canadians travel and they should not commit crimes, whether in Canada or elsewhere; however, we know that some will. We also know that some Canadians may be convicted in contexts where the presumption of innocence has been ignored, where human rights violations, unsavoury policing techniques, and prejudice against foreigners lead to convictions of innocent persons. Should Canadians have the right to be transferred if, indeed, the conditions of their incarceration amount to cruel and unusual punishment? Should they be at the mercy of a minister's whim in the evaluation of such a crucial decision?

Mature democracies tend to seek to limit the potential for abuse of power. We prefer limited discretionary powers as opposed to untrammelled discretion because we recognize that there are dangers in uncontrolled discretion. The minister may be motivated by political convenience – that is, whether or not this transfer or diplomatic intervention will produce votes. We run the risk that the minister may consider factors such as whether the family has voted for the right party, has good connections, has money or the support of important friends. What if the family of the offender has contributed to the campaign of the minister? Indeed, in unstable democracies, this is often the case: discretionary powers are often linked to potential political advantages.

Even in Canada, we see that media appeal may succeed in having one prisoner transferred, while another case may not be able to obtain similar coverage. Even if some Canadians believe that ministers in Canada would never make decisions based on such sordid grounds as political contributions, there is the appearance that they may. The lack of boundaries to such discretion prevents an analysis of whether a decision is fair, sound, and wise, based on a consideration of all factors. It also prevents any legal accountability. Although politicians certainly have the power to conduct international relations on behalf of Canada, they should want to exercise it in a way that is fair and transparent. The absence of rules prevents Canadians from knowing how they will be treated and exposes the government to charges of favouritism when it acts or refuses to act. Indeed, when a white Canadian is repatriated speedily from Mexico while an Afro-Canadian is left in jail in Sudan, Canadians wonder whether the government is acting fairly and reasonably or in a racist manner. A stronger legal framework helps to dispel such accusations and allows for more transparent ruling.

A mature democracy must give itself the tools to prevent abuse of powers and ensure fair and objective decision-making in individual cases. Ministers should debate and implement public policies. However, individual transfers or interventions in individual cases should be assessed objectively; they should not be left to the vagaries of political convenience, which opens the door to too many potential abuses and is dangerous for the rule of law.

THE ALTERNATIVES

In the fall 2009, an NDP bill suggested that the government should (a) recognize its constitutional duty to protect Canadian citizens abroad; (b) enact legislation to ensure the consistent and non-discriminatorily provision of consular services to all Canadians in distress; and (c) create an independent ombudsperson's office responsible for monitoring the government's performance and ordering the minister of Foreign Affairs to give protection to a Canadian in distress if the minister otherwise refuses protection.

Recently, the Federal Court of Appeal recognized that section 6 of the Charter, which protects mobility rights of Canadian citizens, is engaged in the decision to deny a prison transfer from another jurisdiction, but that a denial can be reasonably justified in a free and democratic country.[6] At this stage, it is unclear whether the new amendments will pass constitutional muster. The Canadian Civil Liberties Association (CCLA) has argued that they will not, because they enlarge the minister's decision too widely and are not sufficiently tailored to the objectives.[7]

Time is ripe for a legislative recognition of the duty of the Canadian government toward its citizens. There will be debates as to the scope of this duty, its costs, and the accountability mechanisms that are appropriate. Nevertheless a debate must take place.

The CCLA has suggested that legislation should be enacted to confirm that Canadians have a right to be rescued and protected when:

- They face torture or illegal treatment at international law;
- They face discriminatory treatment;
- Their detention is illegal in accordance with the laws of the country;
- And that in that context, Canada should use all the diplomatic routes available to it, unless they put in jeopardy the lives of other Canadians;
- And that an ombudsman should be created or that the passport ombudsman's role be expanded and improved to provide a measure of accountability to this responsibility.

These measures might have helped Omar Khadr.

The Khadr case will remain a blemish on Canada's history as is the turning back of the SS *St Louis* and the internment of Japanese Canadians. In periods of crisis, such as the events of 11 September 2001, it is hard to maintain a commitment to democratic values. However, it is important to provide in advance for better tools to stop excesses that inevitably occur in times of fear. It is not appropriate for Canadians detained in foreign jurisdictions to have to appeal to the media to get a fair hearing from their government. The process should be objective, apolitical, grounded in international human rights values, and transparent. Legislation may help. This will be too late for Omar Khadr, but Canadians should not have to pray or pay to be protected from unfairness or torture in foreign jurisdictions: Canadian law should protect them.

NOTES

1 A paper by Daphne Keevil Harrold, "Passports and Consular Services Provided to Canadian Citizens Abroad, of the Library of Parliament" (October 2009), laments that the "dearth of academic scholarship and official debate on the subject suggests a need for much more study and analysis of the issues discussed in this paper." At http://www2.parl.gc.ca/Content/LOP/ResearchPublications/prb0919-e.htm#a5.

2 Department of Foreign Affairs and International Trade Act, R.S., 1985, c. E-22.

3 United Nations, Treaty Series, vol. 596, 261.

4 S.C. 2004, c. 21.

5 See Harrold, "Passports and Consular Services," where the author refers to the limitations of the consular services.

6 *Divito v. Canada* (Public Safety and Emergency Preparedness), 2011 FCA 39 (CanLII), http://canlii.ca/t/2fp2d.

7 See the Canadian Civil Liberties Association's Submissions to the Minister of Justice on the Omnibus legislation, http://ccla.org/wordpress/wp-content/uploads/2011/10/CCLA-Brief-C10.pdf, 16–17.

Omar Khadr, the Carceral Net, and the Muslim Body

YASMIN JIWANI

In his now classic treatment of the history of prisons in *Discipline and Punish*, Michel Foucault makes the argument that society has, through time, embraced an increasing reliance on various disciplinary technologies to domesticate the population and shape individuals into docile citizens. Penal institutions are one condensed sign of such disciplinary technologies. However, their logic and rationale has gradually crept into the most intimate crevices of social life in a penetrating gaze facilitated by heightened and pervasive surveillance of quotidian actions. Post-9/11, this surveillance can be conceived of as an actuarial gaze trained upon even the most innocuous behaviours.[1] In the present circumstances, even these behaviours can be construed as potentially threatening and therefore susceptible to entrapment in the ever-widening carceral net.

The carceral net is underpinned by a "law and order" approach that aims to criminalize and, through criminality, contain that which is considered deviant, different, and a threat to the social order. In Foucault's words, "The carceral 'naturalizes' the legal power to punish, as it 'legalizes' the technical power to discipline."[2]

In the post-9/11 climate, certain bodies are more vulnerable to becoming ensnared in the carceral net. However, even prior to the events of 11 September 2001, bodies that were regarded as unworthy were also liable to be captured within that net and contained in penal and other regulatory and disciplinary institutions such as mental hospitals.[3] In his now oft-cited dictum, W.E.B. Dubois argues, "The problem of the twentieth century is the problem of the color-line, – the relation of the darker to the lighter races of men in Asia and Africa, in America and the islands of the sea."[4] Though Dubois did not live to see the twenty-first century, his observation still holds today, especially in light of the contemporary incarceration rates of the Indigenous and people of colour. Dubois's "color-line" also intersects with the globalization of the prison industrial complex, a process that contributes to the ever-widening carceral net. According to Gottschalk, in the United States on "any given day, more than seven million people – 1 in every 32 adults – are incarcerated or on probation or parole or under some form of community supervision."[5]

Guantánamo represents a condensed manifestation of the carceral state. Situated in one of the "islands of the sea" and opposed by the sovereign government of that island (Cuba), the prison deploys all manner of regulatory and disciplinary powers.[6] However, Guantánamo is only the most well known manifestation of the US's carceral network of prisons. In fact, as prison abolitionists have well noted, the United States is populated by a myriad of Guantánamos – prisons that have been known to deploy carceral power in even more extensive and intensive modes that predate the establishment of Guantánamo.[7]

Resonant with Dubois's observation, it is the "color line"[8] that demarcates those who are incarcerated versus those who enjoy the liberty of freedom in an unequal society. For instance, in the United States, "if current trends continue, one in three black men and one in six Hispanic men are expected to spend some time in jail or prison during their lives."[9] In his discussion of prisons in Belgium, Luke Vervaet observes that it is Roma women and Arab men who tend to be imprisoned.[10] He notes that other European states are embracing the American model of prison and argues that, "even if Guantánamo eventually closes, the problem that Guantánamo symbolizes – the lawlessness, racism and imperialist mentality of the powerful – remains."[11]

In Canada, scholars have remarked on the racialized character of the prison population, and the Royal Commission on Aboriginal Peoples has documented the high incarceration rates of native peoples.[12] The contemporary Conservative government in Canada is fervently attached to the law and order agenda. Recent news indicates that the federal government has committed $2.1 billion towards expanding the capacity of federal prisons in various provinces over the next five years.[13] This commitment, combined with the growing evidence of the racial bias inherent in the law, as well as the policies and practices of various law enforcement agencies, attests to the colour line as the defining element separating out those deemed unworthy of protection and due consideration.[14]

The racial underpinnings of the law-and-order agenda are nowhere more apparent than in the treatment that states direct at undocumented migrant workers, refugees, and immigrants. Marie Gottschalk notes that "the number of immigrants held in special detention centers and elsewhere on any given day [in the United States] has increased more than eleven-fold since the early 1970s ... the immigration service has become a mini-Bureau of Prisons."[15] In Canada, there have been numerous accounts of extended detentions and deportations.[16] Sherene Razack has discussed how security certificates have legitimized the long-term detention of potential suspects. Citizenship, as in the official papers one carries to denote membership in a national community, are devoid of meaning in such instances. Omar Khadr's citizenship did not seem to make a difference in protecting him or facilitating his repatriation to Canadian soil. Indeed, as Sunera Thobani has argued, "Canadian citizenship emerged with the clear intention to produce racial divisions among the populations within the territorial bounds of the nation-state, divisions which remain significant to this day and which continue the project of all racial states to produce national/racial homogeneity in the face of actual heterogeneity."[17]

The fibrils of the carceral state extend throughout the body politic. And while some bodies are contained in prisons, others are excluded in a variety of different ways – through deportation, isolation, and ultimately, genocide. A defining aspect of the carceral state is its differentiation between the bodies it chooses to "let live," to use Foucault's terms, and those which it deprives of any basic and political rights – those that it chooses to let die.[18] Philosopher Giorgio Agamben's concept of "bare life" offers a fitting description of the latter, for bare life refers to life stripped of rights and rendered politically impotent. Agamben reasons that *homo sacer*, the "sacred man" (*sic*), is an embodiment of bare life.[19] However, unlike the notion of the sacred steeped in religious eschatology, Agamben's notion of the sacred refers to life that can be killed with impunity and is unworthy of sacrifice. In other words, this is life that has no value, no meaning, and no rights within the political sphere. It is life that can be abandoned or "banned," in Agamben's terms. While Agamben's notion of sacred life as bare life is a useful term, his conjecture that we are all to some extent *homines sacri* glosses over the trenchant divide of the colour line, a process that obfuscates the varied and intersecting influence of race, class, gender, sexuality, and ability, or the degrees to which bare life is produced in different contexts.[20]

Omar Khadr's life has been constituted as "bare life": this is evident in his mistreatment and the profound dispossession of his rights. The state barely acknowledges him except when he is brought to public attention by advocates and international human rights organizations. He remains a figure on the margins. To what can we attribute this disregard for human life, for his life, a life that has been buried within the regimes of the state to the point where formal citizenship is all but abandoned? How can we explain the legitimizing discourse that accompanies this utter abandonment? And how do we account for the lack of a groundswell opposition and public outrage over Omar Khadr's continued incarceration and violation of rights?

These are haunting questions, but their very articulation directs us to an examination of the trenchant nature of the colour line – why Omar Khadr and not anyone else? Why a Muslim youth and not someone else? The mantle of the "War on Terror" has cast a shadow of suspicion on all Muslim bodies, and Omar is no exception. His mediated representation and his continued confinement provide a window through which we can see how the very framing of different bodies as worthy or unworthy, victim or perpetrator, galvanizes both public sympathy and the state's response.

The state and the media often deploy discursive strategies of colour-blind racism where racism is disavowed. Instead, a "common sense" belief that all are equal before the law and equal within society is promoted as the basis for a purported democracy. Within this social world of presumed equality, the "reasonable" person would not be caught in the kind of conditions in which Omar Khadr was apprehended.

Indeed, Omar's illegal confinement is embedded in the denial or erasure of racism. There can be no accountability for the state's actions because the terms of racial discrimination are obscured. Similarly, a "reasonable" person would not belong to the kind of family that Omar does.

With this in mind, the very basis of reasonableness has to be interrogated, especially in light of Omar's status as a child caught in a battle between two unequal nations, one of them equipped with formidable powers. Reasonableness, then, is a construct that has its roots in a civilizational discourse – a way of speaking whereby discrepancies and differences between reasonableness and unreasonableness are attributed to cultural beliefs and practices.[21]

This is a form of colour-blind racism – a racism that camouflages the differential treatment of others based on their phenotypic and/or cultural differences and assumes a universal standard by which to judge these differences.[22] Differences are then inferiorized because they do not match the benchmarks of the universal – the notion that everyone should be a certain way and should practise their beliefs in ways that conform to dominant norms. This new racism or "modern" racism can be distinguished from its older forms by its use of culture, religion, academic performance, civic engagement, and other such seemingly "non-racist," liberal criteria by which to explain away differences and to pejoratively devalue the contributions of those who do not fit into the normative structures.[23] In her analysis of the "War on Terror," Gargi Bhattacharya argues that "the proposition that identities are based on cultures and that cultures are separate and absolutely different enables all kinds of terrible things to be said, and sadly believed. This is a language of racism that has learned to disavow the terms of 'race' in order to relegitimize racist practice."[24] She maintains that whereas blackness historically was construed as a marker of an inferiorized difference and deviance, contemporary discourses of dangerous brown men carry the same mythologies of a deviant difference. Images of bearded mullahs, head-covered Taliban, beheadings, and the quintessential photograph of Osama bin Laden, legs folded and holding a rifle, or of the corrupt dictator Saddam Husein, all come to stand in for the figure of the dangerous brown man – the Muslim Other.[25] These connotations surround Omar Khadr and are concretized in the mediated representation of his family.

Razack contends that three main characters dominate the global theatre of the "War on Terror": the imperilled Muslim woman, the barbaric Muslim man, and the white civilized European whose task it is to rescue Muslim women and tame if not annihilate Muslim men.[26] And thus in understanding Omar Khadr's reception, it is important to turn to the Muslim woman, for she has become a semiotic sign of all that needs to be rectified if the Muslim world is to become postmodern and to transcend its supposedly atavistic cultural heritage. But even here we need to complicate the analysis, for not all Muslim women can be saved. While some are salvageable and can be saved as worthy victims of rescue, other women live "precarious lives," in Judith Butler's words. Their bodies simply do not matter.[27]

Omar's mother, Maha, and his sister, Zaynab, were figures represented in a way that did not solicit much sympathy. Part of this has to do with how we apprehended them. In her groundbreaking analysis, Susan Sontag reasons that "photographs lay down routes of reference, and serve as totems of causes: sentiment is more likely to crystallize around a photograph than around a verbal slogan."[28] Photographs of these two women in the dominant press and on CBC online, for example, portrayed them in black hijabs and niqabs. These head and face coverings, identified in the popular press and imagination with Islam, have incited considerable hysteria among the general public as harbingers of a growing Islamic threat. When combined with the Khadr women's public support of terrorist causes, these photographs invoke a chain of significations pertaining to Islam, tribalism, oppression of women, and the like. Interestingly, in the documentary by directors Luc Côté and Patricio Henriquez on Omar's CSIS interrogation,[29] the Khadr women are portrayed in white hijabs and niqabs. The contrasting associations are different, with whiteness standing in for purity and religiosity, while blackness augers connotations associated with evil, negative differences, and a certain kind of harshness. To reiterate Sontag's point, the photographs are the first visual signifiers that audiences confront, invoking a visceral reaction that the accompanying text may then congeal into an articulate response.

Any Muslim woman's traditional dress has become a site of contestation. In Quebec, for example, an attempt was made to pass a law prohibiting the wearing of the niqab, with the stated punishment that those who chose to wear it would be denied access to government services. In France and Belgium, the hijab has been banned.[30] Jasmin Zine's analysis of the situation in Quebec, more particularly the state-mandated province-wide hearings over the "reasonable accommodation" issue, points to how the veil has come to symbolize a threat, within that context, and – it could be argued – within the nation at large.[31] The threat in this instance is that of cultural dilution signified by the increasing immigration of those who are visibly culturally and religiously different. The fear of being engulfed by another culture – "death by culture" (using Zine's terms) – is then the motivating factor that propels a siege mentality in the dominant population and a xenophobic exclusion that is mediated by racism.

However, there is a structured ambivalence to the hijab.[32] On the one hand, the veil or hijab is considered to be a sign of a premodern, ultra-patriarchal, and archaic cultural system – a system that clearly needs to be brought into modernity, its women released from cultural bondage. This signification becomes the foundational myth underpinning the rescue motif. On the other hand, the veil or hijab stands in for something that is fearsome and threatening – masking a danger, as in the suicide bomber hiding her bomb beneath the folds of her burqa, or disguising behind her face veil her true nature as vengeful Other. In the cluster of images associated with the Muslim woman, the hijab, niqab, and burqa are conflated – interchangeable signs of the religious/cultural affiliation of the Other. The viewer's perception is determined solely by what parts of the body are covered and what is inaccessible to the naked eye.

According to Sharon Todd's reading of the Quebec dailies,[33] this obsession with the veiled body causes considerable anxiety. Along with the disavowal of the veiled woman, there is an avowal or affirmation of her potential liberation – a desire to make her like one of us.[34] However, this desire is always conditional, based on what the Muslim woman's body can do for "us." In the Canadian context, despite all manner of outward assimilation, jobs are not forthcoming, and structural discrimination prevails, effectively impeding Muslim women's acceptance and inclusion within the dominant culture.[35]

The trope of Islamicization as a sign signifying and demarcating the bodies that are not worthy of rescue or that cannot be salvaged and put to use is apparent in a number of other instances. As Felix Odartey Wellington has demonstrated, the case of Suaad Hagi Mohamud is another exemplar of a woman's body whose membership in the nation has been contested. National membership is formalized when one carries a Canadian passport, but this was not considered sufficient for Mohamud to be allowed re-entry into the nation following a visit to her mother in Kenya. On her attempt to return to Canada, she was denied the right to board the airplane.[36] Despite her providing additional pieces of identification, the Canadian government officials in Kenya argued that she was not the person she purported to be. Officials erroneously determined she was an illegal Other, utilizing valid Canadian documentation in an attempt to enter the nation.

The above images appeared in the *Toronto Star*, 1 October 2009, http://www.thestar.com/article/703643.

It was only when Mohamud's legal counsel insisted on DNA verification that her identity and authenticity were affirmed in the eyes of Canadian officials and she was allowed to return, nearly three months after her initial attempt. The *Toronto Star* published two pictures of Mohamud side by side in their 1 October edition. The photographs accompanied a story detailing the views of experts who argued that, upon examination, it was evident that both photos referenced the same woman. Yet Canadian officials deemed otherwise.

Interestingly, Mohamud's photograph prior to her departure (taken from her citizenship documents) shows her as an assimilated (and hence acceptable) Muslim woman (as evidenced by her name). The photograph taken on her attempt to leave Kenya reflects an appearance that shows a considerably darker woman, wearing spectacles and a hijab. All of these accoutrements along with the darkened skin colour mark her as an Other – an Other who is not Canadian. This implicitly invokes an image of what a Canadian "should" look like.

ESCAPING THE NET

One way to escape from the carceral net is to appear to be a docile citizen – in other words, to conform to dominant societal expectations and to "fit in" to the normative order. Another way is to appear as a "worthy" victim, one who can be salvaged and/or rescued. As the crime and media theorists Ken Dowler, Thomas Fleming, and Stephen Muzzatti[37] have noted, race, class, and gender influence who is regarded as worthy victim. Women victims of domestic violence, for instance, are rarely regarded as legitimate victims.[38] Similarly, in the current post-9/11 climate, Muslim bodies are often regarded as "lethal" and toxic to the social body.[39] Indeed, according to Rebecca Wanzo, "the difference between idealized victims and others demonstrates which discourses make victims legible to the state or media."[40] This notion of legibility demands further scrutiny. In other words, how does the media render some bodies worthy of saving while others are considered as disposable "bare life"?

The mass media, as Stuart Hall and others have argued, does not work in a vacuum.[41] It is part of society as a whole, and media personnel are working members who inhabit social worlds immersed in the cross-currents constitutive of both daily realities and historical legacies. Consequently, while some reporters are sympathetic and portray their sentiments through the kinds of stories they tell, others are more conservative.[42] Ultimately, though, the media's role is to generate capital. As a corporate entity, it aims to sell stories that "make sense" – that are legible in the linguistic and cultural frameworks of its audiences. In attempting to sell the news, the mass media thus seeks to cater to the largest audience possible, and it does so by making news palatable to both conservative and liberal audiences. Under the guise of "objectivity," the aim is to present both sides of a story or contrarian views. In this way, the implicit bias of the particular media is shrouded by the façade of objectivity and buttressed by journalistic principles of balance.[43]

Marking some bodies as worthy or deserving and others as unworthy is then the language through which the colour line is coded and communicated by the mass media. Muslim women who seem to be assimilated or who can be used as cheap labour, potential consumers, and the like are more likely to be considered worthy, especially if the ideological goal is to sustain the myth of a civilizational clash within which Islam comes across as ultra-patriarchal and premodern. In this way Muslim men can be derided and their exclusion, isolation, or annihilation legitimized. In contrast, Western women can be paraded as paragons of liberty and gender equality. Their stories of exploitation and gendered violence and the discourses of disposability that frame particular groups of women (as, for example, sex trade workers, women with disabilities, and women who are poor) are erased from the public imagination.

In contrast, Muslim women who appear not to be assimilated, through their wearing of the hijab or other cultural signifiers, are not likely to deserve sympathy. Rather, they are positioned as intransigent Others who cling to barbaric customs and refuse to go along with the pace of postmodernity. These women are perceived as choosing to be oppressed and, like the fanatical Muslim woman who is often regarded as hiding a bomb under the folds of her burqa, these Muslim women are seen as hiding their true natures – not allowing the Western gaze to penetrate into their innermost thoughts and/or visually consume their appearances. Their faces cannot be read, and this, as Natasha Bakht has argued, leads to considerable consternation in the courts and in the media.[44]

CONCLUSION

Omar Khadr's case did not elicit the kind of widespread opposition and outrage that it should have, in part because of the guilt by association. This mantle of guilt is something that the mass media (and by that I do not mean individual reporters or specific editors of various papers) communicated and amplified through their coverage of the Khadr family, the visuals depicting his mother and sister, and the emphasis on the family's connections to al-Qaeda. Taken as a whole, the coverage casts doubt over Omar's innocence, but this shadow of doubt acquires potency in the current climate where the penumbra surrounding the Muslim body is one of criminality and deviance. Ensnared in a carceral net, these bodies are rendered as "bare life" – not worthy enough to be sacrificed to the gods but kept alive as disposable Others whose precarious existence acts as a moral source of instruction for the rest of us.

NOTES

1 Allen Feldman, "On the Actuarial Gaze, from 9/11 to Abu Ghraib," *Cultural Studies* 19, no. 2 (2005): 203–26.

2 Michel Foucault, *Discipline and Punish: The Birth of the Prison* (New York: Vintage Books, 1978), 303.

3 See, for instance, Kirsten Emiko McAllister, *Terrain of Memory: A Japanese Canadian Memorial Project* (Vancouver: University of British Columbia Press, 2010).

4 W.E.B. Dubois. "The Souls of Black Folk," in *Three Negro Classics* (New York: Avon Books, 1965), 213–389.

5 Marie Gottschalk. "Hiding in Plain Sight: American Politics and the Carceral State," *Annual Review of Political Science* 11 (2008): 236.

6 Derek Gregory. "The Black Flag: Guantanamo Bay and the Space of Exception," *Geografiska Annaler Series B: Human Geography* 88(B) (2006): 405–27; Halit Mustafa Tagma, "*Homo Sacer* vs. Homo Soccer Mom: Reading Agamben and Foucault in the War on Terror," *Alternatives* 34 (2009): 407–35.

7 Angela Y. Davis, *Women, Race and Class* (New York: Vintage Books, 1983); Luke Vervaet, "The Violence of Incarceration: A Response from Mainland Europe," *Race & Class* 51, no. 4 (2010): 27–38.

8 Writing in the Canadian context, Sherene Razack in *Casting Out: The Eviction of Muslims from Western Law and Politics* (Toronto: University of Toronto Press, 2008) makes reference to the colour line, arguing that in the contemporary context it operates to separate out those racialized groups that are deemed as not belong to and hence susceptible to being "cast out."

9 Gottschalk. "Hiding in Plain Sight," 236.

10 Vervaet, "Violence of Incarceration," 27–38.

11 Ibid., 31.

12 "Backgrounder: Aboriginal Inmates" (Ottawa: Office of the Correctional Investigator, 2010), http://www.oci-bec.gc.ca/rpt/annrpt/annrpt-20052006info-eng.aspx (accessed 13 January 2011); David Denney, Tom Ellis, and Ravinder Barn, "Race, Diversity and Criminal Justice in Canada: A View from the UK," *Internet Journal of Criminology* (2006): 1–22, http://www.internetjournalofcriminology.com/ijcprimaryresearch.html; Royal Commission on Aboriginal Peoples," *Bridging the Cultural Divide: A Report on Aboriginal People and Criminal Justice in Canada* (Ottawa: Minister of Supply and Services Canada, 1996), ch. 2; Scot Wortley, "Hidden Intersections: Research on Race, Crime, and Criminal Justice in Canada," *Canadian Ethnic Studies* 35, no. 3 (2003): 99–117.

13 *CBC News,* "More Prisons to Be Expanded," 10 January 2011, http://www.cbc.ca/canada/story/2011/01/10/tories-prison-infrastructure.html.

14 Constance Backhouse, *Colour-Coded: A Legal History of Racism in Canada, 1900–1950* (Toronto: University of Toronto Press, 1999);

William J. Closs and Paul F. McKenna, "Profiling a Problem in Canadian Police Leadership: The Kingston Police Data Collection Project," *Canadian Public Administration* 49, no. 2 (2006): 143–60; Gladys L. Symons, "Police Constructions of Race and Gender in Street Gangs," in *Crimes of Colour: Racialization and the Criminal Justice System in Canada*, edited by W. Chan and K. Mirchandani (Ontario: Broadview Press, 2002), 115–25; David Tanovich, *The Colour of Justice: Policing Race in Canada* (Toronto: Irwin Law, 2006); Esmeralda Thornhill, "So Seldom for Us, So Often against Us: Blacks and the Law in Canada," *Journal of Black Studies* 38 no. 3 (2008): 321–37; T. Williams, *Report of the Commission on Systemic Racism in the Ontario Criminal Justice System: Summary of Key Findings*, paper presented at the Background Notes for the Ontario Court of Justice (Provincial Division) Annual Convention, 21–23 May 1996.

15 Gottschalk, "Hiding in Plain Sight," 246.

16 Razack, *Casting Out*; Thornhill, "So Seldom for Us."

17 Sunera Thobani, *Exalted Subjects: Studies in the Making of Race and Nation in Canada* (Toronto: University of Toronto Press, 2007), 102.

18 Michel Foucault, "Society Must Be Defended," in *Lectures at the Collège de France, 1975–1976*, translated by D. Macey (New York: Picador, 2003).

19 Giorgio Agamben, *Homo Sacer, Sovereign Power and Bare Life*, translated by D. Heller-Roazen (Stanford, CA: Stanford University Press, 1998).

20 See, for instance, Parin Dossa, *Politics and Poetics of Migration: Narratives of Iranian Women from the Diaspora* (Toronto: Canadian Scholars' Press, 2004).

21 See Richard F Devlin, "We Can't Go on Together with Suspicious Minds: Judicial Bias and Racialized Perspective in R.v.R.D.S. (Case Comm.)," *Dalhousie Law Journal* 18 (1995): 408–35. See also Sherene Razack, *Looking White People in the Eye: Gender, Race, and Culture in Courtrooms and Classrooms* (Toronto: University of Toronto Press, 1998); Razack, *Casting Out.*

22 Eduardo Bonilla-Silva, "The Linguistics of Color Blind Racism: How to Talk Nasty about Blacks without Sounding 'Racist,'" *Critical Sociology* 28, nos. 1–2 (2002): 41–64.

23 Robert M. Entman, "Modern Racism and the Image of Blacks in Local Television News," *Critical Studies in Mass Communication* 7, no. 4 (1990): 332–45.

24 Gargi Bhattacharyya, *Dangerous Brown Men: Exploiting Sex, Violence and Feminism in the War on Terror* (London and New York: Zed Books, 2008), 96.
25 Yasmin Jiwani, "Covering Canada's Role in the 'War on Terror,'" in *Mediating Canadian Politics*, ed. S. Sampert and L. Trimble (Toronto: Pearson, 2009), 294–316.
26 Razack, *Casting Out.*
27 Judith Butler, *Precarious Life: The Powers of Mourning and Violence* (London and New York: Verso, 2004).
28 Susan Sontag, *Regarding the Pain of Others* (New York: Picador, 2003), 85.
29 Luc Côté and Patricio Henriquez, *You Don't Like the Truth: 4 Days inside Guantánamo* (Montreal: Astral Media and Les Films Adobe, 2010).
30 Joan Wallach Scott, *The Politics of the Veil* (Princeton: Princeton University Press, 2007).
31 Jasmin Zine, "Unsettling the Nation: Gender, Race and Muslim Cultural Politics in Canada," *Studies in Ethnicity and Nationalism* 9, no. 1 (2009), 146–93.
32 See Jiwani, "Doubling Discourses and the Veiled Other: Mediations of Race and Gender in Canadian Media," in *States of Race*, edited by S. Razack, M. Smith, and S. Thobani (Toronto: Between the Lines, 2010), 59–86.
33 Sharon Todd, "Veiling the 'Other,' Unveiling our 'Selves': Reading Media Images of the Hijab Psychoanalytically to Move beyond Tolerance," *Canadian Journal of Education* 23, no. 4 (1998): 438–51.
34 Jiwani, "Helpless Maidens and Chivalrous Knights: Afghan Women in the Canadian Press," *University of Toronto Quarterly* 78, no. 2 (2009): 728–44.
35 See Daood Hamdani, *Triple Jeopardy: Muslim Women's Experience of Discrimination*, Canadian Council of Muslim Women, 2005; Eve Haque, "Homegrown, Muslim and Other: Tolerance, Secularism, and the Limits of Multiculturalism," *Social Identities* 16, no. 1 (2010): 79–101.
36 Felix Odartey-Wellington, "Erasing Race in the Media: The Case of Suaad Hagi Mohamud." Paper presented at the Canadian Communications Association Annual Meetings, Congress of the Social Sciences and Humanities, Montreal, 2010.

37 Ken Dowler, Thomas Fleming, and Stephen L. Muzzatti, "Constructing Crime: Media, Crime, and Popular Culture," *Canadian Journal of Criminology and Criminal Justice* 48, no. 6 (2006): 837–50.

38 See Helen Benedict, *Virgin or Vamp: How the Press Covers Sex Crimes* (New York: Oxford University Press 1992); Marian Meyers, *News Coverage of Violence against Women: Engendering Blame* (Thousand Oaks: Sage, 1997).

39 Shiraz Dossa, "Lethal Muslims: White-Trashing Islam and the Arabs," *Journal of Muslim Minority Affairs* 28, no. 2 (2008): 225–36.

40 Rebecca Wanzo, "The Era of Lost (White) Girls: On Body and Event," *Differences: A Journal of Feminist Cultural Studies* 19, no. 2 (2008): 114.

41 Stuart Hall, "The Work of Representations," in *Representation, Cultural Representation and Signifying Practices*, edited by S. Hall (London: Sage in association with the Open University, 1997), 15–74.

42 See, for example, Michelle Shephard's groundbreaking book on Omar Khadr, *Guantanamo's Child* (Mississauga: John Wiley, 2008).

43 Robert A. Hackett and Yuezhi Zhao, *Sustaining Democracy? Journalism and the Politics of Objectivity* (Toronto: Garamond Press, 1998); Robert A. Hackett, Richard Gruneau, Donald Gutstein, Timothy A. Gibson, and Canada News Watch, *The Missing News: Filters and Blind Spots in Canada's Press* (Ottawa: Canadian Centre for Policy Alternatives/Garamond Press, 2000).

44 Natasha Bakht, "Victim or Aggressor? Typecasting Muslim Women for Their Attire," in *Belonging and Banishment: Being Muslim in Canada*, edited by N. Bakht (Toronto: TSAR Press, 2008).

Stolen Youth: Lost Boys and Imperial Wars

JASMIN ZINE

In these times of neoliberal war and peace, the interconnected fault-lines of race, religion, class, and nationality are shaped by and within "new geographies of exclusion and landscapes of wealth"[1] where some live on the front lines of war, alienation, and oppression, while others live where freedom is simply another commodity purchased through the suffering of others.

The irreconcilability of living in these disparate yet interdependent sites creates feelings of dissonance and angst in the lives of marginalized Muslim youth. The "9/11 generation" bears daily witness to the violence and destruction exported to their lands in the ongoing "War on Terror" and through domestic security policies that label them as potential terrorists and enemies of the state. They are the nameless, faceless masses "over there" who live in militarized playgrounds reduced to being moving targets for sharpshooters and carpet-bombers. "Over here" in the West, these same Muslim youth are transformed from citizens to outlaws by virtue of their religion, ethnicity, and race.

DANGEROUS FOREIGNERS AND ENEMIES WITHIN

In this new world order, the military and security communities along with academics and the media function within a "security industrial complex" to create new ontological categories through which Muslim youth, especially males, can be profiled, studied, policed, disciplined, and "detained." The "radical," the "terrorist," "the extremist," and "the jihadist" are the new identities ascribed to Muslim youth that constitute them as violent, degenerate fanatics hell-bent on the destruction of the West. The construction of these archetypes leaves little room for Muslims to locate themselves outside of these narrow, destructive typologies.

These categories are purveyed without reference to the histories and complex geo-political struggles that shape these terms, and without acknowledging the role of US foreign policies and the "War on Terror" in creating the conditions for reactionary ideologies to give rise to violent movements. Nonetheless the new taxonomies of difference tell us who are to be watched, punished, and exiled for fear they may disrupt "our freedom," "our values," and "our nation." The boundaries of belonging and citizenship and those separating the desirable from undesirable immigrants are anchored on these distinctions. Nationhood, citizenship, and civil and human rights hang in the delicate balance between the fear and moral panic generated among "good citizens" toward the Muslim "anti-citizen."[2] The archetype of the "dangerous foreigner" is a familiar trope in Canadian history, referencing fears of "hindoo invasions" and "yellow peril" in the late nineteenth and early twentieth century; and it is now reactivated in the guise of the bearded, veiled, and dark-skinned bodies of Muslims and those who are "Muslim looking." These images play on the psyche much as earlier colonial narratives did and become the codes through which danger is signified and through which Muslims become the personification of fear and civilizational threat. These Orientalist constructions have gained renewed currency in the current climate of anti-Muslim racism and Islamophobia and are embedded within the fraught social, political, and cultural terrain upon which the 9/11 generation of Muslim youth must negotiate their sense of identity and citizenship.

Caught in this web of militaristic, legal, racial, and epistemic violence is the figure of Omar Khadr. The deep-seated Western fears about "radicalized Muslim" youth are epitomized by Omar: a "homegrown" Canadian who has abandoned the privilege of Western values, norms, and sensibilities in favour of the irrational, backward, religiously inspired terror of al-Qaeda. Many Canadians would regard the entire Khadr clan as having wantonly disavowed liberal democratic values, a view that has situated them outside the boundaries of belonging and citizenship in the public and national imaginary.[3]

The Khadr family have been controversial figures for some time. They served as humanitarian aid workers in Afghanistan in the

1980s and 1990s, but their involvement in Afghanistan's political struggles appears to have taken a different turn and they became accused of involvement with al-Qaeda. Caught in the ideological and military crossfire are the Khadr children, and whatever are believed to be the sins of the parents are now being visited upon them. They have suffered deeply for their parents' choices, and the consequences are lasting. Omar remains Canada's forgotten child, a fifteen-year-old living in a war zone, a victim of torture abandoned by his country, imprisoned and left to languish in conditions that would break many men twice his age. This would be a horrible nightmare for most Canadian parents, were this to happen to their child, yet Omar's case has not garnered much identification and sympathy or even public outrage beyond small ad hoc groups of loyal supporters.[4] According to an Angus Reid poll in early 2008, the issue of his repatriation divided the country, with 41 per cent of Canadians wanting the federal administration to intervene to secure his release and 41 per cent disagreeing.[5] The case has had a polarizing effect on our views of who has a right to belong to the nation and who should be exiled from it. I cannot help but wonder how different public opinion might have been had Omar been identified as a child soldier instead of an enemy combatant – as he should have been designated under international law. Would there be greater public sympathy and support for his repatriation as a child soldier? Or was it his skin colour and religion that made him so easily "disposable" as a citizen? I find it hard to believe that the Canadian government would have been so willing to abandon a seriously injured and traumatized child in a foreign jail if they saw them as "one of their own." Omar clearly was not. He was not one of us: he was the enemy.

DISPOSABLE CITIZENS

Omar is among many other Muslims who have become "disposable citizens" in Canada. I use this term to refer to those for whom being a Canadian citizen is not a guarantee for protection by the state or from the state. Their belonging and acceptability as part of the nation is contingent upon whether or not they raise "suspicion" (real or imagined) or are regarded as otherwise subversive. Race, ethnicity, and religion intervene in the perception of threat and in the profile of those deemed as threatening. These differences are deeply inscribed in the body. The corporeality of belonging is colour coded, but like justice, claims to be colour-blind; yet both rely on the hierarchy of racial inscriptions. Religious difference is also instrumental in the delineation of threat; the wild-looking "angry Muslim man" enraged at the "Western infidel" has become a familiar trope and one that underpins the distinction between those who are deemed friendly to the nation (good Muslims: read secular or religiously moderate) and those who must be kept at bay (bad Muslims: religiously conservative or fundamentalist). The distinction between these categories has been blurred as any form of overt religiosity or excessive "Muslimness" can be coded as potentially dangerous and subversive to the values of a secular nation. For example, movements supporting the banning of headscarves, face veils, minarets, mosques, and Islamic schools in various Western nations demonstrate the way that Islamic symbols are loaded signifiers of danger and difference. Despite the fact that most Muslims are well integrated and productive members within Western nations, the banning of these symbols is linked to the desire to exclude Islam and Muslim bodies from the social and political landscape of the nation.[6]

For those citizen-outsiders, belonging and the guarantee of rights and safety are fragile and precarious concepts. As their rights are sacrificed on the altar of security, they must prove themselves worthy of citizenship or be banished as strangers. Consider the case of Canadian citizens Maher Arar, Abdullah Almalki, Muayyed Nureddin, and Ahmad Abou El Maati, who were "deemed" suspected terrorists and subject to torture. Maher Arar faced extraordinary rendition that involved "the transfer of an individual with the involvement of the U.S or its agents to a foreign state in circumstances that make it more likely than not that the individual will be subject to torture or cruel, inhumane or degrading treatment."[7] The three other Canadian men, Almalki, Nureddin, and El Maati, were detained while in Syria[8] and held in custody by a branch of the Syrian military intelligence. They were subject to brutal beatings and held in grave-like cells and solitary confinement. Maher Arar's case was significant in highlighting the Canadian government's role in the outsourcing of torture that has become a "'tactic' in the 'war on terror.'"[9] While the other men were not subject to an extraordinary rendition, as in Arar's case, they were detained based on information furnished by Canadian authorities.[10] With the exception of Maher Arar's case, the Canadian government has refused to apologize for its complicity in the torture and detainment of these innocent men who, although are now finally free, will forever be imprisoned by the horrific memories of their ordeal. For Canadian Muslims, the slightest hint of terrorist threat can result in the effective dissolution of citizenship through physical removal and torture in such grotesquely Kafkesque scenarios. Despite the fact that extraordinary rendition occurs in violation of international human rights covenants such as the UN Convention against Torture, the image of Canada as a benevolent and just nation manages to remain intact.

What makes it possible for the state to abandon its citizens and facilitate torture and still be considered an example of human rights and democracy? Drawing on the writings of Carl Schmitt, Giorgio Agamben describes a "state of exception" that occurs through the "voluntary creation of a permanent state of emergency" leading to measures that curtail civil liberties and freedoms as being the "dominant paradigm of government in contemporary politics."[11] In other words, the "provisional and exceptional measures" undertaken by the state in times of exceptional political crisis are transformed into a "technique of government" that operates as the basis for modern statecraft. These exceptional temporary measures have become normalized institutional practices that are rendered legitimate on the grounds of necessity conjured through imaginings of a permanent state of siege. The state of exception therefore allows for draconian state policies to become justified through the climate of fear and moral panic. Sherene Razack rightly points out the paradox in the current state of exception that authorizes these draconian policies: "they are laws that suspend the rule of law."[12] She goes on to point out that these practices are shored up by "race thinking," which in the case of Arabs and Muslims is underscored by orientalist notions: "Although race thinking varies, for Muslims and Arabs it is underpinned by the idea that the modern enlightened, secular peoples must protect themselves from the premodern, religious peoples whose loyalty to tribe and community reigns over their commitment to the rule of law."[13] This idea allows a siege mentality to dictate policies that result in a suspension of rights for both citizens and non-citizens.

THE "TORONTO 18"

In Canada's "homegrown" war on terror, the security apparatus of Bill C-36, the Anti-Terrorism Act, allows for sweeping police powers, preventative arrests, and detainment without charge in a trade-off between security and civil liberties that characterizes the conditions under a state of exception. In 2006 seventeen Muslim youths and one adult were arrested under Bill C-36 on charges of alleged terrorism. This case, dubbed the "Toronto 18," involved cloak-and-dagger tactics of spies, moles, and informants planted in the midst of an alleged sleeper cell of young Muslim youths. Their arrests could not have been effected without the use of community informants as moles who impacted the group's actions. A prominent religious leader, Mubin Shaikh, was recruited by the RCMP and "planted" among these young men. As an undercover operative he participated in activities that were later held against these youths, such as the now-infamous paintball camping trip that was refashioned as an al-Qaeda training mission.[14] Shaikh revealed his activities to the media when he only received $70,000 of the $300,000 compensation promised to him by the RCMP. Another mole with a background in agricultural sciences brokered an even more profitable deal for $4.1 million to provide the youths with ammonium nitrate fertilizer used for bomb-making. The fact that they did not possess any of the materials or detonators for such a project or that the fertilizer was never actually in their possession did not detract from the foundation of the case made by prosecutors that they were orchestrating attacks against the Parliament buildings in Ottawa and even planning to "behead" the prime minister.[15]

The sensationalism continued during the trials. From sharpshooters on the roof of the Brampton Court House to frenzied reporters running after women in face veils, the staging of the trial was a bizarre mixture of militarism and carnival. This spectacle militated against any presumption of innocence for those charged. The "theatrical arrests," according to Michael Keefer, "reinforced a media-driven paranoia that home grown terrorists were everywhere." He goes on to correct the negative perception that was being purveyed by arguing: "The threat to Canadian society is not a bunch of Muslim boys playing paint ball, it's an ideologically driven government willing to curtail our civil liberties."[16] Given that eleven of the youth were either convicted or pleaded guilty in this case, Keefer's comments as well as my own reading of this case may appear naïve and dismissive of these facts and therefore outright dangerous to future public safety.[17] Was this case not a distinct warning of the clear and present danger of Islamic terrorism in Canada? Would it not be foolish then to ignore or downplay this threat?

Security and intelligence communities continue to raise heightened concerns about the "radicalization" of Muslim youth in Canada and elsewhere. Cases like the Toronto 18 and Omar Khadr are held up as examples of this trend, along with the "disappearing Somali youth" in Canada and the United States who are being recruited to fight in Somalia for Al-Shahbab, a militant anti-government group branded as a terrorist organization. Each of these cases is different in context and circumstances, but are all used to signal a threat of "homegrown" radicalized Muslim youth. While such cases represent a very small minority of Muslim youth, they nonetheless constitute the dominant paradigm through which these youth are viewed and constructed. Yet the issue is not just the discursive violence enacted through these representational politics: there is of course the real threat of possible terror attacks. What is often overlooked is the connection between these two modalities of violence. The discursive or epistemic violence that is manifest through well-orchestrated campaigns of anti-Muslim racism and Islamophobic representation[18] and the physical violence that is perpetrated through terrorist acts are inter-connected. Islamophobia is the fuel that feeds radical movements and justifies their cause. There is a nexus between Islamophobia and violent formations of Islamism that needs to be addressed.

The issue of whether or not the Toronto 18 youth would have actually carried out the acts they are accused of is not certain, and opinions on this differ, despite the convictions and guilty pleas.[19] The fact that the accused had considered the acts of violence and made some steps toward that end is a concern that involves a deeper examination of what creates the social and political conditions that breed alienation and potential violence among youth in the first place, as opposed to relying upon increased racial religious profiling and curtailing civil liberties in the name of security in ways that promote anti-Muslim sentiments and thus only exacerbate these interrelated tensions.

DISMANTLING RIGHTS OF NON-CITIZENS

The civil liberties of non-citizens have also been dismantled through Canada's immigration law, as in the case of security certificates where individuals can be detained based on secret evidence and secret trials where they not entitled to view the evidence against them. Under the Immigration and Refugee Protection Act (IRPA), the federal government, acting through the Canada Border Services Agency (CBSA), may issue a security certificate to detain or remove a foreign national or permanent resident who poses a danger to Canada's national security or a risk to the safety of any individual. The types of security threats covered under this provision range from espionage to human rights abuses. Five Muslim men (dubbed the "Secret Trial Five"), Mahmoud Jaballah, Adil Charkaoui, Hassan Almrei, Mohammed Harkat, and Mohammed Majoub, have been held on security certificates charges (some since 2000)[20] based on "secret evidence" and have been recently released to even harsher terms of house arrest.[21] They have yet to be charged with any crimes or presented with the full evidence for why they were detained. Security certificates have been criticized for contravening the Canadian Charter of Rights and Freedom that protects the legal rights of citizens and non-citizens from arbitrary arrest, detention, or imprisonment and guarantees their right to be made aware of the charges against them.[22] Nonetheless, the sacrifice of civil liberties is one of the political bargains struck once a state of exception becomes the rule.

In another case that took place in 2003, twenty-three Pakistani nationals residing in Canada on student visas were detained on civil immigration charges and held for five months. In what the RCMP called "Project Thread," pre-dawn paramilitary style raids on the apartments of these Pakistani students created a spectacle of heightened fear, legitimizing the unnecessary use of force. The nefarious image of a "sleeper cell" was invoked to raise alarm over potentially dangerous foreigners abusing the goodwill of Canada and threatening national security. After up to five months of incarceration, the youth rounded up in this sweep were eventually released without any charge, and yet all were deported to Pakistan, not with the pride of having completed professional degrees as they had planned, but as humiliated accused terrorists. Potential repercussions could have been catastrophic in Pakistan where the label of "terrorist" can be a death sentence. The lives of these innocent men were endangered by the actions of the Canadian government that effectively turned them from legitimate migrants to outlaws.

The fear of being profiled, surveilled, and caught in the post-9/11 dragnet of suspicion hindered the public support for Omar Khadr among Canadian Muslims. Many Muslims were afraid of being connected to the case through voicing support for Omar. They were fearful of being deemed guilty by association. The surveillance on Muslims since 9/11 has resulted in a panopticon effect where people become self-surveilling subjects cautiously avoiding suspicion by second guessing and curtailing otherwise innocent actions for fear they might be misread as subversive. Michel Foucault describes this effect within a "panoptic society" where individuals are objectified as subjects that are under constant surveillance and in turn begin to regulate their own behaviour and actions in accordance with the dominant norms and codes.[23] For many Muslims already feeling under siege, the Orwellian hyper-surveillance of the post-9/11 world can limit the kinds of political activities they align themselves with. The internalization of the regulatory gaze makes them wary of being aligned to those bodies that are in any way associated with the spectre of terror or radicalism.

MULTICULTURAL DISCONTENTS

For many, Omar Khadr's case is a reminder of the failure of multiculturalism. Multiculturalism has failed to integrate Muslims like the Khadrs to be more "like us" (read the dominant Anglo culture). Instead, Omar and his family reverted back to a premodern existence in Afghanistan outside the bounds of civilized society to a lawless frontier of violence and religious fanaticism. The fact that decades of foreign occupation and war compounded by warlords, theocrats, neoliberal economics, and imperial geo-politics are part of a complex constellation of forces that has led to the destructive conditions in Afghanistan is not part of the narration of the Khadr saga. Instead they are ahistorical actors in a tale that does not seem to require a back story to be understood. It is enough to argue that "failed states" produce "failed citizens," and the Khadrs, tainted by the political and ideological conditions in Afghanistan, do not possess the requirements for liberal democratic citizenship. They became citizen-outsiders and outlaws, their values and ideologies irreconcilable with Canadian society. They must either be disciplined back to the grid of multicultural conformity and behave as "good immigrants" or be national pariahs.

The construction of the nation as an "imagined community"[24] creates a space of both belonging and banishment where some people are imagined to be rightful citizens of the nation based on shared values and customs while others are rendered simply "un-imaginable" as citizens. Sara Ahmed writes of these contradictory impulses within multiculturalism that create the bifurcations between citizens and "strangers" and reminds us that "multiculturalism can involve a double and contradictory process of incorporation and expulsion: it may seek to differentiate between those strangers whose appearance of difference can be claimed by the nation, and those stranger strangers who may be expelled, whose difference maybe dangerous to the well-being of even the most heterogeneous of nations."[25] Increasingly in the post-9/11 context, Muslims occupy that liminal space between belonging and banishment. Multiculturalism has not provided a guarantee for equality or acceptance and instead serves as a masquerade obscuring the relations of racialized power and privilege that shape the nation.

Yasmin Jiwani unpacks the media's role in creating a "symbolic and discursive universe" where nationalist mythologies are purveyed to secure the benevolence of Canada in the face of dangerous interlopers. She examines the depiction of Arabs and Muslims in Canadian dailies as "angry men of the desert" who are "sophisticated, brutal, hard, fanatical," a representation that "constructs an iconic image of terrorists as deviant bodies that cannot be contained or erased – the ultimate threat to society."[26] Such transgressive Muslims in the national imaginary are further distanced from being identified with the nation. Robert Fisk makes the astute observation that in the media coverage of the Toronto 18 case, the accused Muslim youths were identified as "Canadian-born," not as "Canadians."[27] This subtle yet meaningful distinction signals a difference of being "qualified as a Canadian" by virtue of one's birth (a "borrowed" nationality) versus being unequivocally identified as "rightful" Canadians. This entitlement comes with taking on the role of what Hage terms "nationalist managers" who "perceive themselves as spatial managers and that which is standing between them and their imaginary nation is constructed as an undesirable national object to be removed from national space."[28] Those who see themselves as rightful managers of the nation by virtue of their birthright as white settlers can thus play the role of determining the imagined community of the nation and who has a right to belong to it and who should be deemed outsiders and outlaws. Sunera Thobani expands on this notion by arguing that "having overcome great adversity in founding the nation these subjects face numerous challenges from outsiders – 'Indians,' immigrants and refugees who threaten their collective welfare and prosperity. The nation of citizens has historically imagined itself vulnerable to innumerable such interlopers, compelled to resolutely face down the virulent, chaotic, criminal, and sometimes even deadly menaces posed by them."[29] Therefore the national imaginary has historically been haunted by menacing strangers. In the 9/11 context, the Muslim male has come to represent a central figure haunting and "worrying" the nation as a potential threat, and it is his detention and incarceration that secures "our" freedom and quells the nightmares.

CARCERAL HAUNTINGS

Omar Khadr has come to haunt the public imaginary as a young terrorist/murderer who is being kept at a safe distance in Guantánamo Bay locked away with all the other "monsters." Guantánamo is the last page of a frightening fairy tale where all the monsters are locked up and we can sleep soundly knowing they cannot harm us. It is also a postcolonial tale: civilized society can rest easier as the savages are kept far away, caged and shackled where they no longer can threaten the safety of Western society. Pictures also help tell the story: images of the 2002 temporary detention camp at Guantánamo Bay known as Camp X-Ray show images of "enemy combatants" in orange jump suits hooded and cuffed, bent down on their knees in open air cages. They have been rendered docile, subdued and emasculated by US soldiers whose hyper-masculinity is produced and secured in this encounter. The fact that Guantánamo is used solely to confine Muslims further reinforces the racialized boundaries of the state of exception. The racial inscriptions of dominant white men and debased brown bodies help to rehearse and stage the positional superiority of the civilized West over the barbaric East through this spectacle witnessed in the photographs seen from Camp X-Ray to Abu Ghraib.

Guantánamo has come to epitomize the state of exception: a place that exists outside of the rule of law. According to Agamben, "The camp is the space that is opened when the state of exception begins to become the rule."[30] From colonial plantations, to Nazi concentration camps, refugee detention centres, migrant worker camps, and the outposts of the "War on Terror" – Baghram, Abu Ghraib, and Guantánamo Bay – all of these sites of internment warehouse people who are stripped of freedom and amputated from political and human rights. Those inside are living in a state of indefinite detention and indefinite exile from political community. They occupy what Agamben calls the "zone of indistinction" between "bare life" and political existence: "Whoever entered the camp moved in a zone of indistinction between outside and inside, exception and rule, licit and illicit, in which the very concepts of subjective right and juridical protection no longer made any sense."[31] Agamben's notion of the camp is not dependent on bounded and fenced spaces of confinement; rather, it refers to the borderline between the minimum existence of life and political existence. Judith Butler expands on Agamben's ideas and describes this as living in a "suspended zone, neither living in the sense that a political animal lives in community and bounded by law, nor dead and therefore outside of constituting condition of the rule of law."[32] This "suspended zone" also constructs new ontologies: Omar Khadr entered Guantánamo not as a child soldier or casualty of the "War on Terror" but as an "enemy combatant"; not as a prisoner, as this would entail political rights pertaining to the treatment of POWs that are not afforded to those in Gitmo as they are not subject to the Geneva Convention or any other international laws. In the "suspended zone," Omar and all the other Muslims being held (most without charge) are now "detainees."[33] For Omar, entering Guantánamo meant that he was no longer a child, or a prisoner, or for any real intent or purpose, a Canadian citizen; his subjectivity was reduced to that of "the detainee," one of those who, according to Butler, are "held in waiting, those for whom waiting may be without end. In other words there will be those for [whom] the protection of law will be indefinitely postponed."[34]

Omar is reduced to the bare life of *homo sacer*, a figure from Roman law that Agamben resurrects to embody "*life that cannot be sacrificed and yet may be killed*" (82, original emphasis). Lemke explains that "homo sacer designated an individual that may be killed by anyone without being condemned for homicide since he or she has been banned from the juridical-political community."[35] Agamben is interested in the relation between bare life and sovereign power and sees "the production of bare life is the originary activity of sovereignty."[36] State power as a form of biopower and necropolitics is inextricably bound to the processes of life, death, and banishment. According to Lemke, "Bare life that seems to be located at the very margin of politics, seems to be the solid basis of a political body that decides not simply over the life and death of human beings, but who will be recognized as a human being at all."[37] Sovereign power then is constituted through the act of "deeming" the status of life as existing inside or outside of the bounds and protections of political community. Henry Giroux also contends that the "life unfit for life, unworthy of being lived, is no longer marginal to sovereign power but is fundamental to its form of governance."[38] Omar and the other Muslim men in Guantánamo reside in this space of abandonment and indeterminacy between bare life and political existence that relies on the certainty that they can be shorn of humanity. Lemke takes this further to explain the legal and moral fractures that constitute the conditions of homo sacer: "While even a criminal could claim certain guarantees and legal procedures, this "sacred man" was completely unprotected and reduced to mere physical existence. Because he or she was ascribed a status beyond human or divine law, homo sacer became some kind of 'living dead.'"[39]

Agamben explains that the term used to refer to the "living dead" in the death camps of Auschwitz was "Muselmänner" or Muslims. These were the dying prisoners, sick, malnourished, and emaciated, who had lost the will to live, described as "staggering corpses" or "mummy men"; the horror and misery of their existence made them physically weak and prostrate on the ground. According to some accounts, the term "Muselmänner" was used to liken their comportment to that of Muslims bent down in prayer.[40] While they suffered in the throes of death, Agamben writes, "with a kind of ferocious irony, the Jews knew that they would not die at Auschwitz as Jews."[41] Thus in their prelude to death, the Jews of Auschwitz came to be known as Muslims. In manifestation of related irony, Milo Sweedler observes: "As if by an ironic twist of history it is actual Muslims who find themselves in the position of the *Muselmann* in the New World Order."[42] While he is quick not to conflate the political formation of the US government with National Socialism, Sweedler argues that "the transformation of Guantánamo into a modern day concentration camp and the concomitant reduction of a class of people into subhumans, bears alarming resemblance to the dehumanization of Jews under the Third Reich."[43]

The Muslims of Guantánamo bear this strange and ironic link to a shared human history of encampments as spaces of dehumanization where the loss of political existence renders life as neither sacred nor human. Torture has been part of the arsenal in the "War on Terror" and a practice carried out from Baghram to Abu Ghraib and

Guantánamo. For years, Canadian Forces in Afghanistan have arrested children suspected of working with the Taliban and handed them over to an Afghan security unit accused of torture.[44] Omar and other Muslims at Guantánamo have suffered the indignities of torture to their bodies and spirit. While this treatment does not equal the brutality of the Nazi extermination camps, it nonetheless echoes the dehumanization that makes such atrocities possible. Butler asks some important questions about how life can devolve so easily to a place devoid of human rights and humanity: "It is crucial to ask under what condition some human lives cease to become eligible for basic if not universal human rights. How does the U.S government construe these conditions? And to what extent is there a racial and ethnic frame through which these imprisoned lives are viewed and judged such that they are deemed less human, or as having departed from the recognizable human community?"[45]

STOLEN YOUTH: THE LOST BOYS

Canada's intelligence community has identified the "jihadist generation" as the greatest threat to global security. Muslim male masculinity is connected with violence and terror in the global imaginary and the militarized and securitized context with little consideration of how this may begin to develop as a self-fulfilling prophecy. As mentioned earlier, there is a nexus between rising Islamophobia and Islamism, and Muslim youth precariously navigate this divide. While it is exciting and uplifting to see the revolutionary democratic impulses of youth in the current popular uprisings in Tunisia, Egypt, Libya, and Syria that have struggled to topple the authoritarian regimes in these nations, other youth in the Muslim world are still subject to the dictatorships of their governments and the imperialism of foreign occupation and war. These intersecting sites of domination and oppression are ripe breeding grounds where religious extremism may flourish. There is a global culture of militarism and violence into which young men are being socialized. Whether they fight with armies or in stateless gangs and networks of terror, they are the lost boys who are the by-product of imperial wars. Their youth has been stolen by the brutality of the new world order characterized by war zones, poverty, and physical destruction. They are too easily reduced to ahistorical and decontextualized categories of "radicals" and "jihadis" that tell us little about what circumstances create the conditions for violent reactionary movements to flourish. The "War on Terror" maintains the cycle of violence and reactionary terror. When we are able to see these two sides as part of the same continuum of violence, there may be a chance to work beyond the downward spiral. The irreconcilable spaces that have been forged do not allow for understanding of how they are interconnected and mutually determining. There may be recognition in the mutual suffering endured, but as Susan Sontag warns, this can only happen when the disparities that create the divides are acknowledged as we become witnesses to the pain of others.

"So far as we feel sympathy," Sontag writes, "we feel we are not accomplices to what caused the suffering. Our sympathy proclaims our innocence as well as our impotence. To that extent, it can be (for all our good intentions) an impertinent – if not an inappropriate – response. To set aside the sympathy we extend to others beset by war and murderous politics for a consideration of how our privileges are located on the same map as their suffering, and may – in ways that we prefer not to imagine – be linked to their suffering, as the wealth of some may imply the destitution of others, is a task for which the painful, stirring images supply only the initial spark."[46]

In the end, I draw hope and inspiration from Omar Khadr, who has remained steadfast in his devotion to his faith and has not given up or surrendered to the madness of his conditions despite the burden of intense trauma and political turmoil he has suffered. It is a testament to the kind of young man he is that while his body has been battered and broken by the violence of war, imprisonment, and torture, his faith and spirit have remained remarkably resilient. As the thirteenth-century Muslim poet Rumi often cautioned, the greatest prison is that of the ego, and only when we are released from its trap can we be free to know our true selves. So in Omar's honour I humbly submit the words of Rumi as a prayer of liberation: "Become the sky. Take an axe to the prison wall. Escape. Walk out like someone suddenly born into colour. Do it now."

NOTES

1 Mike Davis and Daniel Bertrand Monk, *Evil Paradises: Dreamworlds of Neoliberalism* (2007), cited in Giroux, "Disposable Youth."

2 Jasmin Zine, "Unsettling the Nation," 146–63.

3 Inflammatory statements made by Omar's mother, Maha Elsamnah, and sister, Zaynab Khadr, proclaiming satisfaction over the 9/11 attacks and condemning Canadian society for its corrupting sexual values and drug use, were met with anger and hostility across Canada. Even Liberal Ontario Premier Dalton McGuinty stated that Maha Elsamnah, who had returned to Canada to seek medical attention for her paralyzed son, should apologize and "repudiate earlier statements that would not be in keeping with our responsibility as Canadian citizens" (Greenberg, "McGuinty Suggests Khadr's Wife Apologize"). Canadians objected to the Khadrs' receiving the benefits of the Canadian health care system since their incendiary rhetoric had placed them outside the bounds of national belonging and they were no longer "citizenship worthy." Their comments were instrumental in creating an ideological backdrop for Omar's case and compromised his claims for repatriation.

4 I want to acknowledge the work of various activists (Muslim and non-Muslim) who developed campaigns of support for Omar and also the efforts of Arlette Zinck and her colleagues at King's College, a Christian university in Edmonton, who have shown unwavering support for Omar's case for his eventual reintegration into Canadian society.

5 See http://www.angus-reid.com/polls/31034/omar_khadr_case_still_splits_views_in_canada/.

6 In many Western nations, Muslims are well integrated into civic and political life. For example, a Muslim mayor, Naheed Nenshi, was elected in Calgary, Alberta, in 2010. Yet in the same way that the election of a black president in the United States has not ended anti-black racism in that country, these positive developments do not counteract the deep institutionalized structures of racism and Islamophobia that persist in Western nations and work toward the exclusion of racial and religious minorities. In fact, the greater presence of racialized and religious minorities accompanied by their claims for accommodation and inclusion within the public sphere has exacerbated right-wing backlash and xenophobia in many Western nations, most recently exemplified by the tragic massacre in Norway by a right-wing Christian terrorist, Anders Breivik, who was motivated by Islamophobia and a hatred of multicultural society.

7 All Party Parliamentary Group on Extraordinary Rendition, "Torture by Proxy."

8 Maher Arar was stopped in a New York City airport in 2002 while enroute to Canada from a vacation in Tunisia. He was deported to

Syria despite his Canadian passport. The other Canadian men were detained while in Syria: Ahmad Abou El Maati was stopped in the Damascus airport in 2001 enroute to prepare for his wedding; Abdullah Almalki was detained when visiting an ailing grandmother in Syria in 2002; Muayyed Nureddin was taken into custody after crossing over to Syria after visiting his family in Northern Iraq in 2003.

9 All Party Parliamentary Group on Extraordinary Rendition, "Torture by Proxy."

10 Former Supreme Court of Canada Justice Frank Iacobucci conducted an inquiry into the events leading to the detentions of El Maati, Nureddin, and Almalki and determined that the actions of Canadian officials did not directly contribute to the detentions abroad of three Muslim-Canadian men, but did indirectly contribute to their mistreatment and torture in Syria.

11 Agamben, *State of Exception*, 2.

12 Razack, *Casting Out*, 11.

13 Ibid., 9–10.

14 While a judge ruled that his actions did not constitute entrapment as defense lawyers for the youths contended, concerns within the Muslim community still remain regarding Shaikh's credibility and conduct as an undercover informant and how this may have affected the events that transpired. Ironically, Shaikh's credibility has been further weakened by CSIS – the very agency that hired him as a paid informant. A 2009 cable from the US embassy in Ottawa, obtained by WikiLeaks and provided to the CBC, revealed that CSIS had placed the name of their own paid informant on a US terror watch list. The *Toronto Star* reported that "CSIS has refused to comment on how the name of one of its paid informants ended up on a U.S. terror list. Defense lawyers for the Toronto 18 are demanding to know if the intelligence agency gave the U.S. information about Shaikh's background that was withheld when he testified at the terror trials, thereby violating the rules of full disclosure" (Contenta, "Who's on the Terror Watch List?"). The defense attorneys noted that this information would be important for appeals in this case.

15 Michael Keefer, "Toronto 18 Frame-Up."

16 Ibid.

17 Since the arrests, four of the seventeen youths and one adult were convicted, seven pleaded guilty, and seven have had their charges stayed.

18 An important study recently released by the Center for American Progress entitled " Fear Inc.: The Roots of the Islamophobia Network in

America" by Ali et al. outlines how a small group of "miseducation experts" such as Daniel Pipes, Steve Emerson, and Frank Gaffney are involved in a heavily funded network that purveys Islamophobia with the support of various American foundations and private endowments, by the media such as Fox News, by various Republican Representatives such as Peter King and Michele Bachmann, and by various right-wing grassroots organizations. The report is significant in mapping this network and revealing the spheres of influence it wields nationally and internationally (Norwegian terrorist Anders Breivik cites many of these players in his anti-Islamic manifesto), as well as sources of its funding (over $40 million dollars from seven foundations over ten years) that sustains these Islamophobic campaigns.

19 My empirical research on the impact of the War on Terror on Canadian Muslim youth has led me to examine these cases and talk to youth, youth workers, and community leaders about this potential radicalization. The stakeholders interviewed included those with personal connection with the Toronto 18 youths and young people recruited to fight in the civil war in Somalia. These discussions made it clear that there is more to the story than the official accounts tell us and suggest a different picture of the youth from what has been portrayed. Nonetheless, initiatives for "de-radicalizing" Muslim youth are growing, positioning "experts" like Mubin Shaikh as the pundits of this new industry offering "ideological rehab."

20 The security certificates against Charkaoui and Almrei were eventually struck down by a judge, while Jaballah and Mahjoub's cases are still in process. Harkat's certificate was upheld in 2010, which comes with a threat of possible deportation. These developments follow the fact that these men were held in custody from two to seven years without full knowledge of the charges and evidence held against them. According to Diab, "Under the terms of criminal law, each of these men among the 'secret trial five' would be presumed innocent until proven guilty. But in this case, it is almost the reverse. Out of an abundance of caution, we have proceeded to treat these men as guilty and to forgo the need to present evidence in a full trial. We have held them in an administrative limbo that is officially neither a detention pending deportation nor a punishment, but simply an indefinite incarceration" (*Guantanamo North*, 10). These conditions have given rise to Canada and specifically Millhaven Penitentiary in Kingston, Ontario, the maximum security facility where the men were held, being dubbed "Guantánamo North." Diab further makes the sobering observation

that as a country that prides itself on high standards of civil and human rights and with the protection of the Canadian Charter of Rights and Freedoms, "We must at some point consider the possibility of their innocence. We must ask: what if even one of these men is innocent?" (ibid.).

21 Mohammed Majoub, one security certificate detainee suspected of having links to al-Qaeda, was released in 2007 after being held for six years without charge. He voluntarily returned to custody in 2009 in protest against his oppressive bail conditions (http://www.cbc.ca/canada/story/2009/08/21/f-security-certificates.html).

22 In February 2007, in the Charkaoui case, the Supreme Court ruled that the security certificate process was unconstitutional. The government introduced a slightly modified law and, a year later in February 2008, new security certificate legislation Bill C-3 entered into force. According to the Justice for Charkaoui website (http://www.adilinfo.org/), the new legislation remains problematic: "In enacting the new security certificate law, the government failed to respect the Supreme Court's ruling that detainees have a right to know the case against them." The modified process now allows that, before the detainee is deported, the security certificate must be reviewed by the Federal Court in what are known as the "reasonability hearings." These hearings (only part of which are held in public) determine whether the government had reasonable grounds to believe an individual is or will in the future be a danger to public safety. The Justice for Charkaoui campaign has noted that what constitutes "danger" and "public safety" remains vague and undefined.

23 Foucault, *Discipline and Punish*.

24 Anderson, *Imagined Communities*.

25 Ahmed, *Strange Encounters*, 97.

26 Jiwani, "Great White North Encounters September 11," 50, 55.

27 Fisk, "Has Racism Invaded Canada?"

28 Hage, *White Nation*, 47.

29 Thobani, *Exalted Subjects*, 4.

30 Agamben, *Homo Sacer*, 168–9.

31 Ibid., 170.

32 Butler, *Precarious Life*, 67.

33 For example, Agamben in *State of Exception* notes, "Not only do the Taliban captured in Afghanistan not enjoy the status of POWs as defined by the Geneva Convention, they do not even have the status of person charged with a crime according to American laws" (3).

34 Butler, *Precarious Life*, 64.
35 Lemke, "Zone of Indistinction," 3.
36 Agamben, *Homo Sacer*, 83.
37 Lemke, "Zone of Indistinction," 2–3
38 Giroux, "Disposable Youth," 170.
39 Lemke, "Zone of Indistinction," 3.
40 Agamben, *Remants of Auschwitz*, 41.
41 Ibid., 45.
42 Sweedler, "Bare Life," 138.
43 Ibid.
44 The Canadian Broadcasting Corporation's investigative unit discovered a document in 2010 outlining how the Canadian Armed Forces routinely handed over juvenile detainees to Afghan National Police whose harsh interrogation techniques were well known and documented in United Nations Human Rights reports: "The document, obtained under an Access to Information request and marked 'secret,' shows that Defence Minister Peter MacKay was briefed on the topic of juvenile detainees in Afghanistan March 30. The 'Canadian eyes only' note informs MacKay of how many children suspected of 'participating in the insurgency' have been arrested by Canadian Forces and how many of them have been transferred into Afghan custody in the previous four years. The note also shows that an undisclosed number of juvenile detainees were being kept in a Canadian transfer facility at Kandahar Air Field for 'a significant period.' The numbers in all cases, however, were blacked out" (http://www.cbc.ca/news/canada/story/2010/11/26/afghan-child-detainees.html).
45 Butler, *Precarious Life*, 57.
46 Sontag, *Pain of Others*, 102.

BIBLIOGRAPHY

Agamben, Giorgio. *Homo Sacer: Sovereign Power and Bare Life*. Stanford, CA: Stanford University Press 1998.
– *Remants of Auschwitz*. New York: Zone Books 2002.
– *State of Exception*. Chicago: University of Chicago Press 2005.
Ahmed, Sara. *Strange Encounters: Embodied Others in Postcolonialty.* London: Routledge 2000.
Ali, Wahajat, et al. *Fear Inc.: The Roots of the Islamophobia Network in America*. Center for American Progress 2011. http://www.americanprogress.org/issues/2011/08/islamophobia.html.

All Party Parliamentary Group on Extraordinary Rendition. "Torture by Proxy: International Law Applicable to 'Extraordinary Renditions.'" New York University Center for Human Rights and Global Justice 2005. http://www.chrgj.org/docs/APPG-NYU%20Briefing%20 Paper.pdf.

Anderson, Benedict. *Imagined Communities: Reflections on the Origin and Spread of Nationalism*. London: Verso 1983.

Butler, Judith. *Precarious Life*. London: Verso 2006.

Contenta, Sandro. "Who's on the Terror Watch List? More Than Just Terrorists, It Seems." *Toronto Star*, 24 May 2011.

Davis, Mike, and Daniel Bertrand Monk. *Evil Paradises: Dreamworlds of Neoliberalism* (2007), cited in Henry Giroux, "Disposable Youth in a Suspect Society: A Challenge for the Obama Administration." 2008. http://www.truth-out.org/112508A.

Diab, Robert. *Guantanamo North*. Black Point, NS: Fernwood 2008.

Fisk, Robert. "Has Racism Invaded Canada?" *Counterpunch* (June 2006). http://www.counterpunch.org/fisk06122006.html.

Foucault, Michel. *Discipline and Punish*. New York: Vintage Books 1995.

– *Society Must Be Defended: Lectures at the Collège de France, 1975–1976*. New York: Picador 2003.

Giroux, Henry. "Disposable Youth in a Suspect Society: A Challenge for the Obama Adminstration." 2008. http://www.truth-out.org/112508A.

Greenberg, Lee. "McGuinty Suggests Khadr's Wife Apologize: Premier Takes Issue with Comments Supporting Terrorism." *National Post*, 15 April 2004, A-16.

Hage, Ghassan. *White Nation*. New York: Routledge 2000.

Jiwani, Yasmin. "The Great White North Encounters September 11: Race, Gender and the Nation in Canada's National Daily, the Globe and Mail." *Social Justice* 32, no. 4 (2005): 50–70.

Keefer, Michael. "The Toronto 18 Frame-Up." *Truthwire* (24 June 2008). http://truthwire.wordpress.com/2008/06/30/the-toronto-18-frame-up/.

"Justice for Charkaoui." n.d. http://www.adilinfo.org/

Lemke, Thomas. "'A Zone of Indistinction': A Critique of Giorgio Agamben's Concept of Biopolitics." *Critical Practice Studies* 7, no. 1 (2005): 3–13.

Razack, Sherene. *Casting Out: The Eviction of Muslims from Western Law and Politics*. Toronto: University of Toronto Press 2008.

Sontag, Susan. *Regarding the Pain of Others*. New York: Picador/Farrar, Straus and Giroux 2003.

Sweedler, Milo. "Bare Life from Auschwitz to Guantanamo Bay." In *The Camp: Narratives of Internment and Exclusion*, edited by Colman Hogan and Marta Marin-Domine. Newcastle, UK: Cambridge Scholars Publishing 2007.

Thobani, Sunera. *Exalted Subjects: Studies in the Making of Race and Nation in Canada*. Toronto: University of Toronto Press 2007.

Zine, Jasmin. "Unsettling the Nation: Gender, Race and Muslim Cultural Politics in Canada." *Studies in Ethnicity and Nationalism* 9, no. 1 (2009): 146–63.

Omar Khadr and the Perils of Canadian Multiculturalism

SHADIA B. DRURY

The story of Omar Khadr is a tragedy in the classic Greek sense of the term – it is a tale of innocent suffering. His first misfortune was being born in 1986 in Toronto to a family with a radical fundamentalist interpretation of Islam. His father, Ahmed Khadr, who had immigrated to Canada from Egypt in 1977, was closely associated with radical elements in Pakistan and Afghanistan, and was constantly moving his family back and forth from Canada to Pakistan and Afghanistan. He was reputed to be one of the founding members and financier of al-Qaeda. This was a time when the organization was obscure and unpopular, even in the Muslim world. The situation changed dramatically after al-Qaeda's successful terrorist attack on the Pentagon and the World Trade Centre in 2001. Less than two months after these attacks, the Americans invaded Afghanistan.

At the time Omar Khadr was living in Afghanistan with his family. He joined his father in fighting with al-Qaeda and the Taliban against the Americans. He was severely injured, captured, and sent to the American prison in Guantánamo Bay, Cuba. He had the further misfortune of being in the clutches of a superpower altogether contemptuous of international law. The United States defined its prisoners of war as "unlawful combatants," with no rights under the Geneva Conventions. Facing heavy-handed interrogation techniques indistinguishable from torture, Omar confessed to killing an American with a grenade. When Barack Obama replaced George W. Bush after the presidential election of 2008, he promised to close the prison at Guantánamo. But in 2010, Omar was still at Guantánamo, the youngest prisoner and the only one from a Western country who had not been repatriated. Finally, as a result of a plea deal with the prosecutors of the American military, and under pressure from the American government, Canada agreed to bring him to a Canadian prison in 2011 to serve eight more years, after which he might be released on condition that he has only the most minimal contact with his family.

It is puzzling that a child born in Canada would suffer such a dreadful fate. Did Omar Khadr have a date with destiny? Was the suffering of this child a function of a series of unusually unlucky circumstances? Or did Canadian multiculturalism have something to do with it?

It is my contention that an unhealthy and exaggerated form of multiculturalism has emerged in Canada in the last few decades. I believe that this new brand of multiculturalism poses greater perils to individuals, especially children. As a child, Omar Khadr was trapped in an intellectually and morally toxic environment created by changes in Canadian multiculturalism corresponding with equally profound and equally perilous changes in Canadian liberalism.

Canada has always distinguished itself from the United States by being a mosaic rather than a melting pot. When immigrants went to the United States, they were expected to shed their old identity and don an American one. They were supposed to abandon the ideas and habits of the Old World and accept those of the New. The Old World was characterized by the primacy of the collective. But in the New World, individuals were to be liberated from the collective; they were to be free to be themselves, free from the burden of conformity required by the group. All newcomers were expected to embrace this liberal individuality. It did not occur to Americans that the burden of freedom may have been more than many could bear.

By offering the mosaic instead of the melting pot, Canadians were not being more liberal, more open-minded, or more accepting of the "other" – they were being more conservative and more realistic about what was involved in an immigrant society. The idea that people can shed their identities and take on new ideas and attitudes the moment they set foot in their new country seemed too much to expect, even a little heartless. The Canadian approach was intended to let immigrants know that they did not have to transform themselves magically in order to live and work in Canada. At the same time, it was natural to expect that the children of immigrants would be different from their parents – they would be Canadian. Even if it was not something clearly defined, it was clear that being Canadian meant being different from one's parents. For young people, it meant listening to different music, dancing, and dating. For people who did not come from European countries (like my parents, who immigrated to Canada from Egypt in the 1960s), all these things were scandalous. It was a difficult transition for parents, but even more difficult for children who had to do battle with their parents in order to become Canadian. Nevertheless, the process of becoming Canadian was taken for granted, even though it was not expected to happen overnight.

The important thing is that immigrants to Canada were not under the impression that they could recreate their old culture in miniature form on Canadian soil. That was out of the question for several reasons. In the first place, immigrants escaping parts of the world with political turmoil and tyranny come to Canada to escape (as was the case with my parents). To recreate the political culture of the old country would defeat the point of immigration. There is no doubt that the Caribbean immigrants who moved to Scarborough, Ontario, are dismayed to find themselves in what has been dubbed "Scarbados." This is why the early multiculturalism of Pierre Elliot Trudeau emphasized things such as food, dances, and costumes as the elements of the Old World that could enrich Canadian society. In other words, Canadian multiculturalism was an effort to embrace an aesthetic plurality that remained only skin deep.

In the last few decades, Canadian multiculturalism has morphed into something more perilous than it was prior to the adoption of the Multiculturalism Act in 1988. The pluralistic inspiration behind the act is that immigrant groups would preserve and cherish their ethnic cultures and values and share them with all Canadians. The assumption was that pluralism is not just a fact about an immigrant society but a definite value worthy of being actively promoted. The pluralist enthusiasts assumed that the Canadian commitment to multiculturalism would strengthen the unity of the country by encouraging people to see it as a colourful salad, its regional differences and loyalties undermined and the threat of separatism diminished. They also hoped that the promotion of multiculturalism would allay the threat of American cultural domination. They were convinced that exposure to diverse cultures would be enriching to the country and its people, expanding horizons and avoiding a narrow parochialism.[1]

It never occurred to these pluralists that many immigrants had no desire to maintain their cultural identity, and that a *policy* of multiculturalism might be an obstacle not only to integration but also to social mobility.[2] It never occurred to them that the plurality of values being preserved and shared with other Canadians might come into conflict with one another and/or with the values of English and French Canada. It never occurred to them that some of the cultural values of the newcomers might not be welcomed by Canadians, or that some of these cultural values might even pose a threat to peace, order, and good government.

In my view, the aspirations of the pluralists were laudable but not realistic. The effect of transforming multiculturalism from a fact into a policy allowed some immigrants to believe that they could preserve their cultures intact without any need to mingle or mix with the rest of Canadian society – contrary to the original intentions of the act. In time, Canadian multiculturalism became a permanent condition that applied not only to new immigrants but also to their children. Omar Khadr went to the Islamic Society of North America (ISNA) Elementary, a private Islamic school in Mississauga, Ontario. It was one of the religious schools that were hoping to become part of the public system in 2007, as proposed by John Tory of the Ontario Conservative Party. This issue was central to the provincial election, and it accounts for the defeat of Tory and his party and the election of the liberals for a second term under Dalton McGuinty. When in 2005, some Muslim groups demanded their own faith-based tribunals that would allow them to settle family disputes (as Jewish and Catholic groups have done in Ontario since 1991) based on Sharia law, McGuinty had the wherewithal to say NO to all faith-based tribunals.

The battle was won, but not the war. The very fact that immigrants to Canada can hope to have their religious schools publically funded, even when these schools inculcate attitudes and customs at odds with the Canadian commitment to gender equality, is a product of the new multiculturalism. For example, ISNA Elementary segregates boys and girls; it encourages girls in Grade 2 to wear the hijab, and by Grade 4, the hijab is *mandatory* for all the girls. No dress codes are required for boys. Islamic schools in Canada, advertising on the web, openly declare that their mandate is to help children "express Islamic attitudes and behavior proudly and openly."[3] If immigrants are led to believe that they can preserve their cultures, then it is not surprising that they would demand not only their own schools but also their own courts. The very fact that immigrants to

Canada can aspire to having autonomous laws (even if they are "voluntary" and subject to challenge in Canadian courts) is an indication that a new and perilous Canadian multiculturalism is on the rise.

The Province of Quebec has so far raised the loudest objections to the new multiculturalism. One reason is that the new multiculturalism rides a wave of religious revivalism around the world. But Quebec is more consciously secular than the rest of Canada – especially since the Quiet Revolution of the 1960s, when the defeat of Maurice Duplessis by Jean Lesage brought an end to the stranglehold of the Catholic Church on Quebec society, politics, and education. The first thing that the new liberal government of Jean Lesage had to do was to create a ministry of education. Until then, education was the exclusive preserve of the Catholic Church. So it was natural for Quebecers to see the new multiculturalism, with its plethora of religious schools, as a threat not only to the French character of Quebec but also to its hard-won liberty from theocratic domination. In response to the concerns of Quebecers, Jean Charest, Quebec's premier, established a Consultation Commission on Accommodation Practices in February 2007. He appointed two intellectuals, Gérard Bouchard and Charles Taylor, to travel around the province, hold forums to consult Quebecers on the issue of cultural accommodation, and come up with a set of policies on what would constitute reasonable accommodation of minorities in Quebec. The result was the Bouchard-Taylor report of 2008, *Building the Future*.[4]

No one old enough to have a memory of the old moderately liberal Canada can help feeling a profound sadness on reading the report on "reasonable accommodation." It is a breathtaking window into the transformation of the soul of a nation. It describes the death of one society and the birth of another. But the authors seem blind to the achievements that have been lost, while being oblivious to the darkness that is taking shape. Instead, they bid us to move forward undaunted even while telling us that the future into which they are hurling us is unknown. But one thing seems to be known to the authors of the report: the old Canada that was somewhat liberal, somewhat individualistic, and somewhat secular, is nothing to lament.

It seems to me that the transformation of multiculturalism into a conscious governmental policy was mirrored by a change in Canadian liberalism itself. A decidedly communitarian spirit has triumphed over individualism, both intellectually and politically. In both theory and practice, Canadian liberalism has morphed into a doctrine in which the collective plays a role of unprecedented importance, while the primacy of the individual retreats – so much so that communitarianism has penetrated the heart and soul of liberalism and transformed it from within. This is clearly evident in the work of liberal philosophers such as Will Kymlicka. For Kymlicka, liberalism must recognize the primacy of the group for the development, completion, and enrichment of the individual. A liberal society must recognize and protect group rights to self-determination, even when these rights involve the oppression of individuals. The oppression involved is supposedly necessary if the group is to maintain its culture, cohesiveness, traditions, and values. Kymlicka is unconcerned about group violations of the rights and freedoms of individuals because he takes it for granted that, in a liberal society, individuals are free to leave communities they find oppressive and join the greater liberal society.[5]

In principle, Kymlicka is right in thinking that there are indeed exit ramps out of these communities, but in reality his vision makes two implausible assumptions. First, it assumes that the exit ramps out of these oppressive enclaves are accessible and not booby-trapped. Second, it presupposes that a robust and vigorous liberal society will always be there to embrace individual refugees escaping oppressive group affiliations.

Unfortunately, for many people within these communities, the exit ramps are either non-existent or treacherous. For example, it would be very difficult for women who are married and have children, especially if they do not speak English, to escape. For a child like Omar Khadr, escaping the toxic brew of death and martyrdom promoted by his family was not possible.[6] After his capture and the death of his father in Afghanistan, his mother, Maha, and his grown sister were interviewed on Canadian television. The two women appeared engulfed in black robes that covered their entire bodies including their faces, their eyes barely visible through the niqab. Maha, a Canadian immigrant from Palestine, married Ahmed Khadr in Canada, and was as radical as her husband. She and her daughter were full of pride over Omar. It was a wonderful thing, they gushed, a badge of honour for the family: Omar was a *shaheed* or martyr for Islam. Maha was full of self-congratulation for having raised a *shaheed* in the corrosive atmosphere of Canadian society, where (in her view) young men are more likely to end up on the streets of Toronto as "drug addicts or homosexuals." If being a *shaheed* meant death, torture, and imprisonment, so be it – it was the will of Allah. Maha's contempt for Canadian society was shocking; her delirious chauvinism and the perversity of her Islamic piety were sheer madness. The interview was not only insulting to Canadians but profoundly detrimental to decent Muslims and other immigrants from the Middle East. I remember being horrified and dismayed, as if this madwoman held my fate in her hands. She gave Canadians the darkest possible window into the mentality of Middle Eastern immigrants in general, and shrouded Muslim women in particular. Clearly, Maha was a mother devoted to bringing up terrorists. As one of Omar's older brothers, Abdurrahman, said in an interview, "I was raised to become a suicide bomber."[7] Canadian audiences could not help but conclude that Omar must also have been raised to become a suicide bomber: so how could anyone insist on his release? Returning the boy to his mother was out of the question. He was trapped. There was no way out.

There was no way out for sixteen-year-old Aqsa Parvez either. Her parents had come to Canada from Pakistan; Aqsa was the youngest of eight siblings. Her older siblings wore the hijab, did not work outside the home, and submitted to marriages arranged by their parents. But Aqsa refused to wear the hijab; she wanted to have a part-time job; and she had no intention of submitting to the marriage arranged for her by her father to a man from Pakistan. She decided to run away from home and live at a friend's house. She went to the movies for the first time two days before her brother lured her back home in December 2007 on some false pretense, and killed her with the help of his father, while the rest of the family was upstairs, unwilling to interfere. Aqsa was not the only victim of this tragedy. Her father and brother received twenty-five year sentences with no parole for eighteen years. Aqsa's mother howled with grief at what had become of her family. Her hopes and dreams were dashed. She was clearly a victim of Canadian multiculturalism. Had she and her husband remained in Pakistan, it would have been unlikely for Aqsa to rebel. If Aqsa did rebel and was killed by her father and brother, the penalty for this "honour killing" would probably have been minimal, depending on the region of Pakistan in which they lived.

Pluralistic enthusiasts assume that knowledge of the "other" will inspire understanding and mutual respect. But surely not all "otherness" can be granted acceptance and recognition. Canadians are not and should not be open to the otherness of Omar's mother or Aqsa's father. I am not suggesting that we should send people like them back to their countries of origin, or that we should admit only immigrants with the "right attitudes." But we can show great disapprobation for certain attitudes and insist that immigrant children go to Canadian public schools where the hijab is prohibited and where religious martyrdom of every variety – including Christian terrorism that goes by the name of "militias" in the United States – is censured and ridiculed. It is simply unfair to tell immigrants that they should preserve their cultural values and impose them on their children by whatever means they see fit, and then to turn against them and their children with fear and suspicion when the results are not what we expected. This is the plight of the Khadr and Parvez families.

When groups are encouraged to preserve their cultural practices in Canada, we should not be surprised to find them imposing these practices on their children with disastrous results. It is no wonder that the founder of the Muslim Canadian Congress, Tarek Fatah, has been calling on Canada to ban the hijab.[8] But he is a voice in the wilderness. Those who are convinced of the nurturing character of group identity prefer to listen to the self-appointed "leaders of the community," even when they are religious bigots.

Kymlicka's confidence that nothing is to be feared from group rights not only assumes that individuals have access to exit ramps; it also presupposes that a robust and vigorous liberal society will always be there to embrace individual refugees escaping their group oppressions. But this reality is by no means assured. As religious and ethnic communities proliferate, liberal society will naturally retreat. In the Bouchard-Taylor report on "mutual accommodation," we encounter a society devoid of a robust liberal centre – a society in which liberal values have no primacy, a society composed only of a multiplicity of groups characterized by a "deep diversity" and engaged in endless negotiations regarding their rightful place in public institutions and spaces such as hospitals, schools, and universities. The report is both a window into the multiculturalism that has taken shape in Canada and the new liberalism that inspired it:

> In any society in which two or more cultures intermingle, the question of the management of diversity inevitably arises, and it has ever been thus. Until recently, it was usually resolved in an authoritarian manner: one more powerful culture attempted

> either to dominate the others or to *eliminate them through assimilation* … Mentalities and legislation have changed in recent decades … Democratic nations are displaying greater respect for diversity and are adopting methods of managing co-existence based on an ideal of inter-cultural harmonization. This ideal is permeating national cultures … harmonization measures are part of the day-to-day life of public institutions such as health establishments, schools, and universities.[9]

In the language of the report, "assimilation" is identified with "authoritarianism" and "domination." This new liberalism is not satisfied with being open to immigrants from foreign lands, allowing them to share equally in Canadian society, giving them equal opportunities to work and thrive in Canada, and providing them with equal protection under the law. This liberal generosity is dismissed as authoritarian domination. The assumption is that real openness is not openness to persons or individuals but to groups, their cultures, and their "otherness." It is fair to say that as a highly esteemed philosopher, Charles Taylor has been an active and successful promoter of the new liberal paradigm.[10]

The Bouchard-Taylor report encourages Canadians to embark on a dramatic journey into the unknown. But for immigrants who grew up in a society where people are divided into clearly demarcated groups defined by religion, the new Canada looks less like a new adventure than something old and dreadfully familiar. The new liberalism resembles the millet system invented by the Ottomans whereby religious communities lived according to their own laws and customs especially where marriage, divorce, child custody, and the like were involved. This system allowed Christian, Muslim, and Jewish communities to live autonomously and therefore avoid conflict; meanwhile, the state attended to foreign policy and wars of conquest, to building roads, and constructing magnificent palaces for the sultan and his harem.

There is no doubt that the millet system was a great advance over the Dark Ages of the West where the Catholic Inquisition was busy inventing fresh horrors in search of an elusive religious conformity of hearts and minds. But the Canadian situation is different. Unlike the Ottoman case, the society described by Bouchard and Taylor is not a collection of autonomous groups, but an *intercultural* state. The full import of this is not totally clear. But as the report indicates, the groups within the society are neither insulated from one another nor totally autonomous. On the contrary, they are perpetually engaged in negotiating their place within a common public realm. The Quebec Charter of Human Rights and Freedoms grants them the right to make all sorts of demands on the public purse, even when these demands require "deferential" treatment – a practice defended by the report.[11] For example, Jews and Muslims must be released from work if they are to celebrate their religious holidays as Christians do. The report insists that these extra days off work do not constitute special privileges or "preferential" treatment. Its authors maintain that different people must be treated differently if fairness is to be attained. Since the intercultural state is also a welfare state, the state will find itself having to decide which demands are "reasonable." For example, the report suggests that if freedom of religion is to be taken seriously, then the state must provide "chapels in detention centers."[12] This transforms the freedom of religion from a negative right requiring only non-interference by the state, into a positive right requiring the state to provide facilities to enhance the activity involved.[13]

The examples show that far from making the groups autonomous – that's how the Ottomans maintained peace – the new liberalism brings them into constant negotiation with one another – negotiation that may be the source of conflict and mutual resentment. What emerges from the report is a picture of a society where almost nothing is settled, nothing is taken for granted, nothing is easily and casually shared, and everything is a locus of contention, so that life is an endless power struggle. There are some minimal norms such as the preservation of the French language, but one gets the feeling that recognition of the most minimal norms is begrudging and that the excluded languages may not accept their subordination for long.

I would like to make three observations about the new liberal paradigm. First, it seems to me that it involves a confusion of domestic policy with foreign policy. But what is appropriate for foreign policy is not appropriate for domestic policy. When it comes to foreign policy, we should be modest enough to recognize that we do not own the world.[14] We should leave strange people in strange lands to live as they please. We have no right to bomb them because we don't like their burqas. We have no right to invade their countries, heap contempt on their religion, send missionaries to convert them, and privatize their oil companies. Diplomacy requires humility and openness to "otherness" in quest of some minimal common ground or some basis of mutual recognition. When the latter proves unattainable, a hypocritical display of mutual respect is still useful – it allows us to deal with foreigners on a basis other than violence. This humility vis-à-vis the world is a lesson that has been lost on liberalism. As a result, it is now forced to pay penance by announcing its new multicultural philosophy to the world, a philosophy that is nothing short of liberal self-annihilation. It is not just a matter of saying to the world, "Come as you are and do as you please."[15] It says, "Come as you are, then apply for government funding to preserve and promote your religion and culture even if they are at odds with the liberal culture of Canada, since the latter has no status whatsoever." In the new multiculturalism, all the cultures that make up the rainbow are to be preserved, but the liberal culture is singled out for annihilation. Yet without the liberal values of freedom, tolerance, limited government, and the rule of law, the multicultural edifice will collapse into sectarian conflict, or even civil war. In short, defending our liberal culture at home and imposing it on the world are entirely different matters that should not be confused.

Second, the infiltration of communitarian principles into the heart of Canadian liberalism has made it easy for illiberal forces in the new Conservative Party of Canada to take advantage of the weakened state of Canadian liberalism. The old Progressive Conservative Party was committed to Canadian liberalism, but the new Conservative Party has a socially conservative agenda inspired by religious fundamentalism. Stephen Harper has vowed to transform Canada into a country that his liberal opponents "will not recognize." His strategy is to unite a plurality of religious groups – Jews, Christians, Muslims, Hindus, and Sikhs – behind a socially conservative agenda in opposition to secular liberal society. The Conservative Party is enticing immigrants into thinking that instead of coming to Canada to enjoy the freedom that it has to offer, they can remake Canada in their own image. As more immigrants are seduced by the prospect of transforming Canada, the basis of the immigrant engagement with Canada will be transformed, and the demise of Canadian liberalism will be imminent.

That demise will be perilous for Canada. As history has shown, religion is not satisfied with freedom; it seeks dominance. In the absence of the liberal basis on which a plurality of religions can coexist in the private sphere, the religious conflicts of the past are likely to be rekindled.

Third, another problem with the new liberalism and its corresponding multiculturalism is that the preservation of identity has replaced the development of character. The difference between character and identity is critical. Whereas character belongs to persons qua individuals, identity belongs to persons qua members of a group. Since identity is a function of one's birth, ethnicity, and language, it is given and inescapable. In contrast, character is developed or cultivated. This is not to say that parents, schools, and communities play no role in the development of character; nevertheless, character belongs only to individuals, who have the sole responsibility for their characters. In other words, the acquisition of identity is passive, whereas the cultivation of character is an active achievement.

In replacing the primacy of character with that of identity, something important is lost. When individuals are defined by their group identity, individual responsibility is lost. The transgressions of individuals implicate their entire community. No one described this dreadful state of affairs more accurately than Anne Frank.[16] Why is it, she asked, that when a gentile commits a crime, only he or she is guilty, but when a Jew commits a crime, then all the Jews of the world are guilty? The primacy of identity over character highlights the concept of collective guilt, where the crime of one or a few individuals implicates the whole group. The burden of identity and "identity politics" may be inescapable in a multicultural society. But the new liberalism aggravates the perils of multicultural societies – especially for a child such as Omar Khadr who has become a prisoner of his identity. In short, the new Canadian multiculturalism is perilous to both Canada and its immigrants.

NOTES

1 David J. Elkins, "The Sense of Place," in *Small Worlds: Provinces and Parties in Canadian Political Life*, edited by David J. Elkins and Richard Simeon (Toronto: Methuen, 1980), 1–30.

2 Neil Bissoondath, *Selling Illusions: The Cult of Multiculturalism in Canada* (Toronto: Penguin Books, 1995).

3 See for example, Ali Ibn Abi Talib School, established in 1991, http://www.ecoleali.com/francais/english.htm (accessed 18 January 2011).
4 Gérard Bouchard and Charles Taylor, *Building the Future: A Time for Reconciliation, Abridged Final Report* (Quebec: Consultation Commission on Accommodation Practices Related to Cultural Differences, 2008), http://www.accommodements.qc.ca/documentation/rapports/rapport-final-abrege-enpdf. All references are to the English edition of the abridged report.
5 Will Kymlicka, *Liberalism, Community and Culture* (Oxford: Oxford University Press, 1991).
6 All he could do to cope with his distress in his early youth was to perfect the expletives of Captain Haddock of *The Adventures of Tintin*: "Oh, billions of bilious blue blistering barnacles!" Thanks to the captain, Omar avoided the capital crime of using the name of the lord in vain, which would have augmented his troubles (Michelle Shephard, *Guantanamo's Child: The Untold Story of Omar Khadr*.
7 "The Khadr Family," CTV *News*, 12 January 2006, http://www.ctv.ca/CTVNews/Specials/20060110/omar_khadr_background_061001/ (accessed 18 January 2011).
8 Tarek Fatah, "It's No Sin to Shun the Hijab," *Globe and Mail*, 17 December 2007. Fatah is also author of *Chasing a Mirage: The Tragic Illusion of an Islamic State* (Mississauga: John Wiley, 2008) and *The Jew Is Not My Enemy: Unveiling the Myths That Fuel Muslim Anti-Semitism* (Toronto: McClelland & Stewart, 2010).
9 Bouchard and Taylor, *Building the Future*, 23 (my italics).
10 See his most recent work, *A Secular Age* (Cambridge: Harvard University Press, 2007).
11 The report defends the practice by distinguishing between "deferential" and "preferential" treatment on the grounds that "rigour in the application of legislation and regulations is not always synonymous with fairness" (25).
12 Ibid.
13 I am using the distinction between positive and negative liberty that was made popular by Isaiah Berlin in "Two Concepts of Liberty," in *Four Essays on Liberty* (New York: Oxford University Press, 1969).
14 See Noam Chomsky, "We Own the World," *Z Magazine*, 1 January 2008.
15 This is Bissoondath's formulation in his brilliant work, *Selling Illusions*.
16 Anne Frank (1929–1945), *Diary of a Young Girl*, trans. from the Dutch by B.M. Mooyaart (New York: Doubleday, 1967).

Omar Khadr as Canadian Icon

RICK SALUTIN

We don't do well with heroes. I speak as someone who has spent part of a writing life dealing with Canadian heroes, some sung and some un: William Lyon Mackenzie, Rocket Richard, labour leader Kent Rowley. My experience is that you start out with laudatory intentions and almost always revert to irony or some form of self-subversion; it's in the national gene pool. Perhaps it comes from seeing from the outside (and just to the south) how ludicrous and self-deluding most attempts at creating national heroes can be. I think the rest of the world is joining us in this reluctance about heroes; it's hard to maintain them in their heroic state under current conditions. Think of Barack Obama.

Icons are different. They're neither praiseworthy nor blameworthy. They tell you a lot about yourself, or the collective self you're part of. Don Cherry is a Canadian icon, though I don't much like what he represents. But there are parts of each of us which we probably aren't very comfortable with. It's not bad to get acquainted with those and think about how you want to deal with them.

I think Omar Khadr is also iconic. This is so, first of all, because he is from an immigrant family, but of a particular set: those who had a harder time than most in coming here, and in integrating once here. This has been especially true for Muslims since 9/11. He belongs to what could be called the new blacks, or the new Jews.

Canada was a terminus of the Underground Railroad from the southern US slave states in the nineteenth century. Ontario, in its early guise as Upper Canada, was the first place in the British Empire to outlaw slavery. Canada became this kind of, er, Mecca, for many groups over the years. In Auschwitz, the least deathly section of the camp, where inmates had at least a slim chance at surviving, was called Canada. When I was in Poland during the 1980s, people still said about someone who had a stroke of luck or acquired sudden wealth, "He got Canada."

For part of official Canada, even in the late 1930s, "none" was "too many" when it came to Jewish immigrants and refugees. Yet the Canadian Jewish community made its way to enormous success in a short time. There is nothing official about the shards of anti-Semitism that remain. It makes more sense to talk about a "new anti-Semitism," directed toward the Muslim population, in terms of its extent, effect, and the role of mainstream voices in it.

I don't mean the cases are the same; nothing ever is. But they illuminate each other and indicate underlying currents. They help to create a sort of national profile in motion. This is more useful than drawing up a table of "Canadian values," of the sort politicians invoke. Such values pretend to a kind of permanence. In reality they're always shifting. Slavery was once permitted; then it wasn't. Jews were pariahs; now they're not. Muslims are vilified or feared; that may change. There are also counterforces. Everything is always in motion; it can go backwards or forwards; it rarely idles. Even medicare, the archetypal Canadian value, was once derided as unCanadian, and not very long ago.

Icons personalize these grand, unstable forces. Individuals become iconic because of larger needs in their society, but the mantle settles on them as particular cases with their own traits. Don Cherry fills certain needs in certain sectors of our society, but he does it his way. What about Omar Khadr?

He is accused of being a "terrorist"; he was arrested in combat during the invasion of Afghanistan. But he was a kid when it happened. So he engages our attention and anxieties in a complex, conflicted way. The anxieties have to do with fear of the jihadist threat, but also fear about what that fear can do to some of the humane bedrocks of our own society. The way a society treats its children is always the best indicator of its own moral level. June Callwood often said we are a society that hates its kids, but June was a part of Canada and worked to change it, to change the profile. It's the dynamic that's crucial.

Omar Khadr is a survivor. Survival is a primal Canadian theme, if you take Margaret Atwood's theory of Canadian literature seriously. He was tortured, broke under it, and survived. He told the military tribunal in Guantánamo that he'd fired his lawyers. When the tribunal pressed him about this, he said, "If I was in a formal court, I wouldn't be doing this." Asked by the judge if he'd ever studied law, he said, "This is a military commission. You don't need to study the law." When the judge asked about his education for this task, he said: "Five years in the military commissions." He'd begun by reading a handwritten statement. He sounded even more articulate in the dialogue with the court on his feet than in the statement he read. The accounts are a little disjointed, and the parties seem to talk past each other, but Khadr gave as good as he got. It's as if something positive happened during the awful years of incarceration and he'd begun to take possession of his fate. That would make him a kind of survivor-plus, which is how we'd like to think of ourselves. Subsequently he pleaded guilty and "confessed" to the murder he'd been charged with. This was part of the plea bargain that may let him return to Canada eventually.

What else do we know? He wrote in a letter that he wants to be useful and help people. Is that implausible? When I was a student in the United States during the 1960s, I knew many people who went into the "weather underground" to lead a violent revolution there. Some of them were involved in violent acts. They were arrested, or surrendered, served time in prison, then were released and in most cases led useful, socially committed lives. Now they're starting to retire and sitting around the pool in Arizona. As you get older, the crazy parts, or the parts you imbibed from influential others, have less hold on you. Khadr said in his written statement, "I have been used many times when I was a child and that's why I'm here taking blame and paying for things I didn't have a chance in doing but was told to do by elders."

As for what actually happened in Afghanistan, the only person who will ever know with certainty – which is often true in such cases – is Omar Khadr.

There is one other element. I was recently in Finland to learn about their remarkable program of reform in public education. It was entirely motivated by the desire for social justice and equality in their school system. But this desire was in turn motivated by their sense that they are a small country, with few resources, and they require the maximum contribution from all their members if they are to thrive. We too are a northern country with a relatively small population compared to our land mass. In our case, unlike Finland, we've always built up our numbers through immigration. We often speak of being a land of immigrants, implying the country has done *them* a favour. But Canada needs its immigrants. This too is a matter of survival. We are guilty of sloppy thinking if we believe we can count out large numbers of potentially productive, ambitious, imaginative, and conscientious people. Everyone counts, if they want to contribute. Omar Khadr is a case at the limit. He tests the proposition. This too makes him iconic.

Afterword: The Mark of Torture

SHERENE H. RAZACK

This anthology has a story of torture on virtually every page: a snippet of a poem by Sudanese journalist Sami al Hajj who was tortured at Bagram; Jean Eméry's recollection of torture in a Nazi concentration camp; Maher Arar's torture in a Syrian prison; tortured Canadians Abdelrazik, Almalki, and El Maati; the Afghan detainees we released to their Afghan torturers with impunity; and, not least, Omar Khadr, detained as a child of fifteen, tortured first at the infamous Bagram prison in Afghanistan and subsequently at Guantánamo. Torture "leaves an indelible mark – not only on the victim but on the torturer."[1] Torturers reject the humanity of those they have tortured and derive satisfaction from the exclusion, a satisfaction that continues as long as the tortured remain alive. When torture is sanctioned, the mark that torture leaves spreads to all members of society.[2] When we know that torture is practised in our name, Tzvetan Todorov writes, and we do nothing to put an end to it, we too participate in the torturer's world. Legally and socially sanctioned torture invites us all into a world that is "colour-lined," a world in which there are humans and subhumans, the latter distinguished by a racial mark.[3]

What mark has the torture of Omar Khadr left on us, those of us who come from the country of his torturers and who acquiesced in his torture by others? The book's contributors, myself included, struggle with the mark that all this torture has left on us. Many of us are haunted by what was done in our name. "How can we stand the sight of what we have done?" Kim Echlin, one of the contributors, asks Canadians. Our anguish, perhaps our guilt, is on every page. When Omar Khadr crosses our minds, our hearts grow heavy and we feel anxious. It is tempting under such circumstances to indulge ourselves in outrage, grief, pathos, a too-easy identification – in short, anything to shield us from the possibility that we have not done enough to put an end to what happened to Omar Khadr.

Janice Williamson, the editor of this collection, explains that her decision to include a variety of literary forms was a deliberate one. Poems, plays, imaginative and academic essays "invite us to see patterns and connection through history and between cultures." It is certain that the creative chapters do just that – more so, perhaps, than the academic essays where there is no easy place for powerful feeling to reside. The creative works and the academic essays together offer multiple paths to accountability, but they also offer multiple narrative shields, ways of protecting ourselves from the things about Omar Khadr's story that we cannot bear to know. When is a narrative about Omar Khadr a path to accountability, and when is it a shield that deflects it? Rather than assess each contribution to this collection in this regard, I offer in this afterword a few broad reflections on the theme of accountability and the role that narrative plays in shaping our moral responses to torture.

How is the moral community that accepts torture created and maintained? By what discursive and representational means, including myth-making, does torture become acceptable in a democracy? How do we come to avert our eyes (in Todorov's words) when we hear that torture has been done in our names?[4] It is through the stories we tell ourselves about torture that we come to make sense of something senseless. We block torture from penetrating our consciousness, Elaine Scarry observes, when we hear enough stories about its necessity.[5] Jamie Mayerfield shows, for example, the power of the ticking bomb story of torture (torturing a suspect will yield vital information about acts of violence that are about to happen) in shaping contemporary morality, in spite of the fact that such a scenario has never occurred.[6] The more we hear about ticking bombs that will explode unless a captured terrorist tells us the bomb's location, the readier we are to accept torture. After all, one torture victim is a small price to pay for saving the lives of many.

When reflecting on the role of narrative in shaping moral attitudes to torture, it is useful to remember that torture itself is a narrative. It is a narrative of power written on the body[7] and on the social body.[8] Torture teaches us who is a part of the human community and who is not. The tortured learn that they are not human, and we, who only come to know of torture through the story of it, are taught who counts and who does not, who is in the nation and who is not. Marnia Lasreg, writing of the torture of Algerians by the French during the Algerian war of independence, stresses that torture provided a source of social integration; the French were bound together affectively as a nation through the shared story of Algerian terrorists whose torture was necessary for the security of France.[9]

A study of narratives of torture can reveal a great deal about the systems that put torture into practice; it can illuminate how torture comes to find a place within democratic systems and in the hearts and minds of people who believe that they are committed to the equality and dignity of all humankind. We can begin by asking what does torture *do*? How does it enable us to become particular kinds of people, particular kinds of national subjects? Who is the subject who thinks that torture is okay? In this collection, Judith Thompson offers brilliant insight into the psyche of the *Canadian* subject who manages to live with torture through narratives that shield her character from seeing its horror. In her one-act play, *Nail Biter*, David, a thirty-year-old CSIS agent who has interrogated Omar Khadr at Guantánamo, reviews the videotape of the interrogation (a videotape that the Supreme Court of Canada, in a moment of sanity, ordered the government to release). David lives with his role as torturer by encasing himself in stories that prevent him from seeing the child whom he tortured. He remembers his own childhood as an awkward, insecure child, and his continuing fear and worry. The bitten-down nails remind him "you are STILL a nervous wreck of a human being, a bit of a joke." He wants so badly to be a man – not just any man, but the kind of man who is like an American intelligence officer in full uniform, "the star of the football team." Thompson suggests that the nail biter is Canada, the Canada that I once wrote about as anxious to prove itself as a grownup nation through participating in wars and peacekeeping ventures.[10] Like David in Thompson's play, Canada will do anything to become (in Robertson Davies's words) the "hero's friend" on the world stage. David tells himself the story of America's power, and Canada's powerlessness, and lets himself off the hook for torture by describing the star footballer's allure: "An American intell officer, in full uniform? Can you say incandescent? It's like being the high school outcast and running smack into the star of the football team you can feel yourself visibly shrinking and blushing like a Southern belle. You just want to say yes sir can I please shine your shoes or get you a coffee." We believed the Americans when they said that Omar was not tortured. Omar looked okay. Omar was even having a good time, "like a kid at Christmas" when he saw Canadian agents and they gave him a Big Mac, a Coke, and a Kit-Kat. Such stories insulate David, and they insulate us as Canadians. David tries hard to block out the kid crying for his mother, insisting that Omar was really only acting.

What are the collective stories that block the cries and moans of a fifteen-year-old child? Thompson reminds us that we seek solace in the story of our national powerlessness. We also circulate stories about Omar Khadr's family as the first family of terrorism, reminding ourselves that there is good reason to treat Omar so badly. After all, he came from very bad stock. Race helps these endeavours along. We say that Muslims fail to integrate and that they bring their misogynist traditions into the country, undermining the purity of Canadian values. With images of dangerous Muslim men and imperilled Muslim women filling our heads, it gets harder to separate fact from fantasy, victim from torturer. We come to believe in a version of the story of the ticking bomb through race: torturing Omar Khadr and others will keep the nation safe from barbaric Muslims who are out to destroy us.

There is so much at stake in this racial story of barbaric Muslims and civilized Europeans. The stories we tell to insulate us from the moral challenge that torture presents operate as a kind of shorthand for conveying our innocence and civility and Muslim guilt and barbarism. Many Canadians have chosen to believe, for example, that we failed to protect Omar's rights as a child soldier because we remembered our mistake in the 1990s when Jean Chrétien interceded on the senior Khadr's behalf with the Pakistani authorities who had detained him on suspicion of working to fund a terrorist group that successfully bombed the Egyptian embassy in Islamabad on 19 November 1995. Ahmed Said Khadr turned out to be a terrorist after all, a close friend of Osama bin Laden. It is reasonable, we tell ourselves, to be suspicious of the son, as we ought to have been about the father. Was there really a "Khadr effect"? Gar Pardy, the diplomat actively engaged in events involving the Khadr family from 1995 to 2003, cautions us to critically interrogate the stuff that myths are made of. Pardy is sceptical of the "Khadr effect" as the reason for our inaction on Omar. He comments that Chrétien only did what was (or used to be) normal for a government to do: ask that one of its nationals be given a fair trial. Further, prominent Canadians and organizations, including the Canadian Arab Federation, the Jewish Civil Rights Educational Foundation of Canada, and the Canadian-Muslim Civil Liberties Association, had all lobbied on Ahmed Khadr's behalf. The foundation for which he worked, Human Concern International, also supported him. If the Pakistanis really believed that he had been involved in the bombing of the Egyptian embassy, they would have immediately shipped him off to Egypt, Pardy writes. In effect, many factors were at work that are not alluded to when we subscribe to the story that the Canadian government was duped by Ahmed Khadr and that we would later take it out on the son, Omar.

The government's own hands are not clean. Human Concern International complained to the Security Intelligence Review Committee that CSIS made a false statement in Federal Court that the senior Khadr had used HCI to funnel money for terrorist purposes. In its 2006–07 report, SIRC recommended that CSIS formally retract this statement. Even the *National Post*, known for its ideological anti-Muslim bent, published an apology to HCI for alleging that Khadr had funnelled funds to terrorists. Pardy notes these details in order to remind us of the many levels of myth-making. If the Khadrs have become the symbol of evil, an evil that only torture will help to defeat, then we are a part of the story. Certainly we knew early on that a fifteen-year-old Canadian national had been shipped to Guantánamo, and we were well informed of his medical condition and of coercive interrogations methods. No easy stories about the Khadr effect can explain why we let it all happen as it did. As Audrey Macklin relates in her essay, when she offered the story of the Khadr effect to a US colleague, that colleague, familiar with the story, nevertheless pressed her, "Yes, but why isn't anyone in Canada doing anything about Omar Khadr?" This indeed is the proper question, and the one that we should keep asking.

If torture becomes acceptable to us through the stories we circulate, we must interrogate the historical, political contexts in which such stories thrive. As Marina Nemat so eloquently puts it in her essay, "Hoping for Omar Khadr," horror doesn't happen overnight. Recalling her own torture in 1982 in Iran as a sixteen-year-old in Evin Prison, she reminds us that there were danger signs then as now. The invasion of Iraq based on lies, the deportation of Muslims without due process: these are signposts on the road to torture. If we can so readily abandon political accountability, truth, and the rule of law, then torture is not far behind.

What are the signs that horror has long been on its way and that torture has become so common that it is banal? Several contributors devote their attention to the law, arguing that the road that takes us to Omar Khadr at Guantánamo is paved with legal procedures. Authors describe the state of exception, the suspension of the law that is accomplished through law itself: trials, for example, where those accused do not have the right to see the evidence held against them. It is this paradox that prompts Giorgio Agamben to define the state of exception as the force of law without law, and to draw a line through the word law.[11]

Spaces of law without law (black sites or secret CIA prisons, Guantánamo, Abu Ghraib, detention hearings of Canadians held as possible security threats), dramatic though they are, operate in a thousand ordinary ways. Audrey Macklin perfectly captures their banality in her chapter when she describes Omar Khadr's "trials" as she experienced them as a lawyer. You gut the rule of law and deny people fundamental rights in a nice, orderly manner. It is through extremely civilized courtroom procedures and rules, Macklin observes, that Omar is rendered without the right to have rights. A hearing at Guantánamo "is not a normal trial." It is a place where you can listen to a torturer testify about how he tortured Omar, but in Guantánamo it is not the torturer who is on trial but the victim. When we look for signs of the horror, we should track these ordinary, "civil" moments when something decidedly uncivil happens.

The law, as contributors remind us, is not behaving as it should. Grace Woo's chapter explores how it came to be that the Supreme Court of Canada reversed a Federal Court order requiring the prime minister to seek Omar Khadr's repatriation. How did Canada become a country that violates the rights of the child and condones torture, in contravention of international law? Were we always like this? (It is instructive to recall residential schools and Aboriginal children whose bodies are still turning up in lakes and fields of snow.) Looking for the answer in the Supreme Court's decision not to order Omar's repatriation, Woo finds an incoherent, poorly reasoned judgment that is full of misconceptions. Conceding that its role is to establish the legal framework with which executive decisions are made, and even acknowledging that it can give specific directions to the executive branch in matters of foreign policy, the Supreme Court nonetheless concluded that it could not order Omar Khadr's repatriation because courts should not interfere with executive prerogative.

What enables incoherence and contradiction to thrive in law? The answer may be found in how narratives of torture travel between the domains of law, politics, and academic and popular culture, and between geographic spaces. In some Canadian university classrooms, students are being asked to read journalist Stewart Bell's book *The Martyr's Oath*. Bell argues that Islamic extremists have a peculiar psyche, that their violence does not emerge from historical, political, and social contexts. Elsewhere I have argued that writers such as Bell rely on racism to give their arguments substance, believing, for instance, that Muslims are predisposed to violence.[12] A similar logic to Bell's is evident in the testimony of the forensic psychiatrists at Guantánamo who testified that Omar Khadr remains a security threat because jihadists are seldom repentant; fanaticism is in their nature. The story that Bell and others circulate about the Muslim psyche is one that informs Canadian judicial responses to Muslim men who are detained on suspicion of terrorism. In detention hearings, Muslims are asked how many times a day they pray. The wrong answer can lead to deportation on the ground of being an Islamic extremist who is a threat to Canada.[13] In security certificate hearings, the government alleges that Muslim men who have a particular profile described as an Islamic extremist have an innate propensity for violence and must therefore be deported or detained indefinitely. The profile suffices as proof of intent to commit terrorist acts.[14]

One of the best responses we can have to the racist logic that underpins so many narratives about torture and terrorism is to ask obvious questions about the humanity of the tortured and about the operation of the rule of law. What are the rights of Omar Khadr as a child, a citizen, and as a human being? How should Canadians abroad be treated by their governments, Nathalie Des Rosiers, counsel for the Canadian Civil Liberties Union, asks in her essay on the transfer of prisoners, answering that we all should have an equal right to our government's protection and to the protection of the law. Is there a pattern of racism visible in the list of names of who is tortured and who the government will protect, as Robert Diab and Alnoor Gova suggest in this volume? Many in this collection ask pointedly: Is torture now acceptable?

This collection includes excerpts from the script for *You Don't Like the Truth: 4 Days inside Guantánamo*, the documentary made by Luc Côté and Patricio Henriquez based on the videotape of then sixteen-year-old Omar Khadr's interrogation by CSIS at Guantánamo. If there is any marker for the Canada of the twenty-first century, it is surely those four days. Torture is now authorized. As Patricio Henriquez baldly puts it, in the videotape of the interrogation we get to see "a child cracking under unbearable psychological pressure."

This is our Canada. We have responded with fear, shame, grief, outrage, and horror. But at the end of the day, we can't stay on these emotional planes, indulging in shared pain. We need to unfreeze ourselves and confront the horror. In this endeavour, it is useful to begin by feeling shock and outrage, as Nate Whitling did on learning that the Liberal government in 2004 continued to reassure Canadians that Omar Khadr was not ill treated, all the while receiving US confirmation that he had been subjected to severe sleep deprivation. But this is only the beginning. Arlette Zinck, an Edmonton based educator, re-established some of Omar's humanity by sending him lesson plans so that he could educate himself. Dennis Edney and Nate Whitling, Omar's long-time lawyers who worked pro bono, kept insisting on the rule of law wherever they could find a forum to do so. Omar himself offered stunning examples of his own humanity, defiantly telling his interrogators that they themselves could not withstand a day in a cell in isolation.

Hasnain Khan writes in this collection that he said nothing to the gentleman who upon approaching him in the bookstore – perhaps presuming that Hasnain was Muslim – denounced Omar Khadr and Muslims. In reflecting and writing about this encounter, Hasnain retrieves a moment of resistance. He finally speaks back here in writing, interrupting the circulation of narratives about Muslims as terrorists.

These are actions making punctures in the story that torture is acceptable, undermining the idea of humans and subhumans. We must challenge the story that is torture, a story that is "colour lined," in law, politics, popular culture, and everyday encounters.

Todorov ends his own challenge with the observation that torture is a cancer that can metastasize, spreading through the social body even among those who thought themselves immune.[15]

What is at stake is everyone's humanity.

NOTES

The author thanks Leslie Thielen Wilson for the conversations that shaped this afterword.

1 Tzvetan Todorov, *Torture and the War on Terror* (London: Seagull Books, 2009), 60.

2 Ibid., 60–1.

3 Sherene Razack, *Casting Out: The Eviction of Muslims from Western Law and Politics* (Toronto: University of Toronto Press, 2008).

4 Todorov, *Torture*, 61.

5 Elaine Scarry, *The Body in Pain: The Making and Unmaking of the World* (New York: Oxford University Press, 1985).

6 Jamie Mayerfield, "In Defense of the Absolute Prohibition of Torture," *Public Affairs Quarterly* 22, no. 2 (April 2008): 111–30.

7 Scarry, *Body in Pain.*

8 Michael Taussig, *Shamanism, Colonialism, and the Wild Man: A Study in Terror and Healing* (Chicago: University of Chicago Press, 1987); Marnia Lasreg, *Torture and the Twilight of Empire: From Algiers to Baghdad* (Princeton and Oxford: Princeton University Press, 2008).

9 Lasreg, *Torture and the Twilight of Empire.*

10 Razack, *Dark Threats and White Knights: The Somalia Affair, Peacekeeping and the New Imperialism* (Toronto: University of Toronto Press, 2004).

11 Giorgio Agamben, *State of Exception*, trans. Kevin Attell (Chicago: University of Chicago Press, 2005): 39.

12 Razack, *Casting Out*, 48.

13 Razack, "The Camp: A Place Where Law Has Declared That the Rule of Law Does Not Operate," *Public* 36 (Fall 2007): 109–20.

14 Razack, *Casting Out.*

15 Todorov, *Torture,* 61.

Contributors

MAHER ARAR, a telecommunications engineer, is a passionate advocate of human rights. He recently founded *Prism* (www.prism-magazine.com), an online not-for-profit magazine that focuses on national security related issues. A victim of "extraordinary rendition" in 2002, he was detained in the United States and deported to Syria, where he was imprisoned and tortured for over a year. In January 2007, a lengthy Canadian commission of inquiry cleared him of any links to terrorism. The Government of Canada offered an official apology and awarded compensation for the "terrible ordeal" he and his family suffered. The Syrian government has declared that Arar is "completely innocent." In spite of this, the US government did not exonerate him and he and his family remain on a watch list. *Time* magazine chose Maher as the 2004 "Canadian Newsmaker of the Year" and three years later named him one of the one hundred most influential people in the world. The *Globe and Mail* called him "the Nation Builder" in 2006. Maher contributes to various publications including the *Globe and Mail*, the *Guardian*, and the *Huffington Post* on issues of national and human security.

GEORGE ELLIOTT CLARKE is the inaugural E.J. Pratt Professor of Canadian Literature at the University of Toronto. A poet, playwright, screenwriter, novelist, and essayist, his scholarship and his writing have won him numerous awards, including a Trudeau Foundation Fellowship, a Governor General's Award for Poetry, appointments to the Order of Canada and the Order of Nova Scotia, and eight honorary doctorates.

LUC CÔTÉ has been directing and producing films for the past thirty-five years. He has travelled extensively around the world, making social documentaries that capture the human spirit. He has co-directed over thirty documentaries, including the award-winning *Turning Sixteen* and *Crash Landing*. He collaborated with Patricio Henriquez in writing, directing, filming, and producing *You Don't Like the Truth – 4 Days inside Guantánamo*, a documentary based on security-camera footage from the Guantánamo Bay prison.

THE HONOURABLE ROMÉO A. DALLAIRE is a Canadian senator who had a distinguished career in the Canadian Forces, achieving the rank of lieutenant-general. In 1994, General Dallaire commanded the United Nations Assistance Mission for Rwanda (UNAMIR). His book on his experiences, *Shake Hands with the Devil: The Failure of Humanity in Rwanda*, was awarded the Governor General's Literary Award for Non-Fiction. Since his retirement from the military, he has worked to bring an understanding of post-traumatic stress disorder to the general public. He has published and advocated on behalf of conflict resolution and worked to eradicate the use of children as weapons of war – the subject of his most recent book, *They Fight Like Soldiers, They Die Like Children.*

GAIL DAVIDSON, a lawyer, is the executive director of Lawyer's Rights Watch Canada, an organization she founded in 2001. She also co-founded Lawyers Against the War (LAW), an international committee of jurists residing in ten countries who oppose war against Iraq and promote adherence to international law. She publishes articles about international humanitarian law.

NATHALIE DES ROSIERS is general counsel for the Canadian Civil Liberties Association. She was dean of the Faculty of Law, Civil Law Section, University of Ottawa, from 2004 to 2008 and president of the Law Commission of Canada from 2000 to 2004. From 1987 to 2000, she was a member of the University of Western Ontario's Faculty of Law. She served as law clerk to Supreme Court of Canada Justice Julien Chouinard from 1982 to 1983 and then worked in private practice until 1987. She is the past president of the Canadian Federation of Social Sciences and Humanities and has been active in other organizations.

ROBERT DIAB, a lawyer, is an instructor at Capilano University in North Vancouver and the author of *Guantánamo North: Terrorism and the Administration of Justice in Canada* (2008).

SHADIA DRURY is a Canada Research Chair in Social Justice, a member of the Royal Society of Canada, and professor in the departments of Political Science and Philosophy at the University of Regina. She is a political theorist whose work focuses mainly on the American right and the intersection between religion and politics. Her books include *Aquinas and Modernity: The Lost Promise of Natural Law* (2008), *The Political Ideas of Leo Strauss* (updated edition, 2005), *Terror and Civilization: Christianity, Politics, and the Western Psyche* (2004), *Leo Strauss and the American Right* (1998), and *Alexandre Kojève: The Roots of Postmodern* (1994). She is also an enthusiastic essayist whose articles can be found on the op-ed pages of *Free Inquiry*.

KIM ECHLIN is a novelist, essayist, and teacher and has written and produced television documentaries. Her doctoral thesis was on Ojibway story-telling and she has published a translation from the Sumerian of the Inanna myth. Her most recent novel, *The Disappeared*, is set in Cambodia and Montreal and was published in nineteen countries. It won the Barnes and Noble Best Novel Award in the United States and was nominated for a Giller Prize in Canada. Her most recent non-fiction work on witness, human rights, and literature, *Tell Others*, will be published by Hamish Hamilton, Penguin in 2012.

DENNIS EDNEY, originally from Scotland, is an Edmonton-based lawyer. He and Edmonton lawyer Nate Whitling began defending Omar Khadr on a pro bono basis in 2002. In 2011, nine months after the conclusion of the military tribunal, Omar Khadr released them. Edney has appeared at all levels of court, including the Supreme Court of Canada and the United States Supreme Court. He received the 2008 National Pro Bono Award that acknowledged his long-term commitment to "an unpopular case [as] a testament to the finest traditions of the legal profession ... [It] increased access to justice for one individual ... [and] impacted human rights the world over." In 2009, the lieutenant governor of British Columbia awarded him the Human Rights Medal. Presently a bencher of the Law

Society of Alberta, he lectures extensively throughout North America on legal issues including the rule of law as it relates to the "War on Terror."

CHARLES FORAN has published ten books. His biography of Mordecai Richler, *Mordecai: The Life and Times*, won the Governor General's Award for Non-fiction. He is the current president of PEN Canada.

DEBORAH GORHAM is Distinguished Research Professor of History at Carleton University. She has published numerous articles and books on social history, childhood, education, women intellectuals and activists, and peace, including *Vera Britain: A Feminist Life*. She is now at work on a biography of Marion Dewar.

ALNOOR GOVA, a PhD candidate in the Faculty of Education at UBC-CCFI, studies Canadian politics in the areas of citizenship, multiculturalism, immigration, national security, race, and law. He was commissioned in 2007–08 to conduct a study on racial profiling. A producer/host on Vancouver Co-op Radio CFRO, he also writes political poetry and essays.

PATRICIO HENRIQUEZ, formerly a director for Chilean television, settled in Montreal after the coup d'état against president Salvador Allende in 1973. His work focuses on social injustice around the world and has won over forty national and international awards. From 1980 to 1993 he worked on dozens of stories for Quebec's benchmark international news magazine, *Nord-Sud*. In 1998 he completed the highly acclaimed *The Last Stand of Salvador Allende,* a film on the last day in the life of the Chilean president. The following year he completed *Images of a Dictatorship*, a unique look at life in Chile under Pinochet, another multiple national and international award winner. Since 2000, he has directed and produced several films in the Extremis collection, including a film on a gay community in Mexico, as well as a highly publicized episode on the death penalty, and one on a handful of soldiers who dared to defy military orders and discipline on ethical and moral grounds. In 2008, he completed *Under the Hood: A Voyage into the World of Torture*, a feature-length documentary. He collaborated with Luc Côté on writing directing, filming and producing *You Don't Like the Truth: 4 Days inside Guantánamo*.

YASMIN JIWANI is an associate professor in the Department of Communication Studies at Concordia University, Montreal. Her doctorate in communication studies from Simon Fraser University examined issues of race and representation in Canadian television news. Her recent publications include *Discourses of Denial: Mediations of Race, Gender and Violence*, and an edited collection *Girlhood: Redefining the Limits*. Her work has appeared in *Social Justice*, *Violence against Women*, *Canadian Journal of Communication*, *Journal of Popular Film and Television*, *International Journal of Media and Cultural Politics*, and *Review of Education, Pedagogy and Cultural Studies* and in numerous anthologies. Her research interests include mediations of race, gender, and violence in the context of war stories, reporting of sexual violence and femicide in the press, and representations of women of colour in popular and mainstream media.

HASNAIN KHAN graduated with a BA Honours in political science and English from the University of Alberta. He is completing an MA in political economy of international development at the University of Toronto.

SHEEMA KHAN is the author of the non-fiction collection *Of Hockey and Hijab*. Since 2002, she has been a monthly columnist for the *Globe and Mail*, writing on issues related to Islam and Muslims. She has spoken at numerous NGO conferences and government agencies on issues of security, civil rights, and Muslim cultural practice. She holds an MA in physics, and a PhD in chemical physics, both from Harvard University, along with patents in drug delivery technology. She has served on the board of the Canadian Civil Liberties Association (2004–08) and is the founder of the Canadian Council on American-Islamic Relations (CAIR-CAN) and its former chair (2000–05). She testified as an expert witness on Muslims in Canada before the Commission of Inquiry into the Actions of Canadian Officials in Relation to Maher Arar (Arar Commission) and has appeared before a number of parliamentary committees. She is currently a patent agent in Ottawa.

CRAIG KIELBURGER is a child-labour activist and co-founder of Free the Children foundation and Me to We. He began researching child labour at twelve years of age and since has built over 650 schools and implemented projects in forty-five countries. He has won many awards, including the Nelson Mandela Human Rights Award and the Officer of the Order of Canada.

W. ANDY KNIGHT is chair of the Department of Political Science and professor of international relations at the University of Alberta. He is a fellow of the Royal Society of Canada and has written and edited several books and essays on aspects of multilateralism, global governance, peace, and the United Nations. His most recent books include *Global Politics* (2010) with Tom Keating, and the *Routledge Handbook of the Responsibility to Protect* (2012), with Frazer Egerton.

AUDREY MACKLIN is a professor at the Faculty of Law at the University of Toronto. She holds law degrees from Yale and Toronto and a bachelor of science degree from Alberta. After graduating from Toronto, she served as law clerk to Mme Justice Bertha Wilson at the Supreme Court of Canada. Her teaching areas include criminal law, administrative law, and immigration and refugee law. Her research and writing interests include transnational migration, citizenship, forced migration, feminist and cultural analysis, and human rights. She has published on these subjects in journals and collections of essays such as *The Security of Freedom: Essays on Canada's Anti-Terrorism Bill* and *Engendering Forced Migration.*

MONIA MAZIGH speaks Arabic, French, and English fluently and holds a doctorate in finance from McGill University. She has worked at the University of Ottawa and taught at Thompson Rivers University in Kamloops, British Columbia. In 2004, she ran in the federal election as a candidate for the NDP, gaining the most votes for her riding in the party's history. In 2002 her husband, Maher Arar, was deported to Syria where he was tortured and held without charge for over a year. During that time, Dr Mazigh campaigned vigorously for her husband's release and later fought to re-establish his reputation and sought reparations, which were won along with an apology after a lengthy inquiry in January 2007. Her 2008 memoir *Hope and Despair* documents her ordeal after her husband's arrest and her successful campaign to clear his name. Her first novel, *Mirroirs et mirages* (2011), is published in French and explores the lives of four Muslim women. She lives with her two children and her husband in Ottawa.

JOHN MCCOY is a PhD candidate and sessional lecturer in political science at the University of Alberta. His primary areas of research include multiculturalism, race and racism, and citizenship. His dissertation examines the role of xeno-racism, or "fear of the stranger," in shaping the contemporary state approach to multiculturalism.

MARINA NEMAT is a non-fiction writer and human rights activist. A native of Tehran, she was arrested at the age of sixteen and spent more than two years in Evin, an Iranian political prison, where she was tortured and came very close to execution. She arrived in Canada in 1991 and published her first memoir, *Prisoner of Tehran*, in 2007. It has since been published in twenty-eight other countries and has been a finalist for many literary awards. She received the inaugural Human Dignity Award from the European Parliament and the prestigious Grinzane Prize in Italy. Her second book, *After Tehran: A Life Reclaimed*, was published in 2010.

GAR PARDY worked initially with the Meteorological Service of Canada in Gander, Goose Bay, and Frobisher Bay (now Iqaluit). He joined the Canadian Foreign Service in 1967 and served in India, Kenya, and Washington, DC. He was ambassador to Costa Rica, El Salvador, Honduras, Nicaragua, and Panama. He was director general of the Canadian Consular Service from 1992 to his retirement in 2003. From 1996 to his retirement, he assisted various members of the Khadr family. He now comments on public and foreign policy issues from Ottawa, and his articles appear regularly in the *Ottawa Citizen*, the *Globe and Mail*, *Embassy-Canada's Foreign Policy Newsweekly*, and the online *Prism Magazine*. He is a regular contributor to the CBC, CTV, and Global television networks.

SHEILA PRATT has been covering the Alberta political scene for more than twenty-five years as a columnist, feature writer, and television analyst and commentator. Former managing editor of the *Edmonton Journal*, she is co-author of *Running on Empty: Alberta after the Boom*. She is a regular contributor to *Alberta Views* magazine.

SHERENE RAZACK is professor of sociology and equity studies in education at the Ontario Institute for Studies in Education of the University of Toronto. Her research and teaching interests lie in the area of race and gender issues in the law. Her most recent book is *Casting*

Out: The Eviction of Muslims from Western Law and Politics. She has also published *Dark Threats and White Knights: The Somalia Affair, Peacekeeping and the New Imperialism*, an edited collection *Race, Space and the Law: Unmapping A White Settler Society*, *Looking White People in the Eye: Gender, Race, and Culture in Courtrooms and Classrooms*, and *Canadian Feminism and the Law: The Women's Legal and Education Fund and the Pursuit of Equality*.

RICK SALUTIN is an award-winning playwright, novelist, and journalist. His column appears weekly in the *Toronto Star*.

HEATHER SPEARS, Vancouver-born writer and artist, has lived in Denmark since 1962. She has published fourteen collections of poetry, four novels, and three books of drawings. She has taught drawing all her life; *The Creative Eye* (Arcturus, September 2007) is the first of a series of books on her method. Heather has won the Pat Lowther Memorial Award three times (latest 2002), and the Governor General's Award for Poetry. Her newest collection is *I can still draw* (2008). She specializes in drawing premature infants, and has exhibited widely in Europe and America.

JUDITH THOMPSON, a professor of drama at the University of Guelph, is one of Canada's most esteemed playwrights for stage and radio, as well as a dedicated teacher. Her plays have been produced around the world and she has also written for film and television. An officer of the Order of Canada, she was awarded two Governor General's Awards, an Amnesty International Freedom of Expression Award, and the Chalmers Award. The Walter Carsen Prize for Excellence in the Performing Arts citation describes her as "a Canadian visionary, whose often disturbing work never leaves audiences unmoved." In 2008, she won the American Susan Smith Blackburn Prize, which celebrates outstanding plays in English by women.

LOLA LEMIRE TOSTEVIN is a bilingual writer who was born into a Franco-Ontarian family. She has published seven collections of poetry, three novels, and a collection of literary criticism. Her eighth collection of poems, *Singed Wings*, will appear in 2012. She is presently working on a book of short fiction.

JANICE WILLIAMSON is professor of English and film studies at the University of Alberta. She writes and teaches about Canadian literature and creative writing. Her recent cultural studies concern trauma, mourning, international adoption, and mothering. Her edited books include *Sounding Differences: Seventeen Canadian Women Writers* and *Up and Doing: Canadian Women and Peace* (with Deborah Gorham). She has also written books and short works of prose and poetry in innovative forms, including *Crybaby!* and *Tell Tale Signs*. She has won national poetry and magazine awards.

RICHARD J. WILSON is a professor of law and founding director of the International Human Rights Law Clinic at American University's Washington College of Law. He has lived or consulted in several Latin American countries and has lectured or consulted in the United States, Eastern and Western Europe, and Asia. He has authored articles and co-edited books and written on international law and human rights. His scholarly interests include the globalization of public interest law, the death penalty and international law, the role of the defence in international war crimes trials, and clinical legal education in developing or transitional countries.

GRACE LI XIU WOO, is a legal historian and a member of Lawyers Rights Watch Canada. She studied international law at l'Université de Québec à Montréal and has taught in the Program of Legal Studies for Native People at the University of Saskatchewan. Her study of judicial reasoning in *Ghost Dancing with Colonialism: Decolonization and Indigenous Rights at the Supreme Court of Canada* (2011) challenges many received assumptions about Canada's constitution and the rights of the First Nations. Her current research focus is on paradigm change and the impact of intercultural misunderstanding on judicial reasoning, education, and governmental practice.

JASMIN ZINE is an associate professor in sociology and the Muslim Studies option at Wilfred Laurier University. She teaches courses in the areas of critical race, gender, ethnic and postcolonial studies, education, and Muslim cultural politics in Canada. Her Canada-wide study of Muslim youth and the politics of empire, citizenship, and belonging post-9/11 was funded by SSHRC. She participated in an expert working group to develop educational guidelines for combating discrimination against Muslims, part of an inter-governmental initiative spearheaded by the Organization for Security and

Cooperation in Europe (OSCE), the United Nations Educational, Scientific and Cultural Organization (UNESCO), and the Council of Europe. In 2008, she published *Canadian Islamic Schools: Unraveling the Politics of Faith, Gender, Knowledge and Identity.*

RACHEL ZOLF's fourth full-length book of poetry is *Neighbour Procedure* (Coach House, 2010). "Child Soldier" comes from *The Tolerance Project* (thetoleranceproject.blogspot.com), what could be the first collaborative MFA in creative writing, recently accomplished at The New School in New York. The poem contains poetic DNA traces from Tolerance Project donors Erín Moure, Gary Barwin, Jordan Scott, Rachel Levitsky, Laura Elrick, Susan Schultz, Emily Beall, Rob Read, Evie Shockley, the Office of Institutional Research, and Communications and External Affairs.

Permissions

MAHER ARAR, "Omar Khadr: America's Injustice, Canada's Shame," originally published online at the *Huffington Post*, 2 November 2010. Reprinted with the permission of the author.

LUC CÔTÉ and PATRICIO HENRIQUEZ, excerpts from the screenplay of *You Don't Like the Truth: 4 Days inside Guantánamo*, a production of Les Films Adobe Inc., 2010. Printed with the permission of the authors.

ROMÉO DALLAIRE, excerpts from "How to Unmake a Child Soldier," in *They Fight Like Soldiers, They Die Like Children: The Global Quest to Eradicate the Use of Child Soldiers*. Reprinted in the US and Philippines with the permission of Walker Books, an imprint of Bloomsbury Publishing Plc.; reprinted in Canada with the permission of Random House Canada; reprinted in the UK, Europe, and the Commonwealth with the permission of Random House UK.

GAIL DAVIDSON, "Torture as Foreign Policy: The Omar Khadr Decision," a portion of which appeared in previous form in *JURIST: Legal News and Research*, 11 February 2010. Reprinted with the permission of the author.

SAMI AL HAJ, "Humiliated in the Shackles," originally published in *Poems from Guantánamo: The Detainees Speak* (2007), edited by Marc Falkoff. Reprinted with the permission of University of Iowa Press.

SHEEMA KHAN, "Politics over Principles: The Case of Omar Khadr," originally published in *Belonging and Banishment: Being Muslim in Canada* (2008), edited by Natasha Bakht. Reprinted with the permission of TSAR Publications.

CRAIG KIELBURGER, "My Encounter with Omar," originally published as "Omar Khadr, Jean Chrétien and Me" in the *Toronto Star*, 17 October 2010. Also published online as "The Day I Met Omar" at the *Huffington Post*, 21 October 2010. Reprinted with the permission of the author.

MONIA MAZIGH, "From Congo to Guantanamo: Omar Khadr, the Invisible Child Soldier," originally published online at *rabble.ca*, 10 Nov 2010. Reprinted with the permission of the author and rabble.ca.

SHEILA PRATT, "Khadr's Canadian Defence," is based on articles previously published in the *Edmonton Journal* and *Alberta Views* magazine between 2010 and 2011.

JUDITH THOMPSON, *Nail Biter: A One-Act Play*, © Judith Thompson, 2008. All rights reserved. Printed with the permission of the author. All enquiries for performance rights should be directed to Great North Artists Management Inc., 350 Dupont St., Toronto, ON, M5R 1V9.

RICHARD J. WILSON, "War Stories: A Reflection on Defending an Alleged Enemy Combatant Detained in Guantánamo Bay, Cuba," originally published in an earlier version in the *Yearbook of New Zealand Jurisprudence*, volume 8 (2005). Reprinted with the permission of the publication.